THE USBORNE
INTERNET - LINKED
ENCYCLOPEDIA
OF THE
ANCIENT
WORLD

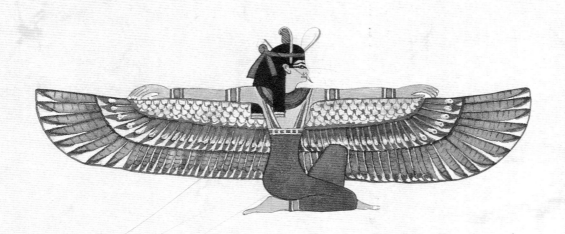

THE USBORNE
INTERNET - LINKED
ENCYCLOPEDIA
OF THE
ANCIENT WORLD

Jane Bingham, Fiona Chandler,
Jane Chisholm, Gill Harvey, Lisa Miles,
Struan Reid & Sam Taplin

Designed by Melissa Alaverdy, Laura Fearn,
Susie McCaffrey, Linda Penny & Stephen Wright

Consultant: Dr. Anne Millard

Illustrated by Inklink Firenze, Giacinto Gaudenzi, Jeremy Gower,
Dominic Groebner, Nick Harris, Nicholas Hewetson,
Ian Jackson, Aziz Khan & Rodney Matthews

Cover design: Zöe Wray

Additional material by Abigail Wheatley   Additional design by Sarah Cronin

Digital images: John Russell   Picture research: Ruth King

CONTENTS

INTERNET LINKS

Throughout this book we have recommended interesting websites where you can find out more about the ancient world. At these sites, you can tour ancient cities and ruins, see beautiful pottery and statues, or even try your hand at ancient recipes and games. On lots of the pages in the book, you'll find Internet Link boxes which contain short descriptions of the sites.

A Roman copy of a Greek statue of Apollo, the god of the Sun, music, prophecy and healing

USBORNE QUICKLINKS

To visit the recommended sites, go to the Usborne Quicklinks Website at **www.usborne-quicklinks.com** and type the keywords 'ancient world'. Then, to reach the Internet links for a particular page, type a page number.

As well as the links described in this book, there are also links to museums, virtual tours, ancient mythology websites and other websites that are useful for research and homework on the ancient world. For the links to these sites, just go to the Usborne Quicklinks Website and click on 'History' and then click on 'Encyclopedias' in the Quicklinks menu.

Here are some of the things you can do at the websites listed in Usborne Quicklinks:

• Browse online encyclopedias of Greek mythology

• Explore the history of writing and take online hieroglyph lessons

• See wonderful works of art in the online collections of famous museums such as the British Museum in London and the Louvre in Paris

• Take virtual tours of ancient Greek, Roman and Egyptian sites.

INTERNET SAFETY

When using the Internet, please make sure you follow these guidelines:

• Ask for your parent's or guardian's permission before you connect to the Internet.

• If you write a message in a website guest book or on a website message board, do not include any personal information, such as your full name, address or telephone number, and ask an adult before you give your email address.

• If a website asks you to log in or register by typing your name or email address, ask an adult for permission first.

• If you do receive an email from someone you don't know, tell an adult and do not reply to the email.

• Never arrange to meet someone you have talked to on the Internet.

All the sites described in this book have been selected by Usborne editors as suitable, in their opinion, for children, although no guarantees can be given and Usborne Publishing is not responsible for the accuracy or suitability of the information on any website other than its own. We recommend that young children are supervised while on the Internet, and that children do not use Internet chat rooms.

SITE AVAILABILITY

The links in Usborne Quicklinks are regularly reviewed and updated, but occasionally you may get a message saying that a site is unavailable. This might be temporary, so try again later. Websites do accasionally close down and when this happens, we will replace them with new links in Usborne Quicklinks. So when you visit Usborne Quicklinks, the links may be slightly different from those described in your book.

WHAT YOU NEED

The websites described in this book can be accessed with a standard home computer and a web browser (the software that enables your computer to display information from the Internet). To hear sounds you will need a sound card and loudspeakers.

To browse the Internet safely and securely, we strongly recommend that you keep your computer operating system up-to-date by downloading the free "patches" offered by the software provider (e.g. Microsoft or Apple).

It is also advisable to make sure you have the most recent version of your web browser. For more information, go to the Usborne Quicklinks Website at www.usborne-quicklinks.com and click on 'Net Help'.

EXTRAS

Some websites need additional programs, called plug-ins, to play sound files or show videos, animations or 3-D images. If you go to a site but do not have the necessary plug-in, a message should appear on the screen.

There is usually a button on the site that you can click on to download a plug-in, or you can go to www.usborne-quicklinks. com and click on 'Net Help'. Here are some plug-ins you might need:

QUICKTIME® – lets you view videos. This is a trademark of Apple Computer, Inc., registered in the US and other countries.

REALONE PLAYER™ – lets you play videos and hear sound files. This is a trademark of RealNetworks, Inc., registered in the US and other countries.

SHOCKWAVE® – enables you to play animations and interactive programs. This is a trademark of Macromedia, Inc., registered in the US and other countries.

COMPUTER VIRUSES

A computer virus is a small program that can seriously damage your computer. A virus can get into your computer when you download programs from the Internet, or in an attachment that arrives with an email.

You can buy anti-virus software at computer stores, or download it from the Internet. For more about viruses, go to www.usborne-quicklinks.com and click on 'Net Help'.

DISCOVERING THE PAST

Our distant ancestors first settled down as farmers about 12,000 years ago, and slowly the first civilizations developed. Many of the buildings and objects they left have been destroyed by wars, natural disasters and decay. But an amazing amount has survived.

BURIED SECRETS

Archaeologists have unearthed thousands of ancient buildings and objects, both on land and beneath the sea. New finds are being made every year in many different parts of the world, and they all help to reveal a little more about ancient life.

This painting from an Egyptian tomb shows people harvesting crops.

Divers using modern sonar equipment have discovered the wrecks of ancient ships, some with their cargoes incredibly well-preserved. Recently, explorers found the remains of ancient Egyptian cities that had been hidden by the waves for hundreds of years.

WORDS AND PICTURES

Thanks to the invention of writing, we can learn something about the thoughts, feelings and beliefs of our ancestors. A surprising number of manuscripts still exist, though sometimes we have to rely on copies made by later generations.

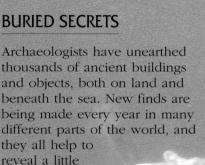

Ancient images are another gold mine of information. People from many cultures painted pictures on the walls of their houses and palaces, showing scenes of everyday life. Some also made mosaic pictures on the floors. All this has revealed vast amounts about ancient clothes, houses and furniture.

Pollen grains from
different plants, magnified
1,300 times

MODERN METHODS

Today, archaeologists use an
amazing range of methods
to help them uncover the
past. Photos taken from
the air reveal the outlines
of buried walls, while
magnetic sensors can
detect structures under the
soil. This type of study is
called a geophysical survey.

The careful analysis of plants
and creatures found at
archaeological sites is just as
revealing. Experts study remains
ranging in size from animal
skeletons to pollen grains. This
painstaking work reveals
fascinating evidence about the
kind of countryside people
lived in and the food they ate.

This marine archaeologist is
exploring an ancient
shipwreck in the Aegean Sea.

Techniques used by doctors can
also help reveal ancient secrets.
Mummies are examined with
CAT scanning machines to
produce 3-D images of the
bodies, and DNA testing shows
how ancient people were
related or where they
came from.

Lion, symbol of the goddess Ishtar, from the
processional way in Babylon, made of
moulded, glazed bricks around 604-562BC

EARLY
CIVILIZATIONS

THE FIRST FARMERS

Until about 12,000 years ago, people everywhere were constantly on the move. They covered huge distances hunting wild animals and collecting wild plants to eat. They lived in caves or in makeshift shelters that could be packed up easily and carried to the next hunting ground. Then an extraordinary thing happened that changed their lives forever: they learned how to farm.

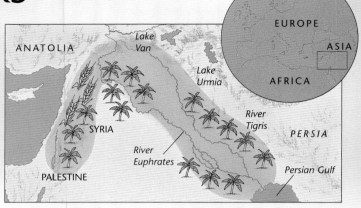

Map showing the Fertile Crescent, the area of the Middle East where farming first began

The land around the banks of the Euphrates, one of the places where the first farms grew up, was much greener in ancient times than it is now.

LAND OF PLENTY

Farming didn't happen overnight - it took hundreds of years of gradual change and happened in different parts of the world at different times. The first farmers appeared in an area known as the 'Fertile Crescent', a great arc of land stretching from the shores of the Mediterranean, through the mountains of Syria and Turkey and down to Iran and Iraq. It had rich, fertile soil which was watered each year by rivers and streams swelled with melted mountain snow.

THE FIRST HARVESTS

The wild ancestors of the first crops and farm animals were probably native to this part of the world. For thousands of years before they started farming, people had been gathering the seeds of wild grasses to eat. People began to plant the seeds and harvest them, instead of searching for wild plants for their food.

This change brought about changes in the crops too. Wild wheat has brittle ears, which break and scatter its

Wild wheat

Domesticated wheat

seeds in the wind. But when the first farmers selected seeds to plant, they chose them from the plants which kept their seeds a bit better, so they could harvest them more easily.

So, very gradually, the wheat changed and a variety called emmer wheat developed, which keeps its seeds much better than wild wheat and is an ancestor of modern types of wheat.

TAMING WILD ANIMALS

Hunters also began to capture young, wild sheep and goats that roamed the craggy hills and deep valleys of the ancient Middle East. They tamed them and raised them to provide milk and wool, as well as meat. The farmers bred from the smaller, more docile animals, until eventually they produced tamer varieties of sheep and goats. Larger and more aggressive animals continued to be hunted and killed to provide extra food.

Auroch - wild ox

Mouflon - wild sheep

Wild goat

 INTERNET LINK

For a link to a website where you can explore a clickable map to find out where lots of different crops and animals were first domesticated, go to **www.usborne-quicklinks.com**

A NEW LIFESTYLE

Once people learned how to farm, other things had to change too. They began to settle in one place for the first time, to look after their animals and crops. They were also forced to cultivate new skills and technology to meet their changing lifestyle.

They made wooden hoes, to prepare the fields for planting, and wooden sickles fitted with sharp flint blades to cut the crops. They made stone querns to grind the grain to make flour for bread, clay ovens to bake the bread, and simple clay pots to carry water and milk.

A pot made by an early farmer

This pot from Turkey dates from around 5700BC.

Stone querns and round pestles like this were used for grinding grain.

Internet link for a link to a website where you can explore Çatal Hüyük, go to **www.usborne-quicklinks.com**

THE FIRST TOWNS

As the farmers were able to grow more food, families were better fed and more children were born. The population of many villages grew so much that some larger ones absorbed smaller villages nearby. In this way the world's first towns began to appear.

MASTER BUILDERS

North of the Dead Sea in Palestine, the lowest and one of the hottest places on earth, lies the ancient site of Jericho, the oldest town ever discovered.

A small group of farmers settled in Jericho in about 8000BC, attracted to the site by a spring of fresh water. A thousand years later, it had grown into a bustling town of over 2,000 people, living in small, round mud brick houses surrounded by a strong, high wall.

Another early town was Çatal Hüyük in Anatolia (part of Turkey), which was inhabited from around 7000BC by about 5,000 farmers and cattle breeders. The people of Çatal Hüyük also appear to have been skilled artists. Beautiful wall paintings have been found in some of the houses.

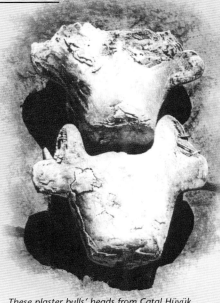

These plaster bulls' heads from Çatal Hüyük would have had real bulls' horns attached, and probably had a religious purpose.

EARLY RELIGIONS

The first signs of religious belief were discovered in these early towns. At Jericho, human skulls were buried under the floors - suggesting people followed some sort of ancestor worship. At Çatal Hüyük, some buildings had paintings and elaborate plaster models of bulls' heads and leopards. Archaeologists think these buildings were probably religious shrines.

Apple trees

This is how Çatal Hüyük probably looked. The town was carefully planned, with neat groups of houses tightly packed together, arranged around courtyards, with narrow streets between them.

People climbed into the houses through a hole in the roof.

Each house had one main room.

The builders used wooden beams and bricks made of mud mixed with reeds which were baked in the sun.

If enemies attacked, the ladders were pulled up.

Cattle and goats were kept for meat and milk.

These walls have been cut away so you can see inside.

THE MESOPOTAMIAN WORLD

Small stone statues of people at prayer,
left in Mesopotamian temples as
offerings to the gods.

MESOPOTAMIA

While Jericho and Çatal Hüyük were growing, great things were happening in another part of the Fertile Crescent, in the region historians call Mesopotamia - which means 'the land between the rivers' in Greek. This vast, fertile plain lying between the mighty Tigris and Euphrates rivers in Iraq, was the birthplace of one of the world's earliest civilizations. The most exciting changes began in the southern part, in an area called Sumer.

PRECIOUS WATER

Every spring the Euphrates river swelled with rainwater from the surrounding hills and flooded its banks. The farmers learned how to make their land more fertile by trapping the floodwater in shallow lakes, and digging irrigation channels to carry it to their fields during the hot, dry summer months.

THE FIRST TRADERS

With these new more efficient irrigation methods, farmers could grow far more crops than they needed. This meant they could trade surplus food with people in the surrounding hills, exchanging it for valuable things they didn't have, such as copper, stone and wood. The earliest farmers of Sumer are sometimes known as Ubaidians, after one of their settlements, Tell al-Ubaid.

This village on the banks of the Tigris is inhabited by river dwellers known as Marsh Arabs. The houses they live in, made of woven reeds, are not so different from the ones the first farmers lived in - about 7,000 years ago.

NEW CRAFTS AND SKILLS

Learning how to irrigate the land was an amazing step forward. It meant extra food, so that not everyone had to spend all their time planting crops, raising animals and cutting irrigation channels. Instead some people became full-time craftsmen, making tools, ornaments and household goods for the rest of the village. Others became priests, praying for a good harvest and overseeing the storage and distribution of food.

The new full-time craftsmen began to create artistic objects, like this Ubaidian clay figure of a woman.

INVENTIONS

From about 4000BC, a new phase began - named after Uruk, one of the earliest settlements - which brought some dramatic changes.

One of these was the invention of the potter's wheel in about 3400BC. Pots became smoother and were much quicker to produce.

Even more important, the wheel was adapted for transport - to produce the first wheeled carts. So farmers could now carry three times as much as they could on the back of a donkey. But the most significant change of all was probably the invention of writing in about 3000BC (see pages 18-19).

This is a decoration from a temple at Tell al-Ubaid, showing bulls which were often used in sacrifices as they were a symbol of power.

THE FIRST CITY

About this time, Uruk began to mushroom into the world's first substantial city. At its height, it covered a huge area, surrounded by a high wall, with wide streets, grand public buildings and two religious areas with large temples.

Uruk stayed an important city for thousands of years. The people who lived there are known as Sumerians, and it was with them that Mesopotamian civilization really took off.

 INTERNET LINK

For links to websites where you can become a Sumerian farmer and find out how the Sumerians invented the wheel, go to www.usborne-quicklinks.com

THE BIRTH OF WRITING

The invention of writing was so significant that it is sometimes seen as the beginning of history, as it enabled people to keep a record of events. Historians and archaeologists disagree about where writing first began, but some of the earliest evidence, from about 3300BC, was found in the Sumerian city of Uruk.

RECORD KEEPING

In the new cities, people gave their crops to the temple, so officials needed to record who had paid what. At first they drew simple pictures, called pictographs, of all the deliveries. Circles and crescents represented numbers. This meant they could record the type and number of the goods.

CLAY TABLETS

Most of the pictures related to farming. An ox's head was used for 'ox', while wheat ears meant 'grain'. The Sumerians wrote on blocks of damp clay using a pointed reed or stick.

This is a clay tablet from around 3000BC, which uses pictographs to record food distribution and is probably from a temple.

When the clay dried, the writing hardened too and the records could be kept for a long time. Some of these clay tablets survive even today.

PICTURE WRITING

Later, other symbols were added to express more complicated ideas. For example, an ear meant 'hear'. Some ideas were made up of a combination of symbols. For example, a mouth and water placed together meant 'drink'.

Another change came when scribes started using the signs to represent short sounds as well as things. This meant several signs could be placed together to spell out a word which did not have its own picture.

It takes time to draw pictures, even simple ones. Scribes discovered that it was quicker to make simpler versions of the shapes by using the end of the writing tool as a stamp, instead of drawing with it.

CUNEIFORM WRITING

The writing sticks the Sumerians used had a wedge-shaped end. So, when they started using it to create shapes, the writing became wedge-shaped too. Historians call this kind of writing 'cuneiform', which means 'wedge-shaped'. It was used in Mesopotamia for more than 3,000 years.

Here you can see a clay tablet including the pictograph for 'grain'.

On this later tablet, the cuneiform sign for 'grain' is used instead.

INTERNET LINK

For a link to a website where you can explore the world of an early Mesopotamian scribe, go to **www.usborne-quicklinks.com**

Assyrian scribes like these would still have used cuneiform, about 3,000 years after its invention.

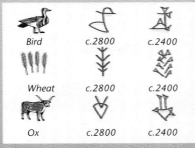

Bird	c.2800	c.2400
Wheat	c.2800	c.2400
Ox	c.2800	c.2400

These three examples show the way Sumerian writing developed from pictures (pictographs) into cuneiform symbols.

Cuneiform was a very successful writing system and was adapted by other Mesopotamian peoples to write down their different languages. The Akkadians, the Elamites and, further afield, the Hittites used cuneiform signs in different ways - sometimes to represent things as pictographs had done, sometimes to represent sounds or even to form the letters of an alphabet.

Henry Rawlinson became the first modern historian to understand cuneiform by studying this 2,500-year-old rock carving at Bisitun, Iran.

CRACKING THE CODE

Cuneiform gradually died out and was forgotten for about two thousand years. When the first archaeologists came across the inscriptions on ancient clay tablets, they had no idea what they meant.

Cuneiform remained a mystery until 1844. That year, an English army officer, named Henry Rawlinson, completed his study of some inscriptions found on a rock at Bisitun in western Iran.

The rock, which had been carved on the orders of King Darius of Persia in the 5th century BC, showed three cuneiform inscriptions recording the same information, but in three different languages - Old Persian, Babylonian and Elamite.

Rawlinson managed to work out which shapes made up the name of King Darius in the Persian part, and used this to guess what some of the cuneiform symbols stood for. This was just the clue he needed, and eventually he was able to decipher cuneiform itself. Even so, it took years of hard work to finish off the job.

THE FIRST CITY-STATES

By about 3000BC, some Sumerian towns, like Kish, Eridu, Nippur and Ur, had grown into vast cities - even bigger than Uruk. Over time, these cities began to control more and more of the surrounding land and villages, and eventually developed into independent city-states.

TAKING OVER

Early Sumerian towns had been governed by elected officials. But, as towns grew into cities, the small local organizations that had looked after daily life grew into huge governments, with hundreds of officials. These began to be appointed directly by powerful men, without consulting anyone.

KINGS AND WARLORDS

City-states squabbled with each other over valuable farmland, and petty disputes sometimes grew into full-blown wars. So rulers built strong fortified walls around their cities. In wartime, people moved inside the walls for protection, and a warlord, or lugal, was chosen to lead the fighting. As wars grew more frequent, lugals stayed in power longer. Eventually, they were recognized as kings and when they died, their sons took over.

This is how the great Sumerian city of Ur would have looked at the height of its power.

This is the huge ziggurat of Nanna, the moon god.

Throngs of people processed up the temple steps, bringing gifts.

The temple staff lived in houses built inside the temple walls.

REACHING FOR THE SKY

At the heart of every Sumerian city was a magnificent temple, dedicated to the city's patron god or goddess. The first temples were simple, rectangular buildings standing on low platforms. But, later, people took to putting up new temples on the rubble of the old - raising the level higher and higher. This created a stepped design, called a ziggurat. Some ziggurats were so enormous that the ruins are still there - 5,000 years later.

The Sumerians prayed to hundreds of different gods and goddesses. But each city had its own special one, and the temple was regarded as the god's home. Priests lived there too, performing ceremonies and reciting hymns and prayers.

Temples were also great employers. Dozens of craftsmen, cooks and cleaners worked there, looking after the priests. The Sumerians believed their land belonged to the gods - not to them. So farm produce was donated to the temple, and the priests were put in charge of collecting, storing and distributing it to everyone. To organize this huge task, a small army of scribes and officials was on hand.

Barley and wheat were grown in fields outside the city walls.

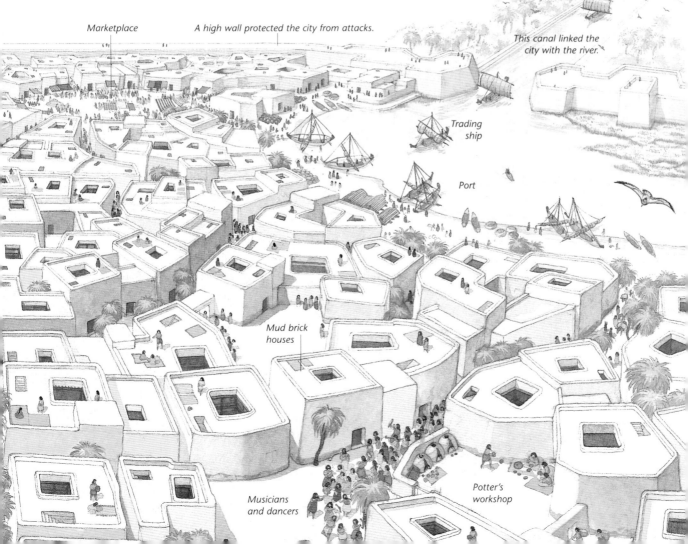

River Euphrates

This canal linked the city with the river.

Marketplace

A high wall protected the city from attacks.

Trading ship

Port

Mud brick houses

Musicians and dancers

Potter's workshop

THE ROYAL TOMBS OF UR

Some of the most dazzling archaeological treasures ever discovered were found in the royal tombs of the Sumerian city of Ur. Excavations there, led by British archaeologist Sir Leonard Woolley, lasted twelve years between 1922 and 1934, and produced a detailed picture of life in one of the world's earliest civilizations.

FIT FOR KINGS

Woolley discovered a cemetery at Ur containing 1,840 graves. Seventeen of these were probably built for important officials or kings, as they were much larger and better constructed than the others.

Although most of the tombs had been robbed centuries ago, luckily two of them managed to survive intact. These tombs belonged to Kings Meskalamdug and Akalamdug of Ur and dated to around 2500BC.

This gold headdress was found in the tomb of Queen Puabi, on a table near her head.

ARTISTS AND CRAFTSMEN

The staggering wealth of the objects in the graves provided evidence of the incredible skill of the artists and craftspeople who worked in Sumerian cities. Judging from what was left in the graves, the royal palaces at Ur must have been decorated with beautiful furnishings and musical instruments.

LUXURY TRADE

Archaeologists found amazing necklaces, headdresses and rings of gold and semi-precious stones. The materials they used - lapis lazuli, carnelian and even gold - were not native to the region and must have been imported from as far away as Afghanistan and northern India. This gives some idea of the vast trading networks that must have existed.

A gold helmet from one of the tombs at Ur

Archaeologists constructed this amazing object (left) from hundreds of pieces of shell, red limestone and lapis lazuli found in the tomb. No one knows exactly what it was for.

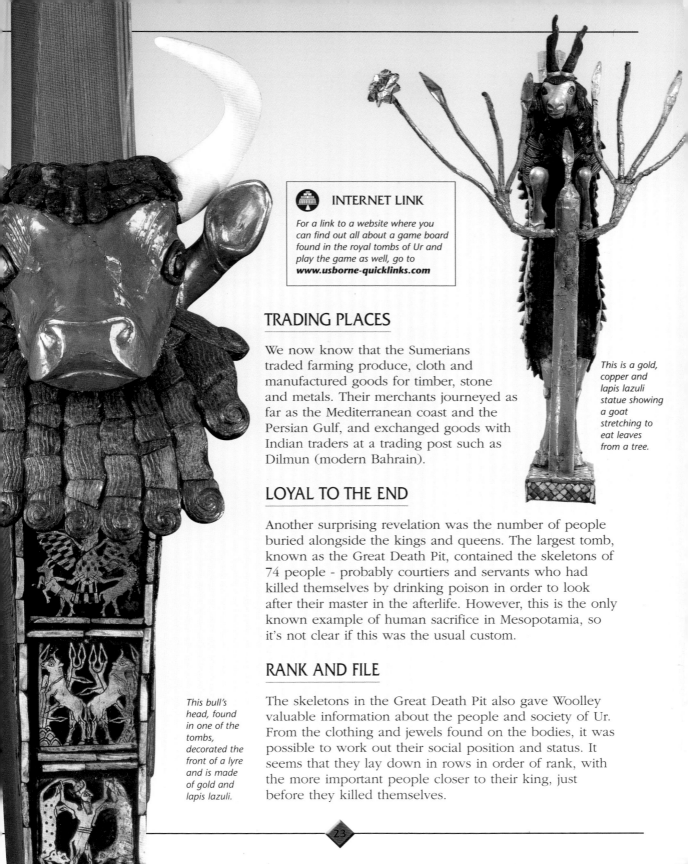

INTERNET LINK

For a link to a website where you can find out all about a game board found in the royal tombs of Ur and play the game as well, go to **www.usborne-quicklinks.com**

TRADING PLACES

We now know that the Sumerians traded farming produce, cloth and manufactured goods for timber, stone and metals. Their merchants journeyed as far as the Mediterranean coast and the Persian Gulf, and exchanged goods with Indian traders at a trading post such as Dilmun (modern Bahrain).

This is a gold, copper and lapis lazuli statue showing a goat stretching to eat leaves from a tree.

LOYAL TO THE END

Another surprising revelation was the number of people buried alongside the kings and queens. The largest tomb, known as the Great Death Pit, contained the skeletons of 74 people - probably courtiers and servants who had killed themselves by drinking poison in order to look after their master in the afterlife. However, this is the only known example of human sacrifice in Mesopotamia, so it's not clear if this was the usual custom.

This bull's head, found in one of the tombs, decorated the front of a lyre and is made of gold and lapis lazuli.

RANK AND FILE

The skeletons in the Great Death Pit also gave Woolley valuable information about the people and society of Ur. From the clothing and jewels found on the bodies, it was possible to work out their social position and status. It seems that they lay down in rows in order of rank, with the more important people closer to their king, just before they killed themselves.

THE FIRST EMPIRES

Early Mesopotamian peoples had well-organized cities and governments, managed huge and complex trading networks, and produced amazing art and technology. However, this burst of activity also made the region unstable, as different peoples competed for power and land.

SARGON AND THE EMPIRE OF AKKAD

The land of Akkad lay to the north of Sumer. Although the people used the same writing as the Sumerians, they spoke a different language, known as Akkadian. Around 2370BC, a great leader called Sargon was born in Akkad.

Legend has it that Sargon's mother put her baby in a reed basket and sent him floating down the Euphrates. Sargon was found and rescued, and grew up to become a powerful official in the city of Kish. But Sargon was ambitious. Soon he overthrew the king of Kish and seized power. He stormed through Akkad at the head of a huge army, conquering each of the cities in turn.

This bronze head may show the face of Sargon, but it could actually be his grandson, the great warrior Narâm-Sin.

GLORY AND DOWNFALL

Not content with this, Sargon set out to conquer Sumer too. Soon, he ruled a vast area of land between the Mediterranean Sea and the Persian Gulf - the world's first empire. Sargon's successors fought hard to keep their empire.

This is a stone carving showing Sargon's grandson at the head of Akkad's armies.

But trouble was brewing. The cities of Sumer began to fight back, and a fearsome mountain tribe called the Gutians invaded Akkad. Around 2230BC, the empire fell apart and the area was plunged into chaos and war.

THE KINGS OF UR

The struggles continued until Ur's third dynasty of kings won control over Akkad and Sumer around 2113BC. The Sumerian kings kept their cities, but they had to follow the orders of the King of Ur.

Ur's kings were rich, and they built many magnificent temples and palaces, as well as a system of canals. They also built the great mud brick ziggurat of Ur, part of which still survives today. For a time, the empire prospered.

These soldiers from the army of Ur are fighting against Gutian tribesmen (left).

THE AMORITES

The barren desert on the southern border of Ur's empire was home to several groups of nomads. They kept flocks of sheep and traded their meat and wool for grain, dates, tools and weapons. Under Ur's third dynasty, nomads called the Amorites began edging their way into the rich farmland within the empire. It soon became hard to keep Ur's empire together.

Kings and important soldiers rode into battle in chariots.

This map shows the empire of the third dynasty of Ur.

- The core of the empire
- Provinces
- Allied states

AKKAD
River Tigris
• Kish
River Euphrates
SUMER   Ur
Persian Gulf

THE END OF AN ERA

Around 2006BC, a kingdom called Elam, which had been part of the empire, attacked and demolished Ur. But, more power struggles in the region were yet to come.

INTERNET LINK

For a link to a website where you can see pictures of the ziggurat at Ur and find out more about Mesopotamian ziggurats, go to
www.usborne-quicklinks.com

THE RISE OF BABYLON

A fter the fall of Ur, Amorites flooded into Mesopotamia's fertile lands. One group settled in a small state with its capital at Babylon, which means 'the gate of the gods'. These Amorites quickly adopted the culture and religion of their new home.

HAMMURABI'S EMPIRE

Around 1792BC, a young man called Hammurabi became King of Babylon. He was a brilliant soldier, and he expanded his territory to bring all of Sumer and Akkad under his rule. He became known as 'King of the Four Quarters' because it seemed to his subjects that his empire covered the whole world.

This dragon is a symbol of Marduk, made Babylon's chief god under Hammurabi.

Hammurabi was also a wise and efficient ruler. The people and land of a city had always been thought to belong to that city's patron god, but Hammurabi seized power for himself. However, he respected the traditions of his different peoples - Akkadians, Sumerians and Amorites.

He also laid down a set of laws for all the people of his empire. Amazingly, these laws still survive, engraved on a huge stone slab - or *stela*. Soon peace and prosperity returned to the region.

A stone head, thought to be a portrait of Hammurabi.

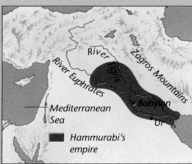

This map shows the Babylonian empire under Hammurabi.

 INTERNET LINK

For a link to a website where you can examine Hammurabi's laws engraved on an ancient stela, go to
www.usborne-quicklinks.com

HITTITE CONQUEST

Hammurabi's successors went on ruling Babylon until around 1595BC. Then the Hittites, a warlike people from the north, sacked the city, and the empire collapsed. When the Hittites eventually left Babylon, a people called the Kassites swarmed in to take their place.

A terracotta head of a Kassite prince

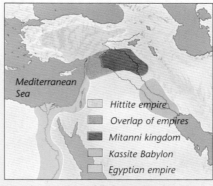

Map showing the Middle East at the time of the Kassites.

Hittite empire
Overlap of empires
Mitanni kingdom
Kassite Babylon
Egyptian empire

KASSITE KINGS

This is a glass bottle, found in a Kassite tomb at Ur.

For centuries, the Kassites had lived in the lonely Zagros mountains and kept themselves to themselves, but now they saw their chance to build an empire. Like the Amorites before them, they adopted the Babylonian culture as their own.

The Kassite rulers made Babylon one of the great powers of the day, though little is known about them. However, we do know that Babylonian kings sometimes gave their daughters to the Egyptian pharaohs as wives.

The Kassites ruled Babylon for more than 400 years, until they were finally overthrown by the Elamites, around 1171BC.

At the top of his law code stela, Hammurabi is shown receiving laws from a god. Lower down is the list of laws.

ALLIES AND ENEMIES

Mesopotamia was surrounded by other peoples and cultures. Sometimes they were allies and trading partners, but often they were rivals and enemies. Here are some of the most important ones.

ELAM

Elam lay between the river Tigris and the Zagros mountains, with its capital at Susa. Its culture goes back as far as 4000BC.

A painted beaker found in the tombs of Elam.

The Elamites were often the enemies of the peoples of Mesopotamia but they adapted cuneiform script (see page 19) and often wrote in the Sumerian language. Elam disappeared when the Persians occupied its land, but Susa remained as the Persian capital.

TRADING PARTNERS

Mesopotamians developed trading links with many places to the east, including Dilmun, Magan and Bactria. Dilmun, in the Persian Gulf, was especially important, as it was strategically placed for trade between Mesopotamia and the Indus Valley.

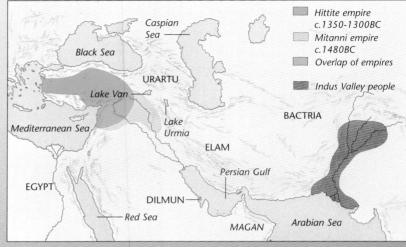

	Hittite empire c.1350-1300BC
	Mitanni empire c.1480BC
	Overlap of empires
	Indus Valley people

Map showing where the civilizations on these two pages were based.

THE INDUS VALLEY

By about 2500BC, an advanced culture was flourishing in the Indus Valley. The Sumerians described it as Meluhha. Well-planned cities were built, with comfortable houses and a good drainage system. The people of the Indus Valley traded with Mesopotamia and invented their own writing, but experts still haven't managed to understand it.

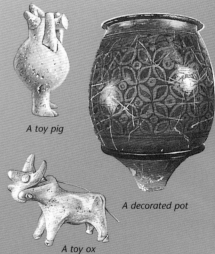

A toy pig

A decorated pot

A toy ox

Indus Valley potters made a wide variety of objects, including cooking pots, drinking cups and children's toys.

This statue probably shows an Indus Valley ruler or priest.

These are carved stone seals showing gods and animals, as well as some Indus Valley writing.

THE INDO-EUROPEANS

Indo-European is a term which describes a group of ancient and modern languages. People who spoke these languages began journeying from southern Europe and Russia to the Middle East sometime before 2000BC. Two of these groups were the Mitanni and the Hittites.

The Mitanni lived in northern Mesopotamia. They were enthusiastic about horses, and wrote books on how to train them. The Hittites were a warlike nation who settled in a region called Anatolia, in Turkey. Around 1350BC, they conquered the Mitanni and many other peoples, building up a large empire.

Hittite warriors leaving their capital city Hattushash (Bogazköy) to go to war

URARTU

The Kingdom of Urartu lay in the high region around Lake Van and Lake Urmia, between the Black Sea and the Caspian Sea. By 1000BC, the Urartians were famed as tough warriors and skilled bronze-workers. They fought many wars against the Assyrians between 900 and 600BC, but were conquered by the Medes (see page 40) around 590BC.

This ruined fortress in present-day Turkey was begun by the Urartians - later peoples added to it.

INTERNET LINK

For links to websites where you can take a photo tour of the Indus Valley or play a Mesopotamian trading game,
www.usborne-quicklinks.com

TRADING AND CONQUERING

Trade with the Mediterranean world was vitally important to the peoples of Mesopotamia, so they tried to keep good relations with the city-states along the trade route to the west. But some rulers had other ideas - and wanted to conquer them instead.

TRADING WEALTH

City-states, such as Mari, Ugarit, and Carchemish, along the Mediterranean trade routes were rich and powerful. Thanks to trade, their cities had huge walls, lavish palaces and towering temples. But this also meant that rival states wanted to conquer them.

A bronze statue of Baal, one of the most important of the Canaanite gods

This gold bowl from Ugarit is decorated with a hunting scene.

Map showing where the peoples mentioned here lived.

THE CANAANITES

Along the east coast of the Mediterranean, people known as Canaanites lived in small kingdoms. They were rich traders, and sold huge amounts of timber, as well as wine and olive oil. They were also skilled craftsmen, who were famous for their exquisitely carved ivory and a purple dye for cloth, which was incredibly expensive and treasured by foreign kings.

Because they were so wealthy, and lived at the crossroads between Africa and Asia, the Canaanites were often under threat from people who wanted their riches and their land. Eventually, around 1550BC, the Egyptians conquered them and ruled them for about 300 years.

PHOENICIAN PURPLE

Around 1100BC, groups of Canaanites who lived in the great northern ports became independent from the Egyptians. These people are known as Phoenicians, from a Greek word for purple - a reference to their famous dye.

The Phoenicians made writing simpler by inventing the forerunner of the alphabet we use today. They also built a fleet of warships which were used by all the great empires that later conquered them.

THE HEBREWS

According to the Bible, the Hebrews, or Jews, were originally nomads who wandered around the edges of Mesopotamia's fertile farming land. After a long stay in Egypt, they escaped to Canaan around 1250BC. About 200 years later, they formed a kingdom.

The Hebrew kingdom flourished under the kings Saul, David and Solomon, but was eventually split into two parts. The north was known as Israel, and the south was called Judah. Israel was later overthrown by the Assyrians, and Judah was conquered by the Babylonians.

The Phoenicians were known for their fine glass, such as these perfume bottles

 INTERNET LINK

For links to websites where you can explore exhibits with information about the Phoenicians and the Canaanites, go to www.usborne-quicklinks.com

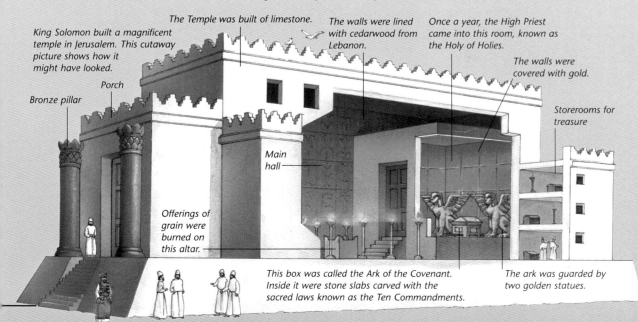

King Solomon built a magnificent temple in Jerusalem. This cutaway picture shows how it might have looked.

The Temple was built of limestone.

The walls were lined with cedarwood from Lebanon.

Once a year, the High Priest came into this room, known as the Holy of Holies.

The walls were covered with gold.

Porch

Bronze pillar

Storerooms for treasure

Main hall

Offerings of grain were burned on this altar.

This box was called the Ark of the Covenant. Inside it were stone slabs carved with the sacred laws known as the Ten Commandments.

The ark was guarded by two golden statues.

NEWCOMERS AND NEW STATES

Around 1195BC, groups called the Sea Peoples arrived in the Middle East. They destroyed the empire of the Hittites, and many city-states. This shook things up in the whole area.

This map shows where some of the peoples mentioned here lived.

THE SEA PEOPLES

The Sea Peoples seem to have come from Mycenaean Greece and its colonies in the eastern Mediterranean. Famine and war at home drove them to search for somewhere new to live, so they invaded the Middle East by land and by sea.

THE PHILISTINES

After many victories, the Sea Peoples were eventually defeated by the Egyptians. They scattered around the Mediterranean, and one group, the Peleset, settled in southern Canaan, giving their name to the area - Palestine. They were great rivals of the Hebrews who had also settled there, and they appear in the Bible as the Philistines.

PHRYGIA

When the Hittite empire was destroyed, new states grew up in Anatolia (present-day Turkey). One was Phrygia, which was ruled for a while by King Midas. According to Greek legend, Midas turned everything he touched to gold.

This strange-looking object is a Philistine coffin, made of pottery.

LYDIA

Another state that rose to power in Anatolia was Lydia. The Lydians mined vast amounts of gold and became extremely wealthy. They were probably the first people to produce coins.

BLACK SEA WARRIORS

By 700BC, a tribe of warlike horsemen called the Scythians had settled in an area north of the Black Sea. For the next few centuries, they traded and fought with the nations of Mesopotamia. The Scythians were fearsome warriors, and the women sometimes fought alongside the men.

The larger tents had two or three rooms inside.

The tents were made of felt.

In this picture of a Scythian camp, one tent has been cut away to let you see inside.

Stews were cooked in a copper pot.

Captured enemy soldiers were made to work as slaves.

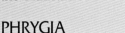

THE ARAMAEANS

Around 1100BC, a group of nomads known as the Aramaeans settled in the Middle East. They took over great cities such as Damascus and Aleppo, and one group - the Chaldeans - settled in what had been Sumer. The Aramaeans settled over such a wide area that their Semitic language became the everyday speech all over the Middle East for the next few centuries. Jesus of Nazareth spoke Aramaic.

THE INCENSE TRADE

Sweet-smelling incense was as valuable as gold in the ancient world. Both the old Mesopotamian states and the new nations burned it at all their religious ceremonies, and states on the south coast of Arabia became very rich by selling it. One group of incense-trading Arabs, known as the Nabataeans, built a beautiful city called Petra in present-day Jordan.

The Khazneh - the treasury - in the Nabataean city of Petra is carved out of solid sandstone.

 INTERNET LINK

For links to websites where you can explore Petra and its peoples with an interactive map, go to **www.usborne-quicklinks.com**

THE ASSYRIAN EMPIRE

The people we now call Assyrians came from a small area on the fertile banks of the Tigris in northern Mesopotamia. Their capital city was Ashur, named after their chief god, Ashur. At times Assyria was small and weak, but it also became a powerful empire with a fearsome reputation for cruelty and violence.

Map showing the smallest and largest areas of Assyrian control

EARLY YEARS

The early Assyrians were rather unimportant, dominated by the nearby civilisations of Sumer and Akkad. But the collapse of Ur (see page 25) made them independent, and they established themselves firmly in northern Mesopotamia.

Riches from around the empire were used to create fabulous jewels, like this bangle, for Assyrian kings and queens.

This colossal statue of a lion is 2.5m (8.5 feet) tall. It comes from an Assyrian temple that was next to the palace of the king.

THE AMORITES

Around 2000BC, the Amorites, who had earlier conquered Ur, attacked Assyria and became its new rulers. The most famous of them was Shamshi-Adad, who ruled from 1813 to 1776BC. He conquered the lands around Assyria and built up trade and an empire which covered most of northern Mesopotamia. Historians usually refer to this period as the first Assyrian empire.

CHANGING HANDS

Around 1740BC, the Babylonians took over and ended the first Assyrian empire. In the years that followed, the Assyrians were sometimes independent, and sometimes ruled by the Babylonians or others. From around 1500 to 1350BC, the Mitanni took control in the area. At its height, their empire stretched to the Mediterranean, but they were eventually wiped out by the Hittites.

A NEW EMPIRE

The Hittites themselves came under attack from the Sea Peoples, around 1200BC. After this, the Assyrians began to regain power. By around 900BC, they had built up an efficient army, which they sent on raids, to demand payment from nearby countries.

This kept the borders of Assyria secure, and supplied important goods, like metal and timber, which the Assyrians did not have in their own lands. It also created a powerful new Assyrian empire, which is often known as the second, or 'great', empire.

This scene shows the Assyrian army attacking a rebel city.

These Assyrian arrowheads were used to attack the city of Lachish.

THE ASSYRIAN ARMY

To keep their subjects under control, the Assyrian army inflicted terrible punishments on anyone who rebelled against the empire. Whole cities were razed to the ground and the ringleaders tortured and killed horribly. Ordinary citizens were made into slaves, or carried off to distant parts of the empire where life was very hard.

BATTLE STATIONS

The Assyrian army was divided up into different kinds of soldiers. Foot soldiers might be lightly armed with bows and arrows or slings, or more heavily armed with spears and shields. The cavalry rode horses without saddles or stirrups, or drove chariots with three or four men to a chariot.

Siege engines were used to attack the city walls.

Rebels fought hard, knowing they would be punished brutally if they lost.

The king gave commands from his chariot.

INTERNET LINK

For a link to a website where you can find out more about the Assyrian army through the story of a real siege, go to **www.usborne-quicklinks.com**

CITIES AND PALACES

A shur was the capital city of Assyria for more than a thousand years. But when the later Assyrian kings created the second empire around 900BC, they made grand new cities or enlarged old ones to celebrate their achievements. Excavations at these cities have revealed many amazing finds, some of which are shown here.

This is a reconstruction, based on finds, of the decoration in the palace at Nineveh.

CAPITAL CITIES

Ashurnasirpal II, who ruled Assyria from 883 to 859BC, was one of the great kings who built the new Assyrian empire. He had magnificent new palaces and temples built on the east bank of the river Tigris, at Kalhu (now called Nimrud). When the building was finished, Ashurnasirpal moved there with all his staff.

This statue of Ashurnasirpal II was found in Kalhu, the new capital he created for the Assyrian empire.

MOVING ON

In 717BC, Sargon II founded his own new city at a place now called Khorsabad. Then Sennacherib, who was king from 704 to 681BC, enlarged Nineveh, making it his most important city.

KING OF THE UNIVERSE

The king had supreme power in Assyria. His subjects addressed him as 'King of the Universe'. The name Ashurnasirpal means 'the god Ashur is protector of the heir'. The Assyrian kings all took names like this, to show that they were close to the gods. It was the king's job to build temples and perform religious rituals.

 INTERNET LINK

For links to websites where you can explore Nimrud Palace and see treasures from its royal tombs, go to **www.usborne-quicklinks.com**

This is a gold necklace, discovered at Kalhu in 1989.

RUNNING AN EMPIRE

Assyrian kings lived in luxury because of the taxes pouring in from around the empire. But they also had to pay for a huge workforce. Officials governed faraway regions, scribes recorded information and relay runners carried messages between the different parts of the empire. With all the construction work making palaces, temples and new cities, the top craftsmen also came from all around the empire to work for the kings.

This scene shows King Ashurbanipal relaxing in the palace gardens at Nineveh.

PALACE LIFE

The Assyrian kings were great warriors, and led their armies onto the battlefield. But they also knew how to enjoy themselves. Several of the kings had zoos of exotic animals. They also hunted lions to prove their skill and bravery. Carvings in the royal palace at Nineveh show this, and also depict the king relaxing in the beautiful gardens.

Kings enjoyed hunting, but the lions were kept in enclosures to make it easier.

THE EMPIRE CRUMBLES

In the end, however, the cruelty of the Assyrian kings united their enemies against them. The Babylonians made an alliance with the Medes from Persia (see page 40), and in 612BC the joint force attacked the Assyrian city of Nineveh and completely destroyed it.

Although many Assyrians fled from the ruins, they were finally defeated by the Babylonians in 609BC. The magnificent empire with all its wealth, finery and power had finally come to an end.

Ashurbanipal, who reigned from 668 to 627BC, was one of the last great Assyrian kings.

THE NEO-BABYLONIAN EMPIRE

For centuries, Babylonia was ruled by a series of shortlived dynasties. Even though some of the rulers were foreign princes, life continued much as usual for the Babylonian people. But then disaster struck.

ASSYRIA STRIKES

After around 730BC, Babylonia became part of the Assyrian empire. Assyria's powerful kings were determined to control the fertile farming land of Babylonia, but the Babylonians kept rebelling. This enraged the Assyrians,

and finally they attacked the city of Babylon, leaving it in ruins. The Babylonians never forgave them, and, led by the Chaldean settlers (see page 33), they continued to struggle for independence.

This is a picture of the city of Babylon during the New Year Festival.

ASSYRIA FALLS

In 625BC, a Chaldean leader called Nabopolassar made himself King of Babylon. Joining with the people of nearby Media, he destroyed the Assyrian empire.

This stepped tower is called a ziggurat. It was built by King Nebuchadnezzar for the god Marduk.

Priests lived here.

The Processional Way led into the city.

The king's throne room

The king's palace

The gate was covered with bright blue tiles.

The Hanging Gardens may have been located here.

This gateway was called the Ishtar Gate.

People watched the procession from the battlements.

This tile picture of a bull, from the Ishtar Gate, represents the weather god Adad.

BABYLON REBORN

Nabopolassar and his son, Nebuchadnezzar II, made Babylon great again. They founded a new ('Neo') Babylonian empire, restored Babylon's influence in the region, and encouraged a revival of religion and culture.

The kings rebuilt Babylon in lavish style, making it one of the most spectacular cities ever seen. It was surrounded by towering walls with huge gates, and there were also splendid temples and palaces.

Machinery carried water to the top of the Hanging Gardens.

Water ran down the terraces and kept the soil wet.

But the most breathtaking part of the city was the gardens. Nebuchadnezzar II married Amytis, daughter of the Median king, and she became homesick for the green hills of her childhood. So the Hanging Gardens of Babylon were built, and they became famous as one of the Seven Wonders of the Ancient World.

The main part of the city was surrounded by two massive walls.

THE NEW EMPIRE

Nebuchadnezzar conquered most of the old Assyrian empire for Babylon. But some peoples were unwilling to be ruled by another foreign power, and rebellions broke out.

After a revolt in 587BC, Babylon's armies launched a ferocious assault on the city of Jerusalem, tearing down the walls and burning down the Temple. Thousands of Jews were carried off to Babylon.

Map showing the Babylonian empire at the time of Nebuchadnezzar II.

THE MYSTERY OF NABONIDUS

The last king of the Neo-Babylonian empire was called Nabonidus. He was an eccentric man, and some of his enemies claimed he was insane. When a famine hit Babylon, Nabonidus left the city and fled into the desert. He stayed away for ten years, and nobody is sure why.

By the time Nabonidus returned, it was all over. The Persians had been growing in strength, and in 539BC they took control of Babylon. But they treated the Babylonians with respect, unlike previous foreign rulers, and they were welcomed into the city.

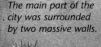

THE PERSIAN EMPIRE

The Medes and the Persians were tribes who spoke Indo-European languages and moved to the Middle East around 2000BC, settling in present-day Iran. At first, the Medes were more powerful, but around 550BC the Persian King Cyrus II defeated the Medes and took control.

THE GREATEST EMPIRE

During the next 60 years, Cyrus II and his successors conquered the greatest empire the Middle East had ever seen. The Persian empire stretched 4,200km (2,600m), from Egypt in the west to Bactria in the east, and even north into Europe.

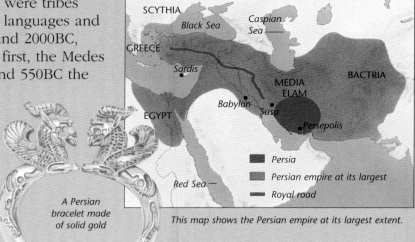

A Persian bracelet made of solid gold

This map shows the Persian empire at its largest extent.

PERSEPOLIS

The Persian king Darius I started building a magnificent palace at Persepolis. His successors completed it, and important ceremonies were held there. Sadly, it was later burned down by Alexander the Great, King of Macedonia.

RUNNING THE EMPIRE

To help them run their enormous empire, Persian kings divided it into smaller provinces ruled by local governors, called satraps. It was important for them to keep in touch with the king, so roads were built to enable royal messengers to carry letters swiftly across the empire. The main Royal Road ran for 2,700km (1,680m).

A statue of a griffin from the ruins of Persepolis

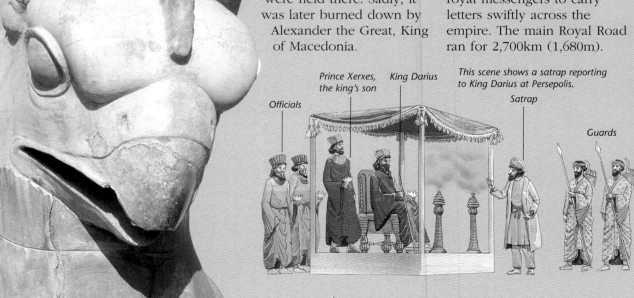

Prince Xerxes, the king's son

King Darius

Officials

This scene shows a satrap reporting to King Darius at Persepolis.

Satrap

Guards

RELIGIONS

Through their vast empire, the Persians had an influence on ideas in many parts of the world. The worship of the Persian god Mithras spread as far as Europe. It was especially popular with the Romans. The Persian prophet Zarathustra (also known as Zoroaster) taught that life was a struggle between forces of good and evil. This belief has attracted followers, right down to the present day.

The chief god of the Zoroastrian religion, Ahuramazda

DECLINE AND FALL

Despite its long rule and great influence, the empire could not last forever. The Persians invaded Europe as far as Thrace and Macedonia, and even attacked Greece. But after a disastrous defeat at Marathon (see page 182), the Greeks fought them off.

The Persian empire was overthrown by Alexander the Great (see page 242) in 330BC. Then, around 171BC, the Parthians conquered Persia and Babylon, and set up a new empire of their own. Persian supremacy had finally ended.

Part of the grand staircase at Persepolis

The carvings show people from all over the Empire bringing gifts to the king.

The Temple of Amun at Luxor in Egypt, built during the reigns of Amenhotep III and Ramesses II

ANCIENT EGYPT

DISCOVERING ANCIENT EGYPT

The ancient Egyptian civilization began to wane in 30BC, when Egypt became part of the Roman Empire. Christianity took over, and the treasures that lay buried in the desert were gradually forgotten. Then, about 200 years ago, European explorers started taking an interest in the ancient sites. For some, this soon became an obsession.

EARLY RECORDS

The ancient Egyptians wrote a lot down, but they wrote to glorify their gods and king, not to create accurate records. So they deliberately left some things out and exaggerated others. The first real history of Egypt was written by a Greek, named Herodotus, who is sometimes known as the Father of History. He visited Egypt in around 500BC. His account was mainly based on what people told him, so some of it was myth rather than fact.

Herodotus

Later, in the Ptolemaic period (see page 75), Ptolemy II paid an Egyptian scribe named Manetho to write a history of Egypt. Manetho divided it into 30 dynasties, or groups of kings, a system we still use today.

This is the Rosetta Stone. Although the French found it, the British claimed it when they defeated Napoleon off the coast of Egypt. It is still in the British Museum in London.

THE VITAL CLUE

For European explorers in the 18th century, it was difficult to make sense of the ancient monuments. They couldn't tell who had built them, when or why, because they couldn't read hieroglyphs, the Egyptian picture writing.

Then, in 1798, Britain and France went to war, and fought in Egypt. Napoleon, the French general, took a big team of scholars with him to study the monuments. But it was his soldiers who made the most important discovery – a slab of black stone, near the Mediterranean sea, at a place called Rosetta. It had three different scripts on it – one Greek, and two Egyptian. The French scholars guessed that the texts were translations of each other. Could this be the key to the mysterious hieroglyphs?

The Pyramids of Giza, which have amazed visitors for thousands of years

THE BIRTH OF EGYPTOLOGY

The Rosetta Stone, as it became known, did indeed make it possible to decipher hieroglyphs. Most of the work was done by a Frenchman, Jean-François Champollion, and an Englishman, Thomas Young. Once people could read hieroglyphs, interest in ancient Egypt shot up, and a new academic subject was created: Egyptology.

BELZONI THE GIANT

Excitement about Egypt's treasures led to what we now think of as reckless plundering. Adventurers thought it fine to ransack tombs and temples, taking whatever they fancied. One was ex-circus strongman, Giovanni Belzoni, who was over 2m (6' 7") tall. He cleared the sand from the big temples at Abu Simbel, and opened many of the tombs in the Valley of the Kings. In his enthusiasm, he caused a lot of damage – but he was probably no worse than other adventurers of his time.

A French coin commemorating Jean-François Champollion's work on hieroglyphs

AUGUSTE MARIETTE

By the mid-19th century, Egypt was attracting more and more enthusiasts. One was a Frenchman named Auguste Mariette. Without permission from the authorities, he began to dig at Saqqara, and soon found a huge underground tomb that became known as the Serapeum.

This was the start of Mariette's great career as an Egyptologist. As well as carrying out many excavations, he set up the Egyptian Museum in Cairo. This meant that most new discoveries stayed in Egypt, where they belonged, rather than being shipped out to European countries.

THE MAN IN PINK UNDERWEAR

Mariette was not as reckless as Belzoni, but even so, careful methods of excavation were only developed later in the 19th century. This was thanks to an eccentric Englishman – William Flinders Petrie. He often worked in just his long, pink underwear to stay cool.

Petrie created a very detailed and disciplined way of working. He saw that as much could be learned from small objects and fragments of pottery as from big monuments. He recorded everything he found and, by comparing thousands of pots with each other, he began to sort out the mystery surrounding Egypt's earliest history.

Flinders Petrie, whose work is still highly respected by Egyptologists today

Belzoni's men hauling off a statue from Luxor, to be transported to England

TREASURE TROVE

By the early 20th century, many Egyptologists had followed in Belzoni's path, hunting for mummies and treasure in the Valley of the Kings. All the tombs they found had been robbed in ancient times, and almost everyone was convinced that there was nothing left to discover. But one man didn't agree...

THE MISSING TOMB

Egyptologists had established which kings had been buried in the Valley of the Kings. All the important ones had been found, but one was still missing: the boy king Tutankhamun (see page 66). A British Egyptologist named Howard Carter was determined to find him. In 1917 he started to hunt, funded by a wealthy man, Lord Carnarvon. For four years he found nothing, and the Egyptian authorities thought it was time he gave up. But Carter begged for one more year. Eventually, they agreed.

One of Tutankhamun's necklaces, inlaid with jewels

WONDERFUL THINGS

The hunt restarted in November 1922. Carter decided to move some ancient workmen's huts – and almost as soon as work began, some steps appeared, leading down to a tomb. Could this be it – success at last? Very excited, Carter sent Lord Carnarvon a telegram saying, *At last have made wonderful discovery in Valley. A magnificent tomb with seals intact. Recovered same for your arrival. Congratulations.* On November 25th 1922, Lord Carnarvon stood waiting while Howard Carter carefully made a hole in the blocked-up door... and looked inside. Impatiently, Lord Carnarvon called, "Can you see anything?" And Howard Carter replied, "Yes, wonderful things."

Howard Carter beginning the long, careful job of cleaning Tutankhamun's coffins

A TEST OF PATIENCE

The first room was full of objects heaped together, such as chariots, statues, chairs and chests. At one end was another sealed door with two statues guarding it. Could the mummy of the king lie behind it? Even though everyone was dying to know, Carter was patient. First, he cleared the first room, taking detailed records of everything. At last, in February 1923, he opened the second door. What he found inside was breathtaking – four wooden shrines, covered in gold, surrounding a solid stone sarcophagus. Beyond was yet another room packed with more amazing objects. But Carter continued to be incredibly patient. It was another three years before he opened the sarcophagus to find three coffins, nestled inside

This pendant, shaped like a scarab, is inlaid with lapis, carnelian and turquoise.

each other. The first two were made of gilded wood, but the third was solid gold, inlaid with precious stones. Inside lay the mummy, its face covered with the beautiful gold mask that is now recognized all over the world.

The treasures in the tomb included this magnificent bed shaped like two golden cows.

INTERNET LINK

For a link to a website where you can read an eyewitness's account of viewing Tutankhamun's tomb in 1923, go to **www.usborne-quicklinks.com**

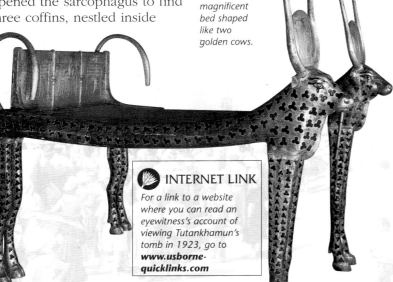

THE MUMMY'S CURSE?

Not long after the discovery of the tomb, Lord Carnarvon developed pneumonia. He died in Cairo on April 5th 1923. Sadly, this meant that he never saw Tutankhamun's stunning gold coffin or mask, because the sarcophagus had yet to be opened. Some newspaper reporters suggested that he had died under a curse, which doomed anyone who disturbed the mummy. People wanted to believe the story, so it spread quickly. But most people who had contact with the mummy, including Carter himself, came to no harm at all.

Tutankhamun's famous mask had yet to be uncovered when Lord Carnarvon died.

RECORDS AND CONSERVATION

Egyptology isn't just about finding new things. Many tombs, buildings and objects have been found that risk being lost forever unless they are recorded and preserved properly. The work can range from making an intricate copy of a small carving to actually moving whole buildings. Many Egyptologists now believe that this is much more urgent than carrying out new excavations.

A stonemason working with restorers at Saqqara

19TH-CENTURY RECORDS

This painting by the 19th-century painter David Roberts shows the temples of Ramesses II at Abu Simbel almost covered in sand.

Making records may not seem as exciting as excavating. But if more of the early explorers had recorded their finds properly, many of the remaining mysteries might have been solved. Even early in the 19th century, though, some records were made. David Roberts, a Scottish painter, made a series of careful oil paintings, and a German named Karl Lepsius carried out a survey of all the major sites.

MODERN DISCIPLINES

As well as excavators, the world of Egyptology includes people who specialize in examining, reconstructing and recording objects such as pots, coffins or ancient writings; mappers, who make plans of ancient sites; restorers, who specialize in preserving fragile paintings or objects; photographers, who provide clear and accurate records; and scientists of many kinds who use modern technology to examine and date objects.

SAVED FROM BEETLES

Not all conservation takes place in Egypt. In 1976, the Egyptian authorities sent a major exhibition of antiquities to Paris. The key exhibit was the mummy of Ramesses II, which was given its own special passport to enter France. When it was discovered that Ramesses was being attacked by beetles, French scientists offered to help, and the king was treated successfully.

The mummy of Ramesses II, now back in Cairo

 INTERNET LINK

For a link to a website where you can read about the history of the conservation of the Sphinx, and the ongoing difficulties of preserving this ancient monument, go to
www.usborne-quicklinks.com

DESERT RESCUE

In the 1960s, one of the world's greatest ever conservation projects took place in Nubia (southern Egypt). To control the Nile's water so crops could be grown all year, a big dam was built, creating a huge reservoir. This would have flooded all the ancient sites in the area, including the temples at Abu Simbel.

The Egyptian government wanted to rescue as much as possible, but the only solution for the temples was to move them. This was too expensive for one government, so UNESCO (United Nations Educational, Scientific and Cultural Organization) helped. The amazing task began in 1964. Over four years, the temples were cut into blocks and moved 60m (197ft) up the cliff face, out of the way of the water.

THE JOB GOES ON

Preserving ancient Egyptian sites is a difficult job. Ones that are open to tourists can easily be damaged – by the moisture in people's breath, for example – and there often isn't enough time or money to preserve the many others. But a great deal of work is still done by the Egyptian Supreme Council of Antiquities and by Egyptologists from around the world.

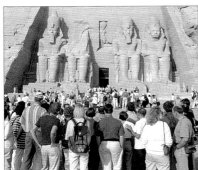

Abu Simbel is now a major tourist site.

Ramesses' temple was cut into 1,036 pieces, each weighing between 7 and 30 tonnes (tons).

Restoration experts worked on the blocks of stone to disguise the seams.

EGYPTOLOGY TODAY

Egyptologists are as busy as ever. They don't expect to find another tomb like Tutankhamun's, but they are always finding vital new information about life in ancient Egypt. As technology develops, new interpretations of the facts become possible, too.

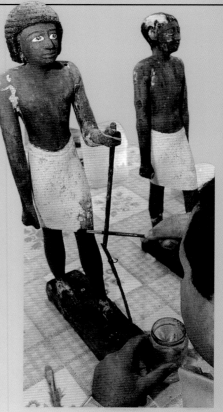

WHAT'S GOING ON?

The Egyptologists' 'season' is generally from autumn to spring, when it's not too hot. Then, Egyptologists of many nationalities work on all sorts of projects. A good way to find out about them is on the Internet. Many do not set out to find new treasures, but to record existing discoveries, or to develop a new theory about why things happened the way they did. Much of the work that goes on is restoration work (see pages 48-49). A recent successful restoration project has been that of the beautiful tomb of Nefertari on the west bank at Luxor, which was being damaged by salty water rising up beneath it.

Excavations are still ongoing at Saqqara. This picture shows an excavation team at the site of a newly discovered tomb in 2001.

A restorer works on the wooden model of an official, found near the pyramids of Saqqara in 1999.

MODERN TECHNOLOGY

Advances in technology have made a big difference to the analysis of Egyptologists' finds. CAT scanners allow them to look at mummies without damaging them, and DNA testing tells us a lot about how people were related, or what diseases they had (see page 101). Computers help Egyptologists to piece together what ruined buildings must have looked like, even when they only have fragments to work with.

 INTERNET LINKS

For links to websites where you can find out about past and present Egyptologists, learn about how Egyptologists deciphered hieroglyphics using the Rosetta Stone and find helpful advice about becoming an Egyptologist, go to www.usborne-quicklinks.com

A DONKEY'S DISCOVERY

One day in 1997, out in the Western Desert at a place called èl Bawati, a donkey trapped his leg in a hole in the ground and fell. His rider realised that the hole might be important, and in March 1999 a major excavation began. The finds have been astonishing – a vast tomb complex containing hundreds of mummies. This is now known as 'The Valley of the Golden Mummies'.

The mummies are mostly in very good condition, and are dated from the Greek period onwards (see page 75). Some are in coffins, while others are simply wrapped in linen; many are richly decorated with gold and other metals.

The face of a golden mummy stares up from its uncovered tomb at el Bawati.

UNDER THE WAVES

Modern sonar and diving equipment open up many possibilities for underwater excavation. Divers working in the bay of Aboukir, near Alexandria, have made some exciting discoveries in the past few years – including a palace that may have belonged to Cleopatra VII herself. Then, in June 2000, two sunken cities called Herakleion and Canopus were found. Work continues to uncover the bay's secrets from underneath many thick layers of silt.

ONGOING WORK

These are some of the most significant discoveries and projects that have happened in Egypt in recent years. Much of the work is still going on.

- Pyramid workers' bakeries and temples have been found at Giza
- Some of the earliest writing in the world has been found at Abydos, and also some 1st dynasty ships
- Another tomb, KV 5, has been rediscovered in the Valley of the Kings
- The ancient city of Memphis is gradually being excavated
- A workmen's village has been uncovered at Tell el Amarna (Akhenaten's ancient capital)
- A hunt is ongoing in the Valley of the Kings for members of Akhenaten's family
- Hatshepsut's temple at Deir el Bahri is gradually being pieced back together.

One of the divers in Aboukir Bay comes face to face with an ancient sphinx.

MAP OF ANCIENT EGYPT

ANATOLIA

R. Euphrates

CRETE

SYRIA

CYPRUS

Kadesh

MEDITERRANEAN SEA

Byblos

LEBANON

Megiddo

Jerusalem

PALESTINE

Rosetta

Alexandria

Tanis

Sais

Avaris
(Per Ramesses)

Siwa

Giza

WESTERN
DESERT

FAIYUM

Memphis

SINAI

R. Nile

E G Y P T

Beni Hasan

Hermopolis

Akhetaten (Amarna)

EASTERN
DESERT

RED SEA

Abydos

Dendera

Thebes (Luxor)

Esna

Edfu

Kom Ombo

Aswan

Abu
Simbel

NUBIA

THE NILE DELTA

Buto

Alexandria

Sais

Tanis

Avaris

Bubastis

Giza

Heliopolis

Abusir

Saqqara

Memphis

Dahshur

FAIYUM

Meidum

Statue of Khafre with the god Horus protecting him, made of black Diorite stone

HISTORY

EARLY EGYPT

The river Nile, snaking its way across the desert and into the sea, first attracted people to its banks many thousands of years ago. At first, they moved around and survived by hunting animals and gathering what they could to eat. Then, by around 5500BC, people started to settle along the riverbank and grow crops.

These are copies of carved ivory labels found at Abydos – examples of some of the earliest writing in the world.

THE PREDYNASTIC PERIOD

Until around 3500BC, things changed slowly. This time is called the Predynastic Period. People farmed the land along the Nile, and began to dig irrigation canals to make more use of its water. They kept animals, too – mainly sheep, goats and pigs.

There were two main groups of villages – one in the south (Upper Egypt), and one in the north (Lower Egypt). These areas gradually became two kingdoms (which means they were ruled by kings). In Upper Egypt, early mud-brick tombs or 'mastabas' have been found that contain beautiful pots and objects. These suggest that a sophisticated culture and religion were already developing, and a belief in life after death.

This Predynastic pot is decorated with a crocodile, common in the Nile at that time.

This Predynastic terracotta dancing woman is nearly 6,000 years old.

WRITING BEGINS

Some historians think that writing began in Egypt earlier than anywhere else, because of some carvings, dating from Predynastic times, that were recently found at Abydos (a town in central Egypt). The Egyptian language was written in pictures or hieroglyphs. Find out more about this on pages 124-125.

TWO CROWNS

The kings of Upper and Lower Egypt had their own separate gods and crowns. The southern king was guarded by the vulture goddess Nekhmet, and wore a tall white crown. In Lower Egypt, the king wore a red crown and was protected by the cobra goddess Wadjet.

White crown of Upper Egypt

Red crown of Lower Egypt

Later kings sometimes combined the red and white crowns to make a single crown, like this.

FIRST KING – OR KINGS?

Around 3100BC, it seems that Upper Egypt defeated Lower Egypt in a battle, and the two areas were united for the first time. The man who then became king is a slightly mysterious figure, because three different names appear in records: Menes, Narmer and Hor-Aha. This could be because kings always had more than one name. It's also possible that Hor-Aha was Narmer's son. Whatever the truth is, the Narmer palette (see below) is one of the earliest records of a king who ruled both Upper and Lower Egypt.

The Narmer palette shows King Narmer wearing the white crown of Upper Egypt. On the other side of the palette, he is shown wearing the red crown of Lower Egypt.

THE ARCHAIC PERIOD

Once Egypt was united, the land was ruled by kings for more than 3,000 years. The 1st and 2nd dynasties form the Archaic period, which lasted about 400 years. Menes (or Narmer) created a capital city for the whole country between Upper and Lower Egypt, at the bottom of the Nile Delta. This was called Memphis, which became a great city with its own special god called Ptah.

The god Ptah

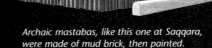

Archaic mastabas, like this one at Saqqara, were made of mud brick, then painted.

FUNERAL CUSTOMS

Some of the remaining features of the Archaic period are rectangular mastabas, which were the burial places for royals and nobles. Some of the royal ones are surrounded by smaller tombs belonging to servants. It's believed that the servants would have sacrificed themselves voluntarily when their master died, and were then buried around him to see to his needs in the afterlife. This practice died out by the end of the 1st dynasty.

The Nile flows from south to north, which is why the north is called Lower Egypt and the south is called Upper Egypt. This satellite image of the river Nile shows how it meanders north from Upper Egypt then fans out into the Nile Delta.

To the east and west of the Nile there is little but harsh, scorching deserts.

INTERNET LINK

For links to websites where you can see early Egyptian objects and take a close-up look at the Narmer Palette, go to **www.usborne-quicklinks.com**

THE OLD KINGDOM

The Old Kingdom was one of the most amazing periods in Egyptian history. For the first time, the Egyptians began building whole buildings in stone, with astonishing results. Many kings made sure that they would not be forgotten in a hurry, with the construction of massive monuments such as the pyramids and the Sphinx.

STABILITY AND WEALTH

The Old Kingdom began in c.2650BC with the start of the 3rd dynasty, and lasted about 500 years. At first, the king ruled all of Egypt, and sent governors to look after specific areas. They had to report back to the king on a regular basis. We now call these local governors 'nomarchs'.

This stable situation was disrupted after the reign of Pepi II. Pepi reigned for so long that he didn't have any successors, and different nomarchs took over instead.

INTERNET LINK

For links to websites where you can explore the Great Pyramid, follow an Egyptian guide into a tomb and find fascinating pyramid facts, go to **www.usborne-quicklinks.com**

THE FIRST GENIUS

The second king of the 3rd dynasty was called Djoser. He is famous because the first ever step pyramid was built for him, thanks to the ideas of an architect called Imhotep. Imhotep was the first recorded genius – as well as being an architect, he was a priest, a doctor, an astronomer and a very wise adviser. He was so admired by ancient Egyptians that, many years after his death, he was revered as a god.

A small carving of the architect Imhotep

SENEFERU

The idea of building a pyramid to rest in after death appealed to many kings after Djoser. The first king of the 4th dynasty, Seneferu, built two pyramids at Dahshur. These are known as the Bent Pyramid, and the Red Pyramid (the first true pyramid). King Seneferu was probably buried in the Red Pyramid.

Mastaba

Step pyramid

Bent pyramid

Djoser's step pyramid at Saqqara began as just a stone mastaba, and the steps were gradually built up.

True pyramid

GIZA

Seneferu's son, Khufu (also known by his Greek name of Cheops), built only one pyramid, but it was the most impressive ever built: the Great Pyramid of Giza. When Khufu died, his son Khafre (Chephren) built another huge pyramid next to his father's. No one matched Khufu's effort, though, and the third pyramid of Giza, built by Khafre's son Menkaure (Mycerinus), is smaller than Khafre's. You can find out more about these three amazing pyramids on pages 104-105.

This tiny carving is the only surviving image of Khufu to have been found.

A DOTTED DESERT

In the 5th and 6th dynasties, kings continued to build pyramids – there are about 90 of them dotted over the west bank of the Nile. However, later kings didn't put as much time and effort into building them, so they didn't last as well. Most of them are now just piles of rubble.

This picture is of the pyramid of Teti at Saqqara, which now lies in ruins.

THE LAST KING

The last king of the 6th Dynasty was called Pepi II. He reigned for a long time, probably until he was about 100. After his death, Egypt fell into a period of confusion as the nomarchs vied for power, and the Old Kingdom came to an end.

THE RIDDLE OF THE SPHINX

The Sphinx sits in front of Khafre's pyramid at Giza, and has a lion's body and the head of a king. Most historians think it was built at around the same time as the pyramid, and is a portrait of Khafre himself.

The Sphinx has always captured people's imagination. Some people still think it has mysterious powers, or that there are undiscovered chambers deep inside it. But, so far, tests carried out by Egyptologists have found no evidence for anything like this.

The Sphinx stares out towards the rising sun. Its front paws have recently been restored.

TIMES OF CHANGE

When the Old Kingdom dissolved, a time known as the First Intermediate Period began. Texts speak of '70 kings in 70 days' because kings came and went like the wind. Then, after about a hundred years, the Middle Kingdom began. This lasted for about 400 years, and was a period of great creativity in Egypt.

Map showing location of Middle Kingdom capital

Memphis•

It-tawy •

Faiyum

Nile

☐ Fertile area

CHAOS AND FAMINE

Nomarchs formed the 7th, 8th, 9th and 10th dynasties. During the 9th and 10th dynasties, some of them were very powerful, but no king ruled the whole of Egypt. It was a period of struggle and civil war. There were also terrible famines. Low annual floods led to droughts in which crops failed and people began to starve.

Mentuhotep II

ORDER AT LAST

After about a hundred years, things improved. The princes of Thebes won control of all Egypt and made Thebes the capital for the first time. This marks the start of the 11th dynasty and the Middle Kingdom. The best known of the 11th dynasty kings, Mentuhotep II, built a magnificent mortuary temple and tomb on the west bank of the Nile, opposite Thebes.

A MYSTERY CAPITAL

Although the Middle Kingdom kings were from Thebes, in the 12th dynasty they moved their capital to a place further north. They called it It-tawy, which means 'Seizer of the Two Lands'.

No one is sure exactly where It-tawy was, but it was somewhere between Memphis and the Faiyum, a huge oasis with a lake forming part of it. One 12th dynasty king, Senusret II, started a massive irrigation project there, so that the land around it could be used for farming.

These models are of Middle Kingdom fishermen, who would have mingled with people enjoying themselves on the river.

 INTERNET LINK

For links to websites where you can read about the excavation of a Middle Kingdom town, see a timeline of ancient Egypt and learn more about the The Tales of Sinuhe, go to www.usborne-quicklinks.com

CONQUERING NUBIA

The Middle Kingdom was a relatively peaceful time, but the kings of the 12th dynasty did expand Egypt southwards and conquered much of Nubia and Kush (part of modern Sudan). To guard their new territory, they built massive forts along the borders.

CREATIVE TIMES

Artistic activity flourished in the Middle Kingdom. Many famous stories were written, such as *The Tale of Sinuhe* and *The Eloquent Peasant*. These were copied over and over again by scribes in future generations, which is why we know about them today.

The model fishermen date from c.2000BC, and were found in the tomb of a man called Meket-Re in Thebes.

Burial practices changed, too, which led to the development of new art forms. Nobles were buried in beautifully decorated tombs cut into the rocks. Those who couldn't afford lavish decoration in their tombs had little models placed in them instead, many of them incredibly detailed and intricate. Some of the best examples were found in central Egypt, at Beni Hasan and Assyut.

INVADERS

After the 13th dynasty, royal power grew weaker and the Middle Kingdom came to an end. Meanwhile, foreigners trickled into the Nile Delta area from the east. The Egyptians called them Hyksos.

The Hyksos adapted well to life in Egypt, taking on its customs and religion. They gradually became more powerful until they controlled most of Egypt from their capital, Avaris. They had a big impact on Egyptian life, and introduced many new objects, including weapons.

THE GROWTH OF EMPIRES

The Hyksos kings were hated by Egyptian princes further south. Once more, it was rulers from Thebes who became powerful enough to act. Three Theban kings – Tao I, Kamose and Ahmose – campaigned northwards and drove the Hyksos right out of Egypt. By 1550BC, a new era of Egyptian history had begun.

LOOKING OUTWARDS

Egypt now began a golden age known as the New Kingdom, which lasted from the 18th to the 20th dynasties. Many of the New Kingdom kings left extraordinary monuments and stories behind them, and the Egyptian empire became big and powerful, especially during the 18th and 19th dynasties.

EGYPT'S MAIN RIVALS

The Near East is the term used for the countries to the north and east of Egypt as far as modern-day Turkey and Iraq. This big area was the home to many great nations at the time of the New Kingdom, such as the Hittites, Mitanni and Babylonians.

In this big melting pot, nothing remained the same for long. Empires grew, shrank, or were taken over. The Assyrian empire (see pages 34-37) was small early in the New Kingdom, but grew when the Sea Peoples defeated the Hittites. By the 20th dynasty, Egypt itself could not keep a grip on its large empire, which by then had begun to shrink.

Gold statue of a Hittite king

GREECE

Hattushash (Bogazköy)

Carchemish

Ashur

CYPRUS

Kadesh

Euphrates

Tigris

MEDITERRANEAN SEA

Byblos

PALESTINE

Babylon

MESOPOTAMIA

•Per Ramesses
• Memphis

Map showing the main great empires during the New Kingdom (c.1552-1069BC)

Egyptian

Hittite

Mitanni

Sea Peoples

Assyrian

Babylonian

Nile

• Thebes

NUBIA

WEALTH AND GRANDEUR

Having a big empire made Egypt very wealthy, because it received a constant supply of goods from the nations it had conquered. Being powerful made trading easier, too. Egypt exported food, and imported horses, timber, metal and many other treasures.

At home, the kings revelled in their power and wealth by carrying out huge building projects. One of the most outstanding was the temple complex at Karnak. There had been temples on this site since the Middle Kingdom, but New Kingdom rulers built around them, adding many new gates (called pylons), halls and obelisks.

The vast temple complex at Karnak as it looks today, showing the sacred lake with the remains of the temple behind it.

The New Kingdom kings lavished some of their wealth on elaborate ornaments, such as this pectoral, worn around the neck.

NEW BURIAL CUSTOMS

Now that Egypt was ruled from Thebes, the pharaohs needed a new burial site. So they started cutting magnificent tombs in a valley on the west bank, which became known as the Valley of the Kings (see pages 106-107). They also built mortuary temples on the west bank, so that they could still receive funeral offerings every day.

THE EARLY NEW KINGDOM

The first 18th dynasty kings (Ahmose, Amenhotep I and Tuthmosis I) consolidated their power by expanding the empire to the south and north, and reforming the administration. This was also a time of powerful women: Tetisheri (Ahmose's grandmother), Ahhotep I (his mother), and Ahmose Nefertari, his wife. Ahmose Nefertari acted as regent when Amenhotep I was too young to rule himself. This paved the way for another remarkable queen later on.

Later, Ahmose Nefertari was worshipped as a goddess, as she is portrayed in this painting.

 INTERNET LINK

For links to websites where you can take a virtual tour of the temple of Karnak and see panoramic views of other sites in the New Kingdom, go to **www.usborne-quicklinks.com**

THE QUEEN WHO BECAME KING

The 18th Dynasty had problems becoming firmly established, because the kings often died young or had sons who died before them. But Tuthmosis II, the fourth king of the dynasty, had a remarkable chief queen who took this matter into her own hands. Her name was Hatshepsut.

A BOY KING

Hatshepsut had no sons, and so her nephew, another Tuthmosis, was heir to the throne. But he was still very young when Tuthmosis II died, so Hatshepsut took over as regent. This meant keeping things under control until the new king was ready to rule.

THE REGENCY ENDS

Hatshepsut was quite a character. Being regent didn't suit her at all, and after a few years the oracle of the god Amun declared she was the true king. She was properly crowned, and began to wear all the royal regalia of a male pharaoh – even a false beard.

A statue of Hatshepsut with a beard

EXPANSION AND TRADE

During Hatshepsut's 20-year reign, she defended Egypt's frontiers in Nubia and Syria, and organized many building projects. She also renewed Egypt's trade with the land of Punt (probably Somalia). This is described on her mortuary temple. The ships had to be carried in pieces from the Nile to the Red Sea and put together again. But it was worth it for Punt's myrrh trees, frankincense, ebony, ivory, leopard skins and even baboons.

This is Hatshepsut's expedition leaving Punt, which was rich and lush, with many trees and plants that did not grow in Egypt.

Myrrh trees were taken on board the ships with all their roots

Hatshepsut's mortuary temple is a dramatic sight, with the cliff-face behind and long avenues leading up to it.

THE BEAUTIFUL TEMPLE

Hatshepsut's mortuary temple was built at Deir el Bahri, next to the temple of Mentuhotep II (see page 58). It is one of the most beautiful temples still standing on the west bank of the Nile. It was designed by Hatshepsut's adviser, a man named Senmut. He also educated her daughter, Neferure.

Some Egyptologists think that Senmut may have been the queen's lover. It's not clear what happened to him – he probably died in the later years of her reign, as he is no longer mentioned in records.

THE NEPHEW'S REVENGE

Throughout Hatshepsut's reign, her nephew Tuthmosis III sat waiting in the wings, furious with her for taking his place. As soon as she was dead, he ordered everything to do with his aunt to be destroyed, including her temple. But now, Egyptologists are gradually rebuilding it.

The warlike king Tuthmosis III

EGYPT AT WAR

Despite having to wait so long to become king, Tuthmosis III had a successful reign, ruling for over thirty years. He built many monuments, but he is best known for waging constant wars and extending the Egyptian empire to its greatest size ever.

The Egyptian empire at its greatest extent

SYRIA

EGYPT

Nile

RED SEA

NUBIA

Extent of Tuthmosis's empire in c.1440BC

THE MITANNI

Every spring, Tuthmosis embarked on a new military campaign, either south into Nubia or north-east into Syria, Canaan, and towards the river Euphrates. He waged a total of seventeen campaigns, many of them against the Mitanni (see page 29). But although he often beat them in battle, he never completely defeated them. The Mitanni were eventually destroyed by a new force from the north – the Hittites.

INTERNET LINK

For a link to a website where you can read more about the feuds, scandals and controversies surrounding Hatshepsut's reign, go to www.usborne-quicklinks.com

RELIGIOUS REVOLUTION

When Tuthmosis III died, Egypt was rich and the empire large. The Mitanni made peace with his grandson, Tuthmosis IV. So Amenhotep III, who followed, was free to enjoy luxuries and concentrate on things at home. This led to such a radical new approach to religion that it shook the whole country.

THE POWER OF AMUN

As the New Kingdom pharaohs came from Thebes, the god of Thebes, Amun, became more and more important throughout Egypt, with rich, powerful priests. So what happened next came as a big shock.

The god Amun

A LEISURELY UPBRINGING

Amenhotep III's long, peaceful reign was ideal for spending time and resources on culture, leisure and building projects. So the heir to the throne, the young Amenhotep IV, would have had a relaxed upbringing, with plenty of freedom to develop his own ideas. He became particularly interested in religion and the arts.

This is one of many statues of Akhenaten that show him with a much longer face than other pharaohs.

 INTERNET LINK

For a link to a website where you can find out more about Akhenaten's world by studying stone carvings and reliefs, go to www.usborne-quicklinks.com

ONE GOD: THE ATEN

Amenhotep IV rejected the worship of Amun and replaced him with the Aten, the sun's disk in its brightest, most visible form. When he became king, he began to put his religious ideas into practice. Soon, he ordered the name Amun to be hacked off temples and told everyone to worship the Aten. He changed his name from Amenhotep to Akhenaten, which means 'Agreeable to the Aten'.

A NEW CITY: AKHETATEN

Akhenaten didn't want to live among all the images of other gods in Thebes, so he built a new city further north and named it Akhetaten ('Horizon of the Aten'). It was on a windswept plain surrounded by cliffs near the area now known as Amarna, so Akhenaten's reign is often called the 'Amarna' period.

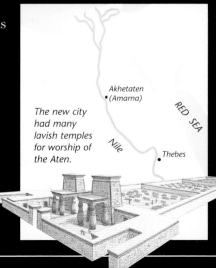

The new city had many lavish temples for worship of the Aten.

THE BEAUTIFUL QUEEN

Akhenaten's main queen was named Nefertiti, and she ruled alongside him for many years. But what became of her is a mystery.

This famous bust, which experts think must be of Nefertiti, suggests she was very beautiful.

Nefertiti faded from view later on in Akhenaten's reign. It has recently been discovered that he had another queen called Kiya, who was given the title 'Greatly Beloved Wife'. This suggests that she was very important to Akhenaten for a while. To confuse matters further, someone else seems to have been close to the king later – Smenkhkare (see page 66). Smenkhkare was probably a young man, but may have been a woman.

STRANGE ART FORMS

Akhenaten encouraged a new style in the arts of sculpture and painting, especially in the first half of his reign. In his portraits, he was shown in happy family scenes, playing with his children and embracing his queen. Before this, most portraits of pharaohs were formal and idealized. The king looked very strange in these images, with big hips, a fat, drooping belly and a long, thin face.

Akhenaten and his family worshipping the Aten. Could his strange shape have been caused by illness?

The whole family was shown with big heads and long skulls. We're still not sure why. One theory is that this style had a special religious meaning, and another is that they had some kind of illness.

THINGS CRUMBLE

Akhenaten was so busy with his religious reforms that he ignored the Hittites, new enemies to the north. This had a profound effect on Egypt's history. The Hittites started stealing provinces from the Egyptian empire, and it began to shrink. Never again did it reach the size it had been under Tuthmosis III.

THE TIMES OF TUTANKHAMUN

The reign of Akhenaten left behind a confusing situation, both for Egypt at the time and for us now. There are still many mysteries surrounding his family and descendents. Tutankhaten took over as king, aged about nine, but he relied on advisers for most of his reign, as he died when he was only nineteen.

AMARNA MYSTERIES

Akhenaten's later years are shrouded in mystery. It seems that someone named Smenkhkare ruled with him for a while. He may have taken Nefertiti's place as co-ruler; or perhaps Smenkhkare was Nefertiti herself under another name.

TOMB KV55

The mystery surrounding Smenkhkare is particularly enticing because of a mummy of a man found in 1907, hastily buried in the Valley of the Kings, in a tomb labelled KV55. It was so fragile it fell apart further when it was handled. This made it difficult to establish who it was. Smenkhkare? The most popular theory is that it is Akhenaten himself, but we may never know.

What's certain is that Tutankhaten came to the throne shortly after Akhenaten's death. Many now believe that he was the son of Kiya and Akhenaten. It was quite acceptable for kings to marry their sisters, and he married Ankhesenpaaten, one of Akhenaten's daughters.

This alabaster canopic jar top is thought to be of the Greatly Beloved Wife, Kiya.

Although the boy king Tutankhamun didn't live long, he was buried with amazing treasures such as this gold statue.

THE BRIEF REIGN OF THE BOY KING

Once on the throne, Tutankhaten soon left the new city of Akhetaten and moved back to Thebes. He changed his name, from Tutankhaten ('Living image of the Aten') to Tutankhamun ('Living image of Amun'). In this way, he showed that he (or his advisers) didn't want anything more to do with Akhenaten's strange religion, and that things were going back to normal. Amun-Re was declared the principal god once more.

For much of Tutankhamun's reign, he was dependent on his older advisers. One, called Ay, was commander of chariotry for years. When Tutankhamun died without any sons, it was Ay who stepped forward to take his place.

INTERNET LINK

For links to websites where you can investigate Tutankhamun's death, see a reconstruction of his face and view treasures from his tomb, go to www.usborne-quicklinks.com

A painting of Akhenaten's daughters, painted in the Amarna style (see page 65).

A DEADLY PLAGUE?

After Tutankhamun's death, a strange thing happened. His young widow Ankhesenpaamun wrote to the king of the Hittites, Egypt's rivals, begging him to send her a husband. The Hittite king obliged, but his son never arrived – he was assassinated on the way.

This story is unusual, as royal Egyptian women didn't usually marry foreigners. However, the queen stated in her letter that she didn't want to marry a 'servant'. This could refer to the old man Ay, who was of lower rank. Another explanation for the shortage of suitable husbands may have been a terrible plague that killed many Egyptians and Hittites, and possibly members of the royal households. This might solve another mystery, too: all Akhenaten's other daughters disappeared without trace.

One of Tutankhamun's thrones shows Ankhesenpaamun rubbing the king with ointment.

MURDER?

Ay reigned for only four years. When he died, a powerful army general named Horemheb wasted no time in grasping the throne. He was a ruthless man who tried to wipe Akhenaten, Tutankhamun and Ay from memory – their names and images were hacked from paintings and sculptures. The finger of guilt also points to Horemheb as the murderer of the Hittite prince.

In Tutankhamun's tomb, Ay is shown performing the ceremony of the Opening of the Mouth (see page 99). This was usually carried out by the dead king's son and heir.

THE REIGN OF HOREMHEB

Despite his shadowy background, Horemheb ruled steadily for about 28 years. He reformed the army, made sure all Egypt's boundaries were made secure, and restored order to local and central government. He also claimed to have carried out a lot of building work – but in fact simply took the credit for Tutankhamun's.

Horemheb

RAMESSES II

The 18th Dynasty came to an end with the reign of Horemheb, who appointed a man named Ramesses to follow him as pharaoh and begin the 19th dynasty. This dynasty's third king, Ramesses* II, had an extraordinary reign. He lived longer than almost any other pharaoh. He was also a great self-publicist, who created as big a name for himself as possible.

Ramesses I, shown here being greeted by gods in the afterlife, was the first of many Ramesses.

RAMESSES I AND SETI I

Ramesses I was an army officer before he became king. He was already old, and reigned for only two years before his son Seti I took over. Seti decided to rebuild the Egyptian empire, which had been lost during the reign of Akhenaten. He led several campaigns to conquer Palestine, reaching right up into Syria and conflicting with the Hittites to the north. But each time he won and returned home, his enemies crept back into the territory he had gained.

A LEGENDARY REIGN

Seti I's son, Ramesses II, had one of the longest reigns in history. He reigned for over 67 years and was probably in his late eighties when he died. He had many wives and children in the course of his long reign. His chief queen, Nefertari, was evidently very well loved and respected. Ramesses had a temple built especially for her at Abu Simbel, and she also had her own beautiful tomb in the Valley of the Queens (see page 107).

A granite statue of Ramesses II holding the royal crook

PROPAGANDA

Ramesses II was a master of the art of propaganda. For one thing, he claimed that the god Amun was his real father. He also commissioned colossal building projects, such as the Ramesseum (his mortuary temple), the hypostyle hall at Karnak, and the temples of Abu Simbel. But many other buildings were just adapted to make it look as though he had built them himself.

 INTERNET LINK

For a link to a website where you can find out about Ramesses I and II, and see photos of their mummies, go to www.usborne-quicklinks.com

THE HITTITES

Ramesses II continued his father's campaign to recapture the Egyptian empire in Palestine and Syria. This soon led to renewed hostilities with the Hittites. In the fifth year of his reign, Ramesses took on the Hittite army along the frontier of Egyptian territory at a place called Kadesh in Syria. He claimed this battle to be a great victory, even though the Egyptian army only narrowly escaped a heavy defeat. He had the battle depicted on the walls of many temples, including Abu Simbel and the hypostyle hall at Karnak.

TRAPPED AT KADESH

At the Battle of Kadesh, the Hittites tricked Ramesses into believing that they had retreated. They trapped one division of the Egyptian army – the Amun division, which had Ramesses at its head – but he showed great heroism in rallying his troops while waiting for reinforcements to arrive. He managed to hold out until eventually both armies withdrew.

The walls of the temple at Abu Simbel show Ramesses slaying his enemies in victorious battles.

A TREATY AND A WIFE

After further disputes, Ramesses came to an agreement with the Hittite king and they signed a treaty. To seal this new friendship, Ramesses married a Hittite princess. This peace lasted throughout the rest of his reign and beyond, until the Hittite kingdom collapsed in c.1196BC.

A NEW CAPITAL

Because of Egypt's interest in Palestine and Syria, Ramesses decided he needed a capital nearer to them. The new capital, Per Ramesses, was built on the site of the Hyksos capital, Avaris. Poets wrote about the beauty of this city, which remained the capital until the end of the New Kingdom.

Amun division and Egyptian camp

Kadesh

Hittite attack

River Orontes

Re division

Map of the battlefield

In the Battle of Kadesh, Ramesses (wearing the blue khephresh war helmet) startled the Hittites by charging at them fearlessly.

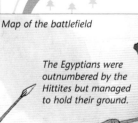

The Egyptians were outnumbered by the Hittites but managed to hold their ground.

THE NEW KINGDOM ENDS

Things would never be the same again after Ramesses II died. The 19th dynasty collapsed within only a few decades. Other New Kingdom kings tried to recreate the glory of his reign, often by taking his name, which meant the 20th dynasty was dominated by kings called Ramesses. But none was able to match him. The New Kingdom came to an end and the Third Intermediate Period began.

FOREIGN THREATS

Ramesses' successor Merenptah had to face new threats to Egypt's security. The first came from the west, what is now Libya. Many people started arriving, hoping to settle in the Delta – probably because of famine. Merenptah had to drive them back.

The second threat was more dangerous. Groups from around the Mediterranean formed what the Egyptians called the 'Sea Peoples' and tried to invade Egypt. Merenptah defeated them, killing 6,000, but more were to return 20 years later.

A Peleset warrior, one of the Sea Peoples

RAMESSES III

The 20th dynasty's second king, Ramesses III, tried to be as great as his namesake, Ramesses II, but he had to deal with many problems. Libyans tried to invade again, and many settled in the Delta. The Sea Peoples attempted another massive invasion, too, and Ramesses battled with them at sea and on land. He won, but Egypt was weakened by the battles and soon lost much of its empire.

THE FIRST STRIKE

Ramesses III carried out a few building projects, including his mortuary temple at Medinet Habu. But his administration was not very efficient and he didn't pay his workers. So they went on strike – the first recorded strike in history.

CONSPIRACY

Even Ramesses' family caused him problems. One of his wives led a conspiracy to kill him and replace him with her son. The plan didn't work and there was a huge trial. Many people were found guilty and at least 17 were executed. Others were allowed to kill themselves, or had their ears and noses chopped off. In the end, Ramesses III was succeeded by a different son. There were another seven Ramesses in the 20th dynasty, but none was very impressive.

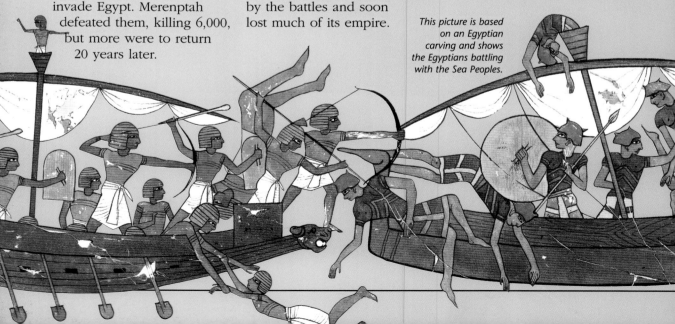

This picture is based on an Egyptian carving and shows the Egyptians battling with the Sea Peoples.

TOMB RAIDERS

During the reign of Ramesses IX, a scandal broke that ran for 20 years. Nobles' tombs were being robbed, and a few royal tombs, too. The great scandal was that some of the robbers actually worked in the local temples. Even the mayor of Thebes was suspected.

Tomb raiders ransacked the tombs as quickly as they could.

There was a big trial, but no one important was found guilty. The convicted robbers were sentenced to a gruesome death – by impalement (being stuck on a spike).

Despite the trial, the problem of tomb robberies continued, especially of the royal tombs. So, in the 21st dynasty, priests decided to move the most important mummies to keep them safe. Two of these were Ramesses II and Seti I, who were hidden in a 'cache' at Deir el Bahri. Others were hidden in the tomb of Amenhotep II in the Valley of the Kings.

The mummies shown here are Seti I, Ramesses IV and Ramesses II, all found in the 'cache' of mummies at Deir el Bahri.

OFFICIALS' POWER

None of the last kings of the 20th dynasty was very strong, and the government structure began to collapse. Nubia broke away, and administration became very disorganized. Because the kings themselves were so weak, officials such as army generals, viziers and priests began to wield more power. By the end of the 20th dynasty, a general called Heri-Hor was more or less ruling Egypt. He also took the title of high priest at Thebes.

> **INTERNET LINK**
>
> *For links to websites where you can find pictures and information about the robberies of ancient Egyptian royal tombs, go to www.usborne-quicklinks.com*

A MELTING POT

Egypt's days of glory were now long past. As the New Kingdom stumbled to an end, the Third Intermediate Period ushered in a time of confusion and division, followed by wave after wave of foreign rulers.

This picture shows the Assyrians plundering the temples at Thebes in 665BC.

TANIS AND THEBES

Ramesses XI died in c.1069BC, leaving two powerful men – Smendes in the capital (Per Ramesses), and Pinudjem, the high priest, at Thebes. They were probably both sons of Heri-Hor.

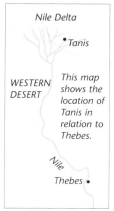

Nile Delta

Tanis

WESTERN DESERT

This map shows the location of Tanis in relation to Thebes.

Nile

Thebes

Smendes made himself king and moved the capital to Tanis, founding the 21st dynasty. Tanis was built along similar lines to Thebes, with temples to Amun and Mut. Pinudjem recognized Smendes as king for a while, then proclaimed himself king too. After this, Egyptian rule was divided between Tanis and Thebes for over 100 years.

The kings of Tanis were buried there. Beautiful treasures have been found at the site, such as this silver coffin belonging to Psusennes I, a 21st dynasty king.

THE LIBYANS

As the dynasty of kings ruling at Tanis began to crumble, powerful Libyan settlers living in the Delta grasped the chance to become rulers. These Libyan pharaohs formed the 22nd dynasty.

The first Libyan ruler, Shoshenq I, married his son to the heiress of Tanis and was Commander-in-Chief of the army before taking the title of pharaoh in c.945BC. He appointed one of his sons as high priest at Thebes. By doing this, he more or less united Egypt again.

The gold mask on the right is made of a single sheet of gold. It was found at Tanis and belonged to Shoshenq II, one of the 22nd dynasty Libyan kings.

THE EMPIRE REGAINED?

The Libyan rulers were keen to establish the Egyptian empire to the east once more, and Shoshenq I carried out some successful raids in Palestine. He looted the city of Jerusalem in c.925BC, carrying off much of the treasure in its main temple. But Egyptian power was never really restored permanently in the region.

Assyrian soldiers were very violent and bloodthirsty and killed many Egyptians.

The Assyrians carried off all the gold in the temples.

What they couldn't take with them, the Assyrians tried to burn instead.

RULERS FROM NUBIA

The Libyan period ended in confusion, with many princes ruling at once. Meanwhile the Nubians, who had freed themselves of Egyptian rule in the reign of Ramesses XI, pushed north in c.728BC, led by a man named Piankhi.

The Nubians had adopted many Egyptian customs, and were more fervent Amun-worshippers than the Egyptians themselves. So Piankhi set himself up at Thebes, starting the 25th dynasty. He fought the princes in the Delta until they all recognized him as king of Egypt.

This sphinx has the face of Taharqa, a 25th dynasty Nubian king.

THE RISE OF ASSYRIA

During the Nubian period, the balance of power in the Near East was changing yet again. The Assyrians had become the major power in the area, and by c.750BC they controlled a large part of Mesopotamia and Palestine. The Nubian kings joined forces with kings in Palestine to try to push them back – but only drew the Assyrians' attention to Egypt instead. The Assyrians invaded the Delta of Egypt twice, but the Nubian kings continued to rebel. Eventually the Assyrians decided to teach Egypt a lesson.

THE SACK OF THEBES

With the help of princes from the Delta, the Assyrians marched as far as Thebes in 665 BC. They plundered the temples and set them alight. The Nubian king of the time, Tanutamen, was forced to flee back to Nubia, bringing Nubian rule in Egypt to an end.

 INTERNET LINK

For links to websites where you can find out more about the ancient Assyrian armies, and Tanis and its tombs, go to **www.usborne-quicklinks.com**

THE LAST KINGS

The 26th dynasty was the last great dynasty of native Egyptian rulers. The final six centuries BC saw the rise of many empires in the Near East and Europe, and Egypt was affected by all of them. In the 4th century BC, Egyptian kings ruled again, but only briefly. After this, the ancient Egyptian civilization was taken over for good.

THE KINGS OF SAIS

After their brutal invasion, the Assyrians went home, but still expected the local princes of Egypt to pay them tribute. It didn't take long for the princes to rebel – only one year later, Psamtek, from Sais in the Delta, refused to pay. In 664BC he proclaimed himself king and reunited Egypt again. He and his descendants formed the 26th dynasty, which marks the start of the Late Period.

The 26th dynasty lasted for about 150 years. In this time, Egypt prospered. The kings of Sais wanted to make Egypt great again, so they carried out a lot of building work and tried to expand to the east once more. One of these kings, Necho II, also started to construct a canal between the Nile and the Red Sea.

These coffins and statue all date from the 26th Dynasty. They show some of the fine artistic work that went on in this period.

PERSIAN TYRANNY

The next great empire to conquer Egypt was that of the Persians. By 525BC, they had defeated the last king of Sais, Psamtek III. They then took control of Egypt for the next 120 years or so, ruling through a *satrap* or local governer. The Persians were very unpopular rulers, even though they ruled from a distance – the only one to visit Egypt personally was Cambyses II. However, the emperor Darius, who followed Cambyses, did make an effort to be fair and to respect Egyptian customs.

The Persian emperor Darius

GREEK SETTLERS

During the Late Period, more and more Greeks came to live in Egypt, first as merchants but later as mercenaries. They were fascinated by Egyptian culture and adopted many Egyptian practices. They also provided Egypt with soldiers. In the Persian Period, Egypt formed a number of alliances with Greece.

Alexander the Great, shown on an ancient Roman mosaic

INTERNET LINK

For links to websites where you can find out about the city founded by Alexander the Great, go to **www.usborne-quicklinks.com**

LAST EGYPTIAN KINGS

The Egyptians constantly rebelled against the Persians and in about 404BC, they managed to get rid of their hated rulers for a while.

This brief, final period of Egyptian independence lasted only about 60 years, but these years were certainly eventful. There were many wars, as the Greeks and Egyptians constantly tried to ward off the Persian threat. Eventually, the Persians invaded again under Ataxerxes II, and the last Egyptian king, Nectanebo II, was forced to flee.

ALEXANDER THE GREAT

In 334BC, another empire was rising – that of Alexander the Great, based in Macedonia (see pagees 242-243). He swept into Egypt and ousted the Persians in 332BC. The Egyptians welcomed him as a hero, and an oracle declared him a son of Amun. Alexander founded a new capital, named Alexandria, on the Mediterranean coast. Then, in 323BC, aged only 32, he died. His empire was divided between three generals. One called Ptolemy (pronounced 'Tollomy') took control of Egypt.

King Nectanebo II making an offering. He had a reputation as a great magician.

PTOLEMY TAKES OVER

Ptolemy and his descendents ruled Egypt for nearly 300 years. All these kings were called Ptolemy, and their queens were called Cleopatra, Arsinoe or Berenice.

The Ptolemies spoke Greek, and made Greek the official language. They saw Greek culture as superior, but at least they lived in Egypt and tried to please their Egyptian subjects. They respected the old traditions and carried out a lot of building work in the Egyptian style.

This is part of the temple of Isis at Philae. This temple was rebuilt in the Ptolemaic period.

THE LAST QUEEN

Although Cleopatra was one of the most important queens of Egypt, she wasn't even Egyptian. She was a Ptolemy, so her origins were Greek. But she was the last ruler of Egypt before it lost independence. She was born there, and her story shows that she saw Egypt as home.

A coin showing Mark Antony's head

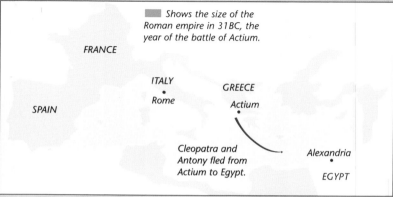

Shows the size of the Roman empire in 31BC, the year of the battle of Actium.

FRANCE

ITALY
• Rome

GREECE
Actium
•

SPAIN

Cleopatra and Antony fled from Actium to Egypt.

Alexandria
•

EGYPT

THE ROMANS

By about 100BC, a new force was gaining power all around the Mediterranean – the Romans. As the Romans grew in strength, Alexander's Macedonian empire slowly crumbled under the pressure. It wasn't long before the Ptolemies were forced to acknowledge the power of Rome. For the time being, the Roman senators just dabbled in Egyptian politics, and allowed the Ptolemies to remain rulers. But this was about to change, too.

CLEOPATRA VII

Cleopatra VII became queen in 51BC, as the wife of her young brother, Ptolemy XIII. She hadn't wanted to marry him and she soon quarrelled with his advisers. The situation grew worse, until war broke out. The Roman general Julius Caesar came to Alexandria to sort things out. Cleopatra won Caesar over to her side – in fact, he became her lover.

Ptolemy was killed, and Cleopatra became sole ruler of Egypt. But then Caesar was murdered, so Cleopatra joined forces with one of his friends, Mark Antony, and became his lover, too. Octavian, Caesar's heir, didn't want any rivals to the east, and war broke out. Cleopatra and Mark Antony were defeated by Octavian's army at Actium in 31BC.

To avoid more humiliation, Mark Antony and Cleopatra killed themselves. He used a sword but, so the story goes, Cleopatra used an asp (a poisonous snake). After this, Egypt became part of the Roman empire (see pages 282-283).

Elizabeth Taylor as Cleopatra in the film Cleopatra. *Behind her is an artist's impression of the Battle of Actium.*

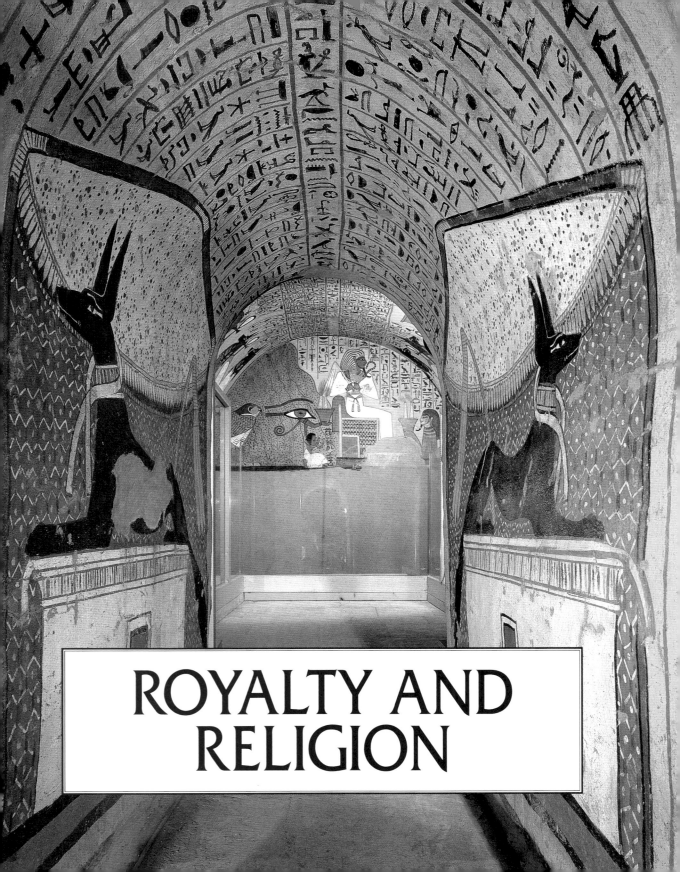

ROYALTY AND RELIGION

THE ROLE OF KING

The king was far more than just a ruler. He represented the gods, and had absolute power. People even believed he could make it rain. But he still had to abide by the principle of *ma'at*, or justice and mercy.

DIVINE ORIGINS

Originally, so it was said, Egypt was ruled by the gods, who lived on Earth like people. Horus, the falcon god, was king, and Osiris ruled the Next World. When the gods no longer ruled on earth, Horus sent his spirit to enter the king instead. When he died, the king became one with Osiris, and the role of Horus passed to the next king.

THE KING'S NAME

The king was considered so important that people didn't refer to him directly. They spoke of the 'Palace' or 'per-aa' instead. This is the origin of the title 'pharaoh'. Kings had two different names: their 'Son of Re' name, received at birth, and their *nsw-bity* name, received when they were crowned. *Nsw-bity* means 'King of Upper and Lower Egypt'. We usually refer to kings by their Son of Re name.

Tutankhamun's head and shoulders from his solid gold coffin. He is holding a crook and flail, and has a cobra and vulture at his forehead.

CROWNING GLORY

The king is often shown wearing either the Red Crown of Lower Egypt or the White Crown of Upper Egypt, or a double crown.

By the New Kingdom, a new bright blue crown had appeared, called the khephresh. It was more of a battle helmet than a crown, and reflects the importance of the king's role as warrior at that time.

Khephresh

Sometimes the king is shown wearing the atef crown – a tall crown adorned with ostrich feathers, which had more religious significance.

Atef

Kings also wore a menes, or long striped head-dress. Like other crowns, this had a vulture's head and a cobra's head attached to it, to represent Nekhmet and Wadjet, the king's protectors.

Menes

ROYAL REGALIA

In paintings and carvings, kings are often shown holding some kind of royal regalia (symbolic item). The most important were the crook and flail. The crook was used by shepherds, so symbolized the king's protection of his people. The flail was used to whip people, so symbolized the king's punishment of his enemies.

A war mace and an ankh, the symbol of life.

There was also a selection of other symbolic items: in scenes of war, the king usually carries a mace (a stick with a stone ball on the end) to smite his enemies. In the afterlife, he holds the *ankh*, a kind of cross that meant 'life', which many of the gods are shown holding.

SYMBOLIC POWER

Egyptian art sometimes demonstrates the king's power by showing him as a powerful animal, such as a lion or sphinx. This was a reminder that he was a god, who could appear in many forms.

The king was also represented as a strong bull, which gave rise to the 'Festival of the Tail' – the Heb Sed. Part of the king's costume was actually a bull's tail, which you can see in some pictures.

During the Sed festival, the king had to perform physical activities, such as a ceremonial run, to renew his strength and show that he was still fit. Sed festivals were supposed to happen when a king had reigned for thirty years. But kings often held them more often, especially if their strength was failing or after some kind of disaster.

The Heb Sed festival taking place in the big courtyard in front of the Step Pyramid at Saqqara. The king runs around to prove he is still fit.

THE ROLE OF QUEENS

The king was almost always a man. He had one chief queen and many minor ones. The chief queen was often the king's sister or half-sister. In early statues and carvings, queens are often shown very small, because they were much less important than the king. But in the New Kingdom they became more important, and were seen as the divine incarnation of the goddess Hathor, Horus's wife.

King Hatshepsut was a woman, here shown as a sphinx to demonstrate her power.

White crown of Upper Egypt

Like all ceremonies in Egypt, the Heb Sed had religious significance and was attended by priests.

GOVERNMENT AND POWER

Even though the king had absolute power, in practice he was surrounded by ministers who did a lot of the work for him. The government of Ancient Egypt was very well organized, with lots of departments and officials. There were strict ways of doing things and everything was written down.

HOW GOVERNMENT WORKED

Ancient Egyptian government was 'centralized', which meant that the king made all the important decisions. When there was a king who wasn't very good at this, the whole government ran into problems.

The king's decisions were carried out by his ministers. Becoming a minister wasn't easy, as most top jobs stayed within families. But if your parents paid for an education and you were talented enough, it was possible to work your way up.

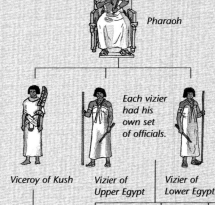

Pharaoh

Each vizier had his own set of officials.

Viceroy of Kush

Vizier of Upper Egypt

Vizier of Lower Egypt

Viceroy staff Treasury Granaries Royal Works Army Priesthood

This diagram shows how the government was structured, with the viziers below the king and everyone else below them.

GOVERNMENT DEPARTMENTS

After the king, the two viziers (for Upper and Lower Egypt) were the most important officials, along with the Viceroy of Kush, who governed Nubia. The viziers were in charge of all government departments and the justice system. They had to collect taxes, supervise irrigation and building projects, receive visitors and much, much more. Below the viziers were the army, the priesthood and overseers of several other departments. The biggest were the Treasury, Granaries and Royal Works (building projects).

In this wall painting, government officials measure how much a peasant should pay the king in tax.

TAXES AND MONEY

Until the Persian Period, Egypt didn't have coins or money as we know it. People paid for things – including their taxes – 'in kind', which means with goods or work. They had to give part of whatever they grew or made to the government, and some of their time, too.

The Egyptian work tax is now described as a 'corvée'. Corvées were very well organized, and were used for many tasks, from digging irrigation channels to carrying out building projects. In fact, if it wasn't for the corvées, the pyramids would never have been built.

PRIESTS AND GENERALS

Two other major aspects of Egyptian life provided some top jobs. These were the army (mainly from the New Kingdom onwards) and the temples.

This striking sycamore statue, found on the West Bank at Thebes, is of a priest named Ka-aper.

The king depended on the army to maintain Egypt's strength, so army generals had a lot of power and influence. They sometimes even became king themselves. Horemheb and Ramesses I are two examples.

Some army generals could afford gold funeral masks like this one.

The temples were important for administration as well as worship, and they collected taxes on behalf of the king. As a result, High Priests had a lot of influence.

INTERNET LINK

For links to websites where you can watch a movie about an Egyptian priest and learn about other officials, go to www.usborne-quicklinks.com

WAS IT FAIR?

Overall, ordinary people were treated well in this system, and they could go to court to settle disputes. People accused of crimes received a fair trial, though they might be beaten to test whether they were telling the truth. There were local and district courts, but if these courts were unable to resolve a dispute, the matter could go before the vizier or even the king himself. Watching trials was a popular public pastime.

Convicted criminals faced a range of punishments. If a crime was serious, they could be executed or mutilated (have their nose, ears or hands cut off). Less serious crimes were punished with floggings, fines, or sometimes exile to a remote place.

In a local court, a panel of judges would decide whether or not the accused was guilty of the crime.

Scribes made records of all that happened.

The accused man had to listen to the charges, but he was allowed to defend himself.

This man reads the charges against the accused.

FIGHTING FORCES

Egypt's army varied enormously in the course of its history. There were times when there wasn't a national army at all, and times when there were several small ones. During the New Kingdom, though, Egypt's army was truly impressive, and struck terror into many other peoples of the Near East.

Golden flies, such as these, were used as symbols of military glory. They were given to reward bravery in battle.

EARLY ARMIES

In the Old Kingdom, Egypt only had a small professional army. In the provinces, local rulers had bands of men that the king could call on if he needed to. It's likely that the first full national army was established by Middle Kingdom kings in the 12th dynasty. They wanted to make sure that Egypt didn't splinter apart in a hurry. However, at this stage the army was probably still quite small.

MEN FROM NUBIA

From as early as the 6th dynasty, men from Nubia moved north into Egypt to join the army. Men who are paid to fight on behalf of a foreign country like this are called mercenaries. In the New Kingdom, one Nubian tribe named the Medjay concentrated more on keeping law and order than on fighting other countries. Because of this, the word 'Medjay' eventually came to mean police force.

This group of model Nubian soldiers was found in a Middle Kingdom tomb.

The soldiers are carrying bows and arrows, as Nubians were famous for their skill as archers.

ARMY STRUCTURE

In the New Kingdom, Egypt went to war regularly. New weapons and chariots were introduced, and the army became a key part of the Egyptian hierarchy. The king was Commander-in-Chief, but there was a whole range of posts beneath him, from royal battle adviser to the humble job of distributing supplies to the soldiers. There was also a navy, for transporting troops and suppressing attacks along the Mediterranean coast.

The New Kingdom army was divided into units, each named after an Egyptian god (for example, Amun, Re, or Set). Every unit had 4,000 foot soldiers and 500 chariots, each with two men – one to drive, the other to fight.

In battle, experienced soldiers fought at the front, with newer recruits behind them. The quick-moving chariots went wherever they were needed. The role of trumpeters and standard-bearers (men carrying flags that soldiers could see) became important for keeping everyone together and passing on orders.

This wall painting shows soldiers in their barracks. Some are being given their weapons, while others are having their hair cut short.

HARDSHIP AND REWARD

Army life was tough. Soldiers were sent on long marches and had to take part in regular wrestling matches. Battles were gruesome, bloody affairs that could leave a soldier horribly maimed or disfigured – if he even survived. But there were definite advantages to being in the army. Soldiers were rewarded for bravery with precious objects such as gold or silver weapons, jewels, or medals in the shape of flies. They also received a share of plunder whenever they defeated an enemy.

The mummy of Seqenenre Tao, a Theban prince who fought against the Hyksos, shows terrible head wounds – probably received in battle.

Part of an Egyptian army division. The charioteers are shown at the front with neat lines of foot soldiers behind them.

TRADE AND DIPLOMACY

The relationship between Egypt and nearby lands was a very complex one. As well as maintaining its power in the region, Egypt needed to guard the trade routes that provided it with vital goods. As a result, Egyptian kings kept tight control of trade coming in and out of the country, and their messengers and ambassadors often dealt with trade agreements as well as diplomatic matters.

GOODS IN AND OUT

Egypt had plenty of resources to trade. It exported grain, wine, linen, papyrus, and manufactured goods. In particular, it was famous for its gold. One of the Amarna letters (see right) shows that other nations thought Egypt was almost dripping with it – 'Send me gold, gold and more gold, for in my Brother's land gold is as the dust,' it says. In fact, the gold came mainly from Nubia.

In return, Egypt imported many goods from the Near East, Greece and Cyprus – oil and resin, silver, copper, slaves and horses; while from Punt it received myrrh trees and other exotic African goods. From the leafy mountains of Lebanon came something that in Egypt was in very short supply – wood.

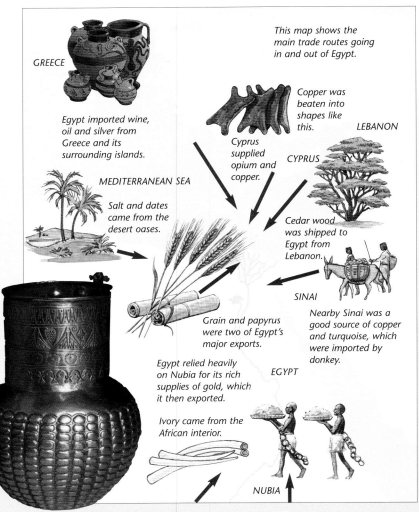

This map shows the main trade routes going in and out of Egypt.

GREECE

Egypt imported wine, oil and silver from Greece and its surrounding islands.

MEDITERRANEAN SEA

Copper was beaten into shapes like this.

LEBANON

Cyprus supplied opium and copper.

CYPRUS

Cedar wood was shipped to Egypt from Lebanon.

Salt and dates came from the desert oases.

SINAI

Nearby Sinai was a good source of copper and turquoise, which were imported by donkey.

Grain and papyrus were two of Egypt's major exports.

Egypt relied heavily on Nubia for its rich supplies of gold, which it then exported.

EGYPT

Ivory came from the African interior.

NUBIA

THE TALE OF WEN-AMUN

The Tale of Wen-Amun was written at the end of the New Kingdom (c.1070BC). It tells the story of an Egyptian ambassador, and shows the links between the worlds of trade and diplomacy.

Wen-Amun was sent on a mission to Byblos in Lebanon to collect some cedar wood, but he was robbed on the way.

Then, when he eventually arrived, he was treated very badly by the authorities in Byblos. Eventually they agreed to give him the wood he needed, but only at a very high price. The story shows how Egypt's power was beginning to wane at the end of the New Kingdom. Other nations weren't afraid of upsetting the Egyptians any more.

FOREIGN TRIBUTE

In the New Kingdom, Egypt's wealth was increased by foreign tribute that conquered nations had to pay. The conquered peoples resented this, and often rebelled. So Egypt adopted 'diplomatic' ploys to encourage payment. One was to take foreign princes' children and bring them to Egypt. They were well treated and educated, so that when they went home they promoted a positive attitude towards their Egyptian rulers.

Nubia, though, was different. It was a conquered territory for much of Egyptian history, and special to Egypt because of its gold. The Nubians did rebel at first, but gradually accepted the benefits of being linked to Egypt and adopted Egyptian customs as their own.

The Egyptians expected to be given the very best goods as tribute.

Everyone was obliged to show great respect in the presence of the Egyptian king.

In this carving, a Libyan captive is brought to Egypt, his hands tied behind his back.

African traders arriving with ivory, animal skins, baboons and other goods

INTERNET LINK

For a link to a website where you can explore an interactive map showing the different goods traded between Egypt and Crete, go to www.usborne-quicklinks.com

THE AMARNA LETTERS

The Amarna letters are about 350 baked clay tablets, found in the ruins of Akhetaten (see page 64). They are mainly letters written to the king of Egypt from the kings and princes of Assyria, Babylonia, Mitanni, Cyprus, Palestine, Syria and Hatti (the Hittites).

The tablets are written in cuneiform script (see pages 18-19) and in Akkadian, the diplomatic language of the day. The more powerful kings called the Egyptian king 'Brother', but their letters could

The clay Amarna letters were small enough for a messenger to carry around his neck.

get very frosty – in one, the king of Mitanni is furious with the king of Egypt for detaining a Mitanni messenger for six years. Lesser kings addressed the Egyptian king with more respect, calling him 'My God', or 'The Great King'. They begged for help, or tried to turn Egypt against their rivals.

THE EGYPTIAN RELIGION

Egyptian religion was a big tangle of beliefs rather than one simple idea. Very early in Egyptian history, in the Predynastic Period, dozens of different gods appeared. Some were only worshipped in people's homes, some in particular areas, while others were worshipped throughout Egypt. There were many myths, too, which varied enormously – even the best-known had different versions.

In this painting, the sun god Re makes his mythical daily journey across the sky in his boat.

WHAT THE GODS WERE LIKE

Most Egyptian gods were gods of a specific object or activity, such as embalming (Anubis), the moon (Khonsu) or water (Sobek). Some, though, represented more abstract ideas such as justice and harmony (Ma'at) or wisdom (Thoth). Many gods and goddesses were associated with a particular animal, bird or plant, and were often represented in more than one way. For example, Hathor is sometimes shown as a cow, a woman, or a woman with the head or ears of a cow.

A statue of Anubis, the god of embalming

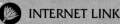 **INTERNET LINK**

For links to websites where you can watch a creation myth and find out more about Egyptian gods, go to **www.usborne-quicklinks.com**

THE CREATION MYTH

Osiris

The best-known Egyptian creation story developed in the city of Heliopolis. Originally, so the story went, there was nothing but chaos. Out of this, the sun-god Re (or Ra) created himself, then created everything else. First of all he created Shu (air) and Tefnut (moisture). Shu and Tefnut had two children, Geb (the earth) and Nut (the sky).

Isis

Geb and Nut had four children: Osiris, Isis, Set and Nephthys. You can read a version of their story opposite. Osiris and Isis were the parents of the falcon god Horus, and Nephthys also had a child by Osiris – Anubis, the jackal-headed god of embalming. Horus's wife was Hathor, the goddess of love, happiness and childbirth.

Nephthys

Every day, Re sailed across the sky in his barque, or boat. Each night, he sailed through the underworld where he had to defeat the monstrous god of darkness, Apep, in order to rise again in the morning.

Hathor

OSIRIS AND ISIS

Osiris took the place of his father Geb on the throne, and ruled fairly and justly. But his brother Set was jealous, and decided to kill him. He made a coffin that only Osiris would fit into, tricked him into getting inside, then quickly shut the lid and threw the coffin into the Nile. It floated away to the sea, and Set was sure he had defeated his brother.

But Isis, the sister-wife of Osiris, wouldn't rest until she found his body. She found the coffin and took it back to Egypt. Set was furious. He hunted down the body, cut it into fourteen

In the final battle between Horus and Set, Horus won, but not before losing an eye.

pieces, then buried each piece in a different place along the Nile. Even so, Isis didn't give up. With the help of her sister Nephthys, she found all but one of the pieces, and Anubis helped her to put Osiris back together again. He came to life briefly, and became the father of Horus. Then Re made him king of the Underworld.

Isis protected Horus from Set by hiding him in the reeds on the Nile until he was old enough to avenge his father's death. After a long battle, Horus defeated Set and became king of Egypt. So Egyptians believed that the spirit of Horus entered every king, and that when the king died, his spirit went to the Next World and was joined to the spirit of Osiris instead.

An udjat eye, or Eye of Horus

THE EYE OF HORUS

One of the Egyptians' best-loved amulets was the *udjat* eye, or 'Eye of Horus'. In his battle with Set, Horus lost an eye, and the god Thoth healed it. So this eye became a symbol for healing, and was believed to bring good health and fitness. It was also a symbol of sacrifice, because Horus had lost it when he was battling against evil.

MORE ABOUT MYTHS

Over the years, the Egyptian religion kept on changing and evolving. Gods would rise to greater importance and then fade into the background, while myths evolved or merged together. Some changes were more significant than others, though, and were often a reflection of the shifts in power that were taking place. For example, the rise of Thebes had a big impact on religion across the country.

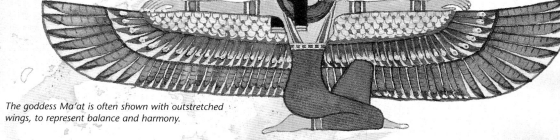

The goddess Ma'at is often shown with outstretched wings, to represent balance and harmony.

THE HERMOPOLIS MYTH

The city of Hermopolis had its own creation myth, in which the world was originally ruled by Ma'at (goddess of justice, order and truth) and her husband Thoth, the ibis-headed god of scribes and wisdom. They had four sets of twins – Nun and Nanuet, Heh and Hehet, Kek and Keket, and Amun and Amunet.

These eight gods were the forces of creation. Of the eight, only Amun became a major god, but Ma'at and Thoth were important throughout Egypt. They had a special role in deciding people's fate in the afterlife, and they were both believed to stand by Re's boat each day as he voyaged across the sky.

Thoth

Amun

Mut

Khonsu

THE GODS OF THEBES

By the end of the Old Kingdom, Amun had been adopted as the god of Thebes. Until the New Kingdom, he was not particularly important elsewhere. Then, as Theban rulers came to power, the worship of Amun began to spread, until he was worshipped throughout Egypt.

Amun's wife was originally his twin, Amunet, but in Thebes she was replaced by Mut, the goddess of motherhood. Mut and Amun had a son called Khonsu, the moon god. Amun, Mut and Khonsu are known as the 'Theban Triad' (a triad is a group of three). As Amun-worship became more important and spread north from Thebes to the rest of Egypt, Amun and Re were seen as the same god – Amun-Re, king of the gods.

THE RIVER OF BLOOD

In one myth, the god Re becomes angry with people for disobeying him and sends the lioness god Sekhmet to punish them. She begins to kill and eat people in a terrible slaughter. Re soon feels sorry for everyone, and regrets his judgement. He tries to stop Sekhmet, but she has developed a taste for blood and continues to destroy people. While she is asleep, Re mixes beer with red ochre and pours it into the river Nile, turning it red like blood. When she awakes, Sekhmet thinks the river is flowing with blood, and so she drinks from it eagerly. But, because she is really drinking beer, she becomes drunk, and loses her desire to kill people. She is transformed into the goddess of love, Hathor, the wife of Horus (see page 86).

In the myth of Re and Sekhmet, Sekhmet is a terrifying lioness who kills all the people in her path.

OTHER GODS

Sobek was the crocodile god, the god of water. He was worshipped in the Faiyum and at Kom Ombo.

Bast was the cat goddess, who represented the healing power of the Sun.

Khnum had a ram's head, and was a potter who made people on his potter's wheel.

Imhotep (see page 56) was one of the few non-royal people to be thought of as a god. He was worshipped by scribes, and as a god of medicine.

TEMPLE LIFE

Much of Egyptian life revolved around the big temples, although only kings and priests could worship in the temple itself. Priests carried out many tasks, from teaching and administration to organizing building projects. Some worked in the temple full time, while others had jobs outside it.

You can recognize priests in paintings because they had shaved heads. Here, a priest brings sacred water and incense to a noble in the afterlife.

TEMPLE LAYOUT

All temples had the same basic layout, because Egyptians believed the gods had designed the first temple when the world began.

Every temple was surrounded by an outer wall. The main gate (now known as a 'pylon') led into a courtyard. This was as far as ordinary people could go.

Beyond this point, the temples became increasingly dark, narrow and spooky. First there was the hypostyle hall, with columns built closely together to look like papyrus reeds. The only light came through little windows around the top.

Beyond this, the sanctuary or 'naos' was even darker. It held a statue of the god, usually stone, but often decorated with precious metal and jewels. Around the edge of the naos were annexes and storerooms.

Each temple also had a sacred lake, where the priests purified themselves.

BECOMING A PRIEST

In theory, the king was the only person who could approach the gods. But he couldn't be everywhere at once, which is why there were priests to stand in for him. Priests had to be educated, so becoming one wasn't easy.

Important priests worked in the temple full time, but most ordinary priests did another job for about eight months of the year. Some were kept busy with the administration and organization of temple life.

Priests took turns carrying out rituals. There were also priestesses, who gave responses in the services.

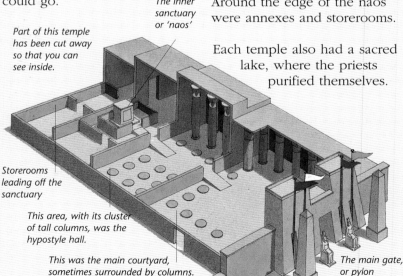

Part of this temple has been cut away so that you can see inside.

The inner sanctuary or 'naos'

Storerooms leading off the sanctuary

This area, with its cluster of tall columns, was the hypostyle hall.

This was the main courtyard, sometimes surrounded by columns.

The main gate, or pylon

THE DAILY RITUAL

The Egyptians believed that the gods sent part of their spirit into the statue in the temple, which the priests had to supply with food, drink and linen. Priests purified themselves by bathing in the sacred lake twice a day, and shaved their whole body.

Every day, the priests woke the god with a hymn. Then they opened the sanctuary to bathe and dress the statue. Next came the offerings, of the best vegetables and meat, while incense was burned and singers and dancers provided entertainment. This ritual was repeated three times a day.

There were professional dancers and musicians in the temples.

During the day, the sanctuary doors were left open. You could peer from the main pylon right through to the sanctuary. At night, the priests closed the doors and backed off carefully. They swept away their footsteps as they went, in case a demon should use them overnight.

The priests and priestesses wore only the finest white linen.

Shafts of sunlight would have glinted dramatically from the ceiling-height windows, lighting up the huge pillars of the hypostyle hall.

 INTERNET LINK

For links to websites where you can make a virtual offering to the gods and learn more about priests and temples, go to www.usborne-quicklinks.com

BUILDINGS FIT FOR GODS

The scale and grandeur of the ancient Egyptian temples was a reflection of the importance of both the gods and the king. Building them took thousands of men and incredible skill, using only very basic equipment.

MONUMENTAL STONE

Quarrying stone for building temples was a difficult, laborious job, so it was often prisoners of war or criminals who had to do it. Granite was the most difficult rock to quarry, because it was very hard. Limestone and sandstone were softer, so most temples were built from these. Granite was kept for details and specific objects, such as the tall spikes known as obelisks.

The Temple of Amun at Karnak is built mainly of easy-to-work limestone.

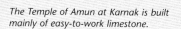

MUSCLE POWER

Hauling the huge blocks of stone to the temple sites needed hundreds of men. Rollers and ropes were used to drag the blocks to the river to be transported by boat. The Inundation helped, as it brought the river closer to the quarries. At the temple site, more men cut the stones to shape.

BUILDING BEGINS

The king himself attended a temple's foundation ceremony. He laid out the ground plan with posts and ropes, while the queen played the role of Sheshat, the goddess of writing, to record what he was doing.

After the ceremony, the first layer of stones was placed in position, and the area inside was filled with rubble. A ramp was made on the outside and the next layer of stones was hauled up. The inside was filled with more rubble and the ramp was raised for the third layer, and so on. Finally, a stone roof was placed over the top.

ARCHITECTURAL DETAILS

Once the temple was basically complete, the rubble and ramps were removed, level by level, so that craftsmen could start the decoration, from the top down. The stone columns were designed to look like palm tree trunks, or bundles of reeds. At the top and bottom, they were carved into the shape of lotus leaves and flowers, papyrus reeds or palm fronds.

Two examples of decoration

INTERNET LINK

For links to websites where you can see lots of Egyptian temples and explore an interactive tomb relief, go to www.usborne-quicklinks.com

While the temple is still full of rubble, work begins on the decoration.

Craftsmen stood on the rubble to decorate the temple.

Taking away the rubble was a big job, and needed many men.

SCULPTURE

No temple was complete without big stone statues of the gods and king. First, the stone was shaped with hard stone pounders. Details of the face and clothing were sketched on the surface, then tapped out by a sculptor with copper and bronze chisels. The completed statues were covered with fine plaster and painted.

RELIEFS

Reliefs are the carvings that you see on the walls of temples. There were two main kinds – raised reliefs and sunken reliefs. For both, the carvers followed a design marked on the stone by a draftsman. Raised reliefs stood out from their backgrounds and were made by cutting away the surrounding stone. Sunken reliefs were made by cutting the figures and inscriptions deep into the stone. When the carvings were finished, they were painted in brilliant shades.

Raised relief

Sunken relief

THE RULES OF DESIGN

Egyptian design followed strict rules, based on a grid. A human figure always had the same proportions, and was divided into 18 parts or squares from head to toe (in the New Kingdom, this changed to 21 parts). Egyptians didn't copy what they saw, but drew what they knew was there. Shoulders and eyes were shown from the front, but the rest of the head, body and legs were shown from the side.

Craftsmen drawing out a scene using the grid

THE GREAT CULT TEMPLES

All the major Egyptian gods had temples along the Nile. These were called 'cult' temples, which just means they were dedicated to the worship of a particular god. Each site was that god's 'home', so new temples were simply built on the foundations of the old ones.

KARNAK AND LUXOR

The temple of Amun at Thebes, now called Karnak, is the biggest of all the temples still standing in Egypt. The complex as you see it today was started by Tuthmosis I, but many later kings added to it. Most of the additions were courtyards and pylons around the edges, so the oldest parts are in the middle.

Amun's consort, Mut, and his son Khonsu had their own temples at Karnak, too, and there was a big sacred lake. If you visit Karnak now, you can sit near the lake in the evening and watch a 'Sound and Light' show about the temple's history.

Luxor temple was another temple to Amun, not far from Karnak. Like Karnak, most of what you can see today was built during the New Kingdom. The two temples were originally connected by a magnificent avenue lined with sphinxes.

The temple of Luxor as it is today, with the Nile in the background.

EDFU AND DENDERA

As far back as the Old Kingdom, the main temple of Horus was at Edfu, and the temple of Hathor was at Dendera. The ones still standing today were built mainly by the Ptolemies.

These temples were linked by a major annual festival – the ceremonial marriage of the two gods. Hathor would travel on a barge all the way up the Nile to Edfu, and everyone would cheer her from the banks.

OTHER TEMPLES

Today, we can only see a small number of the temples that once stood along the Nile. Temples in the Delta haven't lasted so well because the Nile Inundation tended to bury ruins under the rich river silt. There would have been a big temple to Re at Heliopolis, another to Ptah in Memphis, and many others.

Two that have survived, however, belonged to the cult of Isis at Philae, and to Sobek and Horus the Elder (Haroesis) at Kom Ombo. The temple at Kom Ombo is unusual, as it is dedicated to two gods.

A temple complex that still stands out from all the others is that of Ramesses II at Abu Simbel. The two temples there are unique because they were built purely for the glory of the king, not to glorify one of the gods.

Amun, Mut and Khonsu all had their own barques to carry them from Karnak to Luxor. This is Amun's barque.

 INTERNET LINK

For links to websites where you can take virtual tours of Luxor, Karnak and Abu Simbel and find photographs and information about temples, cults and festivals, go to www.usborne-quicklinks.com

FESTIVALS OF AMUN

Amun had two major festivals a year – the Festival of Opet, shown here, and the Festival of the Valley, when the god was taken across the river to visit the tombs and mortuary temples on the west bank.

During the Festival of Opet, everyone gathered to see the magnificent procession as the gods made their way to Luxor.

Amun's statue was carried to his barque in another smaller barque.

RELIGION IN DAILY LIFE

In spite of the fact that they weren't allowed into the big temples, ordinary Egyptians lived and breathed religion. They believed that even the greatest of gods, such as Amun or Hathor, took a personal interest in their lives and in how they behaved. They were superstitous, and looked for deeper meanings in simple everyday events.

The lion-maned dwarf god Bes guarded children and the home.

CLOSE TO HOME

Temples were the homes of gods on Earth, so people would stand outside them to pray. But you didn't have to go to one of the major temples to worship. Each village had its own shrines to its chosen gods, including the major ones, where people could say prayers or make offerings. At shrines and temples, people often erected stones called *stelae,* with ears carved on them to remind the gods to listen to their prayers.

People's homes also had little shrines within them, often in niches in the wall. These would be dedicated to ancestors, or gods such as Bes and Tawaret who protected the home.

The goddess Tawaret was represented as a female hippopotamus. She was the goddess of pregnant women and childbirth.

SPEAKING TO THE GODS

The easiest way to discover the will of the gods was to get a scribe to write down a question. You then gave this to a priest, who would take it into the temple, where the god would answer it. This was known as 'consulting an oracle'. In fact, it was a priest who gave the answers, but he believed that he was inspired by the god. If a prayer was answered, people left a gift of thanks at the temple.

On feast days, when the god's statue was carried out on a barque by priests, people sang, knelt before it or dashed forward to ask it a question. The answer ('yes' or 'no') was shown by the movement of the barque. If the answer was 'yes', the statue would move forwards or back, or become suddenly heavy, forcing its carriers to their knees.

INTERNET LINK

For links to websites where you can see animal mummies and a bird mummy case, and find out about sacred animals, go to www.usborne-quicklinks.com

Some amulets, such as these golden lizards, were fitted into necklaces and bracelets.

Below are examples of other amulets. They were often based on hieroglyphs.

SACRED ANIMALS

People believed that the gods could send their spirits to live in the creatures associated with them. By the Late Period, this applied to whole species – for example, the spirit of Bast was believed to live in every cat. When they died, these creatures were embalmed. Many were buried in animal cemeteries such as the one at Saqqara, where millions of mummified birds, cats, dogs and other animals have been found.

THE APIS BULL

The most important creatures buried at Saqqara were the Apis bulls. They were always black, with a white patch on their forehead and double white hairs in their tail. There was only one Apis bull at any one time. He lived in comfort with his mother in Ptah's temple in Memphis, and was paraded at religious festivals. When the bull died, he was mummified and taken to the Serapeum, a huge tomb underground. Then the search began for the new Apis bull.

Examples of mummified animals – a cat, a dog or jackal, and a young calf

MAGIC, DREAMS AND OMENS

People believed that they were surrounded by the powers of good and evil. There were lucky and unlucky days. Everyone wore good luck charms called amulets, and looked for omens to reveal the future or the gods' wishes. Dreams and signs such as shooting stars were seen as messages from the gods, and priests were asked to interpret them. People turned to priest-magicians to ward off bad luck.

The funeral procession of the Apis bull led to the Serapeum at Saqqara.

The Apis bull was carried on a sacred barque.

DEATH AND THE AFTERLIFE

Death came all too soon to many Egyptians, often before the age of thirty. So it's hardly surprising that they had a strong belief in the 'Next World', where they would go to live. They spent a lot of time preparing for this and had a clear idea of what it would be like, what they would need and what would happen along the way.

This early 'mummy' was preserved by the sand, and is about 5,000 years old.

THE SPIRIT WORLD

The most important parts of a person's spirit were known as the *ka* and *ba*. These both needed the body to survive after death, which is why the Egyptians took such trouble to preserve it. The *ka* was a spirit double, and looked like the person. It could leave the body, but had to return to it for food and refreshment. The *ba* was a person's life force, which needed the body to 'perch' on, like a bird. There was also the *akh*, which could soar to join the stars. A person's name was vital, too – if you didn't have one, it was as though you didn't exist.

The ka (left) was shown as a pair of arms held up in the air. The ba (right) was represented as a bird with a human head.

EARLY MUMMIES

The first mummies weren't made by embalming bodies. When they died, people were laid in the hot, dry sand of the desert, which preserved them quite well. As society developed, rich people were buried in tombs where sand could not preserve them. So methods of embalming the body were developed instead (see page 100).

THE FUNERAL

When someone wealthy died, the body was carried to the west bank of the Nile. There, it was given a purification ritual before being mummified. Then it was placed in its coffin and taken to the tomb. Friends and relatives carried everything the dead person would need in the Next World, while professional mourners screeched and wailed alongside.

This is the funeral of a rich man named Ramose.

Internet link for links to websites where you can prepare for an ancient Egyptian funeral and read ideas about life after death, go to www.usborne-quicklinks.com

THE OPENING OF THE MOUTH

At the tomb, the mummy was placed upright and a priest performed a ceremony called 'The Opening of the Mouth'. By touching the hands and feet, eyes, ears, nose and lips, the priests 'freed' the senses so that they could function in the Next World. Then the coffin was placed in the tomb, surrounded by food, furniture and other necessities, and the tomb was sealed up.

Objects with symbolic meaning, called 'adzes', were used to touch the mummy during the Opening of the Mouth ceremony.

THE JOURNEY TO THE AFTERLIFE

Anubis weighs the heart. Ammut waits hungrily next to him as Thoth writes down the verdict.

The journey to the Next World was a long and dangerous one for the person and their *ba*. First, this involved passing many gateways guarded by monsters to reach the place of judgement.

There, the person had to recite a long list of sins in front of 42 judges, and swear they had not committed any of them. The god Anubis would then take their heart and place it on the scales to be balanced against the feather of Ma'at, or truth, while Thoth stood by to write down the verdict. If the person had led a good life, their heart would be as light as the feather, and they would pass on to meet Osiris and their ancestors in the Next World. If the heart was heavy with sins, it would be eaten by a crocodile-headed monster called Ammut.

Professional mourners wailed and wept at Ramose's funeral.

EMBALMING AND MUMMIES

The embalming process, which prevented bodies from rotting away, was perfected over hundreds of years. If it was done properly, it was a lengthy, messy and gruesome job, but it did work.

Many New Kingdom mummies are still in amazingly good condition today. After the New Kingdom, standards waned, but bodies were still mummified until beyond the time of the Ptolemies.

THE NEW KINGDOM METHOD

Mummification took 70 days altogether. First, a slit was made in the side of the body so that the 'viscera' – the intestines, lungs, liver and stomach – could be taken out.
The viscera were embalmed separately and placed in four 'canopic jars' (see opposite). The heart was left in the body, because Egyptians believed it would be judged in the Next World.

The body is cut open and the internal organs taken out.

Next, the embalmers covered the body with a salt called natron, a preservative that also soaked up moisture. After 35–40 days, the body was completely dried out. Then it was stuffed with materials soaked in oils and resins to make it a normal shape again, and the slit was sewn up.

Embalmers covering the body with natron

The body now had to be wrapped in layers of linen, starting with the fingers and toes.

Jewels and amulets (charms) were placed between the layers, to protect the person in the next life, and each layer was covered in oils, resins and perfumes, too.

The wrapping of the mummy is almost finished.

Finally, a mask was placed over the mummy's head. This was done by the chief embalmer, wearing the jackal mask of the embalming god Anubis. At last, the mummy was ready to be put in its coffin.

The chief embalmer says prayers over the completed mummy.

Over time, the oils and resins used in the wrapping stage became thick and sticky, almost like tar. The local word for this substance was *mumiya*, meaning 'bitumen' (tar is made partly of bitumen). So, this is where the word 'mummy' comes from.

Seti I's amazing mummy shows the effectiveness of the New Kingdom method of embalming.

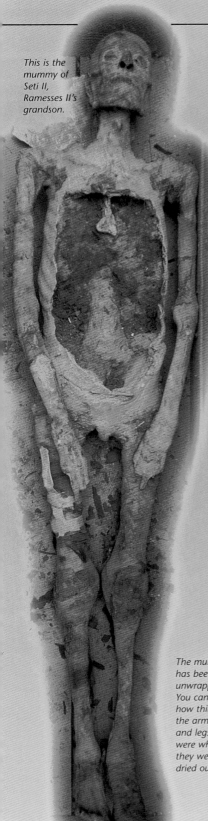

This is the mummy of Seti II, Ramesses II's grandson.

The mummy has been unwrapped. You can see how thin the arms and legs were when they were dried out.

CANOPIC JARS

There were usually four canopic jars with each mummy, containing the mummified liver, lungs, stomach and intestines. Each jar had a different stopper, in the form of one of the four sons of Horus, who protected the viscera.

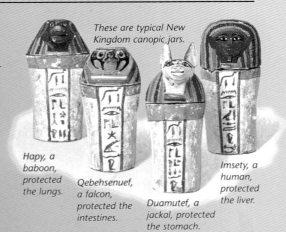

These are typical New Kingdom canopic jars.

Hapy, a baboon, protected the lungs.

Qebehsenuef, a falcon, protected the intestines.

Duamutef, a jackal, protected the stomach.

Imsety, a human, protected the liver.

MUMMIES REVEAL THEIR SECRETS

In the 19th century, mummies were often unwrapped so that investigators could inspect them. Later, it was recognized that this practice damaged them badly, so it was stopped. Now, when scientists want to find out about a mummy, they put it into a CAT scanner, which sees through all the bandages. They can also carry out tests on tiny scraps of mummy flesh to find out about their DNA, the unique blueprint that each of us has in our cells. For example, DNA tests have shown that Tutankhamun and the body found in KV55 (see page 66) were definitely related.

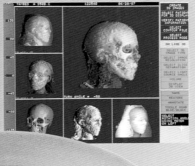

Modern technology: below, a wrapped mummy inside a CAT scanner. Right, images of mummies' faces, reconstructed by a computer.

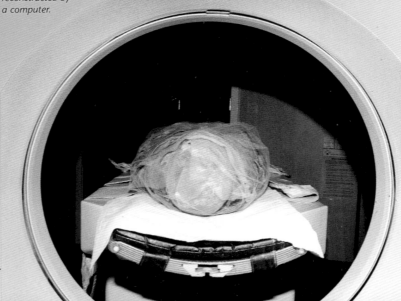

COFFINS AND TOMBS

The coffins and tombs that mummies were placed in were as important as the embalming process itself. They were often lavishly decorated, and the decorations and inscriptions were a vital part of what the deceased person would need on the journey to the Next World.

Sometimes, 'reserve heads' like this one of a princess, were placed in their owners' tombs to help the ka to recognize the body.

COFFINS AND SARCOPHAGI

Anyone who was rich had their mummy placed in a coffin. In the Old and Middle Kingdoms, coffins were rectangular. They were brightly painted, with an *udjat* eye (see page 87) on the outside in the same position as the body's head, so that the dead person could see out. In the Middle Kingdom, people started making human-shaped coffins. An *udjat* eye wasn't needed, as the coffin had its own face, an idealized portrait of the person inside.

If you were royalty or very rich, you might have several coffins that nestled neatly inside each other. Sometimes these were placed in a big sarcophagus, an outer coffin made of stone. Coffins were usually rectangular, but in the Late Period some were human-shaped.

This is the tomb of Ramesses IV, with the king's sarcophagus in its burial chamber.

INSIDE A TOMB

Tombs were made in many shapes and sizes, from the brick mastabas of the early periods to the kings' amazing pyramids and rock-cut tombs. Tombs were only ever for the rich – the poor were buried in the sand.

All tombs had a burial chamber for the sarcophagus or coffin. Some had other chambers, too, such as 'chapels' where food could be left for the dead person's *ka* (see page 98). The burial chamber itself was sealed off, but the Egyptians believed that the *ka* would need to get in and out somehow. So a 'false door' was painted or carved on the inside, through which the *ka* could come and go.

This is a Late Period coffin. A portrait of the dead person is carved into the lid.

READY FOR THE NEXT LIFE

Egyptians believed that life after death would be very similar to life on earth. There would be work to do and houses to live in, so the dead person needed many of the things they used in life, such as food, clothes and furniture.

People obviously hoped, though, that the next life would be much better than the first – that harvests wouldn't fail, and that life would always be relaxed and enjoyable. But just in case they were required to do hard or difficult work, little figures called *ushabtis* were placed with the body. These were the dead person's servants, ready to obey orders and carry out whatever jobs needed doing.

Ushabtis were often placed in their own coffin or box, like these wooden New Kingdom ushabtis. The box is decorated with funerary scenes.

TEXTS FOR GUIDANCE

Writings on the walls of tombs were there to guide the person on the difficult journey to the afterlife. In the Old Kingdom, kings had spells and prayers carved inside their pyramids. These writings became known as the Pyramid Texts. In the Middle Kingdom, ordinary people adapted these for their own coffins. These adaptations are known as the Coffin Texts.

In the New Kingdom, a whole new set of writings appeared, known as the *Book of the Dead*. There were five parts – the *Book of what is in the underworld*, the *Book of gates*, the *Book of caverns*, the *Book of earth* and the *Litany of Re*. Each dealt with an aspect of the afterlife – the *Book of gates*, for example, was for getting past the monsters guarding the twelve gates of the night.

⊛ INTERNET LINK

For links to websites where you can travel through the underworld and see inside tombs and coffins, go to **www.usborne-quicklinks.com**

POWERFUL PAINTINGS

The paintings, writings and carvings on the walls of tombs weren't just for decoration. They were another part of what the person would need after death. For example, a scene of someone baking bread would ensure that the dead person knew how to do this in the Next World.

This wall painting in the tomb of Nakht shows a man rounding up his cattle.

THE PYRAMIDS OF GIZA

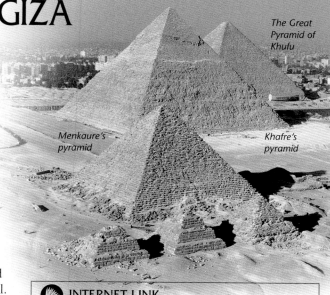

The Great Pyramid of Khufu

Menkaure's pyramid

Khafre's pyramid

Even today, the pyramids of Khufu, Khafre and Menkaure at Giza seem mysterious and awe-inspiring – especially the biggest, Khufu's Great Pyramid. But Egyptologists have solved many of their mysteries. We now have a firm idea of both when they were built, and how.

THE GREAT PYRAMID

Until the 19th century, Khufu's Great Pyramid was the tallest building in the world. It was built in around 2550BC and is made of over 2 million blocks of limestone that were quarried nearby. Its proportions are perfectly symmetrical. Each side is 230m (755ft) wide at the bottom, and is aligned exactly with one of the points of the compass (north, south, east and west).

> **INTERNET LINK**
>
> For links to websites where you can explore Khufu's Great Pyramid, build your own virtual pyramid and find lots of online tours, facts and photos, go to **www.usborne-quicklinks.com**

INSIDE KHUFU'S PYRAMID

The Egyptians never meant it to be easy to get inside the pyramid. They blocked the entrance with huge granite stones, and covered its entire surface with smooth limestone blocks. These blocks were placed together so closely that it was difficult to get even a knife blade in between them. Even so, robbers managed to break in, probably as early as the First Intermediate Period (c. 2150BC). By the time 19th-century explorers came along, the pyramid was empty – apart from a huge granite sarcophagus with no lid.

Three chambers have been found inside the pyramid, and a big hallway known as the Grand Gallery. From the King's Chamber, two small vents point upwards. One suggestion is that these were meant to line up with the stars that the king's spirit would visit in the afterlife. But, in fact, the vents don't reach as far as the open air.

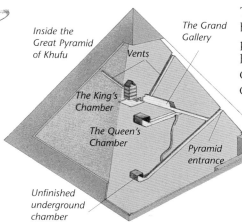

Inside the Great Pyramid of Khufu

The Grand Gallery

Vents

The King's Chamber

The Queen's Chamber

Pyramid entrance

Unfinished underground chamber

HOW DID THEY DO IT?

Each stone in the pyramid weighs about 2½ tonnes (tons). That's heavy. To pull them up the pyramid, the Egyptians used ramps, which were gradually built up as the pyramid grew.

The ramps probably looked like this.

Teams of men hauled the slabs of stone up the ramps.

The teams of men working on the pyramids were highly organized.

KHUFU THE TYRANT?

The Greek historian Herodotus claimed that Khufu used slaves to carry out his staggering task, but he got many facts wrong. Now, we know the Egyptians took great pride in building the pyramids. Skilled craftsmen were employed full time, but most workers were peasants doing their work tax, or 'corvée' (see page 80).

KHAFRE AND MENKAURE

Khafre's pyramid is similar to Khufu's. It is not quite as big, but it looks bigger because it was built on higher ground. You can still see some of its outer limestone casing at the top.

Menkaure's pyramid is smaller than the other two but would have been difficult to build, as its outer casing was of granite. Granite is harder to cut than limestone, and it had to be transported all the way from Aswan in Upper Egypt.

A BUSTLING AREA

Photographs of the pyramids often give the impression that they sit isolated in the desert, but in ancient times, they were surrounded by palaces, temples and other tombs, and there were ports that bustled with boats. Priests and other workers lived close by in busy towns – a recent discovery has been the bakery where the workers' bread was baked. In 1954, some pits were discovered that held the kings' boats or 'barques'. Two boats had survived, including one belonging to King Khufu himself (see page 110).

Overseers made sure the job was done properly.

Accidents were common, but doctors were always available to treat broken bones.

Each stone was placed in position very carefully.

Water carriers supplied plenty of water for thirsty workers.

The rollers underneath the stones made the work a lot easier.

The ramp was made of sand and rubble.

The ramp was probably held in place by a mud-brick wall.

BURIED IN THE ROCKS

Some noblemen had used tombs cut out of rocks from the end of the Old Kingdom. For kings, though, tombs like this didn't replace pyramids until the New Kingdom. Most of the New Kingdom pharaohs were buried in tombs in the Valley of the Kings, opposite Thebes. Some queens were buried there too, but later queens had their own burial valley. Many nobles were buried nearby as well.

VALLEY OF THE KINGS

The Valley of the Kings is set among dramatic limestone cliffs, and the tombs are tucked between folds in the rock. Although they were not as visible as pyramids, most people knew where they were, so they were constantly guarded by the Medjay (police). Even so, by the end of the New Kingdom, most of them had been robbed.

The tombs are decorated with scenes from the *Book of the Dead*. Scenes from everyday life weren't generally shown, as kings wouldn't be expected to do any normal jobs in the next life.

TOMB LAYOUT

The tombs vary in size and shape, but they all have steps and corridors leading deep into the rock. The older, 18th dynasty tombs (such as Tutankhamun's) were built in an L-shape. Later, they had long corridors with annexes leading off and a burial chamber at the end. One example is the magnificent tomb of Seti I.

Burial chambers

Plans of the tombs of Tutankhamun (top left) and Seti I (right). The layouts are not to scale – Seti's is actually much, much bigger than Tutankhamun's.

In this overhead view of the Valley of the Kings, you can see how the tombs are tucked into niches in the cliffs.

Tuthmosis III
Seti II
Tuthmosis I

Amenhotep II
Ramesses III
Horemheb
Ramesses VI
Tutankhamun
Merenptah
Ramesses I
Seti I
Ramesses II

HOW THEY WERE MADE

First of all, a tomb's basic shape was cut out of the rock by stonecutters. Then plasterers applied a layer of fine, smooth plaster to the inside walls. Next, a draftsman drew a grid and outlines of the scene in red, using strict rules of proportion (see page 93). Any corrections were made in black. Then painters came along to fill in the details.

When the rock was hard enough, the tombs had sunken reliefs instead of flat paintings. In this case, the carvers did their job once the draftsmen had finished.

NEARBY TOMBS

South of the Valley of the Kings, scattered among the cliffs facing the Nile, lie the tombs of nobles. They are decorated with religious scenes, both of the owner's funeral and the life the nobles hoped for after death. There are also beautiful tombs at Deir el Medina, made by the workers for their own use.

The reliefs in Horemheb's tomb were never finished, so you can still see the draftsman's grid and drawings followed by the carvers.

NEFERTARI'S TOMB

A little further south of the nobles' tombs lies the Valley of the Queens, where there are tombs of some of the royal children as well as queens. The most beautiful of these tombs belongs to Nefertari, the chief queen of Ramesses II. Many people think it is the most beautiful royal tomb in all ancient Egypt. It has recently been carefully restored to its former brilliance, and a few people are allowed in to see it every day.

This is an image of Nefertari from the walls of her tomb.

The paintings in Nefertari's tomb are amazingly vivid and bright.

Many of the paintings of Nefertari show her wearing very fine white linen that is almost see-through.

Inside the tomb of Pashedu, one of the workers from the village of Deir el Medina

MORTUARY TEMPLES

As well as cult temples, many of the temples still standing today are the New Kingdom 'mortuary' temples. These were built for the worship of kings after their death. Unlike cult temples, mortuary temples were built on the west bank of the Nile, the kingdom of the dead.

A CLUSTER OF TEMPLES

Most mortuary temples were built near the Valley of the Kings at Thebes. Many are now just ruins, but the picture below gives an artist's reconstruction of where they once stood. You can also see where the Valley of the Kings, the Valley of the Queens and the workmen's village of Deir el Medina are situated.

THE COLOSSI OF MEMNON

These two statues once stood in front of Amenhotep III's mortuary temple, which was dismantled by later kings for its stone.

Some time after Amenhotep's temple was dismantled, an earthquake cracked one of the remaining two statues. After this, it began to make a strange noise at dawn. The Greeks thought the sound was the sighing of Memnon, one of their heroes who was killed in battle. In fact, it was probably an effect of the rising sun's heat on air and moisture trapped in the crack in the stone. In 199AD, the Roman emperor Septimius Severus sealed the crack – and the moaning 'Colossus of Memnon' has been silent ever since.

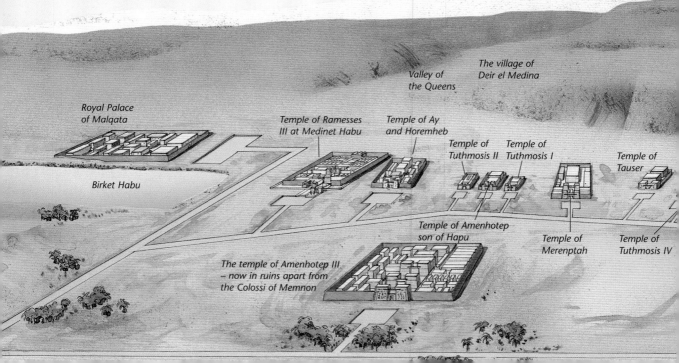

The village of Deir el Medina

Valley of the Queens

Royal Palace of Malqata

Birket Habu

Temple of Ramesses III at Medinet Habu

Temple of Ay and Horemheb

Temple of Tuthmosis II

Temple of Tuthmosis I

Temple of Tauser

Temple of Amenhotep son of Hapu

Temple of Merenptah

Temple of Tuthmosis IV

The temple of Amenhotep III – now in ruins apart from the Colossi of Memnon

Ramesses III's massive temple at Medinet Habu is still in good condition.

THE RAMESSEUM

Like everything that Ramesses II built, his mortuary temple, known as the Ramesseum, is on a huge scale. It included a massive statue of Ramesses himself, about 20m (65ft) high. Now, the statue has toppled over, and its broken remains inspired a poem by an English poet, Shelley. This poem, *Ozymandias*, mocks Ramesses for his arrogance and delusions of grandeur.

MEDINET HABU

Not to be outdone by his predecessor, Ramesses III also built an enormous mortuary temple. It is carved with many battle scenes, showing Ramesses' success in battle against the Libyans and the Sea Peoples. Some scenes are gruesome, showing scribes counting piles of chopped-off hands to calculate how many enemies had been killed.

THE TEMPLES AT ABYDOS

Abydos, halfway between Memphis and Thebes, was Egypt's most holy place. This was because Osiris, the god of the dead, was said to be buried there. It was therefore the ideal place for anyone else to be buried, too, and became a place of pilgrimage.

In the 19th Dynasty, Seti I built a mortuary temple at Abydos. It is now one of the most beautiful temples still standing in Egypt, because much of its paintwork has been preserved. It is unique in that it has seven chapels dedicated to different gods. Seti's son Ramesses II completed it, and built a temple of his own there, too.

Beautiful sunken reliefs can still be seen on Ramesses II's temple at Abydos.

Valley of the Kings (hidden behind the mountain)

Deir el Bahri

Tombs of the nobles

Temple of Siptah

Temple of Tuthmosis III

Temple of Mentuhotep II (Middle Kingdom)

Temple of Hatshepsut

The Ramesseum, Ramesses II's temple

Temple of Seti I

INTERNET LINK

For links to websites with virtual tours, movies and panoramic views of mortuary temples, go to **www.usborne-quicklinks.com**

A ROYAL BARQUE

Boats played an important part in Egyptian life and religious beliefs. Even a king's journey to the afterlife was believed to happen in a boat, or 'barque'. So early kings had a barque placed in or near their tombs to transport them safely to the next world.

INTERNET LINK

For links to websites where you can explore Khufu's barque and watch a movie about tomb boats, go to **www.usborne-quicklinks.com**

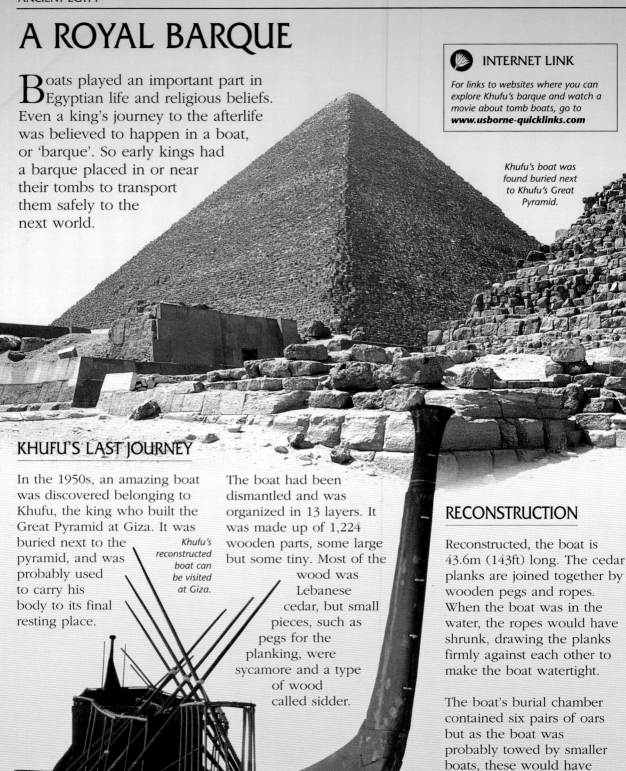

Khufu's boat was found buried next to Khufu's Great Pyramid.

KHUFU'S LAST JOURNEY

In the 1950s, an amazing boat was discovered belonging to Khufu, the king who built the Great Pyramid at Giza. It was buried next to the pyramid, and was probably used to carry his body to its final resting place.

Khufu's reconstructed boat can be visited at Giza.

The boat had been dismantled and was organized in 13 layers. It was made up of 1,224 wooden parts, some large but some tiny. Most of the wood was Lebanese cedar, but small pieces, such as pegs for the planking, were sycamore and a type of wood called sidder.

RECONSTRUCTION

Reconstructed, the boat is 43.6m (143ft) long. The cedar planks are joined together by wooden pegs and ropes. When the boat was in the water, the ropes would have shrunk, drawing the planks firmly against each other to make the boat watertight.

The boat's burial chamber contained six pairs of oars but as the boat was probably towed by smaller boats, these would have been used for steering.

EVERYDAY LIFE

*A Middle Kingdom model of cooks
grinding flour and preparing food*

HOUSES AND HOMES

The very earliest Egyptian houses were made from wooden posts and bundles of reeds. By the time the country was unified, mud brick was used instead. From then on, everyone – rich or poor – lived in mud-brick houses. The difference lay in how big they were, their facilities and how they were decorated. Kings' palaces were big and luxurious, but poor people's houses could be very cramped indeed.

THE PROBLEM WITH MUD

There was never a shortage of mud in Egypt. The annual Nile flood provided plenty of it, but it also meant that houses had to be built on higher ground. Space was limited, so houses were rebuilt on the same site. As a result, not many original houses have survived, but some foundations have been discovered. Whole workmen's villages have been excavated at Karun, near the Faiyum; Deir el Medina, near the Valley of the Kings; and at Tell el Amarna, Akhenaten's abandoned city.

WORKERS' COTTAGES

The village at Deir el Medina was founded in about 1550BC for the craftsmen and artists who were building the royal tombs (see pages 106 and 118). It thrived for about 500 years. This village has given us a good idea of life for many people in the New Kingdom.

The village had one long central street running north to south. It was narrow and airless. The houses themselves, built on either side of the street, were long and narrow, and most had four small rooms in them. About 60 families lived in the village at any one time.

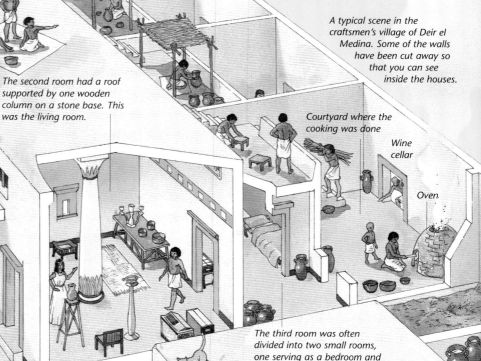

People spent a lot of time on the roof, and slept there in hot weather.

The second room had a roof supported by one wooden column on a stone base. This was the living room.

The front room opened directly onto the street. This is where a lot of the household work was done.

A typical scene in the craftsmen's village of Deir el Medina. Some of the walls have been cut away so that you can see inside the houses.

Courtyard where the cooking was done

Wine cellar

Oven

The third room was often divided into two small rooms, one serving as a bedroom and the other as a storage room.

TOWN HOUSES

Because building land in ancient Egypt was so scarce, houses in towns were built tall and close together. Some were up to four floors high. The streets below were narrow and crowded. There was no public refuse or sewage system, and each household had to dispose of its own waste – in pits, the river, or simply by throwing it into the street. People spent as much time as possible on the roofs to catch the cool breezes, and to get away from the smell of the streets below.

A model of an Egyptian town house, showing several floors.

FURNITURE

Wooden furniture was very expensive, so most houses were very simply furnished. Tables, chairs and beds were usually made from cheap local wood or even reeds.

Rich households, though, had furniture made of expensive imported woods such as ebony and cedar, inlaid with ivory, precious metals, semi-precious stones and a kind of glass called faience. Sometimes it was even covered with gold.

Houses were lit by small oil-burning lamps. These were simply bowls with linseed oil and a wick (a piece of twisted cloth) inside them.

This chair belonged to a queen, so it is much more elaborate than the chairs owned by poorer people. The basic design, however, would have been the same.

INTERNET LINK

For links to websites where you can see all kinds of ancient Egyptian houses, furniture and scenes from daily life, go to
www.usborne-quicklinks.com

HOMES OF THE RICH

Rich people lived in luxurious villas. They had many different rooms, and a big hall in the middle for entertaining guests. Both the inside and outside walls were plastered and painted. These villas often had lovely gardens, with shady trees and pools.

This wall painting is in a tomb at Thebes that belonged to a rich man called Nakht. Here, Nakht is shown with his wife in the garden.

Nakht's house had vents in the roof to keep the house cool, and was built on a platform, to keep the rooms dry.

WOMEN AND FAMILY LIFE

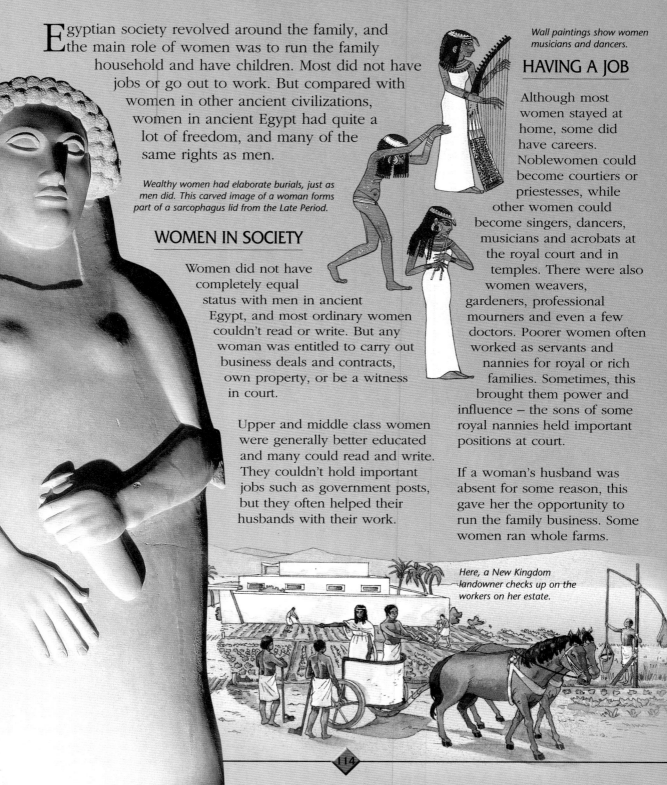

Egyptian society revolved around the family, and the main role of women was to run the family household and have children. Most did not have jobs or go out to work. But compared with women in other ancient civilizations, women in ancient Egypt had quite a lot of freedom, and many of the same rights as men.

Wealthy women had elaborate burials, just as men did. This carved image of a woman forms part of a sarcophagus lid from the Late Period.

WOMEN IN SOCIETY

Women did not have completely equal status with men in ancient Egypt, and most ordinary women couldn't read or write. But any woman was entitled to carry out business deals and contracts, own property, or be a witness in court.

Upper and middle class women were generally better educated and many could read and write. They couldn't hold important jobs such as government posts, but they often helped their husbands with their work.

Wall paintings show women musicians and dancers.

HAVING A JOB

Although most women stayed at home, some did have careers. Noblewomen could become courtiers or priestesses, while other women could become singers, dancers, musicians and acrobats at the royal court and in temples. There were also women weavers, gardeners, professional mourners and even a few doctors. Poorer women often worked as servants and nannies for royal or rich families. Sometimes, this brought them power and influence – the sons of some royal nannies held important positions at court.

If a woman's husband was absent for some reason, this gave her the opportunity to run the family business. Some women ran whole farms.

Here, a New Kingdom landowner checks up on the workers on her estate.

GETTING MARRIED

Kings had several wives, but most men had only one. Men married at about twenty, but girls married earlier – some as young as fourteen. People's husbands and wives were chosen for them by their parents – usually someone from the same background, or the same family. Even so, statues, paintings and love poems show that they often loved each other very much.

A statue of the king Akhenaten, holding hands with his chief queen, Nefertiti.

MARRIED LIFE

A couple's marriage was a legal settlement made up of financial arrangements. A husband gave his wife an allowance to live on and run the household, but both husband and wife could own property separately. The couple also set up a joint fund, the husband putting in two-thirds and the wife one-third. This served as a nest-egg for their children.

If a marriage wasn't a happy one, a couple could get divorced simply by making a statement in front of witnesses. Most people tried to avoid this, though – relatives of the couple would try to persuade them to resolve their differences. If a divorce was unavoidable, children stayed with the mother, and both parents were free to marry again.

INTERNET LINK

For links to websites where you can listen to the dreams and prayers of ancient Egyptian women and discover more about their lives, go to **www.usborne-quicklinks.com**

SONS AND DAUGHTERS

The Egyptians made plenty of toys for children to play with. These are clay balls, and a toy dog with a handle that opens its mouth.

Daughters were valued just as much as sons. When parents died, land was usually left to the sons, while any other property such as a house, furniture and valuables went to the daughters. However, there were no rigid rules and daughters could also inherit land, especially if there were no sons in the family.

This boy and girl form part of a 5th dynasty sculpture of a family group.

THE FARMING LIFE

Farming formed the backbone of Egyptian society. The farmland along the Nile was rich and fertile, so farmers were able to grow far more than they could eat. Some of the extra grain was paid in taxes to the king, who used it to pay servants, finance building projects, or exported it.

This picture shows a 'shaduf' for lifting water, like the ones used in ancient Egypt.

LIFE-GIVING WATER

The farming calendar was based around the rise and fall of the river Nile. Every spring, rain and melted snow from the mountains of Ethiopia swelled the river. Sometime around July, the Nile overflowed its banks, flooding the whole valley. This was known as the Inundation.

There was a lot hanging on the level of the flood. If it was too low, there could be a poor harvest and famine. If it was too high, it flooded villages and sometimes washed them away.

IRRIGATION SYSTEMS

The Egyptians learned to make the most of the Inundation as far back as Predynastic times. The land was divided into fields, with irrigation canals between them. The government used corvée workers (see page 80) to repair the canals properly every year.

People still had to carry water in jars to areas not reached by the Inundation – a heavy, time-consuming job. From the New Kingdom onwards, lifting the water was made slightly easier by devices called shadufs (see above).

AFTER THE FLOOD

By the end of October, the waters had ebbed away, leaving behind a thick layer of fertile mud called silt. Farmers now had to work the fields and sow the seeds. The major crops were wheat and barley, for making bread and beer. After sowing, a herd of sheep was often driven over the ground, so that the seeds were buried and trampled into the soil.

Today, farmers still rely on the Nile to water their crops.

An Old Kingdom painting of geese. These birds were kept by farmers for their meat and eggs.

HARVEST TIME

Once the crop was ripe (sometime between March and June), everyone piled in to harvest it with sickles. Sometimes the army was called in to help. It was vital to finish before the summer heat set in, so that the irrigation ditches could be repaired before the next flood.

The grain was loaded onto donkeys and taken to the threshing floor. Threshing means separating the grain from the stalk, and this was done by cows or donkeys trampling over the crop. Then the grain was 'winnowed' – thrown into the air for the wind to blow away the pieces of straw and chaff.

Tomb painting showing the grain being winnowed

Finally, a tenth of the crop had to be handed over to the king in taxes. The peasants usually had to give a portion to their landlord, too.

MEAT AND MILK

Most land was used for crops, rather than for grazing animals. But sheep, goats and pigs could survive anywhere, so all farmers kept a few, along with geese, ducks and pigeons. Beef was a luxury – only the rich kept cattle for meat and milk.

PLENTY OF VARIETY

Although grain was the most common crop, many farmers grew flax, for making linen. They also grew a wide range of vegetables and fruit, including beans, lentils, onions, garlic, lettuce, cucumbers, leeks, melons, grapes, pomegranates, dates and figs.

SKILLED CRAFTSMEN

The craftsmen of ancient Egypt were well-paid and highly respected members of the community. Although the tools and techniques available to them were very simple, the quality of their work was incredibly high, and much of it has survived to amaze us today.

PLENTIFUL WORK

Most craftsmen worked for the king, on the tomb and temple projects or on the palace and temple finery. Some nobles could afford to have workshops, too. Craftsmen increased their income by taking on private work in their spare time.

DEIR EL MEDINA

We know a lot about craftsmen's lives from the village of Deir el Medina, home to the men who built the tombs in the Valley of the Kings. They were wealthier than average craftsmen, with enough leisure time to make beautiful tombs for themselves as well

This unshaven stonemason was quickly sketched on an ostracon by another worker at Deir el Medina.

as the kings. They also had fun using their skills at home, doodling on ostraca (limestone flakes).

The craftsmen weren't paid in money, but in grain, fish, vegetables, meat, salt, beer and oil, with occasional 'extras' such as silver and wine. They were given so much grain that they could trade some of it for other goods. The village was in the desert, so they had people to bring them water, and they were also given slave girls to grind their grain.

Craftsmen's tools, like this carpenter's adze, were strong and very well made.

AT THE TOMBS

The craftsmen stayed in huts in the Valley of the Kings while they worked on a tomb. They did an eight-hour day with a long midday break, and had a day off every ten days. They also had time off for the many religious festivals.

The men worked in two groups, one on each side of a tomb, with a foreman in charge of each group. A scribe kept records of materials and tools, the men's attendance and wages. Two other men looked after the storerooms.

A Middle Kingdom model of a carpenters' workshop

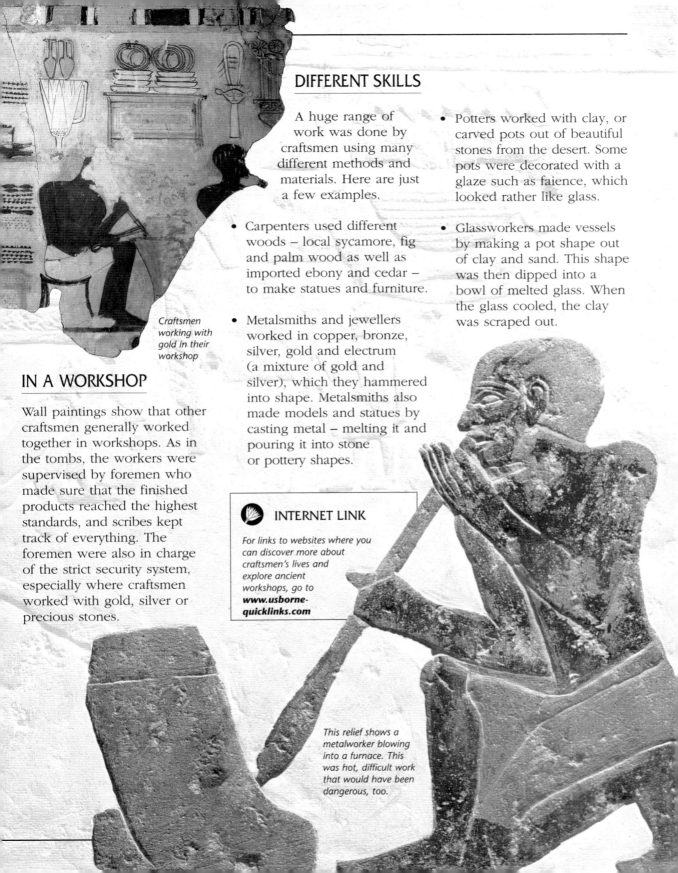

Craftsmen working with gold in their workshop

IN A WORKSHOP

Wall paintings show that other craftsmen generally worked together in workshops. As in the tombs, the workers were supervised by foremen who made sure that the finished products reached the highest standards, and scribes kept track of everything. The foremen were also in charge of the strict security system, especially where craftsmen worked with gold, silver or precious stones.

DIFFERENT SKILLS

A huge range of work was done by craftsmen using many different methods and materials. Here are just a few examples.

- Carpenters used different woods – local sycamore, fig and palm wood as well as imported ebony and cedar – to make statues and furniture.

- Metalsmiths and jewellers worked in copper, bronze, silver, gold and electrum (a mixture of gold and silver), which they hammered into shape. Metalsmiths also made models and statues by casting metal – melting it and pouring it into stone or pottery shapes.

- Potters worked with clay, or carved pots out of beautiful stones from the desert. Some pots were decorated with a glaze such as faience, which looked rather like glass.

- Glassworkers made vessels by making a pot shape out of clay and sand. This shape was then dipped into a bowl of melted glass. When the glass cooled, the clay was scraped out.

INTERNET LINK

For links to websites where you can discover more about craftsmen's lives and explore ancient workshops, go to **www.usborne-quicklinks.com**

This relief shows a metalworker blowing into a furnace. This was hot, difficult work that would have been dangerous, too.

JOBS FOR ALL

There were a number of things that Egyptian society really couldn't do without. These included bread, oil and beer, linen, which everyone wore, and mud bricks, which everyone built their houses with. Making these may not have been the most skilled or respected work, but it kept a lot of people very busy.

This wall painting from the tomb of Khaemwese shows the different processes involved in making wine.

BAKING BREAD

Whether you were rich or poor in ancient Egypt, bread was an important part of your diet. Loaves came in all shapes and sizes, and the types of flour varied, too. Richer people ate white bread, but most people ate a coarser brown version. Sweet pastries were popular, often made into fancy shapes.

Bread was made by adding water to flour to make dough. Most of it was made in the home by women and servants. On building projects, though, large amounts of bread were made on site for the workers to eat.

In this Middle Kingdom model, the figure on the left is making beer.

DRINKS ALL ROUND

The most popular drink in Egypt was beer. Grain and bread were soaked in water, then mashed, put through a sieve and left to ferment. Sometimes things such as spices and dates were added to the beer, then it was sieved again. It was stored in large pottery jars sealed with clay stoppers, but it had to be drunk soon as it went flat quickly.

Richer people also drank wine. The grapes were grown on trellises and taken for pressing as soon as they were ripe. Then they were trampled underfoot, and finally the juice was poured into pottery jars to ferment into wine.

The two right-hand figures are kneading dough to make bread.

PRECIOUS REEDS

The reeds that grew along the Nile had many uses. They were chopped and used to make boats and roofs; and they were dried and woven to make mats, baskets, chests and sandals. One special reed called papyrus was also used to make the precious papyrus scrolls used by scribes.

Papryus plant

To make paper, the outer skin was peeled away.

The pith was cut into strips and soaked.

The strips were arranged on top of each other, hammered and pressed together with weights.

MAKING LINEN

Linen, made from the flax plant, varied from very coarse, rough cloth to the finest 'royal linen', which was so fine it was almost transparent. Only highly skilled workers made royal linen.

When the stalks of flax were harvested they were first soaked in water, then beaten. The strands were separated out with a comb and dried, then sticks called spindles were used to spin them into long threads. Finally, the threads were woven into cloth on looms.

These samples of ancient Egyptian linen were found at the craftsmen's village of Deir el Medina.

INTERNET LINK

For links to websites where you can watch a slide show to see how papyrus is made and find out how papyrus changed Egyptian society, go to **www.usborne-quicklinks.com**

MUD, GLORIOUS MUD

Most building work was done with mud bricks, not stone. Sand and chopped-up straw were added to mud to help bind it together. Then this was made into brick shapes, which were left to dry in the sun for a few days. And that was it — the bricks were ready.

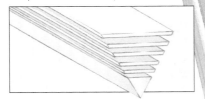

SERVANTS AND SLAVES

Before the New Kingdom, there weren't many slaves in Egypt, though rich people had servants to do the chores and wait upon guests. But, when Egypt became a powerful empire, many prisoners of war were captured and slavery became very common. Even ordinary people like craftsmen had slaves.

Life as a slave varied. If you worked at a quarry or building site, it was tough. But some slaves worked for kind people and were well treated. Some were set free, and a few even married into local families.

A servant carrying his master's belongings

THE EDUCATED FEW

Although most people couldn't read and write, Egyptian society was based on written records, so if you could write you were never short of work. The life of a scribe, or writer, was probably envied by other people – you didn't have to toil under the hot sun, and you were highly regarded in society, too.

In schools such as this temple school, the lessons were strict and pupils were beaten for behaving badly.

WHO WENT TO SCHOOL?

Anyone could pay to go to school, so having an education depended on whether you could afford it. Peasants did their best to educate their sons, as this was the only way to improve their lot in life. Girls from poor families were rarely educated, but in rich families they learned to read and write like boys.

There were several kinds of schools. If you were from a noble family, you might be educated in the palace with the royal children. Next down were temple schools. There were village schools, too, attached to local shrines.

IN THE CLASSROOM

Boys started school aged about five, and learned both the hieroglyphic and hieratic scripts (see pages 124-125). They spent a lot of time copying and reciting texts to perfect their writing and reading skills. To teach younger pupils, teachers used a book called *Kemyt*, which means 'completion'. This was a very simple text of model letters,

There were plenty of these limestone flakes, called ostraca, for pupils to write on.

phrases and expressions. Older students studied more advanced books. These were often classics of Egyptian literature, such as the *Books of Wisdom*, which gave advice to young men about how to behave. Other texts talked about how wonderful it was to be a scribe rather than a craftsman, which must have given scribes a big sense of their own importance.

 INTERNET LINK

For links to websites where you can discover more about scribes, their lives and their schooling, go to **www.usborne-quicklinks.com**

THE NEXT STEP

Once a pupil had mastered the basic arts of reading and writing, he could become a scribe. Many never went beyond this position. If you could afford it, though, you might go on to further studies, which could include mathematics, history, literature, religion, geography, languages, surveying, engineering, astronomy, medicine or accounting.

THE BUSY SCRIBE

Even if you never progressed from being a scribe, there was always plenty of work to do composing letters or legal documents such as wills, marriages and business deals. Scribes also copied out documents in temple libraries, or wrote down questions for people who wanted to ask a god for advice.

There were scribes in every government department. If you were clever and had good connections, you could better yourself. If you kept tax and legal records, or worked in the foreign office, you might be able to become an adviser or even, eventually, a minister.

A seated scribe holds a papyrus in his lap, preparing to read it.

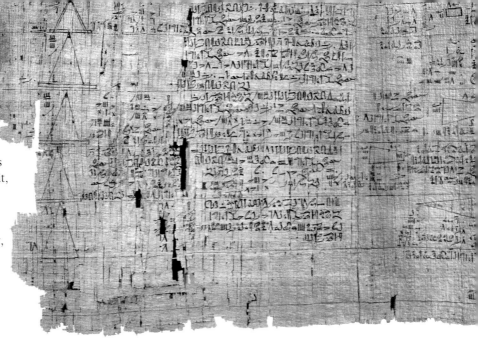

The Rhind Mathematical Papyrus describes different practical and mathematical problems and how to solve them.

TOOLS OF THE TRADE

Important documents were written on papyrus (see page 121), the first kind of paper in the world. This was expensive so unimportant writing was done on wooden tablets coated with plaster that could be wiped clean, or on pieces of broken limestone known as ostraca. There were two kinds of ink: black and red. These were stored in dry blocks on little palettes, and were moistened with water. Pens were made of reeds, and were rather like paintbrushes.

A scribe's ink palette. His equipment also included a little pot of water for moistening the ink.

Blocks of red
and black ink   Reed pens

WRITING OF THE GODS

The ancient Egyptian language was written down in two ways. The picture writing you see carved on monuments is known as the hieroglyphic script. But there was also a simplified version, known as hieratic, which was easier and faster to write on papyrus.

THE HOLY SCRIPT

The Egyptians believed that writing had been given to them by Thoth, the god of wisdom. They called the script *mdw ntr*, which means 'the words of the god'. They thought that the signs had a magic power of their own and could come to life.

Later, the Greeks called the script *hieroglyphs*, which means 'sacred sculptures'. This was because hieroglyphs were usually sculpted onto stone or painted onto the walls of tombs, not written down on papyrus.

Hieroglyphs carved on the walls of a tomb in the Valley of the Queens, with the paint still visible

HOW HIEROGLYPHS WORK

The hieroglyphic script is a very complex system of more than 700 pictures. Below are some of the simpler ways in which they work.

Many of the pictures stand for an actual object. When this is the case, there is often a small stroke near to it to confirm this.

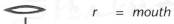

r = mouth

But as well as an object, each picture may represent a sound. It can appear in a word as just this sound, and not as the actual object. There are only 24 pictures that represent a single letter-sound.

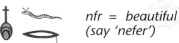

nfr = beautiful
(say 'nefer')

Here, this means 'r', not 'mouth'.

Many of the other signs represent more than one letter and sound, or have some other meaning.

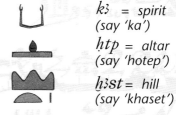

$k3$ = spirit
(say 'ka')

htp = altar
(say 'hotep')

h3st = hill
(say 'khaset')

Often, it was difficult to tell what a word meant from just the 'letter' signs, so another sign was added at the end of the word to show what kind of word it was. These signs are called 'determinatives'.

hpi = to walk
(say 'khepi')

Determinatives

miiw = cat
(say 'mioow')

3
i
y
ꜥ
w
b
p
f
m
n
r
h
ḥ
ḫ
ẖ
s
s
ḳ
k
g
t
ṯ
d
ḏ

These are the 24 signs that represent a single letter-sound.

ADDING THE VOWELS

The hieroglyphic 'letters' didn't include vowels, although there were a few semi-vowels, such as 'y'. The vowel sounds only appeared in the spoken language. This might seem odd, but there are still many languages like this (modern Arabic is one). In the case of ancient Egyptian, though, we are still not entirely sure how it sounded, so we have to guess at the vowel sounds, too. This is why you may see Egyptian words written differently in different books.

READING HIEROGLYPHS

It takes a long time to learn to read hieroglyphs properly. A good place to start, though, is to learn some of the kings' and queens' names. They are easy to spot because they are written in an oval frame that we call a 'cartouche'. This was there to give protection to the royal name.

Hieroglyphs can be read from left to right, right to left, or top to bottom. You can tell which way to read from symbols such as birds, which always face the beginning of the sentence.

This reads from left to right and says 'Son of Re, Lord of Appearances, Seti beloved of Ptah'.

These are the same as the hieroglyphs above but are read from right to left.

These hieroglyphs are read from right to left and top to bottom. The right-hand column says, 'King of Upper and Lower Egypt, Lord of the Two Lands, User-Kheperu-Re beloved of Amun'.

HIERATIC AND DEMOTIC

The hieratic script, a kind of shorthand, developed in the Old Kingdom. The Greeks gave it this name, which means 'priestly', because it was mostly priests who used it. Then, during the Late Period (about 700BC), a new shorthand developed, simpler than either hieratic or heiroglyphics.

An example of the hieratic script

An example of the demotic script

Because it was easier to write, this script became known as demotic, which means 'the people's'.

WHAT HAPPENED NEXT?

After the fall of the Ptolemies, Egyptian culture began to decline as Christianity took over as the main religion. The Egyptian language began to change, because it was difficult to describe Christian beliefs with it.

This new Christian language was called Coptic, and Egyptian Christians are called Copts even today. In fact, the language used in Coptic churches is the closest language in the world to ancient Egyptian.

A temple pillar intricately carved with hieroglyphs

FEASTING AND FUN

The Egyptians loved having fun. This is clear from their tombs, which show scenes of banquets, making merry, and leisure pursuits such as hunting. These pictures were there to ensure that the dead person had a good time in the afterlife, but they show the Egyptians knew how to enjoy themselves while they were alive, too.

EXTRAVAGANT PARTIES

Rich Egyptians would often throw elaborate parties for their friends. They provided huge amounts of meat, vegetables and fruit, not to mention wine and beer. The dining area was decorated with flowers and bowls of fruit, and the best plates and cups were taken out of storage.

Guests were welcomed with a garland of flowers and taken to wash their hands in basins filled with scented water. Then they sat down on cushions, stools or chairs and had their first cup of wine. A servant went around the room and placed a small cone of perfumed ointment on everyone's heads. As things got going, the ointment melted and dripped down their wigs, keeping the guests cool and sweet-smelling.

Then the feasting began. People didn't do things in moderation. They ate and drank far too much and thoroughly enjoyed themselves.

Food would have been served on bowls such as this 18th dynasty faience bowl.

A servant carries a goose to be slaughtered.

This wall painting in the tomb of Neb-amun shows guests being entertained at a banquet. They all have cones of perfume on their heads.

MUSIC AND DANCING

As well as good food and wine, the best parties always had lively entertainment. As the guests arrived, and throughout the meal, musicians played on harps and lyres, flutes, pipes and drums. When the food was finished, it was the turn of the singers and storytellers, dancers, acrobats and jugglers to perform.

Here, a flute player and a singer provide entertainment at a party.

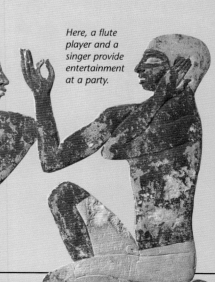

INTERNET LINK

For links to websites where you can play the Egyptian game of senet and examine tomb paintings with scenes of banquets and festivals, go to **www.usborne-quicklinks.com**

EXOTIC ANIMALS

Wild animals provided more sport for noblemen. Those who could afford it went hunting in the desert for hares, foxes, antelopes, ostriches and sometimes lions. At first this took place on foot, but in the New Kingdom they usually went in horse-drawn chariots. The hunt served as another excuse to have a party, with picnics, drinking and more fun.

RELAXING AT HOME

In contrast to their livelier leisure activities, the Egyptians also enjoyed sitting around playing board games. The most common game was called senet, a board game played with different pieces. This was played by everyone, from the royal family to farmers.

The ancient rules for playing senet have been lost, but the most likely rules have now been established.

THE SPORTING LIFE

Hunting and fishing were vital for many Egyptians, but richer people hunted simply for sport. The most dangerous sport was hunting crocodiles and hippos. A team of hunters harpooned the animals, then dragged them ashore with ropes and nets.

Mainly, though, noblemen went hunting for birds, accompanied by their servants. They took their pet cats, too, which were trained to flush out the game. The noblemen used specially-shaped throwing sticks, which could easily break a bird's neck.

Throwing sticks were used to break birds' necks.

Wall paintings show the Egyptians' interest in different birds and animals.

ALL DRESSED UP

The Egyptians went to a lot of trouble over their appearance, but their clothes were simple and didn't change much over the centuries. They did wear plenty of showy ornaments, though. Richer people wore fancier clothers and a wider range of accessories, too.

DAY-TO-DAY WEAR

Most clothes were made of linen. Rich people wore very thin, fine linen, while ordinary people wore a thicker, coarser cloth. Until the New Kingdom, women wore a simple, tight-fitting ankle-length dress, with two shoulder straps. Men wore a kilt, made from a piece of linen wrapped around the waist and tucked in. This could be knee or ankle length. In winter, men and women sometimes wore cloaks made from thick linen.

A servant girl wearing a brightly patterned dress

Egyptians went barefoot most of the time. They sometimes wore sandals made of papyrus reeds, and nobles had sandals made of richly decorated leather.

A CHANGE OF STYLE

During the New Kingdom, tunics and cloaks made of very fine pleated linen became fashionable for both men and women. The pleats would have made the fabric hang very elegantly. Women began to wear another garment over their basic tunic, which as well as having pleats sometimes had a bright fringe with little ornaments attached to it. Some men had two kilts – a longer one made of the finest, almost transparent linen, was worn over the basic short tunic.

These statues are of an Old Kingdom couple, Rahotep and Nofret. Rahotep wears a simple kilt ánd Nofret a dress, wig and cloak.

This New Kingdom tomb painting shows the more elaborate fashions for men and women, which used much more fabric, with many pleats.

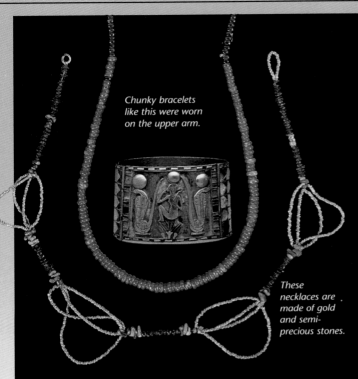

Chunky bracelets like this were worn on the upper arm.

These necklaces are made of gold and semi-precious stones.

FINE ORNAMENTS

No Egyptian's costume was complete without a selection of amulets, necklaces, bracelets and other ornaments. Poor people's were made from cheaper substances such as copper or faience. The rich wore spectacular pieces made from gold, silver and electrum, often set with semi-precious stones and glass.

The most striking items were the big decorative collars that were often worn by servants as well as their masters. These were usually made of several strings of beads or jewels that sat in a big semi-circle around the neck. Women wore them more often than men, but they were popular among both sexes.

WIGS AND HAIRCUTS

Most men kept their hair very short, though noblemen often had longer hair. They were generally clean-shaven (Rahotep's moustache is unusual – see left). Boys shaved their heads, apart from one section that formed a kind of pony-tail to one side. This was called the 'side-lock of youth'. Women wore their long hair either loose or braided in a variety of styles, and decorated it with flowers, pins and beads.

At parties, both men and women wore wigs. Among the rich these could be amazingly elaborate, especially in later periods, with lots of braids and curls. The wigs also had ornaments hung over them, or were decorated with beads and jewels. The best wigs were made of real hair, but there were cheaper ones of black wool.

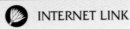

INTERNET LINK

For links to websites where you can create hairstyles with an Egyptian barber and see how Egyptians dressed, go to **www.usborne-quicklinks.com**.

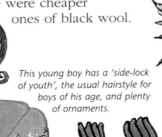

This young boy has a 'side-lock of youth', the usual hairstyle for boys of his age, and plenty of ornaments.

This painting is of a New Kingdom woman wearing a long, elaborate wig, decorated with a sacred blue lotus flower.

The cone on top of her head is made of perfumed fat.

TRAVEL AND TRANSPORT

The river Nile was like a big main road that stretched from one end of the country to the other. Real roads would have been a waste of precious farming land in the Nile valley, and in any case the annual flood would have washed them away. So most travel in ancient Egypt happened in boats.

SHORT TRIPS

Ordinary people didn't travel very much. They only needed to cross the river, and go short distances up and down. From the earliest times, they made small boats out of bundles of reeds, and went on using these for getting around and fishing throughout ancient Egyptian history. From the Old Kingdom onwards, though, all boats of any size (such as passenger ferries) were made of wood.

UP AND DOWN RIVER

Sailing north by river was easy, because this is the way the Nile flows. Luckily, though, the wind usually blows from the north. This means that with a sail you can travel south, against the flow of the river. So, when you see carvings or paintings of Egyptian ships, you can tell which way they're going by whether their sail is up or not.

The hieroglyph for 'going south' showed a ship with its sail up.

The hieroglyph for 'going north' showed the sail rolled down.

THE BUSY RIVER

People used the Nile a great deal for getting around, but it was also the place where they relaxed and had fun. For nobles in particular, being on the river in a nice boat was a pleasant way to pass some time. These boats often had a cabin with a canopy in front, to shield their passengers from the sun.

Hunting birds, crocodiles and hippopotamuses were all popular pastimes, and people loved playing around in the water. Groups of boatmen often held competitions, where two teams on boats would try to knock each other into the river.

A nobleman's boat with a canopy to protect him from the sun

A small local passenger ferry

CARRYING CARGOES

The Egyptians depended on the Nile to help them transport goods, and they needed particularly big, strong boats to carry heavy loads. Some of the heaviest loads of all were the blocks of stone used in building projects. For the larger ones, huge barges were used. These barges were too big to be rowed, so they were towed by as many as 27 smaller boats.

One of the biggest barges on record was used to transport Hatshepsut's granite obelisks from Aswan to the temples at Karnak. It was estimated to be 82m (270ft) long.

The Nile was always busy, with many different kinds of boats making their way up and down.

THE OPEN SEA

Egypt's traders sailed from the Mediterranean coast to other eastern Mediterranean countries, and crossed the eastern desert to the Red Sea to reach places such as Punt. Sea-going ships for trading expeditions to the Red Sea were sometimes built along the Nile, dismantled and carried to the sea, where they were reassembled. They were strong, and had plenty of storage space. You can see what they looked like on page 62.

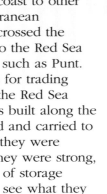

A huge barge carrying an obelisk up the river. These barges were too big to row, so they were towed by lots of little boats.

TRAVEL ON LAND

Although the Egyptians used the Nile whenever possible, overland travel was sometimes unavoidable. Generally, this had to be on foot, though on journeys across the desert, people and small loads were carried by donkey.

For the rich, overland travel was a bit more comfortable. Nobles sometimes travelled in special carrying chairs carried by slaves, or in litters, which were slung between donkeys. Some of them also owned horse-drawn chariots.

INTERNET LINK

For links to websites where you can watch a short movie about ancient Egyptian boats and find pictures and information about exciting discoveries, go to www.usborne-quicklinks.com

Fishermen used small wooden boats like these.

Boatmen playing the popular game of pushing each other off their reed boats

Reed boat

This nobleman is being carried in his chair by Nubian servants.

MEDICINE AND MAGIC

Egyptian doctors were highly respected throughout the Middle East. Sometimes, they were even summoned abroad to treat foreign princes. Egyptian medicine was closely linked to religion, so when science didn't work, doctors turned to magic instead.

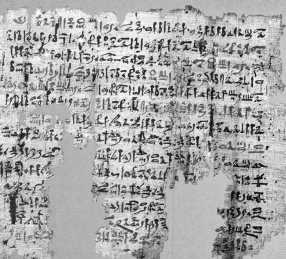

This papyrus, now known as the 'London Medical Papyrus', gives recipes and spells for curing different illnesses.

WHO WERE DOCTORS?

Doctors may have passed their knowledge from father to son, although there were probably medical schools as well. Once they had finished their training and were officially recognized as doctors, they received a salary from the government.

Most doctors worked as general practitioners in the community. Others worked in temples, or as army surgeons or specialist consultants. The most skilled doctors were appointed physicians to the royal court.

WHAT THEY KNEW

Egyptian doctors understood quite a lot about the body. They knew that the heart pumps blood around, and they had some understanding of the nervous system. They were also skilled at setting bones. But there were big gaps in their knowledge. They thought that water, air and nerves passed through the heart. They also believed that people thought with their hearts and that the brain was useless.

A bone showing clearly where it broke and healed again. There were no plaster casts, so bones often didn't heal quite straight.

TRIAL AND ERROR

Egyptian doctors learned about drugs and treatments through trial and error. They knew that a good diet was important, and believed that too much food caused diseases and polluted the body. They understood that rest and hygiene could prevent illnesses, and could also help cure them.

⬤ INTERNET LINK

For links to websites where you can find lots of information about ancient Egyptian doctors, medicine, magic spells and remedies, go to
www.usborne-quicklinks.com

BOOKS AND POTIONS

Doctors had textbooks they could consult on how to diagnose and treat illnesses. There were also books on anatomy, women's diseases, dentistry, surgery and veterinary science.

When treating someone, doctors followed a strict procedure. They looked for the symptoms, then asked questions, inspected, felt, smelled and probed. They took detailed notes, and recorded the treatment and the results. These notes were then used in future cases.

The castor oil plant, shown here, was often used in Egyptian remedies. Many of the other ingredients are unknown, because we still can't read their particular hieroglyphs.

Honey and garlic, like castor oil, appear in many Egyptian remedies. Honey was also used for keeping wounds clean.

Medicines were made from different plants, minerals and sometimes parts of animals. These were either mixed with water, beer, wine or milk and drunk, or mixed with oil and applied to the skin.

THE ROLE OF RELIGION

To the Egyptians, illness was caused by evil spirits entering the body, so prayers to the gods were recited over the patient during treatment. If their efforts with medicines failed, doctors turned to religion and magic for a solution. For this reason, Egyptian doctors consisted of three groups: surgeon-healers, priest-doctors, and pure magicians.

GODS AND MAGICIANS

The gods Thoth, Sekhmet, Isis and Imhotep were particularly associated with healing, and people often went to their temples to find a cure. Sometimes, they were allowed to spend the night in a room next to the temple, so the gods could visit them in dreams – another source of information about how to treat someone. If everything failed, a magician could be called in. He recited spells or used ivory wands to draw magic circles of protection around the sick person.

This ivory magic wand was meant to give protection during childbirth.

An opium bottle. Opium was an early anaesthetic, used to deaden pain.

BEAUTY CARE

The Egyptians kept themselves very clean, and paid a lot of attention to the finer details of their looks. Both men and women wore perfume and cosmetics which they kept in elegant little pots.

FINISHING TOUCHES

Many cosmetics were made from finely ground minerals mixed with oils. Egyptians were particularly fond of eyeliner. Malachite (copper ore) was used to make green or grey eyepaint called kohl. This emphasized the beauty of someone's eyes, and also cut down the glare of the sun. Lipstick and blusher were popular as well. These were made with red ochre, a type of clay.

Red-brown henna, made from the leaves of the henna tree, was used to paint nails, and possibly hands and feet as well.

Images on coffins, like the one above, suggest how women wore eye makeup.

Mirrors, like this bronze one, were just highly polished metal.

Rich people kept their toiletries in elaborate boxes like the one below.

This glass container was probably used to hold perfume.

SMELLING SWEET

It was important to keep clean in the hot climate. Most people washed in the river, or used a basin and jug of water at home. Instead of soap, they used a cleansing cream made from oil, lime and perfume. They also rubbed scented oils into their skin to stop it from drying out in the fierce sun.

Perfumes were made from flowers, seeds and fruits soaked in oils and animal fats. In wall paintings, perfume is often shown as little cones that people wore on their heads at parties (see page 127).

Lotus blossoms were used to make perfume, and were also worn in women's hair.

⬥ INTERNET LINK

For a link to a website where you can watch a short movie about Egyptian cosmetics, and the beautiful containers that were made for them, go to **www.usborne-quicklinks.com**

ANCIENT EGYPT FACTFINDER

A sphinx outside the Temple of Amun at Luxor in Egypt

KINGS & DYNASTIES

Here are the names and approximate dates of most of the kings, queens and dynasties that ruled ancient Egypt. The reign dates can be confusing because sometimes several kings ruled different parts of Egypt at the same time. Kings may also have two names, as they are sometimes known by the names the Greeks gave them (shown in brackets). Names marked * show kings crowned in the lifetime of the previous king. Those marked ** are queens ruling as kings. The evidence for Egyptian dates comes from lists of kings compiled by the Egyptians themselves. Some dates may vary a little in other books. This is because experts disagree about how to interpret the available evidence, and often use slightly different dating systems.

Dynasty I
Very few dates are known for this early period in Egyptian history. Dynasty I consisted of seven or eight kings starting with:

Menes	c.3100

Narmer and Hor-Aha

Dynasty II
Eight or nine kings including:
Hetepsekhemwy, Re'neb, Peribsen and Kha'sekhemui

Dynasty III
Sanakht	c.2649-2630BC
Djoser	c.2630-2611BC
Sekhemkhet	c.2611-2603BC
Kha'ba	c.2603-2599BC
Huni	c.2599-2575BC

Dynasty IV
Seneferu	c.2575-2551BC
Khufu (Cheops)	c.2551-2528BC
Ra'djedef	c.2528-2520BC
Khafre (Khephren)	c.2520-2494BC
Menkaure (Mycerinus)	c.2490-2472BC
Shepseskaf	c.2472-2467BC

Dynasty V
Userkaf	c.2465-2323BC
Sahure	c.2458-2446BC
Neferirkare	c.2446-2426BC
Shepseskare	c.2426-2419BC
Ra'neferef	c.2419-2416BC
Neuserre	c.2416-2392BC
Menkauhor	c.2396-2388BC
Djedkare	c2388-2356BC
Unas	c.2356-2323BC

Dynasty VI
Teti	c.2323-2291BC
Pepi I	c.2289-2255BC
Merenre	c.2255-2246BC
Pepi II	c.2246-2152BC
Nitocris**	c.2152-2150BC

Dynasties VII and VIII   c.2150-2134BC
These dynasties were made up of numbers of kings who reigned only for short periods.

Dynasties IX and X   c.2134-2040BC
These kings ruled from the city of Herakleopolis.

Dynasty XI
A line of kings reigned independently at Thebes, at the same time as the kings of Herakleopolis. This family later became Dynasty XI, ruling over Egypt under the Middle Kingdom.

Mentuhotep II	c.2040-2010BC
Mentuhotep III	c.2010-1998BC
Mentuhotep III	c.1998-1991BC

Dynasty XII
Amenemhat I	c.1991-1962BC
Senusret I*	c.1971-1926BC
Amenemhat II*	c.1929-1892BC
Senusret II*	c.1897-1878BC
Senusret III*	c.1878-1841BC
Amenemhat III*	c.1844-1797BC
Amenemhat IV*	c.1799-1787BC
Sobek-neferu**	c.1787-1783BC

Dynasty XIII   c.1783-1640BC
Dynasty XIII was made up of about 70 kings, most of whom had very short reigns.

Dynasty XIV
Dynasty XIV is the name given to princes from the western delta who broke away, ruling at the same time as Dynasty XIII.

Dynasty XV
This dynasty was made up of Hyksos kings including:
Apophis	c.1585-1542BC

Dynasty XVI
Minor kings who ruled at the same time as Dynasty XV.

Dynasty XVII   c.1640-1552BC
This dynasty contained fifteen Theban kings including: Tao I, Tao II and Kamose (c.1555-1552BC).

Dynasty XVIII
Ahmose	c.1552-1527BC
Amenhotep I	c.1527-1506BC
Tuthmosis I	c.1506-1494BC
Tuthmosis II	c.1494-1490BC
Hatshepsut**	c.1490-1468BC
Tuthmosis III	c.1490-1436BC

Amenhotep II	c.1438-1412BC
Tuthmosis IV	c.1412-1402BC
Amenhotep III	c.1402-1364BC
Akhenaten	c.1364-1347BC
(Amenhotep IV)	
Smenkhkare*	c.1351-1348BC
Tutankhamun	c.1347-1337BC
Ay	c.1337-1333BC
Horemheb	c.1333-1305BC

Dynasty XIX

Ramesses I	c.1305-1303BC
Seti I	c.1303-1289BC
Ramesses II	c.1289-1224BC
Merenptah	c.1224-1204BC
Amenmesse	c.1204-1200BC
Seti II	c.1200-1194BC
Siptah	c.1194-1188BC
Tawosret**	c.1194-1186BC

Dynasty XX

Set-nakht	c.1186-1184BC
Ramesses III	c.1184-1153BC
Ramesses IV	c.1153-1146BC
Ramesses V	c.1146-1142BC
Ramesses VI	c.1142-1135BC
Ramesses VII	c.1135-1129BC
Ramesses VIII	c.1129-1127BC
Ramesses IX	c.1127-1109BC
Ramesses X	c.1109-1099BC
Ramesses XI	c.1099-1069BC

By the end of Dynasty XX, Egypt was divided and a line of priests, beginning with Heri-Hor, was ruling from Thebes.

Dynasty XXI

This line of kings ruled part of the country from Tanis.

Smendes I	c.1069-1043BC
Amenemnisu	c.1043-1039BC
Psusennes I	c.1039-991BC
Amenemope	c.993-984BC
Osochor	c.984-978BC
Si-Amun	c.978-959BC
Psusennes II	c.959-945BC

Dynasty XXII

This line of Libyan kings began reuniting the country.

Shoshenq I	c.945-924BC
Osorkon I	c.924-889BC
Shoshenq II	c.890BC
Takeloth I	c.890-874BC
Osorkon II	c.874-850BC
Takeloth II	c.850-825BC
Shoshenq III	c.825-773BC
Pimay	c.773-767BC
Shoshenq V	c.767-730BC
Osorkon IV	c.730-715BC

Dynasty XXIII & Dynasty XXIV

These were two separate lines of kings ruling at the same time as the later kings of Dynasty XXII. They included:

Tefnakhte I	c.727-720BC
Bakenranef	c.720-715BC

Dynasty XXV: The Nubian kings

Piankhi	c.728-716BC
Shabako	c.716-702BC
Shebitku	c.702-690BC
Taharqa	c.690-664BC
Tanut-Amun	c.664-663BC

Dynasty XXVI: The Saite kings

Psamtek I	c.664-610BC
Necho II	c.610-595BC
Psamtek II	c.595-589BC
Apries	c.589-570BC
Amasis	c.570-526BC
Psamtek III	c.526-525BC

Dynasty XXVII

525-404BC

A line of Persian kings including:

Cambyses	525-521BC
Darius I	521-485BC
Xerxes	485-464BC

Dynasty XXVIII

Amyrtaeus	c.404-399BC

Dynasty XXIX

Nepherites I	c.399-393BC
Achoris	c.393-380BC
Psammuthis	c.380-379BC
Nepherites II	c.379BC

Dynasty XXX

Nectanebo I	c.379-361BC
Tachos	c.361-359BC
Nectanebo II	c.359-342BC

Dynasty XXXI

341-323BC

A second line of Persian kings.

The Macedonian kings

Alexander the Great	332-323BC
Philip Arrhidaeus	323-316BC
Alexander IV	316-305BC

The Ptolemies

Ptolemy I	305-284BC
Ptolemy II	284-246BC
Ptolemy III	246-221BC
Ptolemy IV	221-205BC
Ptolemy V	205-180BC
Ptolemy VI	180-164BC, 163-145BC
Ptolemy VII	145BC
Ptolemy VIII	170-163BC, 145-116BC
Queen Cleopatra III and Ptolemy IX	
	116-107BC
with Ptolemy X	107-88BC
Ptolemy IX	88-81BC
Queen Cleopatra Berenice	81-80BC
Ptolemy XI	80BC
Ptolemy XII	80-58BC
Queen Berenice IV	58-55BC
Ptolemy XII	55-51BC
Queen Cleopatra VII	51-30BC
with Ptolemy XIII	51-47BC
with Ptolemy XIV	47-44BC
and with Ptolemy XV	44-30BC

GODS AND GODDESSES

The Egyptians worshipped hundreds of gods and goddesses. There were so many of them that it is sometimes difficult to work out which was which. As the Egyptian religion evolved over the centuries, the identities of some early gods disappeared, as they merged together in people's minds, while other gods split up their roles to form separate new gods.

Many gods and goddesses were associated with certain animals, and they were often shown in paintings as that animal or with an animal mask. Major gods, like the sun god, were worshipped throughout Egypt, but some others were local gods, linked to a particular town or temple.

AKER

Aker was the double-lion god, guardian of the sunrise and sunset. Often shown as two lions back-to-back, with the disc of the Sun between them, balanced between the east and west horizons.

AMUN

Amun

In his earliest form, Amun was god of air and wind. Later he was worshipped as a fertility god and Creator of all things. In the New Kingdom, Amun became king of the gods and father of all the pharaohs. He was associated with the Sun god Re and so became known as Amun-Re.

Temple: Karnak
Animals: goose and ram

AMMUT

A female demon. She was known as 'the devourer' and ate the hearts of dead people judged not to have led good lives.

ANUBIS

Anubis was the god of the dead and of magic and embalming. He guided the dead through the darkness of the underworld. He was the son of Osiris and Nepthys.

Animal: jackal

Anubis

ANUKIS

Anukis was the goddess of the First Cataract on the River Nile. She was the daughter of Khnum and Satis.

ATEN

Represented as the Sun's disc with rays, Aten was the Lord of the Heaven and the Earth. He became the most important god during the reign of Akhenaten.

BAST

Bast was a sun and mother goddess. She was the daughter of the sun god Re and represented the life-giving power of the Sun to heal sickness and to ripen the crops.

Temple: Bubastis
Animal: cat

BES

Bes was a dwarf and jester to the gods. He was also the protector of people's homes and of children.

Bes

GEB

Twin brother and husband of Nut, Geb was god of the Earth. He was known as the Great Cackler and was often represented as a goose. He was said to have laid the egg from which the Sun was hatched. Father of Osiris, Isis, Seth and Nepthys.

HAPI

God of the Nile, with special responsibility for the annual floods, Hapi was therefore very important to everyone throughout the land. His followers regarded him as even more important than the Sun god.

HATHOR

Hathor, the wife of Horus, was one of the earliest goddesses and was identified with many local goddesses. She was the goddess of love, beauty and joy, and a mother and death goddess.

Temple: Denderah
Animal: cow

Hathor

HORUS

Horus, god of the sky, was said to have inherited the throne of Egypt from Osiris.

Temple: Edfu
Animal: falcon

IHY

Ihy was the god of music and musicians. He was the son of Horus and Hathor.

ISIS

One of the earliest and most important goddesses, Isis was worshipped as the great mother-goddess and goddess of crafts. The daughter of Nut and Geb, she was married to her brother Osiris.

Temple: Philae

KHEPI

A Sun god linked to sunrise, he was often shown as a scarab beetle pushing a dung ball. This was a symbol of the Sun, as Egyptians believed Khepi pushed the Sun across the sky each day.

KHNUM

Khnum was a potter who created people from clay on his potter's wheel. He was believed to control the source of the Nile.

Temple: Elephantine
Animal: ram

KHONSU

Khonsu was the moon god. He was the son of Amun and Mut.

Temple: Karnak

MA'AT

Ma'at was the goddess of truth and justice. She represented the balance and harmony of the universe.

Symbol: feather

MIN

Min was worshipped by men as the god of fertility and later as a rain god who helped crops to grow.

Temple: Coptos
Animal: bull
Plant: lettuce

MITHOS

Mithos was the lion-headed god and son of Bast.

MUT

Mut was a mother goddess and wife of Amun. She was the queen of all gods and the mother of all living things.

Temple: Karnak
Animal: lioness

Mut

NEFERTEM

Nefertem was the god of oils and perfumes. He was the son of Ptah and Sekhmet.

Flower: sacred blue lotus

NEITH

Neith was the goddess of hunting, war and weaving. Later she was worshipped as a protector of the dead and as a guide in the underworld. She was also guardian of the Red Crown of Lower Egypt. She was the mother of the Sun.

Temple: Sais
Symbol: shield and arrows

NEPHYS

Nepthys was a protector of the dead. She was married to her brother Set, god of deserts.

Ma'at

NUT

Nut was goddess of the sky. She was the daughter of Shu and married to her brother Geb, god of the Earth. She is often shown stretching from one horizon to the other, only her fingertips and toes touching the ground. Her husband Geb is often shown stretched out beneath her.

OSIRIS

Egyptians regarded Osiris as King of Egypt. He introduced vines and grain to the land, and became supreme god, judge and ruler of the dead. Son and heir of Geb and Nut, and the symbol of eternal life.

Temple: Abydos

PTAH

Ptah was patron of the city of Memphis, and patron of artists, sculptors and architects. He was himself an architect and was responsible for building the framework of the universe.

Temple: Memphis
Animal: Apis bull

RE

Re was the most common form of the Sun god, although there were many different versions. Each day Re was born again and began a journey across the sky.

Temple: Heliopolis

RENENUTET

Renenutet, a protector of children, was a goddess of great powers. Her gaze could destroy her enemies, but it could also make crops and livestock grow and fatten.

Temple: Medinet el Fayum
Animal: snake

SATIS

Satis was patroness of hunters. As guardian of Egypt's southern border with Nubia, she was responsible for killing the pharaoh's enemies. She was married to Khnum.

SEKHMET

Sekhmet represented motherhood and the burning, destructive power of the Sun. A fierce goddess of war, she was the wife of Ptah and the daughter of Nut and Geb.

Animal: lioness

SET

Set was god of deserts and trouble, also known as Lord of Upper Egypt. Son of Geb and Nut, he was Osiris's evil brother. Set killed Osiris, and took his place on the throne of Egypt. Later dynasties worshipped Set as a protector from desert storms. He was married to his sister Nepthys.

Animals: donkey, pig and hippopotamus

SHU

Shu was the god of atmosphere and of dry winds. He was the son of Re, brother and husband of Tefnut, and the father of Geb and Nut.

SOBEK

Sobek was the god of water, and admired but feared for his ferocity. Often shown with the head of a crocodile. Husband of Renenutet.

Temples: Faiyum and Kom Ombo
Animal: crocodile

Sobek

TAWERET

Taweret was a female hippopotamus. She was the goddess of childbirth and was responsible for looking after pregnant women and babies.

THOTH

Thoth was the moon god and god of wisdom. His role was to be vizier and scribe to all the gods and he was keeper and recorder of all knowledge. He was married to Ma'at.

Temple: Hermopolis
Animal: baboon
Bird: ibis

Tawaret

THE HISTORY OF EGYPTOLOGY

Egyptology means the study of the history and archaeology of ancient Egypt. Egypt was the world's first tourist destination. The Egyptian monuments were the object of awe and admiration ~ and of plunder too ~ almost from the moment they were first constructed. Many of Egypt's conquerors ~ the Greeks, the Romans and the Arabs ~ studied the ancient ruins with great interest, and the country attracted visitors from other parts of the Mediterranean as well.

But it was not until late in the 19th century that European archaeologists began introducing scientific methods of excavation, which dramatically improved our understanding of Egyptian civilization. Here are some of the landmarks in the history of Egyptology.

Great Sphinx and pyramids of Giza by David Roberts, the Scottish artist who journeyed to Egypt in 1838. His paintings of the great monuments did much to encourage European interest in the subject.

c.500BC Greek historian Herodotus visited Egypt and made the first record of Egyptian history and civilization by a foreigner. But his account was mainly based on what people told him, so some of it was myth rather than fact.

Herodotus, the Greek historian, known as the 'father of history'

c.290BC An Egyptian priest named Manetho wrote the *History of Egypt* for Pharaoh Ptolemy II. This divided Egypt's history into 30 dynasties, a system which is still used today.

c.59BC Greek writer Diodorus Siculus wrote a 12-volume *Universal History*. The last volume dealt with the history and customs of Egypt.

25BC A Roman geographer named Strabo visited Egypt. He wrote the 17-volume *Geographia,* which included information on Egyptian tombs, temples and pyramids.

c.AD50 Roman historian Pliny the Elder was the first Roman to describe the Great Sphinx at Giza. He made records of the monuments in Egypt, and of those brought out of Egypt to Rome, such as obelisks.

AD378-388 A Christian nun known as Lady Etheria from Gaul (France) voyaged to Egypt and described the monuments around Thebes.

c.1200 Arab doctor Abd' el-Latif from Baghdad visited Giza, entered the Great Pyramid and saw the Great Sphinx. He wrote that the word 'mummy' comes from the Persian term *moumiya,* meaning pitch or bitumen.

1646 John Greaves, Professor of anatomy at Oxford University, wrote *Pyramidographia*. This tried to find the real purpose of the pyramids, comparing the facts with the stories that had grown up around them.

1657 French voyager Jean de Thevenot wrote about his journey to Egypt in a book called *Voyage au Levant.*

1692 Benoit de Maillot, French consul in Egypt, explored the Great Pyramid at Giza and argued for scientific exploration of Egypt and its monuments.

Between **1707** and **1726** Jesuit priest Claude Sicard voyaged around Egypt. He went as far south as Aswan, recording monuments and collecting information on 20 pyramids, 24 temples and over 50 decorated tombs. This was the most extensive coverage at that time. His most important work was to identify the temples at Karnak and Luxor as part of the ancient capital at Thebes.

1755 Frederick Nordern, Danish engineer and artist, published a book called *Voyage*. This gave a detailed description of Egypt with accurate plans and drawings of many of the monuments.

1768 Scottish explorer James Bruce sailed up the Nile and discovered the tomb of Ramesses III in the Valley of the Kings.

1798 Napoleon Bonaparte arrived in Egypt with an invading army and defeated the Egyptians at the Battle of the Pyramids. But he had also brought scholars with him to collect information about Egypt.

Various members of this commission stayed for three years and worked in different parts of the country, mapping and collecting information about its natural history, ancient monuments and the customs of the people. The books that were published made a huge impact in Europe and served as the foundation for modern Egyptology.

1799 The Rosetta Stone was discovered by French soldiers at Fort Rachid near Rosetta in Egypt. A large slab of basalt carved with identical texts in Greek, Egyptian hieratic and hieroglyphics, it later provided the clue to deciphering the mystery of Egyptian hieroglyphs.

1815 English physician Thomas Young published *Remarks on Egyptian Papyri and on the Inscription of Rosetta*. This was a vital step towards deciphering Egyptian hieroglyphs.

1815 Henry Salt was appointed British consul-general in Egypt and collected a number of ancient Egyptian works of art for British museums. He employed Giovanni Battista Belzoni to help him. Belzoni sent back many pieces that are now in the British Museum in London, including the colossal head of Ramesses II from Thebes. He also explored the temples at Abu Simbel, opened up many tombs in the Valley of the Kings and the pyramid of Chephren at Giza, and discovered the ancient port of Berenice on the Red Sea.

1821 John Wilkinson sailed to Egypt and spent the next three years there. He is

A portrait of Giovanni Belzoni, the Italian treasure hunter

often described as the founder of Egyptology in Britain. Wilkinson excavated tombs at Thebes, and his copies of paintings and inscriptions are still among the best ever made.

1824 French scholar Jean François Champollion published *Précis du Système Hiéroglyphique*. This built on Thomas Young's work and finally unlocked the secret of hieroglyphics.

1824 Scottish scholar Robert Hay made drawings, plans and copies of inscriptions on Egyptian monuments.

1825 English physician Augustus Granville performed a scientific autopsy on a mummy named Irtyersenu, showing how much could be learned from mummies.

1834 Italian adventurer Guiseppe Ferlini found a collection of gold jewels in the tomb of Queen Amanishakheto (1st century BC) at Meroë: the largest collection of Meroitic jewels ever found.

1840s German scholar Karl Lepsius and his team of draftsmen made numerous recordings of drawings and inscriptions from temples and tombs in the Valley of the Kings.

The Egyptian Museum in Cairo, founded by Auguste Mariette, has the largest collection of Egyptian antiquities in the world.

1850s Scottish scholar Henry Rhind set up new methods for excavation, in contrast to the 'treasure hunting' that had been conducted so far. He spent two years excavating tombs at Thebes, recording for the first time the precise location of each find.

1858 French archaeologist Auguste Mariette was appointed the first director of ancient monuments in Egypt and head of the new museum near Cairo, the first national museum in the Middle East. He also set up the world's first national antiquities service. From this point on, most of the objects excavated were kept in Egypt rather than taken away to foreign museums. The Cairo Museum now contains the world's largest Egyptian collection.

1871 A family of local treasure-hunters discovered a tomb at Deir el Bahri, containing 36 mummies belonging to members of New Kingdom royal families.

1873 Amelia Edwards, an English writer, made the long journey up the Nile, inspiring many others to follow. She became a founder member of the Egypt Exploration Fund, established in **1882**.

1884 English archaeologist William Flinders Petrie began excavating in Egypt for the British Egypt Exploration Fund. Over a period of 40 years, he made many important discoveries, but his most significant contribution was in the introduction of scientific methods for the recording of archaeological finds. He introduced stratigraphy (the study of the relative positions of rock strata) and 'sequence dating', for dating and arranging material. His best known digs include Naucratis, a Greek city in Egypt, and Kahun and Gurob, which increased experts' knowledge of daily life in towns. He also studied the famous Amarna Letters ~ found by a peasant woman in a field ~ which revealed new information about Akhenaten.

1893 Farmers stumbled across over 300 fragments of papyrus from the pyramid complex of 5th dynasty King Neferirkare at Abusir. These papyri provided archaeologists with information about the staff, duties and equipment in Egyptian temples.

1898 French archaeologist Victor Loret discovered 13 more royal mummies in Amenhotep II's tomb in the Valley of the Kings.

1898 English archaeologist James Quibell found the palette of King Narmer at Hierakonpolis: a major record of the unification of Egypt.

1913-1914 A German expedition led by Ludwig Borchardt uncovered the house of sculptor Thutmose at Amarna, containing the famous bust of Nefertiti.

1917 A French archaeological expedition began work at Deir el Medina, which led to the discovery of the royal workmen's village.

1919-1920 Herbert Winlock excavated the tomb of Meket-Re in Thebes. Inside were models of the man's house and workshops, giving a detailed glimpse of life at the time.

1922 Howard Carter, backed by Lord Carnarvon, discovered the tomb of King Tutankhamun containing its fabulous treasure.

1920s-1940s Egyptian archaeologist Sami Gabra excavated the human and animal cemeteries at the site of Tuna el-Gebel in Middle Egypt.

1930s Pierre Montet uncovered spectacular treasures from the royal burials of the little-known 21st and 22nd dynasties at Tanis.

1936-1956 William Emery excavated mastaba tombs of 1st and 2nd dynasty officials at Saqqara.

1954 A dismantled and perfectly preserved 4th dynasty funerary ship was found in a large pit south of the Great Pyramid at Giza. It had been buried for 4,600 years.

1960s UNESCO funded an international rescue operation to move the temples at Abu Simbel, so they would not be flooded by the building of a dam at Aswan.

From 1966 Excavations in the Nile Delta, led by Austrian archaeologist Manfred Bietak, found the Hyksos capital of Avaris and Ramesses II's city at Per Ramesses.

From 1975 The Akhenaten Temple Project uncovered blocks from Akhenaten's destroyed temples at Amarna, which are being slowly reconstructed.

1978 Hierakonpolis Expedition uncovered the charred remains of a potter's house, providing vital information about Egyptian life in about 3500BC. In **1985**, the remains of Egypt's earliest known temple were uncovered at the same site.

1995 American archaeologist Kent Weeks discovered the huge family tomb of Ramesses II in the Valley of the Kings. It contains at least 118 rooms, most identified by sonar as they were filled with rubble.

1996 Underwater archaeologists led by Franck Goddio started recovering remains of the city of Alexandria, now submerged under the sea, and nearby cities of Canopus, Herakleion and Menouthis, destroyed by earthquake in AD746.

1999 At least 200 mummies, some with gold masks, were discovered at Bawati in the Western Desert, dating from the early Graeco-Roman era. The burial ground, thought to contain over 10,000 mummies, may be the biggest ever found.

1999 An Egyptian-German team uncovered some of the world's oldest stables on the edge of the Nile Delta. Housing up to 460 horses, they are the biggest stables ever found in the ancient Middle East and have been linked to Pharaoh Ramesses II.

2000-2001 Important underwater archeological finds at Herakleion, in the Bay of Aboukir, include colossal statues, a stela with an inscription of Nectanebo I, a Ptolemaic shrine to Amun, and the remains of 10 ancient Egyptian ships.

One of the huge granite statues being recovered from the sea near Alexander the Great's ancient city of Alexandria. This one may show the Pharaoh Ptolemy II.

The remains of the Temple of Apollo at Delphi, Greece, built in the 4th century BC

ANCIENT
GREECE

MAP OF ANCIENT GREECE

THRACE

ILLYRIA

MACEDONIA

Methone
Vergina
Pydna
CHALCIDICE

Hellespont

Aegospotami

Granicus

Troy

Mount
Olympus

EPIRUS

Dodona

THESSALY

Iolkos

AEGEAN SEA

LESBOS

Pergamum

CORCYRA

ITHACA

Thermopylae

EUBOEA

SKYROS

CHIOS

Smyrna

IONIA

Ephesus

Delphi

Chaeronea
Leuctra

Thebes
Plataea

Eretria

Marathon

ACHAEA

Elis

Corinth

Athens
Salamis

ATTICA

SAMOS

Mycenae
Mantinea
Olympia

Argos
ARCADIA   Tiryns ARGOLIS

Aegina
Epidaurus

DELOS

Miletus

MESSENIA

Sparta

CYCLADIC ISLANDS

NAXOS

Halicarnassus

KOS

Cnidus

Pylos

LACONIA

THERA

MEDITERRANEAN SEA

CRETE   Knossos
Mallia

Hagia Triada   Zakro
Phaestos

EARLY GREECE

THE FIRST GREEKS

Greece is a hot, dry, country in southern Europe with a craggy, mountainous landscape. Its long, jagged coastline, peppered with bays and inlets, juts out into the Mediterranean Sea and is surrounded by hundreds of islands. Around 40,000 years ago, the first inhabitants started moving into the area.

THE STONE AGE

The first Greeks lived in caves and used tools of bone and flint. They hunted bison and reindeer - which have long since died out in southern Europe - and gathered wild plants. This period is known as the Stone Age.

THE FIRST FARMERS

Some time before 6000BC, farmers settled in eastern Greece. They grew wheat and vegetables, and kept sheep. The landscape wasn't quite the same as it is now: it was much more wooded, and the only good farming land was in narrow valleys and coastal plains. So people relied on fishing for extra food.

THE BRONZE AGE

Around 3000BC, people in Greece discovered how to make bronze by mixing copper and tin. They used it to make tools and weapons that were hard and sharp. This made farming and building easier. This period, from around 3000BC to 1100BC, is known as the Bronze Age.

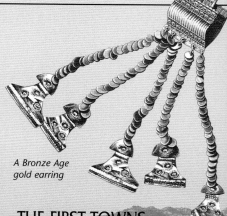

A Bronze Age gold earring

THE FIRST TOWNS

As farming became more efficient, many farmers grew more food than their families could eat. This extra food could be exchanged for other goods, such as tools or pottery. Some people began to make a living as craftsmen, making objects instead of farming. The population increased and some villages grew into towns.

Fish-hook

Scraper

Dagger

A selection of bone tools

INTERNET LINK

For links to websites where you can see carved figures from the Cyclades, as well as pots shaped like animals, go to **www.usborne-quicklinks.com**

THE CYCLADES

Archaeologists have identified a thriving culture on the Cyclades islands from about 2600-2000BC. Craftsmen there produced fine carvings and there was active trade between the islands. But the Cyclades were too small for the way of life there to develop further.

This map shows the Greek mainland and islands.

This stretch of the Greek coastline, looking out onto the Aegean Sea, looks much the same as it did when the first Greeks settled here.

A marble figure from the Cyclades, dating back to about 2500BC

THE MINOANS

The first ever European civilization developed on Crete, the largest of the Greek islands. It began to flourish around the year 2000BC, but mysteriously died out less than a thousand years later. Its remains were first discovered in the 1920s, by a British archaeologist, Sir Arthur Evans. He named it the Minoan civilization, after a legendary king of Crete named Minos.

MINOAN LIFE

Minoan civilization was based around several large palaces, each of which was at the heart of a thriving local community - with skilled craftsmen, artists, and professional writers known as scribes. The Minoans also had a highly organized economy and system of trade. Their goods have been found all over Greece, the Cyclades islands, Egypt and the eastern Mediterranean.

Much of what we know about the Minoan way of life comes from frescoes (wall paintings). It appears that most people made their living from farming, but fished and hunted for extra food. We also know that men usually wore a loincloth and a short kilt made of wool or linen, while women wore bright dresses with frilled skirts.

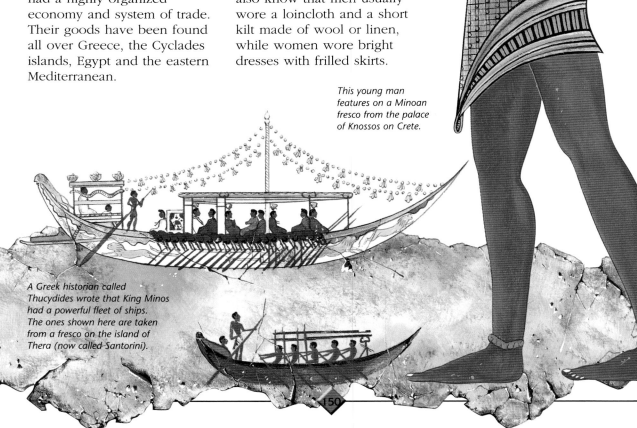

This young man features on a Minoan fresco from the palace of Knossos on Crete.

A Greek historian called Thucydides wrote that King Minos had a powerful fleet of ships. The ones shown here are taken from a fresco on the island of Thera (now called Santorini).

THE LEGEND OF MINOS

According to Greek legend, the god Zeus fell in love with a beautiful princess called Europa. Zeus turned himself into the shape of a bull and swam to Crete with her on his back. One of their three sons, Minos, became the King of Crete. Although Minos was the name of the king in the legend, scholars think *Minos* may have been a Cretan title for all kings, like the Egyptian word *Pharaoh*.

Europa riding on the back of Zeus

 INTERNET LINK

For links to websites where you can see Minoan pottery, paintings and jewels, and explore an interactive map about trade, go to www.usborne-quicklinks.com

MINOAN HOUSES

At the heart of Minoan life was the palace, where the royal family lived. Courtiers and people who worked at the palace also lived there, but most people would have lived in houses outside the palace grounds. The storage and cooking areas were downstairs, with the living and sleeping areas above.

This model house, found at the palace at Knossos, is made of faience (glazed earthenware). It shows what Minoan town houses probably looked like.

DATING THE EVIDENCE

Archaeologists sometimes use information from other cultures to help them date newly excavated sites. Minoan pots had been found in Egypt, long before any major sites were found on Crete. So, when similar pots were eventually discovered on Crete, experts were able to date them according to the Egyptian finds.

This Minoan jar, dated 1450-1400BC, was dug up in Knossos.

MINOAN PALACES

Around 2000BC, the Minoans built several large palaces, each with its own king and royal family. These remained the focus of their communities and their way of life until around 1700BC, when disaster struck the island and the palaces were destroyed by a series of earthquakes. The Minoans remained undeterred, however, and built new, even grander, palaces right on top of the ruins of the old ones.

The major archaeological sites on Crete

CRETE
Knossos
Mallia
Zakro
Hagia Triada
Phaestos

Mediterranean Sea

▲ Palace
■ Villa

FRESCOES

Each palace had apartments set aside for its royal family. These were spacious rooms decorated with wall paintings known as frescoes, made by applying paint to wet plaster. The frescoes at Knossos have given archaeologists lots of valuable information about Minoan life. Most of the frescos you can see there today, however, are actually modern reconstructions.

INTERNET LINK

For a link to a website where you can go on a virtual tour of the palace of Knossos, go to **www.usborne-quicklinks.com**

KNOSSOS

The largest of the Minoan palaces was at Knossos, which was built and rebuilt several times. The walls were mainly stone, with wooden roofs, ceilings and doors. The design of the palace was light and airy, with a good drainage system, and it was decorated with bulls' horns – which appear to have been a Minoan religious symbol. At its height, over 30,000 people may have lived in Knossos and surrounding areas.

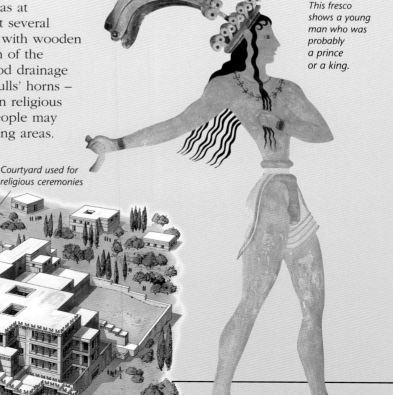

The palace at Knossos

Courtyard used for religious ceremonies

This fresco shows a young man who was probably a prince or a king.

THE KING

The King of Knossos may have had some authority over the rulers of the other palaces, and played an important part in the religious life of the whole island. He had a number of state apartments, including a throne room where state business and religious ceremonies took place.

These dolphins are from a fresco in the queen's apartment at Knossos.

MINOAN SCRIPTS

The Minoans developed writing systems to help them keep records for trading purposes. The first, from c.2000BC, was a form of hieroglyphic (picture) writing. From c.1900BC, they began using a script which we call Linear A. So far, however, no one has been able to decipher either of the scripts.

Linear A clay tablet from Hagia Triada, dated c.1900BC

THE HARVEST

As a form of tax, the king retained part of the annual grain harvest, which was stored at the palace. A portion of it was used to feed the people who lived there, and to pay officials and craftsmen.

The rest was exported around the Mediterranean, and the profits were used to pay for imports from other countries, such as precious metals, jewels, ostrich feathers, ivory and amber.

A large pot, called a pithos, used for storing food and wine

The throne room at Knossos was discovered almost intact. This is what it looks like today.

MINOAN RELIGION

Although there are no written records of the Minoans' religious beliefs, we know certain things from their paintings, pots and statues.

This bull's head is actually a vessel, called a rhyton. It was used for pouring liquid offerings to the gods.

SACRED SYMBOLS

There appear to have been two main sacred symbols. One was the bull, sacred to the sea god. Images of its horns were found all over Knossos. The other sacred symbol was a double-headed weapon, known as a *labrys*. Both of these were used to decorate pots and tombs, as well as palaces.

Double-headed weapon, called a labrys

RELIGIOUS CEREMONIES

Religious ceremonies were led by priests and priestes while musicians played. Rooms were set aside for worship in the palaces, bu Minoans also used outdoor shrines in caves and on mountain tops.

It seems likely that goddesses and priestesses were more important than gods and priests. We know this because females are shown more prominently in religious statues and paintings.

INTERNET LINK

For a link to a website where you can find out more about Minoan religion and see pictures of Minoan priests, go to **www.usborne-quicklinks.com**

Bulls' horns symbol from the palace of Knossos

This small marble statue is probably a Minoan priestess.

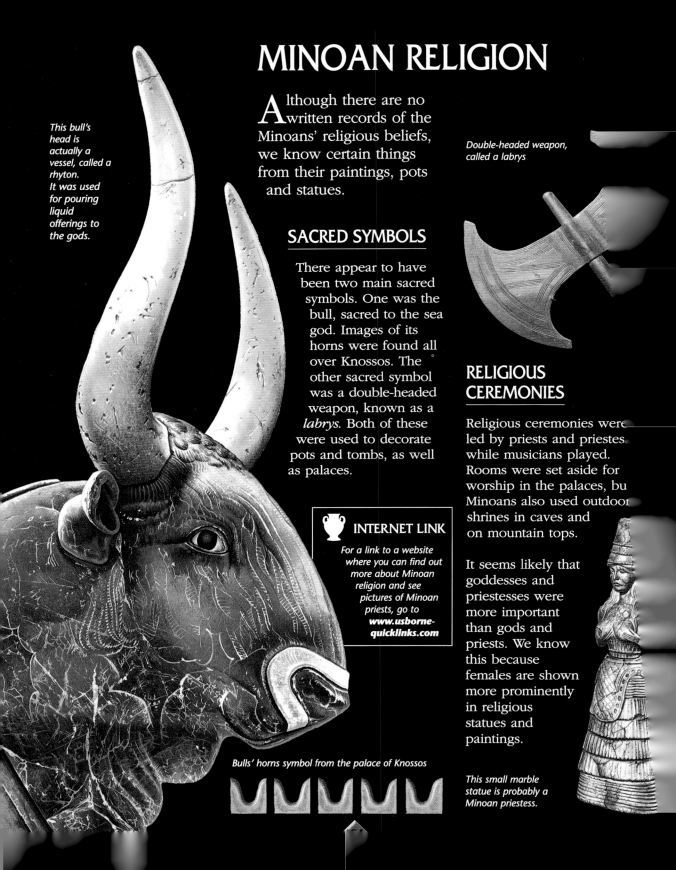

ULL-LEAPING

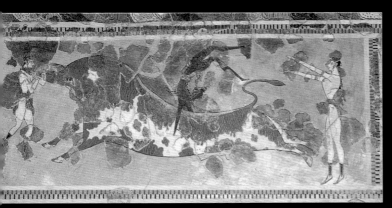

s fresco from Knossos shows a man leaping over a bull's back. The figure on the left held
e bull's horns, while the figure on the right caught the leaper.

e Minoans appear to have
d a daring custom, which
volved leaping over a bull.
om images on Minoan
intings, it seems that teams
men and women took
rns to approach a charging
ll. They grasped its horns
and catapulted themselves
onto its back, and then onto
the ground. This dangerous
sport may have been a
religious ritual, as the bull
was a sacred animal. It
probably took place in the
courtyard of the palace.

DEATH AND THE AFTERLIFE

The Minoans believed in li
after death. They buried th
dead with food and
possessions, for use in the
afterlife. In early times, the
rich were buried in stone
tombs with other bodies.
Later on, they were buried
individual coffins.

This coffin, dated c.1400BC, was fou
in Hagia Triada on Crete. It is decora
with a funeral scene, showing people
making offerings.

HE LEGEND OF THE MINOTAUR

ccording to legend, an Athenian prince named
heseus sailed to Crete, where he fought and
verpowered a terrible monster
nown as the Minotaur. The
onster was half man and half bull
nd was kept in a labyrinth – an
nderground maze.

his tale may be based
artly on fact. The palace at
nossos was so maze-like that
could be described as a
abyrinth. The king may also
ave worn a bull's mask in
eligious ceremonies, linking
im to the idea of the Minotaur.

EXPLOSIONS AND INVASIONS

Around 1600BC, the once golden age of Minoan culture went into decline. Although we don't know exactly why this happened, it seems that Crete suffered a series of natural disasters which must have contributed.

THERA EXPLODES

Scientists have discovered that, around 1450BC, the nearby island of Thera was blasted to pieces by a massive volcanic eruption. At about the same time, the palaces on Crete were destroyed. The cause may have been tidal waves and earth tremors, created by the eruption - but, whatever the reason, the whole Minoan way of life was thrown into chaos.

 INTERNET LINK

For a link to a website where you can explore the ruins of Akrotiri on Thera and look at more frescoes and pottery, go to **www.usborne-quicklinks.com**

Thera before the eruption

Thera after the eruption

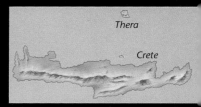

Thera

Crete

Thera (the main part of which is now called Santorini) is 110km (70 miles) from Crete.

The explosion on Thera may have b the biggest volcanic eruption 10,000 years. People would have b killed, farmland ruined by falling and houses destroy

MYCENAEANS INVADE

After the Thera eruption, the Minoans seem to have reoccupied their palaces for a time - until, around 1350BC, when most of the palaces and villas were destroyed for good, this time by fire. We don't know what caused this, but it is likely that Crete was invaded by Mycenaeans from mainland Greece, who overthrew the Minoans and took control of the island, destroying the Minoan civilization in the process.

Mycenaean pot, discovered on the Greek mainland, showing a military scene

THE END OF KNOSSOS

Knossos became the focus of Mycenaean society on Crete, but around 1100BC it was burned down and never rebuilt. No one knows what caused the fire, but it could have been the result of a violent confrontation between Mycenaeans and Minoans, or between different Mycenaean groups.

AKROTIRI

In the 1960s, Greek archaeologists Spyridon Marinatos and Christos Doumas started excavations on Thera. They unearthed the remains of a Minoan village at Akrotiri, which had been completely buried in volcanic ash. Houses, frescoes and pottery were all preserved, revealing in great detail how Minoan people lived their lives.

Minoan houses in Akrotiri on the island of Thera

A fresco showing blue monkeys, from a house in Akrotiri

THE LEGEND OF ATLANTIS

According to the Greek philosopher Plato, there was a once thriving civilization on an island named Atlantis, which had sunk beneath the ocean without trace. Over the centuries, many people have been captivated by the legend - with some suggesting that the eruption and the departure of the Minoans might be the source of the story.

17th century map, based on Plato's story, showing Atlantis in the Atlantic Ocean, between Europe and North America

THE MYCENAEANS

From about 1600BC, mainland Greece was dominated by a people we call the Mycenaeans. They are named after the city of Mycenae, where evidence of their culture was first discovered.

INTERNET LINK

For a link to a website where you can take a virtual tour of Mycenae, go to **www.usborne-quicklinks.com**

GREECE
Iolkos
Orchomenos
Gla   Thebes
Mycenae• Athens   Miletus
Pylos   •Dendra
Sparta

Mediterranean
Sea   CRETE

Map of Mycenaean cities

THE ACROPOLIS

The acropolis at Mycenae was similar to those of other ancient cities. Inside the walls was the royal palace and houses for courtiers, soliders and craftsmen. The main gateway was decorated with two lions, possibly symbols of the royal family.

This is a reconstruction of the acropolis of Mycenae in around 1250BC.

City walls, extended in the 13th century BC

Houses

Circular wall enclosing graves

Royal palace and megaron

North gate

There was an underground reservoir at this end.

The Lion Gate

WHO WERE THEY?

The Mycenaeans lived in small kingdoms, each based around a separate city. These kingdoms were never united, but they traded together and shared a language and way of life. Mycenae itself was probably the leading city.

Historians are not sure where the Mycenaeans came from. They may have come to Greece from central Europe around 2000BC, or they may have already been in Greece for some time before that.

WHERE DID THEY LIVE?

Most Mycenaeans lived in walled cities which were built on high ground, to make them easy to defend. The important buildings were situated in the *acropolis* (meaning "high city" in Greek) on top of the hill. Most people lived in the lower town, outside the walls of the acropolis.

FOOD AND TRADE

As in Crete, the palace was at the heart of the island's economic life. Craftsmen's goods and produce from farming were stored in the acropolis, for distribution around Crete, or export.

A gold pot, called a rhyton, shaped like an animal's head

MYCENAEAN PALACE LIFE

This is a reconstruction of a megaron, based on excavations from several cities.

The royal palace at Mycenae was made up of several brightly painted buildings - often with more than one floor - arranged around a vast central courtyard. A Mycenaean palace was far more than just a royal residence. It was a military headquarters, an administrative base, and a workplace for craftsmen. Palace life revolved around a large hall, called a megaron, where the king held court and conducted state business.

This fresco shows a woman courtier, from Mycenae.

MYCENAEAN SCRIPT

The Mycenaeans adapted Minoan forms of writing to devise their own script, which we call Linear B. Archaeologists have unearthed thousands of Linear B tablets, which they have been able to decipher, because the Mycenaeans spoke an early form of Greek.

Linear B clay tablet

The results have not been that exciting, though, as the tablets mainly contain lists - of livestock, farming produce and craft items, as well as details of palace officials and their tasks.

MYCENAEAN ROYAL TOMBS

In 1876, a German businessman and passionate amateur archaeologist named Heinrich Schliemann made an exciting discovery at Mycenae. He unearthed six royal tombs, dating back to around 1600BC, which provided a great step forward in our knowledge of the Mycenaeans, their religious beliefs and way of life.

RELIGION

From the many objects found in the royal tombs, archaeologists concluded that Mycenaean religious beliefs were similar to those of the Minoans. Both cultures seem to have believed in life after death, and rated goddesses more highly than gods.

Pottery figure of a Mycenaean goddess

SHAFT GRAVES

The earliest royal tombs were shaft graves. These are very deep holes in the ground where several bodies, usually from the same family, were buried. The graves could be as deep as 12m (40ft). Objects such as pots and weapons were buried with the dead for use in the afterlife.

This shaft grave is marked by a tombstone above ground.

THOLOS TOMBS

By about 1500BC, beehive-shaped tombs, known as *tholos* tombs, were being used to bury members of the royal family. The dead person was buried with great ceremony, along with valuable possessions, such as weapons and ornaments.

Pausanias, a Greek historian, believed these tombs were treasuries, rather than tombs, because of the magnificence of the things inside. Unfortunately, they were easy to break into, so very few have been found with their treasures intact.

INTERNET LINK

For a link to a website where you can see photographs of Mycenaean tombs and some of the spectacular treasures found in the tombs, go to **www.usborne-quicklinks.com**

The scene here shows a reconstruction of a funeral procession to a tomb known as the Treasury of Atreus, after a legendary Mycenaean king.

Many of the king's possessions, including his war chariot, were buried with him. Mourners and musicians accompanied the body, and a sheep was led in to be sacrificed.

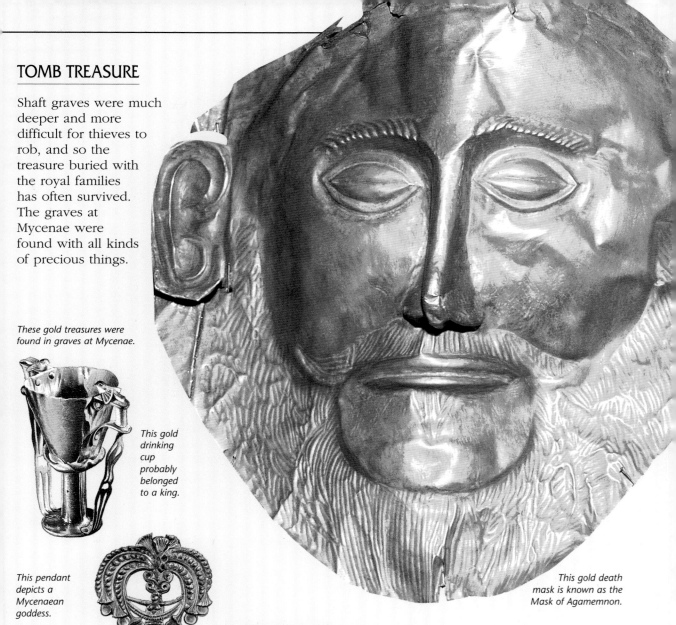

TOMB TREASURE

Shaft graves were much deeper and more difficult for thieves to rob, and so the treasure buried with the royal families has often survived. The graves at Mycenae were found with all kinds of precious things.

These gold treasures were found in graves at Mycenae.

This gold drinking cup probably belonged to a king.

This pendant depicts a Mycenaean goddess.

This duck-shaped crystal vessel may have been used in religious ceremonies.

This gold death mask is known as the Mask of Agamemnon.

DEATH MASKS

The faces of five kings in the Mycenae burial chambers were covered with masks of gold or electrum (a metal made of gold and silver). To make the mask, the metal was heated, then beaten into shape. Experts believe these masks were attempts at real portraits of the kings. The most famous one, shown here, is often named after Agamemnon, the legendary king in Homer's tale of the Trojan War (see pages 164-165). But, sadly, it can't really be Agamemnon himself. The mask dates back to about 1550BC, but the Trojan War, if it happened, took place later - around 1250BC.

WARRIORS AND TRADERS

Judging from what they left behind, the Mycenaeans seem to have been a very warlike people. Archaeologists have dug up masses of weapons and images of war and battle scenes.

This carved head from Mycenae shows a soldier in a helmet made from boars' tusks.

WARRIOR KINGS

The king of a Mycenaean city was expected to be a warrior too. He had to look after his soldiers, and to supply them with food, housing, land and slaves. This was arranged by officials in the palace, where many of the soldiers lived.

In battle, kings and nobles wore helmets and protective clothing made of bronze. Ordinary soldiers just wore leather tunics.

The king leading his soldiers into battle

Nobles rode into battle in chariots. Soldiers marched on foot.

WHAT SOLDIERS WORE

Most of what we know about what the soldiers wore comes from contemporary pictures - although one nearly complete bronze suit was found in a tomb in a place called Dendra (see the map on page 158).

The suit is made of bronze plates. With it was a boars' tusk helmet, some bronze greaves (leg guards), two swords, and the remains of a wooden- framed shield. The whole find dates back to around 1400BC.

> **INTERNET LINK**
>
> For links to websites where you can see Mycenaean metalwork, weapons and goods from a shipwreck, go to **www.usborne-quicklinks.com**

This soldier's suit was found in a tholos tomb.

Boar's tusk helmet

Bronze high neck guard

Shoulder pieces

Bronze protective clothing, called a cuirass

Bands to protect the stomach and lower body

SHIELDS AND SWORDS

The shields that the Mycenaeans used were made of oxhide stretched over a wooden frame. There were three different shapes. Shields were large and heavy, and warriors carried them into battle slung on their backs.

Shield shaped like the number eight

Tower shield

Round shield

Daggers and swords were made from bronze. Some were highly decorated and look similar to those found on Crete. They may even have been made on the island.

A Mycenaean gold sword hilt. Above is a bronze dagger, inlaid with a scene of a lion hunt.

MEDITERRANEAN TRADERS

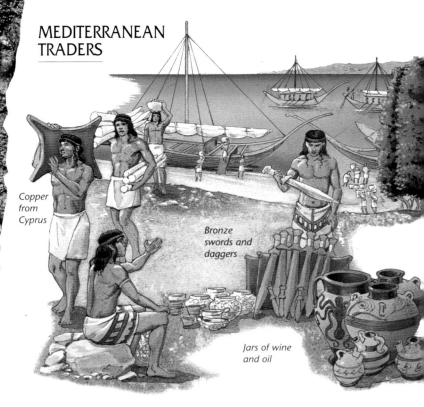

Copper from Cyprus

Bronze swords and daggers

Jars of wine and oil

This scene from a Mycenaean port shows traders unloading goods.

The Mycenaeans were great traders. At first, there was fierce competition from the Minoans, but after the Mycenaeans invaded Crete, they took over the Minoan trade for themselves. They had trading posts all along the eastern Mediterranean coast - in Asia Minor (now Turkey) and Lebanon - but they also traded goods from as far away as Scandinavia and Africa.

The Mycenaean world in 1400BC

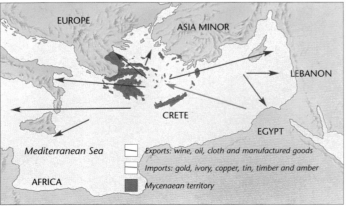

EUROPE
ASIA MINOR
LEBANON
CRETE
EGYPT
Mediterranean Sea
AFRICA

Exports: wine, oil, cloth and manufactured goods

Imports: gold, ivory, copper, tin, timber and amber

Mycenaean territory

TROY AND THE TROJAN WAR

The *Iliad*, an epic poem by Homer, a Greek poet who lived around 800BC, tells of a war between Greece and Troy – a city in Asia Minor (now Turkey). There was a war around 1250BC, but we don't know if it was the same one that Homer described in his poem.

THE LEGEND

Legend has it that the Trojan War was caused by Helen, Princess of Sparta – the most beautiful woman in the world. All the Greek kings wanted to marry her, but her father made them swear to support the man he chose as her husband – Menelaus of Sparta, brother of Agamemnon of Mycenae.

HELEN MEETS PARIS

King Priam of Troy sent some men to Greece to bargain for the return of a Trojan princess who had been kidnapped. Among them was Paris, Priam's son. When Helen and Paris met, they fell in love and ran away together to Troy. Furious, Menelaus and Agamemnon organized a great military expedition to bring Helen back.

THE TROJAN HORSE

For ten years the Greeks laid siege to Troy and a battle raged outside the city walls. At last, the Greek king Odysseus thought of a trick to win the war. He got his men to build a huge wooden horse, which they left outside the city gates. The Greeks then sailed away under cover of darkness.

GREEK VICTORY

The Trojans thought that the horse was a gift to the goddess Athene. They dragged it inside the city, unaware that Greek soldiers were hidden inside it. That night, the Greeks crept out and opened the city gates. The Greek army returned to storm in and destroy the city.

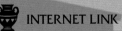

INTERNET LINK

For links to websites where you can read about the story and characters of the Trojan War, go to **www.usborne-quicklinks.com**

This is a portrait of Helen of Troy, carved in about 1819 by the Italian neoclassical sculptor, Antonio Canova.

FACT OR FICTION?

According to Homer, Troy stood overlooking the Hellespont – a channel of water that separates Asia Minor and Europe. In the 1870s, Heinrich Schliemann (see page 160) set out to find it.

Following Homer's description, he started to dig at Hisarlik in Turkey, and uncovered the ruins of several cities, built one on top of the other. Several of the cities had been destroyed violently, but it is not clear which was the Troy of Homer's legend. Experts are now certain, though, that Troy was a real place.

Greek soldiers climbing out of the Trojan horse in the dead of night

PRIAM'S TREASURE

In 1873, Schliemann made an incredible discovery. He found a copper bowl, which turned out to have a hoard of gold, jewels, weapons and ornaments inside. He nicknamed it Priam's Treasure.

This photograph of Schliemann's wife Sophia wearing the jewels was for many years the only record of them that existed.

Although Schliemann believed the treasure to date back to the Trojan War, it was in fact more recent - but it was still a remarkable find, and revealed much about ancient metalworking. It was lost in the chaos at the end of World War Two, but has recently resurfaced in Russia.

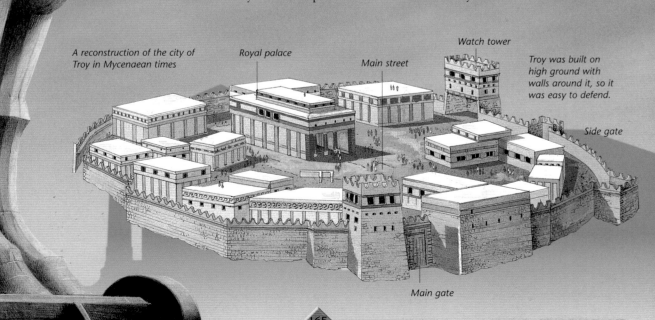

A reconstruction of the city of Troy in Mycenaean times

Royal palace

Main street

Watch tower

Troy was built on high ground with walls around it, so it was easy to defend.

Side gate

Main gate

THINGS FALL APART

By around 1200BC, the world of the Mycenaeans was falling apart. Ancient Egyptian records show that, in the second half of the 13th century BC, there was a long run of poor harvests, food shortages and famine in the Mediterranean, which put the whole Mycenaean way of life under threat.

This portrait of one of the Sea Peoples was carved on a temple built by the Egyptian pharaoh Ramesses III.

TROUBLED TIMES

During this difficult period, groups of starving Mycenaeans probably attacked each other's cities and villages to steal food and other goods. At around this time, many people built strong defensive walls around their cities, to protect themselves from raiders.

Thick stone walls at the Mycenaean fortress of Tiryns, built in the 11th century BC

THE SEA PEOPLES

In desperation, as their trade and economy disintegrated around them, some groups of Mycenaeans may have gone on raids overseas. This may have been the real cause of the Trojan War, described by Homer in his poem *The Iliad* (see pages 164-165).

Some Greeks may even have been driven away from their homes altogether. There are Egyptian reports of groups of people on the move in the eastern Mediterranean in 1190BC. Some were marching overland, while others set sail in a large fleet of battleships.

The Egyptians named these migrants the 'Sea Peoples'. Experts don't know exactly who they were or where they were from, but it's possible that some of them may have been Mycenaean refugees.

As they advanced, the Sea Peoples' fleet seized the island of Cyprus. Meanwhile, on land, their army destroyed many cities, and overthrew the powerful Hittite empire in Asia Minor (Turkey).

This reconstruction of a sea battle between Egyptians and Sea Peoples is based on a carving at Luxor in Egypt.

Sea Peoples' ship

Egyptian ship

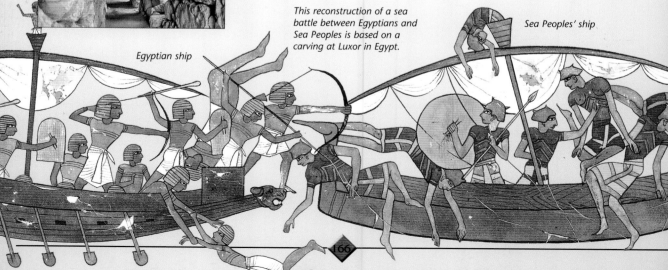

EGYPT'S VICTORY

The Sea Peoples' army and fleet were decisively defeated by the powerful Egyptian pharaoh Ramesses III. After this final blow, the Sea Peoples scattered over the Mediterranean. Some may have become the ancestors of the Etruscans, who later settled in Italy. Others moved to Sicily, or to Palestine, and became the ancestors of a people known as the Philistines.

THE DORIANS

One by one, the Mycenaean cities were abandoned and destroyed, either by earthquakes or by enemy conquest. Then, a people called the Dorians became dominant in the Peloponnese in southern Greece. They took advantage of the troubles to increase their power.

Dorian Greek
Ionic Greek
Aeolic Greek
Arcadian Greek

ASIA MINOR

Aegean Sea

GREECE

PELOPONNESE

CRETE

INTERNET LINK

For a link to a website where you can find out more about the Sea Peoples, go to **www.usborne-quicklinks.com**

This map shows the different routes taken by the Sea Peoples.

This map shows where the main Greek dialects were spoken.

ITALY

ASIA MINOR

Sea Peoples' fleet
Sea Peoples' army
Route after defeat

SICILY

GREECE

CYPRUS

CRETE

PALESTINE

Mediterranean Sea

EGYPT

Wherever the Dorians settled, their dialect took root, and it was from this that the Greek language later developed. But the Dorians did not adopt the artistic skills of the people they conquered, and many of the cultural achievements of the Mycenaeans were lost, including the art of writing.

THE DARK AGES

The period in Greece from 1100 to 800BC is sometimes described as the Dark Ages, as we know very little about what was happening - although new excavations are starting to reveal more. The Greeks lost the art of writing, so they left no written records, and foreigners, such as the Egyptians, hardly mention them either.

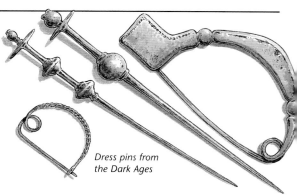

Dress pins from the Dark Ages

GREECE IN DECLINE

By the beginning of this period, the population in Greece had fallen hugely. This was most probably due to the widespread famine and warfare that hit the region at the end of the Mycenaean period. The palaces were destroyed, and a whole way of life crumbled with them. Old styles of metalwork and pottery died out, and skills such as fresco-painting and gem-cutting were forgotten.

DAILY LIFE

Most people were very poor and probably grew just enough to eat. They would have lived in small huts made of mud brick, with thatched roofs. As these materials do not last long, few buildings from this period have survived.

Mud brick house

Vase in the new geometric style that developed in the Dark Ages

EUBOEA

One exception to this picture of poverty was on the large island of Euboea (now called Evia). As early as 900BC, the Euboeans were trading abroad, but wars between the two main cities on the island eventually brought an end to this properous culture.

The island of Euboea

Terracotta centaur from Euboea

A statue of a man carrying a calf from about 570BC, found on the Acropolis in Athens

ARCHAIC GREECE

THE ARCHAIC PERIOD

Sometime after 800BC, Greek culture began to show the first signs of a revival. This new era, which lasted until around 500BC, is known as the Archaic Period. The Greek population grew and there was increasing contact with other lands. Greek art improved and the skill of writing was rediscovered and developed (see page 186).

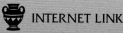

INTERNET LINK

For links to websites where you can see an animated map showing the spread of Greek colonies and design a Greek amphora online, go to **www.usborne-quicklinks.com**

This vase, called an amphora, was painted in about 560BC. It is decorated with a scene from a wild boar hunt, which was typical of the style of the time.

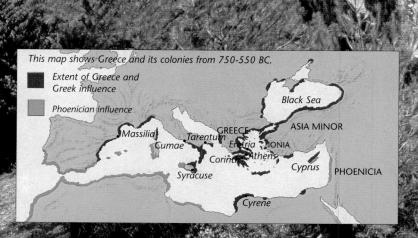

This map shows Greece and its colonies from 750-550 BC.

- Extent of Greece and Greek influence
- Phoenician influence

Massilia
Cumae
Tarentum
GREECE
Eretria
Corinth
Athens
IONIA
Syracuse
Black Sea
ASIA MINOR
Cyprus
PHOENICIA
Cyrene

This pottery model of a horse and its rider was made in Greece in about 600BC.

THE FIRST COLONIES

As early as 1000BC, groups of people had begun leaving the Greek mainland, in search of new land overseas. They were driven by different things: famines, struggles between states, and overcrowding as the population grew.

The areas where these people settled, known as colonies, soon grew into independent states. The first of these, Ionia, was on the coast of Asia Minor (now Turkey). Later groups settled all around the Mediterranean, from France to the Black Sea. The colonies were often in places with a natural port and good farmland, where the locals were friendly.

TRADE AND COMMERCE

Trade grew between the Greek cities and their colonies, and with the Phoenicians from the eastern Mediterranean (see page 31). Merchants sailed from port to port, buying and selling goods. The Greek colonies acted as staging posts for Greek trade with foreign lands.

This photograph shows the ruins of a fortress on the Ionian coast, where the Greeks established their first colonies.

THE GRAIN TRADE

Many of the Greek cities could not grow enough to feed all their people, so grain - mainly barley - was the most crucial import. Athens had to import as much as two-thirds of all its grain from abroad, mostly from Greek colonies around the shores of the Black Sea.

GREEK CITY-STATES

By the Archaic Period, mainland Greece was made up of a cluster of small city-states, politically independent from each other. The word the Greeks used for a city-state was *polis* - which is the origin of our word 'politics'. Although these states were often rivals, and sometimes fought wars against each other, they shared the same Greek identity - a common language, culture and religion - which created strong links between them.

This map shows the city-states in around 500BC. The most powerful cities were Athens, Corinth and Sparta.

This image from a Greek vase shows an Athenian slave and his owner.

WHAT WAS THE CITY-STATE LIKE?

The Greeks liked to keep their political units fairly small - even the largest city-state, Athens, had no more than a few thousand citizens (see opposite page). Each *polis* consisted of a single city, enclosed by walls, and its surrounding countryside. Inside the walls was an area of high ground, called an *acropolis*, and an open area, called an *agora*, which was used for markets and meetings.

FREE MEN AND SLAVES

Greek society was made up of two main groups: free men (and their wives and families) and slaves. Slaves were workers who were owned by free men and had no legal rights. Many lived closely with their owners, like members of the family, but were very rarely granted their freedom.

WHO RULED?

At the beginning of the Archaic Period, most Greek states were governed by groups of rich landowners, called aristocrats. This kind of government is known as an aristocracy, which means 'rule by the important people'. Sometimes, if they were unpopular, the aristocrats chose respected, important men to rule instead. This is called an oligarchy, which means 'rule by the few'.

As trading activities increased, a middle class of merchants and craftsmen began to prosper. They resented the aristocracy and demanded a role in politics. This often led to riots between different social groups.

THE TIME OF TYRANTS

To bring peace, the people were sometimes prepared to let one very powerful man rule alone. This sort of leader was known as a tyrant.

In 621BC, the people of Athens appointed a man called Draco to lead them. He drew up a set of very severe laws. Even minor crimes, such as stealing food, were punished by death.

INTERNET LINK

For a link to a website where you can find out more about the city-state of Corinth and choose which kind of ruler you would have preferred, go to **www.usborne-quicklinks.com**

SOLON THE REFORMER

In 594BC, an aristocrat named Solon was given power and introduced popular reforms. He provided food for the poor, stopped people who owed money

Solon

from being sold as slaves, and gave citizens a say in the city's affairs. But this didn't satisfy everyone. Solon was forced to leave Athens and unrest broke out again. Then, in 508BC, an aristocrat named Cleisthenes came to power, introducing a radical new system of government, known as democracy (see pages 192-3).

CITIZENS AND METICS

In Athens, free men were eventually divided into two groups: citizens, which meant men who were born in Athens, and metics, who were not.

Citizens could take part in politics, but they were also expected to serve in the army, act as officials and volunteer for jury service. Metics had to pay tax and serve in the army, but they could not own property or get involved in politics.

Metics often worked as craftsmen. This scene from a painted pot shows a cobbler.

SPARTA – A WARRIOR STATE

In the 10th century BC, a group of Dorians settled in Sparta, in Laconia, southern Greece, which became the nucleus of a thriving state. The Spartans soon acquired a reputation for toughness and military strength. After overpowering the local people, they extended their frontiers by conquering nearby Messenia in 740-720BC. Sparta was now one of the largest Greek states of its day.

This Spartan cup, made around 560BC, shows a busy North African trading scene. Not much pottery now survives from Sparta.

The Spartans themselves produced fine metalware and vases, and were also said to have played a role in the development of Greek music.

Unlike other states, the Spartans were slow to adopt coins as currency. Instead they used these iron rods.

Map showing Sparta and Argos

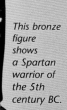

This bronze figure shows a Spartan warrior of the 5th century BC.

TRADE AND PROSPERITY

Not only was Sparta one of the largest states, it also had enough fertile land to make it self-sufficient in food. At the start of the Archaic Period, the Spartans were trading with other Greek states, importing luxury goods, such as ivory, amber and cloth.

SPARTA WEAKENED

Their early success was not to last. In 668BC, they were defeated in a war against Argos, another local state. In 630BC, the Messenians began a revolt which dragged on for 17 years. This convinced the Spartans they must make drastic changes - both to keep the population under control and to protect themselves from foreign invasions.

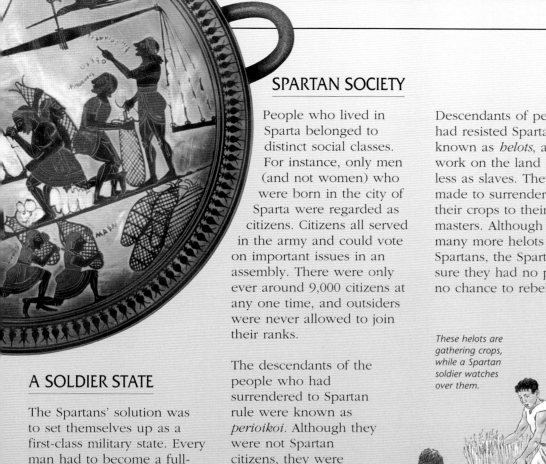

SPARTAN SOCIETY

People who lived in Sparta belonged to distinct social classes. For instance, only men (and not women) who were born in the city of Sparta were regarded as citizens. Citizens all served in the army and could vote on important issues in an assembly. There were only ever around 9,000 citizens at any one time, and outsiders were never allowed to join their ranks.

The descendants of the people who had surrendered to Spartan rule were known as *perioikoi*. Although they were not Spartan citizens, they were free and were allowed to trade and join the army.

Descendants of people who had resisted Spartan rule were known as *helots*, and forced to work on the land - more or less as slaves. They were made to surrender most of their crops to their Spartan masters. Although there were many more helots than Spartans, the Spartans made sure they had no power - and no chance to rebel.

These helots are gathering crops, while a Spartan soldier watches over them.

A SOLDIER STATE

The Spartans' solution was to set themselves up as a first-class military state. Every man had to become a full-time soldier and devote his life to training and fighting. All Spartans lived very hard lives, and had little contact with the outside world.

This huge bronze pot, as tall as a man, was made in Sparta in the 6th century BC. It was found in the grave of a Celtic ruler at Vix in France.

The handles are shaped like mythological beasts called gorgons.

The rim is decorated with a scene showing hoplites and horse-drawn chariots.

GREEK ARMIES

Cavalry
soldier

At the beginning of the Archaic Period, the most important part of any Greek army was the cavalry - the soldiers on horseback. Soldiers had to provide their own horses and weapons, so early armies were dominated by rich men who could afford to do this.

Auxiliary
soldiers

FOOT SOLDIERS

In these early times, foot soldiers tended to be fairly poor, so their weapons and equipment were poor as well. By the 7th century BC, however, there was a new elite class of foot soldiers, called hoplites, who were better equipped and better trained (see pages 178-179). Once the hoplites had grown in importance, cavalry units became smaller.

AUXILIARIES

Poor men who could not afford the full battle kit and weapons of a hoplite soldier usually served instead in lightly armed auxiliary units. These units included archers, stone slingers, and men called *psiloi*, who were armed with clubs and stones.

SIEGE WARFARE

In wartime, a common tactic was to lay siege to a city by surrounding it - even going to the lengths of building walls around it. The idea was to starve the city into submission - although this could take months. In 305-304BC, the city of Rhodes managed to hold out for a year against the Macedonian army, which was eventually forced to withdraw.

INTERNET LINK

For links to websites where you can examine battle scenes on a Greek pot, and see pictures of Greek weapons, go to **www.usborne-quicklinks.com**

A trumpeter blares out to encourage the attackers and give orders.

These soldiers are swinging a battering ram, suspended on ropes to help the swinging action.

An archer

A stone slinger

SIEGE WEAPONS

Another tactic was for the army to try to storm the city and take it by force. By about 400BC, the Greeks were using a heavy wooden beam, called a battering ram, to smash into walls or gates. The ram was attached to ropes inside a wooden covering, and was moved back and forth by a team of men.

The attacking army also used siege towers – huge wooden structures that could be moved up against the city walls, as platforms for attack.

Attackers climb up the tower, so they can clamber onto the city walls.

Defenders throw rocks and spears and shoot arrows.

Hoplites in formation, ready to storm the city

Towers were sometimes divided into floors.

Each level housed archers or a catapult.

A catapult could fire arrows or javelins.

The main body of the battering ram was made of wood.

The battering ram took its name from the bronze ram-shaped head.

HOPLITES

B y the 7th century BC, foot soldiers called hoplites were the elite corps of any Greek army. Hoplites all used similar clothing and weapons, but most armies did not have a special uniform.

EQUIPMENT

To protect his body, a hoplite wore a joined breast and back plate known as a cuirass. Early models were made from two bronze plates, attached with leather straps at the side.

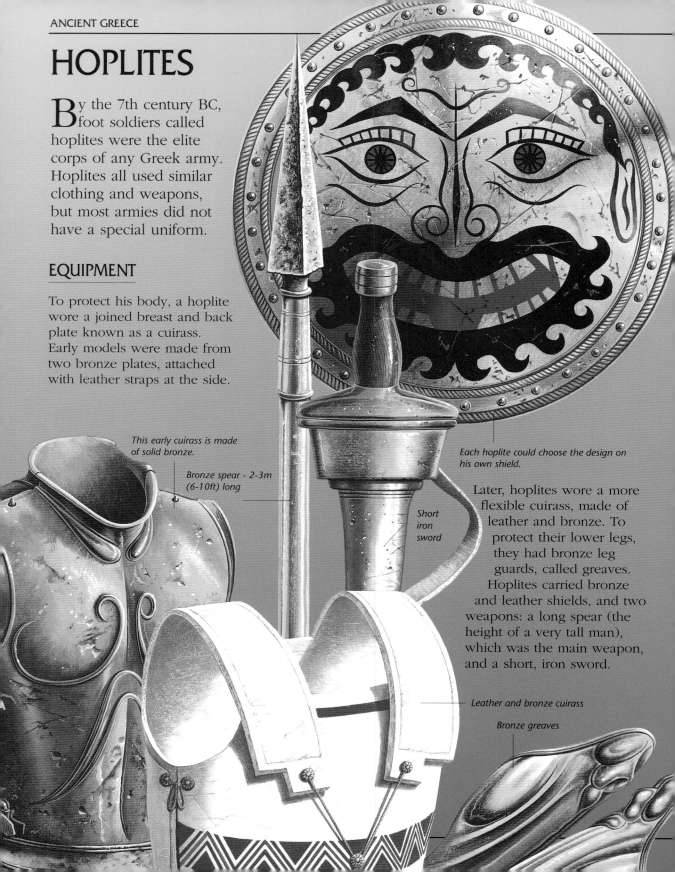

This early cuirass is made of solid bronze.

Bronze spear - 2-3m (6-10ft) long

Short iron sword

Each hoplite could choose the design on his own shield.

Later, hoplites wore a more flexible cuirass, made of leather and bronze. To protect their lower legs, they had bronze leg guards, called greaves. Hoplites carried bronze and leather shields, and two weapons: a long spear (the height of a very tall man), which was the main weapon, and a short, iron sword.

Leather and bronze cuirass

Bronze greaves

HELMETS

Helmets were made of bronze and often had horsehair crests on top. Designs changed over the years: here are just a few of them.

The most basic kinds were the Kegel and the Corinthian, both worn in the 7th century BC. Different types evolved from these, one of which was the Illyrian helmet.

The basic Corinthian helmet developed into one with ear holes, so that soldiers could hear better in battle. The Chalcidian helmet left both the ears and the mouth uncovered.

Between the 5th and the 2nd centuries BC, the Thracian helmet became popular. It had a peak at the front and long cheek pieces.

Kegel

Illyrian

Corinthian

Later Corinthian

Chalcidian

Thracian

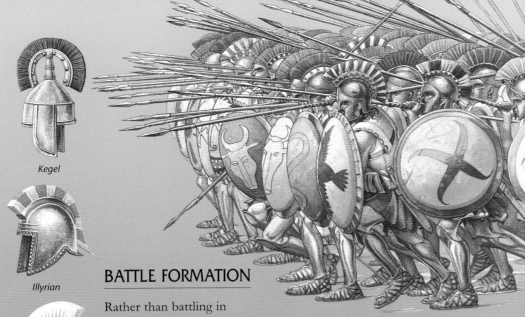

A phalanx charging forward in battle

BATTLE FORMATION

Rather than battling in one-to-one combat, as warriors had done in earlier times, hoplites fought in an organized formation called a phalanx. The phalanx was a long block of soldiers, usually eight ranks deep. Each man was protected partly by his own shield and partly by the shield of the soldier on his right hand side.

The man on the far right was left partly exposed. Because of this, the right wing of a phalanx was vulnerable. In battle, a general would often try to attack the enemy on this weak side.

ATTACK

In attack, a phalanx charged forward so that the full weight of men and shields smashed into the enemy. The two opposing phalanxes would then push against each other until one gave way.

This hoplite soldier was painted on a Greek plate, dated around 560BC.

🏺 **INTERNET LINK**

For a link to a website where you can find out lots about the weapons of the Greek hoplite, go to **www.usborne-quicklinks.com**

GREEK WARSHIPS

The most powerful and famous warship in the ancient world was a Greek design known as a trireme. As Greek cities grew rich and powerful, they built fleets of triremes to patrol the eastern Mediterranean and wage war on their enemies.

A MODERN TRIREME

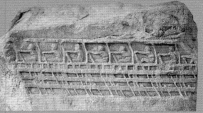

This Athenian carving of a trireme dates back to around 400BC.

In 1985, a group of ship-lovers from all over the world constructed a full-size replica trireme, named *Olympias*. Building the ship taught them a lot about the design of these ancient warships. During sea trials, the team discovered more about how the ship and crew performed. *Olympias* is now on permanent display at Neon Faliron, near the port of Piraeus in Greece.

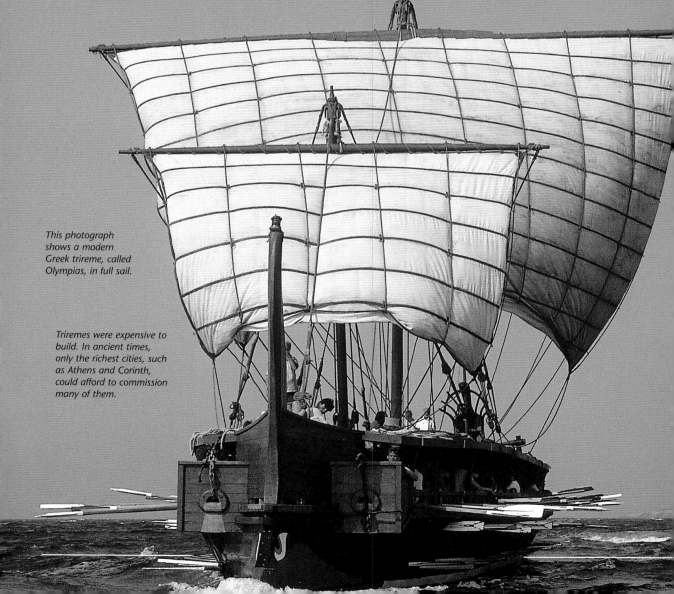

This photograph shows a modern Greek trireme, called Olympias, in full sail.

Triremes were expensive to build. In ancient times, only the richest cities, such as Athens and Corinth, could afford to commission many of them.

FAST AND FIERCE

Triremes were formidable in battle, because they were fast and easy to steer. Although they had sails, they always put them away and rowed into battle, because it was easier to start, stop and turn. The oarsmen propelled the ship through the water at up to 15km (9 miles) an hour – much faster than it could move under sail.

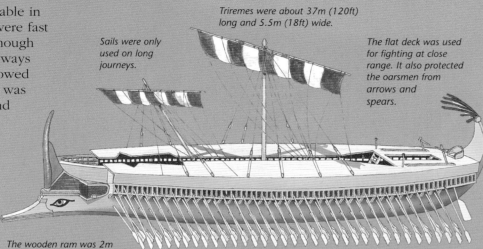

Triremes were about 37m (120ft) long and 5.5m (18ft) wide.

Sails were only used on long journeys.

The flat deck was used for fighting at close range. It also protected the oarsmen from arrows and spears.

The wooden ram was 2m (6.5ft) long and covered in bronze, to punch holes in enemy ships.

There were three tiers of long oars inside the hull.

Two huge oars at the back were used for steering.

THE CREW

Triremes carried crews of up to 200 men, most of whom were oarsmen. The name trireme came from the Latin for 'three oars', because the men sat on three levels inside the hull. Also on board were naval officers, soldiers, archers and deckhands.

INTERNET LINK

For links to websites where you can see photographs of full-size replicas of Greek triremes, go to www.usborne-quicklinks.com

The upper rowers, called thranites, sat in two rows of 31.

The middle rowers were called zygites. They sat in two rows of 27.

The bottom rowers were called thalamites. They also sat in two rows of 27.

BATTLE TACTICS

At the start of battle, enemies often faced each other in two long lines. The main tactic was to attempt to ram an enemy ship and sink or disable it.

The best places to aim for were the back and sides of an enemy ship. Four different ways of doing this are described below.

1 *Sweep around the far end of the line and attack from behind.*

2 *Swerve away from the opponent at the last moment, pull the oars on board and then sweep past the enemy ship, breaking its oars.*

3 *Make for a gap in the line and then veer to the side at the last moment, smashing into the side of the enemy.*

4 *Dart through a gap in the line, wheel around and attack the enemy from behind.*

THE PERSIAN WARS

In the 6th century BC, the rising stars on the scene in western Asia were the Persians. As they carved out an empire for themselves, they sparked a series of clashes with the Greek city-states, which lasted for over 50 years.

King Darius I

Map of the Persian empire in about 500BC

WHO WERE THE PERSIANS?

The Persians were a people from a small kingdom called Persia, at the heart of the country which is now Iran. Their expansion took off in 550BC, when they conquered the nearby kingdom of Media. By 485BC, under Darius I, they had built up a vast empire - one of the largest and most powerful in the ancient world.

Conflict with the Greeks first looked likely in 546BC, when the Persians succeeded in conquering the Greek states in Ionia, on the western coast of Asia Minor, in the area which is now Turkey.

At first, the Greek city-states did little to protest, until 500-499BC, when the Ionians rebelled. This time, they were backed by Athens and Eretria, who provided both men and ships. The Greeks destroyed the Persian city of Sardis, but the revolt collapsed when the Athenians and Eretrians withdrew their support.

THE BATTLE OF MARATHON

The Persians never forgave Athens and Eretria for helping the Ionians. In 490BC, King Darius led an invasion against Eretria and crushed it. Then his army landed at Marathon, just northeast of Athens.

The Athenians and their allies marched an army of 10,000 men to meet them. Although the Greeks were heavily outnumbered, they won a tremendous victory, by means of superior tactics and the strength of the hoplite phalanx (see page 179).

A runner was sent to Athens, 25 miles away, with the news. Right after announcing it, he dropped dead from exhaustion. Modern marathon races are named after this.

The first marathon runner

Persian relief from the palace at Persepolis, seat of the Persian kings

THE SECOND INVASION

King Darius I died soon after the Battle of Marathon, but memories of the Persian defeat festered in the mind of his son, King Xerxes. In 480BC, Xerxes led another invasion into Greek territory - this time overland. To cross the Hellespont, a thin stretch of water separating Europe and Asia, Xerxes had his engineers construct two huge bridges, entirely from ships.

The first confrontation took place in a narrow mountain pass called Thermopylae. At first, a small army of Greeks was able to hold back the Persian advance. But a Greek traitor showed the Persians a secret route around the pass.

Realizing there was no way out, Leonidas, the Spartan commander, stayed on with a small force to fight and be slaughtered, allowing the rest of the Greek army to flee to safety. It was one of the greatest, and most famous, gestures of self-sacrifice in ancient history.

The Persians then marched on an undefended Athens. Excited by their victory, they ran riot in the city, and looted and set fire to the Acropolis.

This monument at Thermopylae is to Leonidas, the Spartan commander who led the Greek army in the battle there.

This is a reconstruction of one of the boat bridges built by the Persians across the Hellespont.

The bridges built by the Persians were made up of more than 600 ships.

The huge Persian army was said to have taken seven days to march across.

THE DECLINE OF PERSIA

The destruction of Athens marked a low point for the Greeks in their conflict with Persia. However, while the Persians were celebrating their victory on land, trouble was brewing for them at sea.

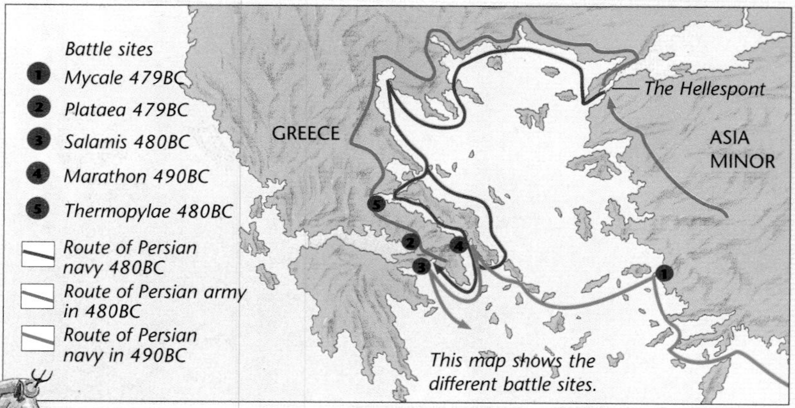

Battle sites
1 Mycale 479BC
2 Plataea 479BC
3 Salamis 480BC
4 Marathon 490BC
5 Thermopylae 480BC

Route of Persian navy 480BC

Route of Persian army in 480BC

Route of Persian navy in 490BC

GREECE

The Hellespont

ASIA MINOR

This map shows the different battle sites.

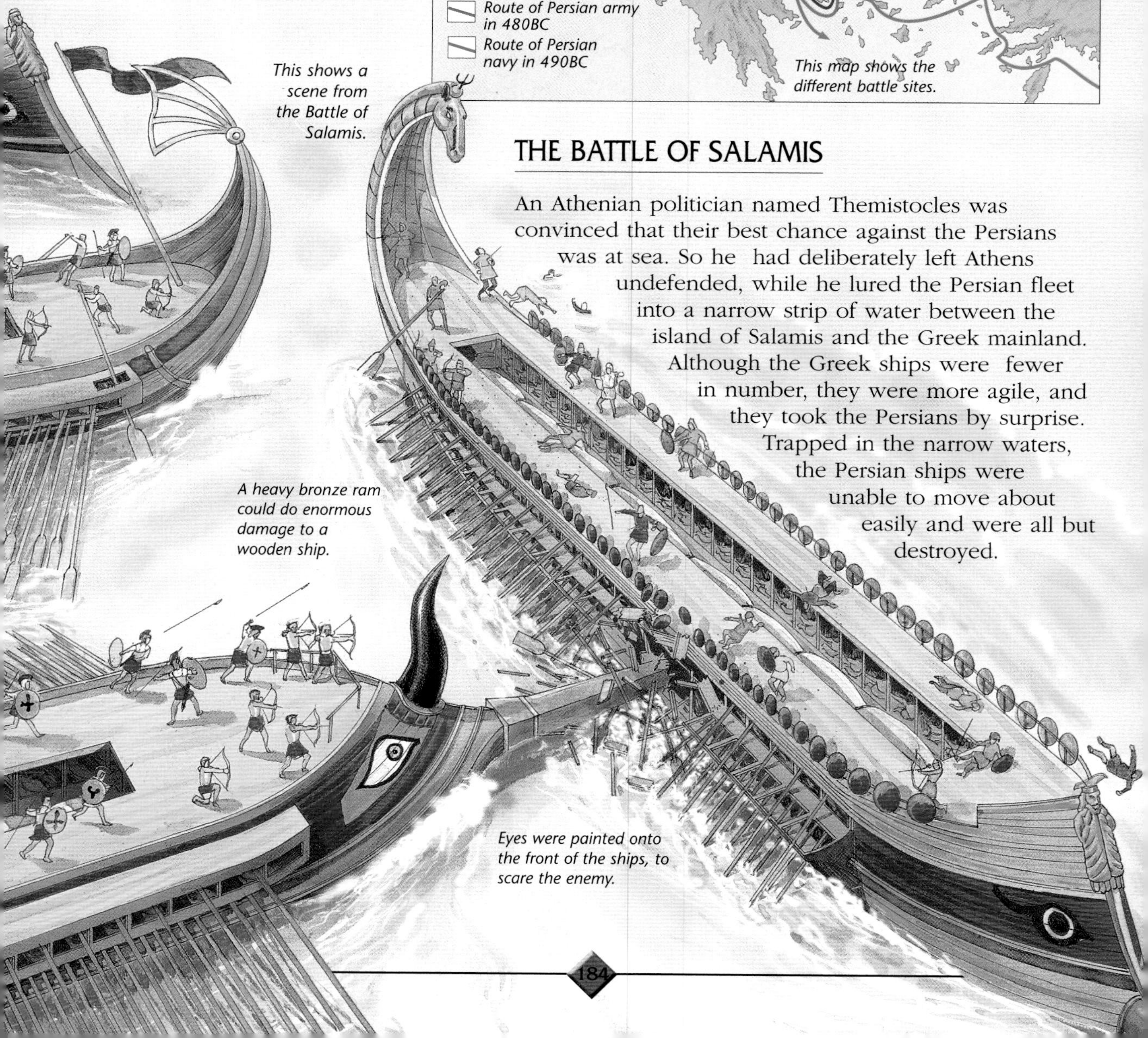

This shows a scene from the Battle of Salamis.

THE BATTLE OF SALAMIS

An Athenian politician named Themistocles was convinced that their best chance against the Persians was at sea. So he had deliberately left Athens undefended, while he lured the Persian fleet into a narrow strip of water between the island of Salamis and the Greek mainland. Although the Greek ships were fewer in number, they were more agile, and they took the Persians by surprise. Trapped in the narrow waters, the Persian ships were unable to move about easily and were all but destroyed.

A heavy bronze ram could do enormous damage to a wooden ship.

Eyes were painted onto the front of the ships, to scare the enemy.

THE INVASION ENDS

In 479BC, the Greeks amassed an enormous army, led by the Spartan general Pausanias, and defeated the Persians on land at a place called Plataea. Meanwhile, Greek forces attacked and burned the entire Persian fleet while it was moored at Mycale, off the coast of Asia Minor. The Persian invasion was finally over.

MEETING ON DELOS

Most Greeks believed it was only a matter of time before the Persians struck again - and they wanted to be ready for an attack. In 478BC, representatives from Athens and allied states gathered together on the Aegean island of Delos to discuss the problem. There they formed the Delian League, an alliance against any future Persian aggression. Members promised ships and money, to defend each other's territories in times of war.

Map showing Delos and the Delian League

GREECE

ASIA MINOR

Athens

Delos

League members

This painting of one of the Persian elite warriors, known as the Immortals, is taken from the palace at Susa, Persia.

WAR IS OVER

After this, the Greeks and the Persians continued to squabble over various territories in the Mediterranean. Egypt, Cyprus and Ionia all became battlegrounds in the struggle between the two powers. Then, in 449BC, the Greeks and the Persians made peace at last.

PERSIA FALLS

By this time, however, the Persian empire was already sliding into decline. King Xerxes had been murdered in 465BC, and his successors were weak, making the empire unstable. Greek power grew as Persian power waned.

King Xerxes taken from a Greek vase dated 330BC

By 330BC, the once all-powerful Persian empire had been overrun by the next great conqueror of the ancient world - Alexander the Great, the King of Macedonia (see pages 242-243).

THE BIRTH OF LITERACY

The skills of reading and writing first developed in Mesopotamia (in modern Iraq) and Egypt, before 3000BC. Literacy helped civilizations to develop because it allowed rulers to keep records and pass messages, helping them to organize large societies and develop trading links with other peoples.

This Greek inscription comes from a memorial stone beside the Sacred Way at Delphi, Greece.

THE GREEK ALPHABET

After the Mycenaean age, the art of writing was lost in Greece. Later, around 800BC, the Greeks adapted an alphabet used by the Phoenicians from the eastern Mediterranean (see page 31). The new script contained fewer letters than previous scripts, which made it much easier to learn. It also included vowels, which made it clearer to read. All modern European alphabets - Roman, Greek and Russian - developed from this Ancient Greek one.

THE SPOKEN WORD

Before the spread of literacy, stories and information about the past were passed down by word of mouth. Professional poets, known as bards, journeyed widely throughout Greece, passing on stories of the gods and Mycenaean heroes.

HOMER

Little is known about Homer's life, although tradition relates that he was blind. His poems were probably written down in his lifetime, or soon after his death, but we don't know exactly how.

The most famous bard was Homer, whose epic poems, the *Iliad* and the *Odyssey*, retold the traditional tales of the Trojan War. Composed between 850BC and 750BC, they are the earliest surviving examples of Greek literature.

INTERNET LINK

For links to websites where you can learn how to speak like an ancient Greek and translate Greek names in an online game, go to **www.usborne-quicklinks.com**

Left: some of the letters from the new Greek alphabet

This Roman bust of Homer is based on a Greek original.

The porch of the
Erechtheum temple,
built around 420BC
on the Acropolis in
Athens

CLASSICAL GREECE

THE GOLDEN AGE OF ATHENS

This period from about 500 to 336BC is known as the Classical period in Greek history. For much of this time, the city-states were dominated by the great city of Athens.

CITY OF CULTURE

Athens prospered in the years of peace following the end of the Persian Wars. The city was magnificently rebuilt, and became the focus for business and culture. At its peak - from about 479 to 431BC - Athens attracted the best artists and scholars of the time. They developed ideas about art, architecture, literature, politics, philosophy, science and history that laid the basis for modern European civilization.

THE EARLY YEARS

The earliest settlement, known as the Acropolis, or 'high city', was built high on a rocky hill. The first Athenians settled there because it was easy to defend and there was a freshwater spring.

INTERNET LINK

For links to websites where you can explore ancient Athens with an interactive map and discover what it was like to live there, go to www.usborne-quicklinks.com

NAMING THE CITY

According to legend, Poseidon, god of the seas, and Athene, goddess of wisdom and war, fought over the naming of the greatest city in Greece. Poseidon promised the people riches through trade, but Athene planted an olive tree. The people decided that this was the more valuable gift, so the city was named Athens after her.

This is a reconstruction of Athens in Classical times. There were probably about a quarter of a million people in the city and surrounding countryside.

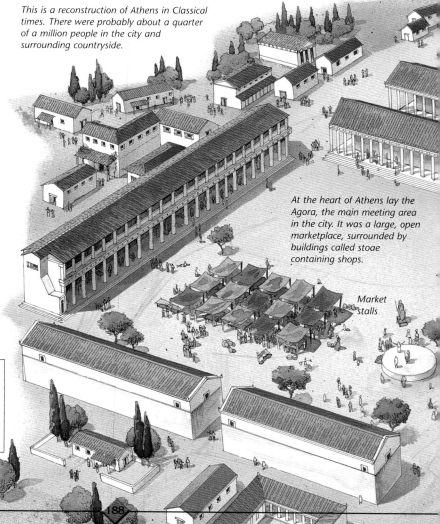

Athene's olive tree, from a Greek vase painting

The area around the olive tree on the Acropolis became a sacred place. Later, when the city grew, people built their homes around the base of the hill, reserving the Acropolis for temples and shrines.

At the heart of Athens lay the Agora, the main meeting area in the city. It was a large, open marketplace, surrounded by buildings called stoae containing shops.

Market stalls

Acropolis

The main route from the city up to the Acropolis was called the Panathenaic Way. This was used during a festival called the Panathenaea (see page 234).

The Court of Justice was situated on a hill called the Areopagus. It was named after Ares, the god of war, who was believed to have been tried there for murder.

Carving of Athene, goddess of Athens

The leaders of the city council held their meetings in this building, called the Tholos.

This is the Bouleterion, where the city council held its meetings.

Behind the Bouleterion was a temple dedicated to Hephaestos, god of metalsmiths and craftsmen. It was also known as the Theseum, after the hero Theseus.

Many craftsmen lived in these houses near the Agora.

THE ACROPOLIS

Towering over the ancient city of Athens was the Acropolis, or 'high city', the site of all the main temples to the gods. In 449BC, Pericles, the political leader of Athens, began a massive rebuilding of the Acropolis, to repair the damage done by the Persians.

This Roman copy of the statue of Athene from the Parthenon is made of unpainted marble. The original was made of wood and ivory, covered with gold.

THE PARTHENON

The main temple on the Acropolis, the Parthenon, was dedicated to Athene, patron goddess of Athens. It was designed by an architect named Ictinus and constructed of white marble, brightly painted. Although it is now in ruins, with few sculptures and no paint left in place, it is still one of the most famous buildings in the world.

TRICKS OF THE EYE

Looking at the columns of a temple can play funny tricks on the eye. From below, a column with absolutely straight sides can look thinner in the middle - even though it's not. So Greek architects designed their columns to bulge slightly in the middle.

 INTERNET LINK

For links to websites where you can explore the main temples of the Acropolis, including the Parthenon, with panoramic movies, go to **www.usborne-quicklinks.com**

THE GOLDEN STATUE

There were statues of Athene - portrayed in her different roles - all over the Acropolis. The most magnificent, and expensive, was probably the enormous statue of Athene Parthenos (Athene the Virgin), that stood just inside the Parthenon. About 12m (40ft) high, it was made of wood and ivory, with robes of pure gold, which were removed whenever there was a risk of the city being attacked. The statue is said to have cost more to make than the Parthenon itself.

This is a reconstruction of the Parthenon, as it would have looked when newly built.

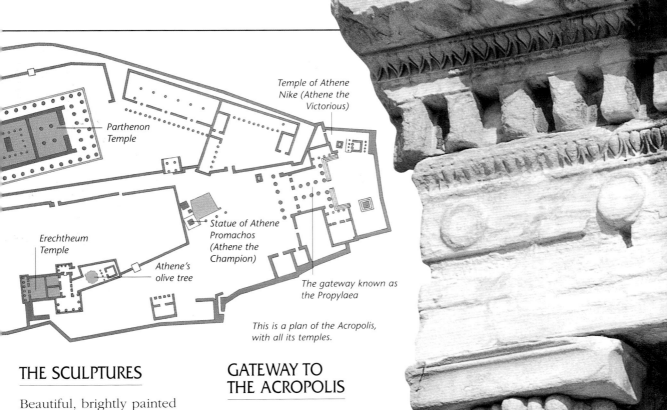

Temple of Athene Nike (Athene the Victorious)

Parthenon Temple

Erechtheum Temple

Statue of Athene Promachos (Athene the Champion)

Athene's olive tree

The gateway known as the Propylaea

This is a plan of the Acropolis, with all its temples.

THE SCULPTURES

Beautiful, brightly painted marble sculptures adorned the outside of the Parthenon. They were designed by Pheidias, one of the greatest artists of the 5th century BC.

These horsemen are part of the carved frieze on the outside of the Parthenon. The paint has long since worn away.

The carvings formed a horizontal band, or frieze, showing scenes from Athene's life, and from other Greek legends, such as the struggle between good and evil.

GATEWAY TO THE ACROPOLIS

Inside the gateway was a gallery of paintings and a huge bronze statue to Athene Promachos (Athene the Champion). Nearby, on the Acropolis walls, was a small temple dedicated to Athene Nike (Athene the Victorious), which was carved with scenes telling the story of the Trojan War (see pages 164-165).

ATHENE'S CONTEST WITH POSEIDON

This is one of the caryatids from the porch of the Erechtheum.

On the site of Athene's legendary contest with Poseidon (see page 188) was the Erectheum temple, named after Erechtheus, a mythical king of Athens from Mycenaean times. Athene's olive tree grew in the courtyard, and six graceful statues of young women, known as caryatids, decorated the side porch.

THE FIRST DEMOCRATIC STATES

At the end of the Archaic Period, some Greek cities overthrew their tyrants and replaced them with a radical new form of government. The new system - which provided a model for political systems in the modern world - is called democracy, from the Greek words *demos* (people), and *kratos* (rule). Unlike modern democracies, though, only citizens had a say. Women, slaves and men born outside the city were all excluded.

THE ATHENIAN MODEL

The Athenian system was introduced in 508BC, by an aristocrat named Cleisthenes. He set up an Assembly, where every citizen could speak and vote. It met every 10 days, on a hill called the Pnyx, and debated proposals made by the Council (see opposite).

The Assembly required 600 citizens for a meeting to take place. If there were too few people, police were sent to round up more.

PERICLES

Pericles was an enormously popular politician in Athens. He dominated the political scene from around 443BC, and was responsible for rebuilding the Acropolis. He was elected *strategos* (see opposite) nearly every year, until his death in 429BC.

🏺 INTERNET LINK

For a link to a website where you can find out lots more and watch short films about Pericles and Cleisthenes, go to **www.usborne-quicklinks.com**

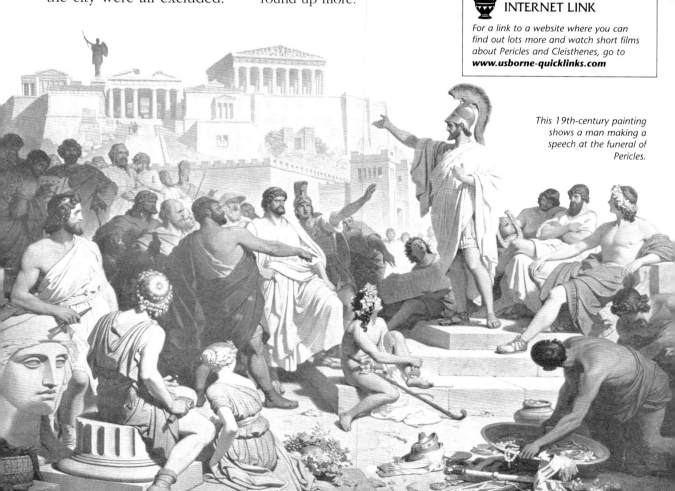

This 19th-century painting shows a man making a speech at the funeral of Pericles.

THE OFFICIALS

The people of Athens were divided up into 10 tribes. The Council was made up of 500 citizens - 50 elected from each tribe. The tribes took turns running the Council and the daily affairs of the state.

Under the democratic system, the most important officials were the *strategoi* who were 10 military commanders, elected annually, one from each tribe. Popular *strategoi*, like Pericles, were reelected many times.

There were also 9 archons, also chosen annually, but their duties were mostly ceremonial rather than political. Three of them, shown below, had special roles in the government of Athens.

The Basileus Archon presided over the law courts, arranged religious sacrifices and the renting of temple land, and supervised festivals and feasts.

The Eponymous Archon chose the men who financed the choral and drama contests. He was also responsible for lawsuits about inheritance and the affairs of heiresses, orphans and widows.

The Polemarch Archon was in charge of athletic contests held to commemorate men killed in battle. He also dealt with the legal affairs of metics.

OSTRACISM

The Athenians had an interesting system for getting rid of unpopular politicians. A vote was held once a year, at which any citizen could write down the name of a politician he wished to see banished on a piece of broken pot called an *ostrakon* (plural: *ostraka*). If more than 6,000 votes were cast against someone, that person would have to leave Athens for 10 years. This procedure is known as ostracism, after the pottery on which the name was written.

These ostraka show the names of two Athenian soldiers and politicians, Aristeides and Cimon. They were both ostracized, and then later recalled to help out in wartime.

THE LAW

One of the duties of an Athenian citizen was to take part in the legal system, because there were no professional lawyers. All citizens over 30 were expected to volunteer for jury service. Each jury had over 200 men, which made it too difficult to bribe or intimidate all the jurors.

These bronze tokens were used for voting. A token with a solid middle meant "innocent".

A token with a hollow middle meant "guilty".

Citizens had to conduct their own cases, but they could hire speechwriters to help out. Metics (see page 173) could not speak in court. They had to ask a citizen to speak for them.

LIFE IN SPARTA

By the Classical Period, Sparta had become the strongest military power in Greece: its soldiers were celebrated for their bravery throughout the Greek world. But because the Spartans concentrated their efforts on military superiority, the artistic life of the people never had a chance to develop. Artists and philosophers were actively discouraged.

A bronze figure of a Spartan girl, dated around 530BC.

Spartan girls competed in athletic events, wearing short tunics. This shocked the Athenians, who didn't let women take part in sports.

This misty and mountainous landscape is at Mistra in Sparta.

HEALTH AND FITNESS

The Spartans valued good health and physical strength above all else, because all the men were destined to become soldiers. Each new baby was examined by officials and, if it showed signs of weakness, it was left outside to die. Women were expected to keep fit by training in athletic events, so that they would give birth to healthy babies.

A SOLDIER'S LIFE

Until the age of 20, boys were educated by the state. Then they had to join the army and were elected to one of Sparta's military clubs. Soldiers lived, ate and slept at the club's barracks - where life was cold, hard and uncomfortable. Men did not usually marry until they were 30 and, even then, were very rarely allowed to go home to see their families.

Many Spartan sculptures, like this bronze figure, depict warriors.

All soldiers were given land, and helots to work it, by the state. This left them free to devote themselves to the army. Part of the produce that came from their land was kept to support the soldiers' families. The rest went to the barracks to feed the soldiers.

GOVERNMENT IN SPARTA

The Spartan government included two kings, a council of elders, and an Assembly. According to legend, a man called Lycurgus established the Spartan laws and system of government, although experts are unsure whether or not he was a real historical character.

KINGS AND OVERSEERS

Sparta's two kings belonged to the two most important families, called the Agiadsand the Eurypontids. They always ruled together and led the army in war, but at home their powers were strictly limited to religious duties. The actual running of the state was carried out by five ephors, or overseers, who were elected every year.

THE COUNCIL

The Council, or *gerousia*, consisted of the two kings and 28 council members. These were men over the age of 60 who were elected for life. They drew up the laws, acted as judges, and decided what policies the state should adopt.

THE ASSEMBLY

The Council's proposals had to be passed by the Assembly, or *apella*, which was made up of all citizens over 30. Experts think that the Assembly probably could not debate or amend anything: they could only vote for or against measures. They did this by shouting "yes" or "no", and the loudest group won.

This photograph shows a man dressed as a Spartan warrior at a Greek Independence Day celebration.

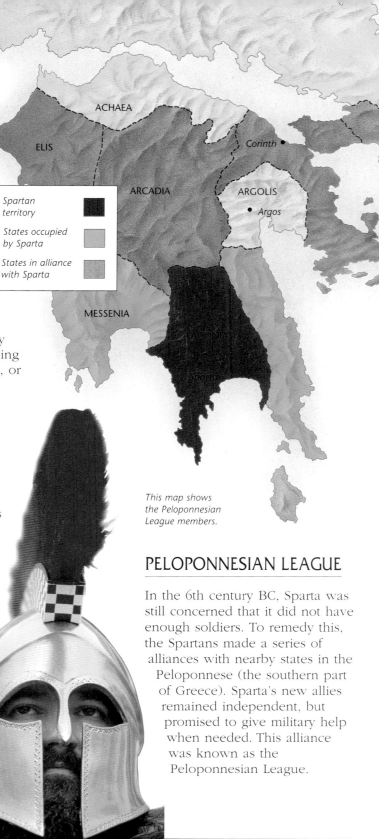

This map shows the Peloponnesian League members.

Spartan territory

States occupied by Sparta

States in alliance with Sparta

ACHAEA

ELIS

Corinth

ARCADIA

ARGOLIS

Argos

MESSENIA

LACONIA

Sparta

PELOPONNESIAN LEAGUE

In the 6th century BC, Sparta was still concerned that it did not have enough soldiers. To remedy this, the Spartans made a series of alliances with nearby states in the Peloponnese (the southern part of Greece). Sparta's new allies remained independent, but promised to give military help when needed. This alliance was known as the Peloponnesian League.

THE PELOPONNESIAN WARS

While Athens grew richer and more powerful, the other city-states began to feel threatened. Relations grew worse, especially between Athens and her great rival, Sparta. An atmosphere of suspicion and uneasy peace dragged on until 431BC. Then a war broke out, which tore the Greek world apart, and weakened the city-states beyond repair.

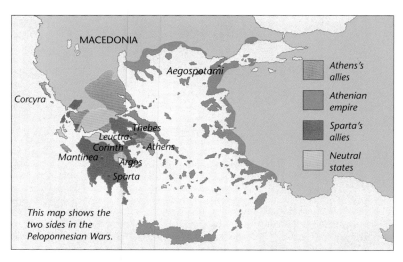

MACEDONIA

Aegospotami

Corcyra

Thebes
Leuctra
Corinth · Athens
Mantinea
Argos
Sparta

☐ Athens's allies

☐ Athenian empire

☐ Sparta's allies

☐ Neutral states

This map shows the two sides in the Peloponnesian Wars.

THE LONG WALLS

In 460BC, the Athenians began building vast walls to enclose their city and its sea port at Piraeus. The walls were designed to stop an enemy from cutting Athens off from its navy. The Long Walls, as they were known, effectively turned Athens into a fortress. The Spartans were nervous: they were sure the Athenians must be preparing for war. In 435-433BC, fighting broke out between Corinth and its colony of Corcyra (Corfu).

Sparta and Athens backed opposing sides. Sparta (supported by its allies in the Peloponnesian League) then declared war directly on Athens (and its allies in the Delian League). In 431, the mighty Spartan army marched into the province of Attica, the area immediately around Athens.

This scene shows the Athenians behind the Long Walls defending themselves from a Spartan attack.

THE SIEGE OF ATHENS

While the Athenians could rely on their navy to import food, they could retreat behind the Walls and avoid a land battle. But in 430BC, the city was struck by plague: it lasted four years, killing a quarter of the population, while the Spartans destroyed land all around them. By 421BC, both sides were exhausted and signed a truce.

BETRAYAL AND DEFEAT

In 415BC, a politician named Alcibiades persuaded the Athenians to attack Syracuse in Sicily. But, before the attack, he was recalled to Athens to face charges brought against him by his enemies. He fled to Sparta, Syracuse's ally, and betrayed his city. His treachery spelled disaster for Athens: 175 ships were destroyed or captured, and 40,000 men were killed.

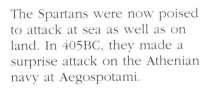

INTERNET LINK

For links to websites where you can read a cartoon story about one of the battles and find out more about the wars, go to
www.usborne-quicklinks.com

DEMOCRACY IN PERIL

Life in Athens became very unstable after this. For a while, democracy was even abolished. Desperate for a strong leader, they recalled the traitor Alcibiades from exile. But he failed to solve their problems. Support for the Athenians declined, and some of their allies in the Delian League turned against them.

SPARTA BUILDS A FLEET

For the Athenians, the final nightmare came when their old enemies, the Persians, joined forces with their rival Sparta. The Persians agreed to fund a fleet of ships: in return, Sparta had to to agree to recognize Persia's claim to Ionia.

The Spartans were now poised to attack at sea as well as on land. In 405BC, they made a surprise attack on the Athenian navy at Aegospotami.

This coin was issued in Syracuse to commemorate its victory over Athens.

FINAL SURRENDER

Led by their admiral, Lysander, the Spartans won a crushing victory: they captured 170 Athenian ships and executed about 4,000 prisoners. Then they laid siege to Athens itself. Without a fleet of ships, the city was unable to import food. The Athenians were finally starved into surrender in 404BC.

THE END OF AN ERA

The conclusion of the Peloponnesian Wars didn't bring peace or unity. Instead it spelled the end of the great days of the city-states, and eventually of the Classical Age. Other squabbles and conflicts followed, in which the Greek cities were far too absorbed to notice a new power rising in the northeast: Macedonia. Within 50 years, the Macedonians would control most of Greece, making it the core of a great empire.

SPARTA IN CONTROL

After the Wars, Athens was ruled by a group of pro-Spartan aristocrats, led by a man named Critias. The Thirty Tyrants, as they were known, made themselves so unpopular that the King of Sparta allowed democracy to be restored in 403BC.

This bronze helmet came from Sparta.

The figure from this painted pot is a Persian archer. Notice how different the costume is from that of a Greek soldier.

WAR BEGINS AGAIN

Spartan supremacy did not last. Wars broke out again and Sparta lost much of the land it had won. The Persian alliance collapsed too, when the Persians declared war on Sparta over the former Greek colonies in Ionia. Within 10 years, Athens, Thebes, Argos and Corinth were all at war with Sparta. The Spartans were defeated by Thebes at the Battle of Leuctra in 371BC and Thebes took on the role of leading Greek state. Less than 10 years later, the Thebans themselves were beaten by Spartans and Athenians at the Battle of Mantinea in 362BC.

 INTERNET LINK

For a link to a website where you can see a timeline of the major events in the history of ancient Greece, go to www.usborne-quicklinks.com

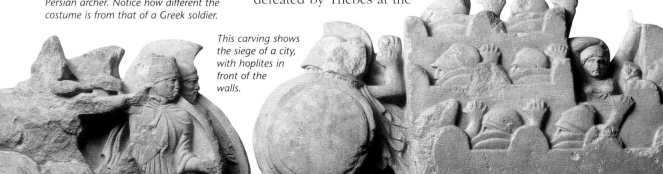

This carving shows the siege of a city, with hoplites in front of the walls.

Grave stele of an Athenian woman, late 5th century BC.

EVERYDAY LIFE

GROWING UP

Greek citizens were taught that it was their patriotic duty to marry and have children. Sons were always preferred, as they would become the next generation of citizens. They would also be able to look after their parents in old age. Daughters could not do this, because they were not allowed to inherit money or property of their own.

This scene from a water jar shows a nurse handing a baby to its mother.

This portrait of a woman and her grandchild was carved on a tombstone.

LIFE OR DEATH

A father could reject a baby if he believed it wasn't his, or if it was disabled. Baby girls were often rejected too. The baby was left to die in an exposed area, such as the top of a mountain. Some babies were abandoned because their parents couldn't afford to keep them. In this case the baby might be adopted and brought up as a slave.

CELEBRATIONS

Seven days after the birth of a baby, friends and family were invited to a party to celebrate the birth. Sacrifices were made to the gods and the guests brought gifts for the child. The door of the house was decorated with garlands - olive branches for a boy and wool for a girl. A special ceremony, called the *Amphidromia*, was held. This was usually when the baby was given its name.

When children reached the age of three, they were no longer regarded as infants. In Athens, this stage of the child's life was celebrated at a spring festival in honour of the god Dionysus, called the *Anthesteria*, or festival of flowers. The children were presented with small jugs during the festivities.

CHILDREN'S TOYS

This odd-shaped feeding bottle (left), bed and potty belonged to a Greek child.

Babies were given rattles and dolls, while older children played with spinning tops, yo-yos and hoops. Richer families even had small-scale furniture, such as stools and cots, made for their children.

EDUCATION

To the ancient Greeks, the purpose of education was to bring up good citizens to take part in running the state. Inevitably, this meant school was limited to boys only. Girls stayed at home, and usually only learned to read and write if their mothers could teach them. School began at the age of seven, but it was not free, so most boys only received a basic education. Richer boys could stay on until the age of 18.

This scene from a Greek pot shows a pupil and his teacher, writing on something that looks like a laptop computer. It's actually a wooden slate coated with wax, which is what children wrote on.

THREE SCHOOLS

There were three types of schools. At the first, the boys were taught reading, writing and arithmetic by a teacher called a *grammatistes*.

At the second school, poetry and music were taught by a teacher called a *kitharistes*. Boys had to learn pieces of poetry by heart, and were taught musical instruments, such as the lyre and the pipes.

At the third school, boys were taught dancing and athletics by a man called a *paidotribes*. Boys took part in competitive games at a training ground called a *gymnasium*.

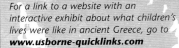

INTERNET LINK

For a link to a website with an interactive exhibit about what children's lives were like in ancient Greece, go to **www.usborne-quicklinks.com**

This Greek statue of a boy wearing a short cloak was found in Asia Minor (Turkey).

HIGHER EDUCATION

The ancient Greeks did not have universities as we do today, but from the 5th century BC teachers called sophists went from city to city, instructing young men in the art of public speaking. In the 4th century BC, philosophers such as Plato and Aristotle set up schools at *gymnasia* in Athens (see page 257).

WOMEN AND THE HOME

This piece of pottery shows two women deep in conversation. It was made in Asia Minor (Turkey) in about 100BC.

Women in ancient Greece led very sheltered lives - even by the standards of other ancient civilizations. They couldn't take part in politics, or own property. Their lives were always under the control of male relatives: fathers, husbands, brothers, and even sons.

This painting of a wedding procession has been magnified hugely, as it was painted on a tiny pottery box. A bride is being driven to her new home in a chariot.

MARRIAGE

A girl usually married when she was only about 15 years old, but her husband could be much older than she was. The philosopher Plato suggested that 30-35 was the best age for a man to marry. The husband was chosen by the girl's father, who provided her dowry. This was a gift of money and goods, which was looked after by the husband.

CHILDHOOD ENDS

The day before the wedding, the bride sacrificed her toys to the goddess Artemis, to symbolize the end of her childhood. Then she bathed in water from a sacred spring, carried to the bath in a special vase called a *loutrophoros*. These vases were often decorated with scenes of the wedding ceremony.

THE WEDDING DAY

On the day, both families made sacrifices to the gods and held feasts in separate houses. Then, in the evening, the groom went to his bride's home. This was often the first time that they had met.

The couple then made their way back to the groom's house. If they were rich, they were driven by chariot, led by torch-bearers and musicians. Poorer people had to make do with a simple cart.

The bride was carried over the threshold, as a symbol that she was joining the religious life of the new family. The family scattered fruits and nuts over them for luck.

 **INTERNET LINK**

For links to websites with information on the lives of women in ancient Greece, go to **www.usborne-quicklinks.com**

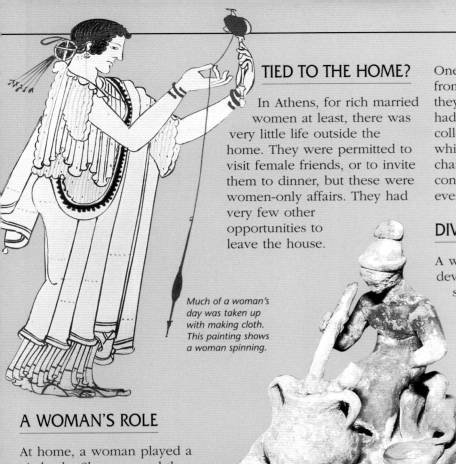

TIED TO THE HOME?

In Athens, for rich married women at least, there was very little life outside the home. They were permitted to visit female friends, or to invite them to dinner, but these were women-only affairs. They had very few other opportunities to leave the house.

Much of a woman's day was taken up with making cloth. This painting shows a woman spinning.

A WOMAN'S ROLE

At home, a woman played a vital role. She managed the finances, food, housework, spinning and weaving, and cared for the children and for anyone else in the family if they fell ill.

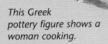

This Greek pottery figure shows a woman cooking.

One compensation for women from poorer families was that they could get out more. They had to go shopping and collect water from the wells, which gave them more of a chance to see life outside the confines of their home. Some even had jobs as innkeepers.

DIVORCE

A wife was expected to be devoted to her husband. If he suspected her of being unfaithful, he could divorce her and keep her dowry - and the children as well.

A DIFFERENT LIFE

Not all girls were brought up to be good, obedient wives. Some, known as *hetairai*, became companions to rich men. They lived in great comfort and could even attend men's dinner parties.

GREEK HOUSES

Very few Greek houses have been excavated, because they were built of mud brick, which does not last. But we have a good idea of what they were like from the ones that have been found, and because the design of houses in the Mediterranean has changed so little over the centuries.

A COURTYARD HOUSE

A typical house was built around a courtyard, with doors to each room, and a few small windows in the outside walls. The walls were made of mud brick, on stone foundations, with wooden doors and window shutters. There were stone slabs on the floors of the courtyard, and mosaics or stone slabs on the floors downstairs on the inside. The roof was covered with clay tiles.

The walls were usually plain, but were sometimes hung with tapestries.

Bedroom

This is what the house of a fairly rich family would have looked like - except that the front walls have been taken away so you can see inside.

This is the bathroom. It has a bathtub of baked clay, with a drain which leads outside.

Household altar

Inner courtyard

SEPARATE LIVES

The men and women in a wealthy Greek household lived very separate lives, in separate parts of the house.

Floors were sometimes decorated with patterns like this, called mosaics, made from tiny pieces of stone.

Although most houses had a single floor, some had two. The men ate and entertained in a downstairs room called the *andron*. The kitchen and bathroom were also downstairs, as well as a special room, dedicated to Hestia, goddess of the hearth, which was used for family gatherings.

This baked clay, or terracotta, statue is of a woman making bread.

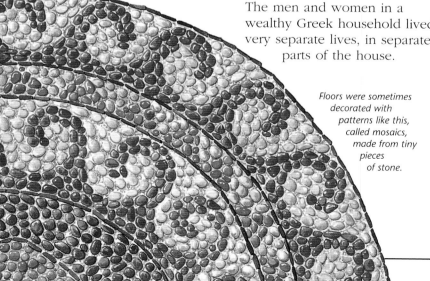

The women's room, called the gynaeceum

This wall has been removed, so you can see inside the kitchen.

The walls of the house were made of mud bricks, sometimes reinforced with wooden beams.

The dining room, or andron

In winter, portable metal stoves which burned charcoal were used to heat the rooms.

FURNITURE

Most houses were very simply furnished, with plain wooden tables, chairs and beds. In richer households, the furniture might be decorated with elaborate patterns, with ivory, gold or silver inlaid into the wood.

Most people sat on stools, like this one, except the head of a rich household who had an armchair called a thronos (right).

Tables were usually low, so that they could be pushed under couches when not in use. They were either round, oval or rectangular, with three legs or a single support.

Wooden couches and beds were strung with cords or leather thongs, with mattresses, pillows and covers on top.

Clothes and bedding were stored in wooden chests, while smaller items were kept in boxes and baskets.

UPSTAIRS ROOMS

In a house like the one here, the family bedrooms, the servants' quarters, and the women's rooms, known as the *gynaeceum*, were all upstairs. Women from the richer families led very sheltered lives. They spent most of their time confined to their rooms, organizing the household, spinning, weaving, and talking to other women friends.

LIGHTING

Greek houses were lit by small oil-burning lamps, made of pottery, bronze or even silver. Oil was poured into the round body of the lamp. Then you lit a wick (a piece of string coated with wax), which was sticking out of the spout.

Spout

Oil-burning lamp

CLOTHES AND FASHION

Greek clothes were extremely simple in design. Men wore tunics and women wore a robe called a *chiton*. Both were made from one or two rectangular pieces of cloth, sewn up the sides and fastened at the shoulders with pins and brooches.

MEN'S CLOTHES

Tunics were normally knee-length for young men, and ankle-length for older men. They were often worn with a belt and hitched up over it to keep them in place. When the weather was particularly hot, craftsmen and slaves often wore nothing more than a loincloth tied around the waist, to keep them cool.

This is the sort of plain, short tunic many men would have worn.

In cold weather, people sometimes wore cloaks as well. A long one was called a *himation*, a short one was a *chlamys*. Out in the sun, people often wore shady, wide-brimmed hats.

A chlamys was usually worn by soldiers, or by younger men for hunting or riding.

WOMEN'S CLOTHES

There were two styles of chiton: Doric and Ionic. The Doric chiton was a single piece of cloth, folded over at the top and wrapped loosely around the body, with a belt, and brooches at the shoulders to make armholes.

The Ionic chiton was made from two pieces of cloth, stitched up the sides and fastened along the shoulders and arms with brooches.

This woman is wearing an Ionic chiton. This style may have come from the Greek colony of Ionia.

This woman is wearing a shawl called a himation, over an Ionic chiton. A himation could be a thin, light scarf, or a thick, heavy cloak for cold weather or journeys.

The woman in this statue is wearing a Doric chiton. The dress was usually left hanging open, unstitched, down one side.

CHANGING FASHIONS

These women weaving on a loom, wearing highly patterned dresses, were painted on an Archaic Period vase.

Most people's clothes were made of plain wool or linen, although richer people could afford to dye or decorate them. Bright, patterned fabrics were popular in the Archaic Period. Later, clothes were often of one shade, sometimes with a patterned border.

 INTERNET LINK

For links to websites where you can see clothing and ornaments worn by the ancient Greeks, go to www.usborne-quicklinks.com

HAIRSTYLES

Fashion in hairstyles changed over the centuries. As time went on, men's hair and beards grew shorter and tidier, and women's hairstyles became higher and more elaborately styled.

Simple styles from the Archaic Period

In Classical times, women put up their hair with ribbons, hairnets, scarves or gold bands. Men's beards were tidier.

In the Hellenistic Period, men shaved off their beards and women styled their hair with waves and curls.

SHOES

These Greek scent bottles, shaped like feet, show us what their sandals looked like.

Most Greeks went barefoot for much of the time, or wore strappy leather sandals. But they did have other styles of shoes, such as calf-length boots for horsemen.

BEAUTY REGIME

Rich women bathed every day and rubbed themselves with perfumed oils. Powdered chalk was used to make their skin look fashionably pale. They also used a red powder on their cheeks and a darker one for emphasizing their eyebrows.

This Greek pottery model shows a woman in a bathtub. It is only big enough for sitting up in.

Mirror glass had not been invented in ancient times, so hand mirrors like this one were made of highly polished bronze.

FARMING AND FOOD

Most people in ancient Greece lived by farming, although the land wasn't always easy to cultivate. There was good farmland by the coast and in the valleys. But the rest of the country was rugged, rocky and mountainous - suitable only for grazing mountain sheep and goats.

A TYPICAL FARM

Ancient Greek farms were usually fairly small and only produced enough food to feed one family, with a little extra to sell at the local market. They were worked by the owner, his family, and a few workers or slaves. Citizens from the towns often owned farms too, and paid a manager to look after them.

WHEAT AND BARLEY

Wheat and barley were the most important crops. They were used to make bread and porridge, which formed the major part of the diet - at least for poorer people. The grain was sown in October and harvested in April or May. After this, the field was left fallow (unplanted) for a time, so that the soil could regain its goodness.

This is a modern photograph of a typical Greek landscape. It still looks much as it would have in ancient times.

OLIVES AND GRAPES

Olives and grapes were among the most important crops. Most olives were crushed in a press to make oil, which the ancient Greeks relied on for a great many things: medicines, cosmetics and lighting, as well as cooking. Grapes were grown for eating, or pressed to be made into wine.

This Greek vase shows people picking olives.

FARM ANIMALS

Farmers kept pigs and poultry for their meat, and sheep and goats for their milk and hides too. Cows were not common. Horses were bred in the region of Thessaly, where there was a lot of good pasture. Oxen and mules were used as working animals on farms. The oxen pulled heavy equipment and mules pulled carts and carried loads.

 INTERNET LINK

For links to websites where you can find ancient Greek food facts, pictures and recipes, go to **www.usborne-quicklinks.com**

WHAT PEOPLE ATE

The ancient Greeks ate many of the same sorts of things that we do. The main difference was that most people ate more porridge and bread than anything else. Greek bread was usually made from barley, as it was cheaper than wheat.

This is a hunter and his dog, from a Greek vase painting.

The Greeks also ate fish, cheese, vegetables and fruit, but relatively little meat - apart from wild animals that they could hunt, such as hares, deer and boars. Coriander, sesame and honey were often used to add taste, but not sugar - because they didn't have any.

THE MARKETPLACE

At the heart of every Greek city was a main square, or marketplace, called an *agora*. It was the focus for business life and a hub of local gossip - a meeting place, where people gathered to shop, do business, catch up on the latest news and chat with their friends.

BUYING AND SELLING

Storekeepers often sold their goods in open rooms, with a counter across the front, behind a row of columns in a building in the *agora* called a *stoa*. Local farmers also set up temporary stalls in the middle of the square. Meat and fish were often displayed on marble slabs, which kept the food cool in the hot sun.

This is an agora in a typical Greek city. Notice the acropolis above the main square.

Friends could meet in the shade under the columns of the stoa.

The men usually did the shopping. Most women only went out accompanied by their male relatives.

A statue of a local god, a politican or an athlete often stood in the main square.

Altar for sacrifices to the gods

Slaves being sold on a platform called a kykloi

Workers for hire

Local farmers and craftsmen selling goods such as pots, olives, and vegetables

WEIGHTS AND MEASURES

Traders in the *agora* were controlled by different officials. In Athens, ten *metronomoi* were chosen annually to check weights and measures, to ensure that the customers were not cheated with short measures. Officials called *agoranomoi* checked the quality of the goods, while *sitophylakes* were specifically in charge of keeping an eye on the grain trade.

The coin on the left is an electrum coin from Cyzicus, a Greek colony in Ionia. It shows the god Poseidon with a fish.

THE FIRST BANKS

By the 6th century BC, each city was issuing its own coins, which became a sign of its independence. People who wanted to do business in another city had to change their money with a moneychanger. These people charged a fee, and often made such a profit that they lent money too.

A moneychanger sometimes helped people who had money to spare. He would find a suitable venture for them to invest in, and pay them interest from the profits.

This silver coin is from Athens and is called a didrachm. It shows an owl, a symbol of the city.

These Hellenistic Period gold coins show Ptolemy I of Egypt (left) and Alexander the Great in a chariot drawn by elephants.

THE FIRST COINS

Coins were probably invented at the end of the 7th century BC in Lydia, a kingdom in Asia Minor. They were made of electrum (a mixture of gold and silver). The idea spread to the Greek colonies in Ionia and then to mainland Greece. Sparta was the only state that didn't adopt coins until later, in the 4th century BC.

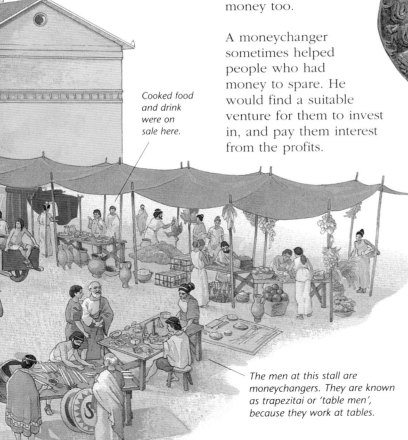

Cooked food and drink were on sale here.

The men at this stall are moneychangers. They are known as trapezitai or 'table men', because they work at tables.

📯 **INTERNET LINK**

For links to websites where you can watch a movie about Greek coins and tour a Greek agora, go to **www.usborne-quicklinks.com**

ARCHITECTURE

The architects of Classical Greece built according to strict mathematical rules, carefully calculating proportions - such as the height and number of columns - to give their buildings a feeling of balance, simplicity and elegance. Their results were so successful that they have been seen as a model for architecture ever since.

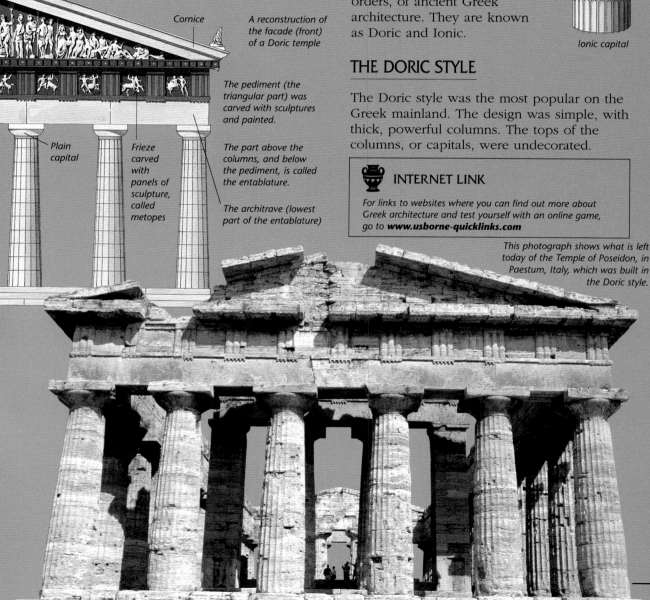

Cornice

A reconstruction of the facade (front) of a Doric temple

The pediment (the triangular part) was carved with sculptures and painted.

Plain capital

Frieze carved with panels of sculpture, called metopes

The part above the columns, and below the pediment, is called the entablature.

The architrave (lowest part of the entablature)

THE BASIC DESIGN

The design of most temples and other public buildings in ancient Greece was based on a series of vertical columns, with a horizontal beam across them. This idea may have developed from much earlier times, when tree trunks would have been used to support a roof. There were two main styles, or orders, of ancient Greek architecture. They are known as Doric and Ionic.

Doric capital

Ionic capital

THE DORIC STYLE

The Doric style was the most popular on the Greek mainland. The design was simple, with thick, powerful columns. The tops of the columns, or capitals, were undecorated.

INTERNET LINK

For links to websites where you can find out more about Greek architecture and test yourself with an online game, go to **www.usborne-quicklinks.com**

This photograph shows what is left today of the Temple of Poseidon, in Paestum, Italy, which was built in the Doric style.

THE IONIC STYLE

The Ionic style was a more elegant, decorated style than the Doric, using slender columns with bases and decorated capitals with spiral curls known as volutes. It was particularly popular in the eastern colonies of Asia Minor and on the Aegean islands.

These are the ruins of the Erectheum temple, built in the Ionic style, which is on the Acropolis in Athens. The pediment and roof have worn away with time and pollution.

These are caryatids, female statues used as columns

Pediment (triangular space)

The frieze went all the way around the building in a continuous band.

Ionic capitals were decorated with a curl on each side, called a volute.

Stepped base

Above is a reconstruction of the front of a typical Ionic temple, with its parts labelled.

OTHER STYLES

The Aeolic capital was an early form of Ionic capital, found at Smyrna in Asia Minor (Turkey) and on the island of Lesbos. It dates back to the 6th century BC.

Aeolic capital

The Corinthian capital was a later, more ornate style, decorated with a leafy pattern. Although the Greeks rarely used it, it became very popular later with the Romans.

Corinthian capital

A LASTING INFLUENCE

Ancient Greek architecture has had a lasting influence on the architecture of the world. It impressed the Romans so much that they copied and adapted it, but it has also inspired countless other imitations over the centuries, in many different countries. Buildings in the Classical Greek style of architecture are often known as Neoclassical.

The 19th-century Capitol building, in Washington D.C., has Corinthian capitals and a facade like a Greek temple.

BUILDING

The Greek city-states commissioned architects and sculptors to construct magnificent public buildings and monuments. Most of them were made of marble or limestone, with wooden beams to support the roof, which was covered with tiles made of marble or terracotta (a type of baked clay). The insides were decorated with sculptures and the outsides with panels of carved stone, called reliefs.

Mythological beasts, like this winged monster called a griffin, were among the things the Greeks carved on temple walls.

This Greek head, shaped like a lion, would have decorated the side of a temple. There are still traces of paint attached to the stone.

CARVING IN MARBLE

Greek sculptors worked in marble because it is hard enough to last and fine enough for carving detail.

Blocks of stone were dug out of a quarry and carved into a rough shape at the site, before being transported to the sculptor's workshop. Most statues we see today are bare stone, but they were originally brightly painted. It's just that all the paint has long since worn off.

Sometimes bright glass, stone or metal was used for eyes, and details such as jewels or weapons were made of bronze.

This sculpture of Nike, goddess of victory, came from the temple of Apollo at Delphi.

BUILDING A TEMPLE

Temples were the most important buildings in ancient Greece. They were the focus both for religious feeling and local pride. Here you can see how the Greeks constructed a temple, without the help of cranes or cement.

Workmen cut the stone into cylindrical pieces for the columns, leaving stone handles on the sides so they could be lifted with ropes. The handles were chipped off later.

Metal rods known as dowels joined each block to the one above and below.

For a link to a website where you can build a temple
online, go to **www.usborne-quicklinks.com**

Workmen climbed up
on wooden ladders
and scaffolding.

Ropes and pulleys were
used to lift the blocks
of stone and hoist
them into position, one
on top of the other.
Then they were eased
into place with levers.

Carts like this one
carried large blocks
of stone from the
quarry to the
building site.

Blocks of stone were joined with
pieces of metal called cramps.

SCULPTURE

The ancient Greeks carved some of the finest sculptures ever made. They set a standard for the portrayal of the human body that has been imitated and admired ever since. Many of the original sculptures were lost, or carried off by invaders at the end of the Classical era. But we know what many of them were like, because the Romans made thousands of copies that still survive (see page 340).

The features on this Archaic Period limestone head look quite Eastern.

To decorate their temples, the Greeks carved figures and mythological scenes, known as reliefs, on flat slabs of stone. This one shows the gods Poseidon and Apollo and the goddesses Artemis and Athene.

ARCHAIC PERIOD c.800-480BC

Early sculptures were carved in a simple, formal style, copied from Egyptian art (see page 93). Figures stood stiffly, with the left leg forward and the arms at the side. The face was carved with a half-smile. There were two main types: a male nude, called a *kouros*, and a clothed female, called a *kore*.

Later sculptors began carving figures in more relaxed poses, to make them look realistic.

A statue of an Egyptian queen

The figure of a young woman, or kore, on the left is from Greece, c.650BC. If you compare it with the figure above, you may notice her hairstyle looks Egyptian.

INTERNET LINK

For links to websites where you can see lots of Greek sculptures and explore a timeline, go to **www.usborne-quicklinks.com**

CLASSICAL PERIOD c.480-323BC

This marble discus thrower is a Roman copy of a bronze statue of c.450BC, by a well-known Greek sculptor named Myron.

The sculptors of the Classical period perfected the art of portraying the human body in a realistic, natural-looking way.

Their figures were noted for their beauty and serenity. There was a growing interest in portraying the female body. Many sculptors became skilled at showing facial expressions and emotions, and produced recognizable portraits of famous people. To demonstrate their skill, figures were often shown in active poses, such as taking part in sports.

This marble head of the goddess Aphrodite is one of the most famous works of a sculptor named Praxiteles.

The reputation of Athenian artists soon spread abroad, and their work was exported all around the Mediterranean. Factories were set up near marble quarries, to try to meet the demand.

This headless statue of the goddess of victory, the Victory of Samothrace, was carved c.190BC to commemorate a victory at sea.

It was originally part of a larger sculpture, which had the goddess landing on a ship's prow - which explains her outstretched wings and swirling clothes.

HELLENISTIC PERIOD c.323-100BC

In the Hellenistic Period, sculptors began to portray a much wider range of characters. Where Classical artists had concentrated on gods and famous men, children, foreigners and old people were now possible subjects. Sculptures from this time could be very dramatic too. Instead of just calm, serene poses, Hellenistic sculptors tackled subjects such as old age, pain and even death.

POTTERY

The ancient Greeks are famous for their painted pottery, often known as 'vase painting'. The amazingly detailed and varied scenes they painted on their pottery have given us an enormous a mount of information about their daily lives and their myths and legends.

GEOMETRIC STYLE

From about 1000-700BC, during the Dark Ages, Greek pots were decorated with zigzag and geometric patterns. Later in this period, figures of animals and people began to be added to the designs, painted in between the bands of geometric decoration.

This Dark Age pot is painted with intricate geometric patterns.

ORIENTAL STYLE

From about 720 to 550BC, contacts with foreigners, such as the Egyptians, led to what is called the "Orientalizing" style. Many designs included motifs, such as lotuses, palms and mythical monsters, that were common in Egyptian art. Later in the period, scenes from Greek mythology and daily life started to appear on pots. The figures were also more detailed and realistic than they had been earlier.

Greek pots came in many different shapes. Here are the most common styles.

Kylix

Skyphos

The first three pots shown here were drinking cups used at parties.

Kantharos

Kraters were large two-handled pots for mixing wine with water. The two main types were calyx kraters and volute kraters (with spiral handles).

Calyx krater

Volute krater

The wine and water mixture was then poured into a jug known as an oinochoe. It was then poured into cups to drink.

Oinochoe

This animal-headed jug dates back to about 600BC.

A kylix painted by a well-known Athenian artist named Exekias

ATHENIAN POTTERY

Some of the most detailed and sophisticated vase painting was produced in Athens between 550-300BC. Artists decorated pots with scenes from daily life, as well as from Greek mythology.

The earliest Athenian pottery, from about 550BC, is known as black-figure ware, because black figures were shown on a red background. From about 530BC, they also made red-figure ware: red figures on a black background. A few pots were painted on white backgrounds too.

INTERNET LINK

For links to websites where you can see lots of Greek pots, try a quiz and watch a video of how they were made, go to **www.usborne-quicklinks.com**

MAKING BLACK- AND RED-FIGURE WARE

Athenian potters used a clay that turned red when fired. The areas of the pot that were to be black were filled in with a black paint made from clay, ash and water. Red-figure pots were painted black, with the figures left bare, or cut into the surface, so that they showed through in red after the clay was fired. Touches of white and dark red paint were used for fine details.

During the firing process, the openings to the kiln were shut. This cut off the oxygen supply, turning the pot black. The temperature was left to drop and the air vents were reopened - the painted areas stayed black, and the rest turned red.

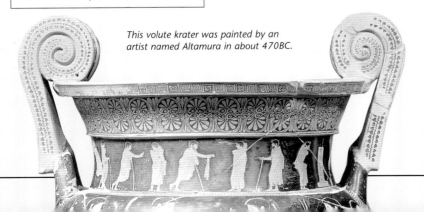

This volute krater was painted by an artist named Altamura in about 470BC.

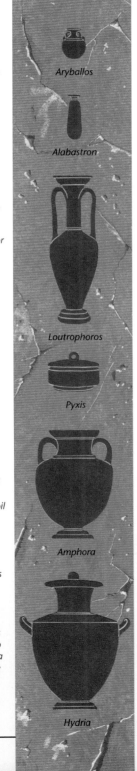

An aryballos and alabastron were delicate flasks for perfumed oils and ointments.

Aryballos

Alabastron

This is a loutrophoros, a large vase with a long neck, used for carrying water for a bride's ceremonial bath.

Loutrophoros

This flat round box, known as a pyxis, was used for storing medicines.

Pyxis

This is an amphora, a two-handled jar used to store wine, oil and other liquids.

Amphora

A hydria was a jar for carrying water from fountains. Two handles were used to lift it, while a third, on the neck, was used for pouring.

Hydria

METALWORK

Bronze was the main metal used by the Greeks for their weapons and tools from Mycenaean times on. Iron was introduced in the Dark Ages. Gold and silver were used too, but only for more precious items.

METALSMITHS

Most metalsmiths worked in small workshops at home, but in Athens they had their own quarter near the temple of Hephaestos, the patron god of metalsmiths.

The picture on this pot shows a metalsmith at work on a helmet.

BRONZE

Bronze is a valuable metal, made by mixing a small amount of tin with copper. Many of the larger statues that were made of bronze were melted down for reuse, so very few still exist today. Two larger than life-size statues that have survived were fished out of the sea off southern Italy in 1972. They date back to 450BC and are known as the Riace warriors.

This is the head of one of the Riace warriors. The lips were made of copper, and the eyelashes and teeth of silver.

WORKING BRONZE

HAMMERING
The earliest bronze statues were made from flat sheets of bronze which were hammered out and riveted over a wooden core, sometimes called a shape.

CASTING
Later, small statues were made of solid metal, cast inside a shape. Larger statues were made in several sections, then joined together afterwards.

LOST WAX
Some statues were made by a method called lost wax.

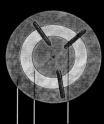

Pins hold core in place.

Wax shaped around clay core

Outer clay shape

1. The statue was shaped in wax around a clay core.

2. The model was covered with more clay and heated. The wax melted and ran out, leaving a gap between the two layers of clay.

3. Molten bronze was poured into the gap. When it cooled and set, the clay shape was removed, revealing the statue.

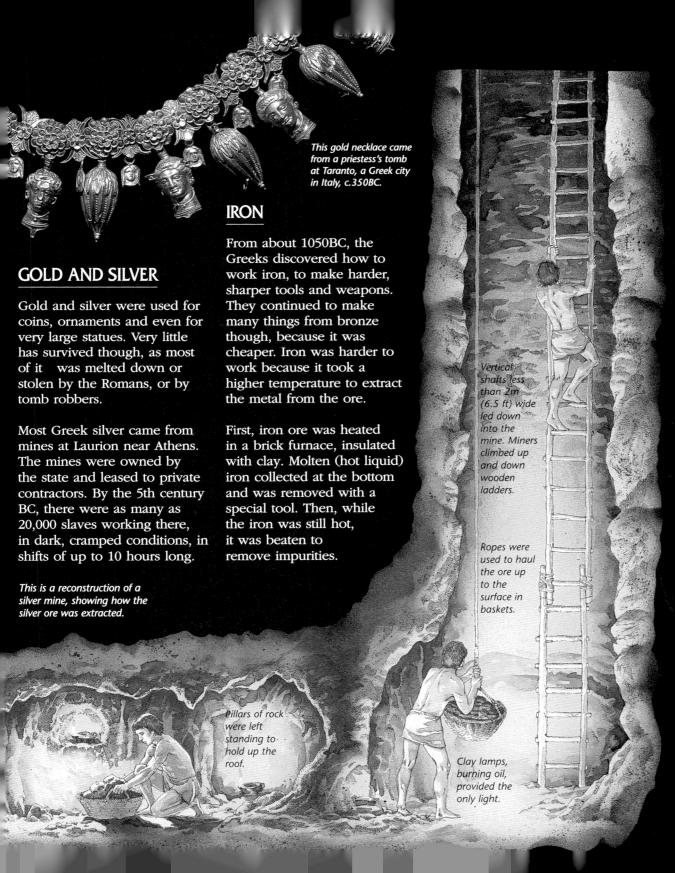

This gold necklace came from a priestess's tomb at Taranto, a Greek city in Italy, c.350BC.

GOLD AND SILVER

Gold and silver were used for coins, ornaments and even for very large statues. Very little has survived though, as most of it   was melted down or stolen by the Romans, or by tomb robbers.

Most Greek silver came from mines at Laurion near Athens. The mines were owned by the state and leased to private contractors. By the 5th century BC, there were as many as 20,000 slaves working there, in dark, cramped conditions, in shifts of up to 10 hours long.

This is a reconstruction of a silver mine, showing how the silver ore was extracted.

IRON

From about 1050BC, the Greeks discovered how to work iron, to make harder, sharper tools and weapons. They continued to make many things from bronze though, because it was cheaper. Iron was harder to work because it took a higher temperature to extract the metal from the ore.

First, iron ore was heated in a brick furnace, insulated with clay. Molten (hot liquid) iron collected at the bottom and was removed with a special tool. Then, while the iron was still hot, it was beaten to remove impurities.

Vertical shafts less than 2m (6.5 ft) wide led down into the mine. Miners climbed up and down wooden ladders.

Ropes were used to haul the ore up to the surface in baskets.

Pillars of rock were left standing to hold up the roof.

Clay lamps, burning oil, provided the only light.

TRAVEL BY LAND AND SEA

The Greek interior is rugged and mountainous. Some remote areas can be perilous and difficult to pass in winter, even now, but in ancient times it was far worse, as there were hardly any roads. With a coastline full of natural ports and inlets, it was much easier to travel by sea - although it was laden with all kinds of dangers nevertheless, either from the weather and natural difficulties, or from other sea voyagers.

INTERNET LINK

For links to websites where you can read about the incredible tales of Odysseus and Jason, and see ancient Greek ships, go to **www.usborne-quicklinks.com**

PIRATES, STORMS AND SHIPWRECKS

People who didn't have their own ship could pay merchant seamen to take them, but all sea journeys were fairly risky. Once the ship had set sail, dishonest sailors might rob their passengers, or the ship might be attacked by pirates. Piracy was a real and constant fear, until the 5th century BC, when the Athenian navy began to patrol the Aegean and reduced the number of attacks. Another potential danger was that of being sunk in a storm. Marine archaeologists have explored the remains of several ancient wrecks off the Greek coast.

THE KYRENIA SHIP

One merchant ship, discovered in the waters off Kyrenia in Cyprus in 1967, was raised to the surface and restored. Known as the Kyrenia ship, it originally sank around 300BC.

This is a reconstruction of the Kyrenia ship. The side of the ship has been cut away so you can see the cargo.

The ropes were made of flax or hemp.

The mast was made of spruce wood and the hull of pine. This timber had to be imported from the woods of Thrace or Macedonia.

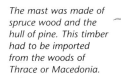

The large, square sail was made of linen.

Two large oars at the back to steer the ship

MAPPING THE WORLD

The Greeks were skilled at navigating and making maps. In the 6th century BC, a man named Thales who was from Miletus went to Egypt to study mathematics and astronomy He brought his specialist knowledge back to Greece and became the first person there to find a method of measuring the distance of a ship from the sea shore.

Another Greek scholar, named Anaximander, became the first to draw a map of the world, although it does not survive today for us to check its accuracy.

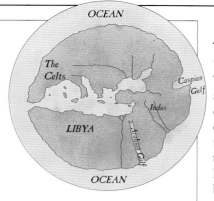

This 6th century BC map by Hecataeus shows that Greek knowledge of the world extended as far as North Africa, Western Europe and Asia Minor.

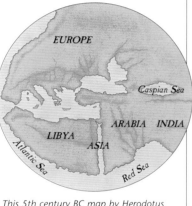

This 5th century BC map by Herodotus shows that, by then, knowledge of Asia had increased and the Greeks knew the Caspian Sea was bordered by land.

There are many images of sea creatures in Greek art and legend. This bronze figure is of a boy riding a dolphin.

TRAVEL OVERLAND

Travel overland was painfully slow, as most people had no choice but to walk everywhere. Donkeys were used to carry goods, but only the rich could afford to ride horses. Carts could be used, but only when the roads were good enough for them - which was not often. Then there was the added danger of attacks by bandits and wars between states, which often meant people were forced to make detours lasting many days, just to travel in safety.

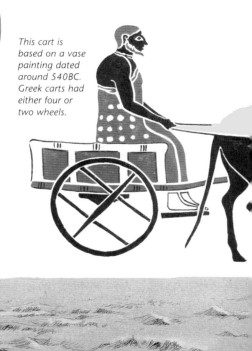

This cart is based on a vase painting dated around 540BC. Greek carts had either four or two wheels.

FEASTING AND FUN

For the ancient Greeks, dinner was the most important meal of the day, and it was always eaten late in the evening. For people who could afford it, it was also an opportunity to entertain friends.

This Greek plate shows the sort of fish that would have been eaten at dinner parties.

A GREEK DINNER PARTY

Greek dinner parties were generally all male-affairs. Women were forbidden to join in, except at family gatherings, although male guests could bring female companions, called *hetairai*.

Guests were met at the front door of the house by slaves, who washed their hands and feet, and put garlands of leaves or flowers on their heads. Then they were led into the dining room, where they reclined on couches.

THE FOOD

The food was served by slaves from small tables. There were no forks, so the guests used their fingers, or pieces of bread, to scoop it up. However, table manners were imporant, and they were sometimes written down to help people. Each course had several dishes to choose from. There was probably a fish dish, followed by a meat course, such as mutton, beef, pork or small birds. The meal finished with fruit, such as figs, grapes, pears and apples, and sweet cakes made of honey and nuts.

Grapes, both eaten and drunk as wine, featured on the menu at Greek dinners.

WINE AND DISCUSSION

The most stimulating part of a dinner party was called a *symposium*. This was when the food was cleared away and the guests concentrated on serious conversation. The discussions usually covered weighty topics, such as politics, philosophy or morals. They drank wine, which was mixed with water in a large vase called a krater and then ladled into cups. Three offerings of wine, known as libations, were made to the gods before the guests themselves began drinking.

A kithara, an elaborate stringed instrument rather like a lyre, and a timpanon, an early tambourine

MUSIC, POETRY AND DANCING

The symposium was usually a solemn occasion, but at some dinner parties this part of the evening was much more relaxed. Guests sometimes played musical instruments, sang songs, recited poems or told jokes. At some parties, professional dancers, musicians and acrobats were hired to amuse the guests.

This scene showing after-dinner activities comes from a 5th century BC drinking cup. One musician is playing the double pipes, an instrument seen in many Greek paintings.

GAMES

Although most Greeks worked very hard, they seem to have had time to play games. Several board games, similar to chess, were popular. Apart from the athletic competitions (see page 228), the Greeks also played more informal sports, including a type of hockey, using a ball and sticks.

Some people also enjoyed cruel sports, such as cat or dog fights. Games such as dice, or knuckle-bones, in which small animal bones were thrown like dice, were played at home or in special gaming houses.

These pottery figures show two women playing a game called knuckle-bones.

INTERNET LINK

For links where you can watch a movie about Greek parties and listen to a poem, go to **www.usborne-quicklinks.com**

PLAYS AND PLAYERS

The Western idea of drama is deeply rooted in ancient Greece. In Europe, the very first plays probably developed from songs and dances, performed as part of a Greek religious festival held for Dionysus, the god of wine.

THE DIONYSIA

In Athens, the early religious festival grew into a much larger dramatic festival, the Dionysia, held for five days each spring. Processions and sacrifices were followed by drama competitions. Everyone was allowed to stop work so that they could attend. Aspiring writers submitted their plays to the archon, who chose which ones would be performed.

INTERNET LINK

For a link to a website where you can go on a trip to watch plays in ancient Greece, go to **www.usborne-quicklinks.com**

THE EARLY PLAYS

The early festivals consisted of a group of men, known as the chorus, dancing and singing. Later, an actor was brought in to exchange dialogue with the leader of the chorus. As more actors were introduced, the role of the chorus dwindled, and the dialogue between the actors became the most important part of the play. In this way the modern idea of a play was born.

This is a chorus member dressed as a bird.

Comedies, like the one shown here which comes from a Greek pot, contained a lot of clowning around and rude jokes.

TRAGEDIES AND COMEDIES

Greek plays soon evolved into two distinct types: tragedies and comedies. Tragedies were usually about heroes of Greek myths and dealt with moral choices, passions and conflict, and often had unhappy endings. Comedies were about ordinary people, and often mocked leading politicians and personalities of the day.

THE STAGE

In Athens, the first plays were performed in the agora - but, as the festival grew bigger, a huge open-air auditorium was built near the Acropolis. This idea was soon copied all over Greece, and some venues could hold over 18,000 spectators.

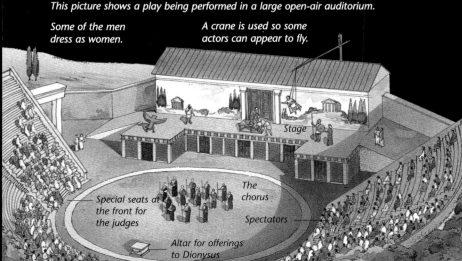

This picture shows a play being performed in a large open-air auditorium.

Some of the men dress as women.

A crane is used so some actors can appear to fly.

Stage

Special seats at the front for the judges

The chorus

Spectators

Altar for offerings to Dionysus

IDENTITY MASKS

Greek theatres were cleverly designed so that everyone could hear well, but the auditorium was so large that people sitting at the back were too far from the stage to see clearly. So the actors, who were always men, wore masks to show who they were - man or woman, young or old - and what mood they were in. Some masks were reversible: they had calm expressions on one side and angry ones on the other, so the actor could change moods with a twist of his hand.

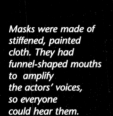

Masks were made of stiffened, painted cloth. They had funnel-shaped mouths to amplify the actors' voices, so everyone could hear them.

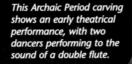

This Archaic Period carving shows an early theatrical performance, with two dancers performing to the sound of a double flute.

COSTUMES

The actors wore special costumes - wigs, thick padded tunics and shoes with thick soles - to make them look larger and taller. Bright clothes meant they were playing happy characters, and dark clothes were for tragic roles. In comedies, the chorus also wore special outfits and sometimes dressed up as birds and other animals.

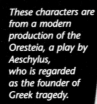

These characters are from a modern production of the Oresteia, a play by Aeschylus, who is regarded as the founder of Greek tragedy.

THE GAMES

Athletic competitions were held in ancient Greece as part of a religious ceremony for a god or goddess. They were enormously popular and everyone was encouraged to take part. Most of the competitions were local affairs, but some attracted athletes and spectators from all over the Greek world.

This athlete was painted on a Greek pot. None of the contestants wore any clothes.

THE OLYMPIC GAMES

The Olympic Games - the ancestor of the modern Games - was the most famous of all the games. It lasted five days, and was held every four years at Olympia, as part of a festival for the god Zeus.

Wars were brought to a standstill, just so that people could travel to the Games in safety, and magnificent temples and stadiums were built for the occasion. Often, as many as 50,000 people came, some from as far away as Spain and Egypt.

THE MAIN EVENTS

One of the most challenging events in the Games was designed to find the best all-round athlete. This was the *pentathlon*, from the Greek words *pente* (five) and *athlon* (contest). There were five events: discus and javelin-throwing, running, jumping and wrestling.

Running was the oldest event and opened the first day of the Games. There were three main races: the *stade* (one length of the track), *diaulos* (two lengths), and the *dolichos* (20 or 24 lengths). The track was about 192m (640ft) long.

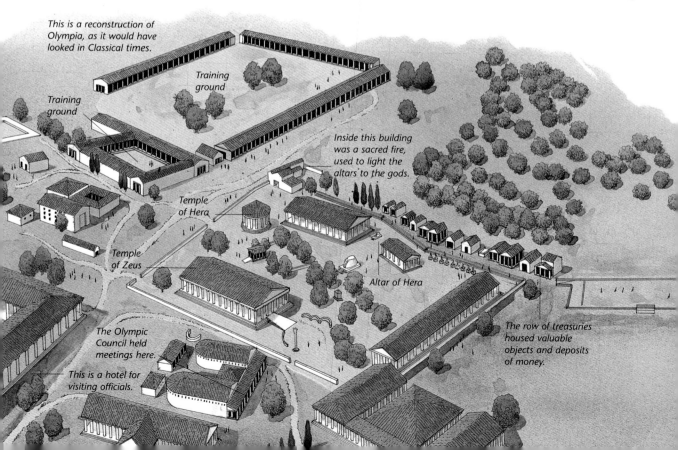

This is a reconstruction of Olympia, as it would have looked in Classical times.

Training ground

Training ground

Inside this building was a sacred fire, used to light the altars to the gods.

Temple of Hera

Temple of Zeus

Altar of Hera

The Olympic Council held meetings here.

The row of treasuries housed valuable objects and deposits of money.

This is a hotel for visiting officials.

HORSE AND CHARIOT RACING

Horse races were run over a distance of about 1200m (nearly a mile). In one race, the rider ran part of the way beside his horse. Jockeys rode bareback (without saddles) and accidents were common.

Chariot racing was probably the most popular event. Chariots, pulled by teams of two or four horses, were raced 12 laps. Up to 40 chariots could take part in one race, so collisions were inevitable.

This life-size bronze statue of a horse and boy jockey was found in a shipwreck.

INTERNET LINK

For links to websites where you can watch the ancient Games and see how they've changed, go to **www.usborne-quicklinks.com**

WRESTLING AND BOXING

There were three types of wrestling events: upright wrestling, ground wrestling, which lasted longer, and a highly dangerous combination of wrestling and boxing, called the *pankration*. This could last for several hours, and absolutely any tactic, apart from biting and eye-gouging, was allowed. The boxers wore leather straps with metal studs, and they could make a terrible mess of their opponents. Some of them died.

The scene on this Greek vase shows two men engaging in upright wrestling.

The running events took place in the stadium. About 40,000 spectators could watch from embankments around the track.

This is the hippodrome, a large oval-shaped racetrack, where chariot and horse races were held.

THE WINNERS

After each event, a herald announced the name of the winner, but prizes were not awarded until the last day. The prizes, which were simple laurel wreaths, were only meant to be symbolic. The real prize lay in competing and in the glory of winning. Huge celebrations were held when the winners returned home. A victorious athlete won prestige for his city, and he was often handsomely rewarded by the city itself.

RELIGION AND MYTHOLOGY

The ancient Greeks had dozens of different gods and goddesses, each in charge of a different aspect of life or death, as well as many figures who were spirits, and some who were half-gods. Although the Greeks were very religious, they didn't follow a strict set of rules, as modern religions often do. People worshipped the gods they found most useful.

MYTHS AND LEGENDS

Myths were an important part of ancient Greek religion. Many myths were tales of the lives of the gods and their dealings with humans. Others were stories which explained natural phenomena, such as why day turned into night, why the seasons changed, or how the world began. Now, many of these ideas would be explained scientifically.

THE CREATION

According to legend, before anything existed, there was a nothingness called Chaos. Out of this dark and empty state, Gaea, Mother Earth, slowly emerged to form the world. She gave birth to Uranus, the sky.

This is a carving of Gaea, mother earth goddess

Aphrodite - the goddess of love

THE FAMILY OF GIANTS

Gaea and Uranus married and had many children. The most important were the Titans, who looked like humans but were vast in size. They were the first gods and goddesses.

Uranus banished some of his children to the Underworld, a dark, gloomy place under the Earth. Gaea was furious, and encouraged the Titans to rise up against him. Led by Cronos, they attacked and overthrew their father.

THE BIRTH OF ZEUS

Cronos then became King of the Titans. He married his sister Rhea and they had five children. Before the children were born, Cronos was warned that one of them would kill him. So he snatched and swallowed each baby at birth. Then, when Rhea was giving birth to her sixth baby, Zeus, she tricked Cronos by giving him a stone wrapped in clothes instead of the baby. So, Zeus survived.

THE REVENGE OF ZEUS

When he was fully grown, Zeus visited his parents in disguise, and slipped a potion into Cronos's drink. This made him cough up all the babies he had swallowed: his two sons, Poseidon and Pluto, and his daughters: Hera, Hestia and Demeter.

 INTERNET LINK

For links to websites where you can try online games and quizzes about Greek gods and find out more about them, go to www.usborne-quicklinks.com

---

This photograph shows the summit of Mount Olympus, in Greece, where the gods were supposed to live.

This carving from Delphi c.525BC shows the battle between the gods and giants.

THE NEW GODS

The new Greek gods were known as Olympians, because people believed they inhabited a land high above the clouds on Mount Olympus. They lived like a large family, with Zeus as the head. No humans could visit Olympus, except by special invitation. The gods often visited the Earth, though. Sometimes they even fell in love with humans, and had children with them. Many heroes in Greek myths were born in this way and were half-human and half-god.

Zeus then led his brothers and sisters in revolt against Cronos and the other Titans. After a bitter struggle, the younger gods defeated the older ones and divided the world among themselves. Zeus became ruler of the sky and King of all the gods, with Hera as his queen. Poseidon was King of the Ocean; Pluto, King of the Underworld; Hestia, goddess of the hearth and home; and Demeter, goddess of plants and harvests.

This scene from a vase painting shows Pluto, god of the Underworld, and Persephone, Demeter's daughter.

This giant bronze statue of Poseidon, god of the sea, was found in the Aegean. The eyes are missing, but they would have been inlaid with jewels or semi-precious stones.

MPLES AND WORSHIP

cient Greek temples were not built for people to
worship in, like churches, synagogues and
ues. The Greeks thought of them as somewhere
e gods and goddesses to live comfortably when
visited Earth. So each temple was dedicated to a
cular god or goddess.

This shows a woman beir
carried off by the god Zeu
disguised as an eagle, on
of his visits to Earth.

MPLE DESIGN

e design of a Greek
mple was based on the
al halls in the palaces of
cenae. The early ones
re just a simple room,
led a cella, with a statue
the god or goddess. Later,
mples became much more
phisticated. The largest and
ost ornate ones were built
the Classical Period.

This is a Greek pottery
model of a Dark Age
temple. Temples at this
time were made of wood
or mud brick, and
consisted of a single
room, called a cella.

This stone temple is
from the Archaic
Period. It had a
porch at the front
and at the back.

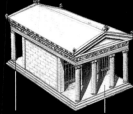

Back porch, or
oisthodomus

Front porch,
or pronaos

This a more
sophisticated, Late Archaic
Period temple. It had seve
steps up to the entrance,
and a covered row of
columns, called a peristyle
around the outside.

This is a reconstruction of a m
Classical Period temple, base
the Parthenon in At

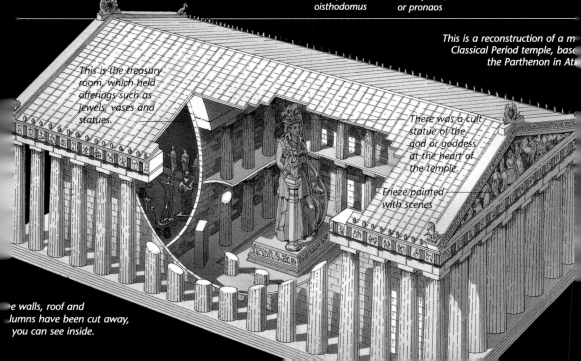

This is the treasury
room, which held
offerings such as
jewels, vases and
statues.

There was a cult
statue of the
god or goddess
at the heart of
the temple.

Frieze painted
with scenes

e walls, roof and
lumns have been cut away,
you can see inside.

DAILY PRAYER

Religion played an important part in daily life. Greek families began the day with prayers at an altar in the courtyard of their house. During the prayers, they poured a libation (an offering of wine) over the altar.

Who they prayed to depended on what they were doing that day. For example, someone going on a journey would pray to Hermes, god of voyagers. A person with a special request would go to the temple of the appropriate god to make an offering.

This carving shows a procession of people making offerings to Demeter, goddess of harvests.

FOLLOWING THE RULES

Although religion was informal, there were strict rules on how to pray. Gods and goddesses had their own priests, who made sure the rules were followed correctly. If they weren't, the god might be offended, and the prayers rejected.

Different gods preferred offerings of different animals, and the rules about how the animal was to be killed, or sacrificed, varied too. For praying, the right appearance and gesture were of great importance.

Most gods were addressed with raised arms and hands turned up toward Heaven.

This marble statue is not from ancient Greece, but it shows the influence of the Greeks - both in style and subject.

It was made by a 16th century Italian artist named Michelangelo. The figure is supposed to combine the Greek god Apollo with David from the Bible.

 INTERNET LINK

For links to websites where you can make a model temple and see an animation, go to www.usborne-quicklinks.com

To address a sky god, the worshipper had to face the East.

For Underworld gods the worshipper's palms had to face the ground.

For a marine god, the worshipper had to face the sea.

TALKING TO THE GODS

The Greeks held festivals at various times right through the year, to pay respect to their gods, and persuade them to grant people's wishes, such as providing a good harvest, or winning a victory in war. Festivals were much more than just religious ceremonies: plays, music, dancing, athletic events and good food played a large part too. Some were small local events, but others drew crowds from miles around.

This sculpture shows water carriers at the festival of Athene in Athens. It is taken from a frieze on the Parthenon.

This woman, shown on a Greek vase painting, is bringing offerings to an altar.

THE GREAT FESTIVAL OF ATHENE

One of the most important dates in the Greek calendar was the Panathenaea, the festival held in Athens for Athene, patron goddess of the city. It took place each year, in the Greek month of Hekatombion (July/August), but every four years, it was celebrated on a much grander scale. Then, it lasted six whole days and was known as the Great Panathenaea

The celebrations began with music and singing, followed by athletic competitions, called the Panathenaic Games. The winners were presented with pots of the finest olive oil, from Athene's sacred olive tree. A grand procession led up to the Acropolis, where 100 cattle were slaughtered as an offering, and a magnificent new dress was draped around the statue of the goddess.

 INTERNET LINK

For a link to a website where you can have a look at the sacred site of Delphi, go to www.usborne-quicklinks.com

ORACLES AND OMENS

For major decisions, the Greeks always sought the advice of the gods. One way was to consult an oracle. An oracle could be a priestess who spoke for a god, the holy place where this happened, or the message she gave.

The most famous oracle was at Delphi, where the god Apollo was believed to speak through his priestess, called the Pythia. The Delphi oracle was so well-known that many Greek states sent delegations there for political advice.

Another skilled art, only undertaken by trained priests, was reading signs, or omens. An omen could be seen in such things as the entrails of sacrificed animals, the flight patterns of birds, or in flashes of lightning and earth tremors.

SOOTHSAYERS

Soothsayers were people who were thought to be able to see into the future. One famous and tragic example in Greek legend was the Trojan princess Cassandra, who was punished by Apollo for breaking a promise. He gave her the power to see the future, while ensuring that no one would believe her. When she warned the Trojans about the dangers of the wooden horse, they ignored her with fateful consequences: their city was destroyed by the Greeks.

This is a painting of the god Dionysus, subject of one of the wilder mystery cults.

MYSTERY CULTS

People who wanted a deeper religious experience could join a mystery cult, a group of people dedicated to a particular god. Members had to undergo strict training, including purification rituals and processions at night. Once admitted to the cult, they were sworn to secrecy, so no one is really sure what was involved.

These are the ruins of the temple of Apollo at Delphi, site of the most famous oracle.

DEATH AND THE UNDERWORLD

The ancient Greeks believed that when they died their souls were taken to Pluto's kingdom, known as Hades, or the Underworld. It was supposed to lie deep under the Earth's surface. People thought caves and cracks in the ground were doors leading into this secret world.

DRIFTING AWAY

The god Hermes guided the dead person's soul through one of these entrances, down to the banks of a river called the Styx. This marked the boundary between the worlds of the living and the dead. People were buried with a coin to pay the ferryman, whose name was Charon, to take them across the river. Once across the water, they were met by a three-headed dog called Cerberus.

This is an imaginary view of the Underworld, painted by a 16th century artist from the Netherlands.

His duty was to keep the living out of the Underworld, and prevent dead souls from escaping. Next, they reached a crossroads, where their destinies would be decided. Three judges inspected the new arrivals and directed them to one of three places: the Elysian Fields, the Asphodel Fields, or Tartarus.

Cerberus, from a Greek vase

The next life could be blissful, horrifying, or just plain dull. It all depended on how the person had behaved when he or she was alive.

The lucky few, who had led good and blameless lives, were allowed to enter the Elysian Fields: a happy place full of sunshine, warmth and laughter.

The wicked ones were flung into Tartarus, where they were condemned to eternal punishment, pain and misery.

Most people ended up in the Asphodel Fields, a drab and misty place, where the inhabitants drifted around aimlessly. The only relief from boredom came when they received offerings from their living relatives.

INTERNET LINK

For links to websites where you can play an Underworld myth game and see a movie about gravestones, go to
www.usborne-quicklinks.com

LOVE AND DEATH

This is a Roman mosaic from Turkey, showing Orpheus, a character from a Greek myth, playing his lyre to some wild animals.

A well-known Greek myth tells of two lovers, Orpheus and Eurydice, who were separated and then joined by death. Orpheus was famed as the best musician in all of Greece. When Eurydice died from a snake bite, he went to the Underworld to beg Pluto to give her back. The god was so impressed when Orpheus played his lyre that he agreed to free Eurydice - but on one vital condition: Orpheus must not look at her - even once - on their journey back to the land of the living. But the temptation was too much for him. As Orpheus turned to gaze at her, Eurydice disappeared forever. He was so upset that he refused to play any more happy music. This made the gods so angry they sent creatures called Maenads to tear him to pieces. So, he was finally able to join his beloved in the Underworld.

FUNERALS AND BURIALS

When it came to the customs and rituals surrounding funerals and burials, the ancient Greeks were careful to follow very strict rules. They believed this was essential to make sure the dead person's soul reached the Underworld. For, without a proper funeral, the soul would wander lost and forgotten forever.

Pottery figure of woman holding her head in grief

BEFORE BURIAL

First, the dead person's body was washed, rubbed with perfumed oils, and dressed in white robes. Then, it was laid out for a day, so friends and relatives could come and pay their respects. A coin was put in its mouth, to pay the ferryman for the journey to the Underworld. Anyone buried without a coin was doomed to remain in this world as a ghost.

Mourners wore black clothes, cut their hair short, and displayed their grief very noisily. They cried and moaned and clapped their hands to show how sad they were.

This long-necked vase, called a loutrophoros, shows mourners weeping.

THE PROCESSION

Before dawn the next day, the body was taken away for burial. It was carried on the shoulders of male relatives or, if the family was rich enough, transported on a horse-drawn carriage. The procession was accompanied by friends and family, crying and wailing. To amplify the sounds of grief, rich families sometimes hired professional mourners to make even more noise at the funeral.

Offerings to the dead were left in pots, like this one.

AT THE TOMB

The dead were either buried or cremated in cemeteries outside the city walls, where each family had its own plot of land. Personal belongings were usually buried with the corpse, as well as food and drink for use in the afterlife.

Even after death, the family was expected to look after its ancestors by making offerings of food. This was done at birthdays and anniversaries, and at festivals for the dead.

This illustration of a dead person being visited by relatives comes from a Greek pot.

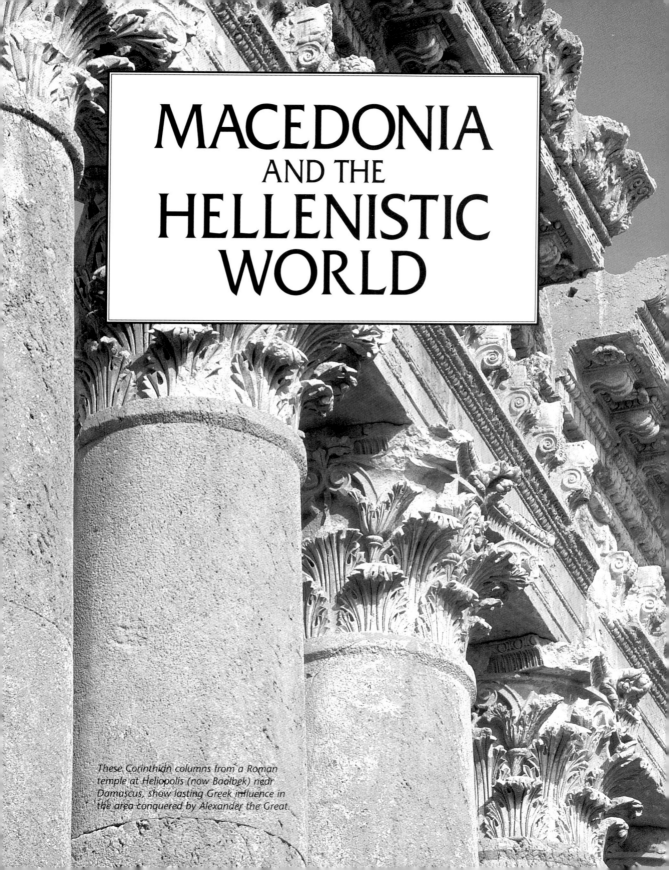

MACEDONIA
AND THE
HELLENISTIC
WORLD

These Corinthian columns from a Roman temple at Heliopolis (now Baalbek) near Damascus, show lasting Greek influence in the area conquered by Alexander the Great.

THE RISE OF MACEDONIA

The ancient kingdom of Macedonia lay in the northeast part of Greece. In Classical times, most Greeks regarded it as a culturally and politically backward place, inhabited by people who were little better than barbarians. They would scarcely have believed it would be possible that, in the 4th century BC, Macedonia would become the greatest military power of the day, posing a serious threat to Athenian democracy and independence.

This map of the Macedonian empire shows dates when Philip gained control of each region or city.

Macedonia at the start of Philip's reign

Allied state

Macedonian territory by Philip's death

Carved head of Philip II, made of ivory (elephant tusk)

ORDER OUT OF CHAOS

Macedonia had had an unstable history. It was invaded repeatedly in the 6th and 5th centuries BC, and in 399BC the country collapsed into civil war after the murder of its king. Decades of turmoil ended in 359BC, when Philip II became king and set about restoring order. Once he was firmly in control of his new kingdom, Philip began expanding his frontiers through military campaigns, taking over the regions to the east and south.

By 342BC, Philip had extended Macedonia to include all of Thrace, Chalkidike and Thessaly. Meanwhile, the other Greek states, led by Athens and Thebes, were growing very nervous of this rising power in the north. So, in 342BC, they formed the Hellenic League against Macedonia.

THE COLLAPSE OF THE CITY-STATES

In 338BC, Philip won a decisive victory against the Hellenic League at Chaeronea. This gave him control of Greece and marked the end of the city-states. He united the states into the League of Corinth, with himself as leader. To strengthen their unity, he planned an attack on the Persians.

The head (right) and butt (left) of a Macedonian spear

THE NEW ARMY

Philip reorganized the Macedonian army, making it the most efficient in Greece. It was led by elite units of foot soldiers and horsemen, called the Companions. Philip gave his troops heavier fighting clothes and long spears, and trained them in a particularly effective version of the phalanx (see page 179).

 INTERNET LINK

For a link to a website where you can play a game based on Philip's tomb, go to **www.usborne-quicklinks.com**

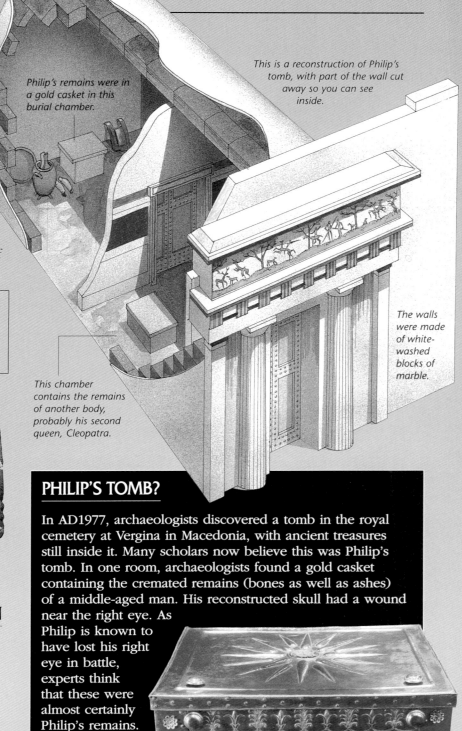

Philip's remains were in a gold casket in this burial chamber.

This is a reconstruction of Philip's tomb, with part of the wall cut away so you can see inside.

The walls were made of white-washed blocks of marble.

This chamber contains the remains of another body, probably his second queen, Cleopatra.

A carving of one of Philip's mounted bodyguards, the Companion Cavalry

PHILIP'S ASSASSINATION

Philip had several wives but only one queen, Olympias, mother of his heir, Alexander. In 337BC, Philip took another wife, replacing Olympias as queen. The next year, Philip was murdered, as he was about to attack the Persians. The killer might have been paid by the Persians, or by Olympias.

PHILIP'S TOMB?

In AD1977, archaeologists discovered a tomb in the royal cemetery at Vergina in Macedonia, with ancient treasures still inside it. Many scholars now believe this was Philip's tomb. In one room, archaeologists found a gold casket containing the cremated remains (bones as well as ashes) of a middle-aged man. His reconstructed skull had a wound near the right eye. As Philip is known to have lost his right eye in battle, experts think that these were almost certainly Philip's remains.

This gold casket held Philip's bones and ashes.

ALEXANDER THE GREAT

When Alexander became King of Macedonia in 336BC, he was only 20. Despite his youth, he immediately embarked on a military campaign that won him the greatest empire the world had ever seen and earned him the title "Alexander the Great". He was a military genius of extraordinary energy and courage, who inspired great loyalty in his soldiers.

This Ancient Roman mosaic, from Pompeii in Italy, shows Alexander on horseback at the Battle of Issus.

VICTORY OVER PERSIA

Alexander continued the task of expanding Macedonian territory that his father had begun. In 334BC, he led 35,000 soldiers into Asia Minor and set out to destroy the Persian army (see page 41). He beat the Persian rulers of Asia Minor at the Battle of Granicus, and went on to defeat Darius III, the Persian king, at the Battle of Issus in 333BC. Darius fled and Alexander marched on to Egypt, where he overpowered the Persian governors and was crowned King of Egypt. But his greatest battle was yet to come. In 331BC, he destroyed the entire Persian army at Gaugamela. Once again, Darius escaped, but the Greeks pursued him and he was finally murdered by his own troops. Alexander was crowned Great King of Persia.

INTERNET LINK

For links to websites where you can watch movies and find out more about Alexander, go to **www.usborne-quicklinks.com**

This photograph shows the landscape of the Indus Valley, in northern India. It still looks much as it would have when Alexander's troops got there.

BUILDING AN EMPIRE

Alexander's army marched over 8,000 km (5,000 miles) and acquired an empire that stretched as far as northern India. Along the way, he founded several cities, including Alexandria in Egypt (see page 246).

This map shows the extent
of Alexander's empire.

☐ Alexander's empire

→ Alexander's route
to India

Granicus

Issus

Gaugamela

Alexandria

PERSIA

EGYPT

INDIA

LOCAL RULE

Alexander had never
planned to build an
empire - only to rid
himself of the Persian
threat. The more land he
acquired, the more he
realized he couldn't control it
from Greece. He replaced
local rulers with Greek ones,
but otherwise tried to
cooperate with the local
people. He wore Persian
clothes and married a Persian
woman named Roxane.

THE END OF AN ERA

Alexander's soldiers won
every battle they fought, but
by the time they reached
India many of them refused to
go on. So Alexander turned
back to Persia with part of his
army. In 323BC, they reached
Babylon, but he caught a
fever and died, aged only 32.

ALEXANDER'S ARMY

Alexander had
inherited a highly
efficient army from
his father. The
main part, known
as the Royal Army,
was from
Macedonia, but
there were soldiers
from other states in
the League of Corinth
too, and professional
soldiers from other
parts of Greece.

CAVALRY AND INFANTRY

Alexander's
cavalry was made
up of 5,000
horsemen, mostly
from the horse-
breeding plains of
Thessaly, led by the
elite Companion
Cavalry (see page
241). His infantry
consisted of 30,000
foot soldiers, some
armed with spears,
others with javelins,
bows and arrows or
slings and stones.

The cavalry was divided
into units of 49 men. Each
unit charged in a wedge-
shape, to break up a
phalanx of enemy foot
soldiers. His foot soldiers
moved in from behind to
finish off the enemy with
hand-to-hand fighting.

THE HELLENISTIC WORLD

For several hundred years after Alexander's death, the territories of his former empire remained influenced by Greek culture. They are often described as the Hellenistic World, from the word *Hellene*, meaning "Greek". The period until the Roman conquest in 30BC (see page 250) is known as the Hellenistic Age.

This gold Hellenistic diadem, or headband, was made in Apulia, Italy in the 3rd century BC.

AFTER ALEXANDER

As news of Alexander's death reached Greece, rebellions broke out in many Greek cities, which turned into a full-scale war. After a year, the revolt was subdued by

Ptolemy III, a descendent of one of Alexander's generals

soldiers from Alexander's army returning from Asia. The empire itself was officially inherited by Alexander's infant son and half-brother Philip Arrideus, but it was ruled on their behalf by his generals, known as the Diadochi, meaning "successors".

THE EMPIRE DIVIDES

As rival Diadochi fought to grab the lion's share, the political unity of the empire was soon shattered by a terrible power struggle. By 301BC, Alexander's mother, wife, son and half-brother had all been murdered in the conflict. By 281BC, three separate kingdoms emerged from the chaos. They were ruled by descendants of three Diadochi: Antigonas, Seleucus and Ptolemy.

INTERNET LINK

For links to websites where you can find interactive timelines of ancient Greece and read about the Hellenistic world, go to **www.usborne-quicklinks.com**

HELLENISTIC ART

Although the peoples of Alexander's empire preserved their own culture and worshipped their own gods, Greek art and architecture often had an influence, even in places far from Greece. Statues of the Buddha from Gandhara in northern India show elements of style that are Greek, rather than traditionally Indian.

The features on this carving of the Buddha, including the expression, the tilt of the head and the curly hair, show signs of Greek influence.

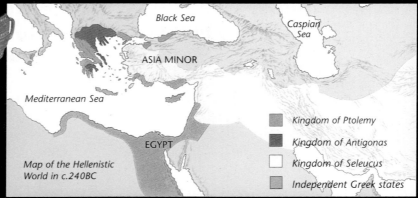

THE ANTIGONIDS

Antigonas founded a new Greek dynasty, the Antigonids, who ruled from Macedonia. They kept the rest of Greece under their control by maintaining garrisons of soldiers in the main cities. In the 3rd century BC, however, the Greek colonies in southern Italy were threatened by the Romans, who were pursuing a policy of aggressive expansion. The Antigonids were soon dragged into a fatal series of wars with Rome.

THE SELEUCIDS

The ambitious leader Seleucus seized a huge part of Alexander's empire in the Middle East and Central Asia, but it was so big that his successors were never able to control it properly. Large parts soon began to break away. Wars, rebellions and disputes between the leaders of the Seleucid family all helped to weaken their hold on their dwindling empire.

Black Sea

Caspian Sea

ASIA MINOR

Mediterranean Sea

EGYPT

Map of the Hellenistic World in c.240BC

⬛ Kingdom of Ptolemy

⬛ Kingdom of Antigonas

⬜ Kingdom of Seleucus

⬛ Independent Greek states

THE PTOLEMIES

The dynasty founded by Ptolemy was in many ways the most successful of the three. He only took charge of Egypt, a relatively small portion of Alexander's empire (see page 75). As a result, he was able to keep his kingdom intact for longer. Ptolemy also won great prestige by having Alexander's body buried in Alexandria, the Ptolemaic capital. Eventually, however, quarrels over the succession, and the expanding Roman empire, brought this final Greek dynasty to an end.

Even under Greek rule, the Egyptians continued to build in their own style. The temple at Kom Ombo (shown here, as it looks today) is entirely Egyptian in design.

ALEXANDRIA

When Alexander the Great arrived in Egypt in 332BC, he ordered the building of a new capital city, to be named after him, on the Mediterranean coast. Although he died before he was able to see it, the city of Alexandria became one of the leading cities in the ancient world.

CITY OF CULTURE

Alexandria owed its fame and prestige to outstanding achievements in science and scholarship. In the 3rd century BC, the Greek ruler, Ptolemy II, founded the first 'museum' - not a museum in the modern sense, but a temple to the Muses, nine goddesses of the arts and sciences. Next to the temple was a huge library, with writings from Greece, Egypt and beyond.

Over several centuries, around half a million works were collected in the library. After Greek civilization declined (see page 250), this collection played a big part in preserving knowledge of Classical Greece for future generations.

THE PHAROS

Probably the greatest building in all Alexandria was a fabulous marble lighthouse, called the Pharos, overlooking the city's busy port. Named by ancient writers as one of the Seven Wonders of the World (see right), it stood until the 14th century AD, when it was destroyed by earthquakes. In 1480, some of its stones were used to build an Arab fort.

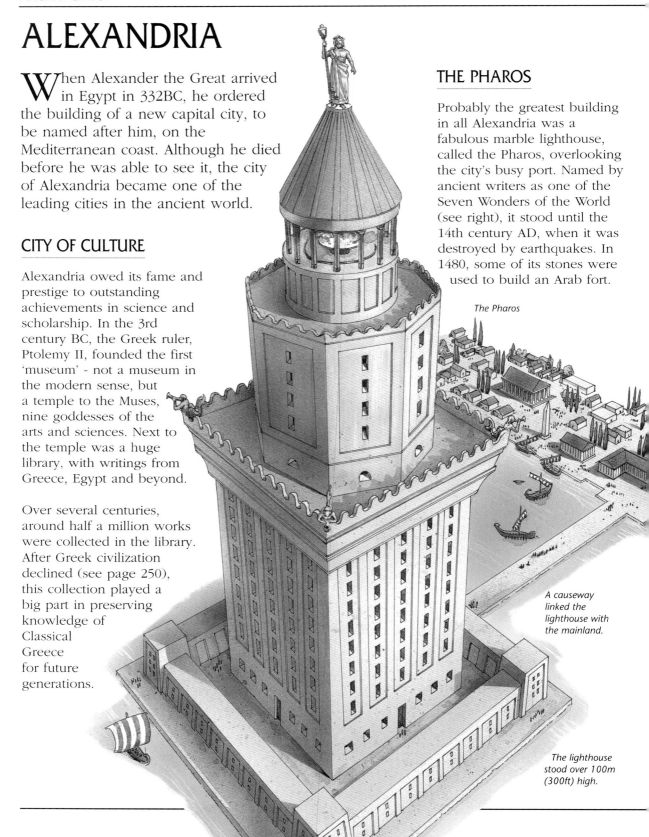

The Pharos

A causeway linked the lighthouse with the mainland.

The lighthouse stood over 100m (300ft) high.

THE SEVEN WONDERS

Great feats of engineering and architecture captured the imaginations of people in ancient times - just as they do today. The greatest of these were the famous monuments which the Greeks called 'the Seven Wonders of the World'. Only one of the seven survives, so we have to rely to some extent on written accounts to give an impression of what they looked like.

INTERNET LINK

For links to websites where you can watch underwater discoveries in Alexandria and play a game about the Seven Wonders, go to **www.usborne-quicklinks.com**

IN SEARCH OF THE LIGHTHOUSE

In 1994, a team of archaeologists began to explore the port of Alexandria, hoping to find evidence of the celebrated lighthouse. Divers examined huge piles of debris, and made an accurate map of the seabed.

Most of the underwater discoveries predated the Greek arrival in Egypt. But there was a giant statue and some massive blocks of stone that were from the right era.

Archaeologists believe the statue is very likely to be Ptolemy II, and that the stone blocks could be all that is left of the illustrious lighthouse, lost to the world for five centuries.

This diver may be gazing into the eyes of a statue of Ptolemy II.

The Seven Wonders of the Ancient World

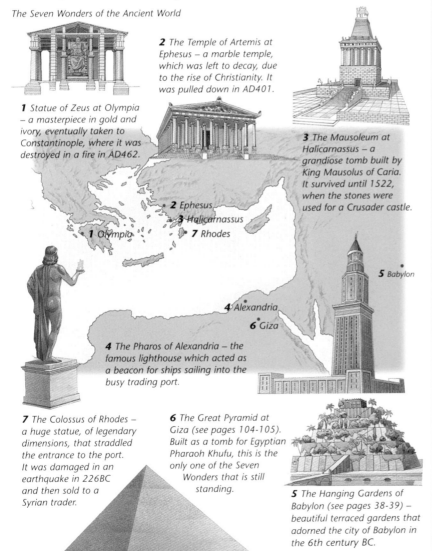

1 Statue of Zeus at Olympia – a masterpiece in gold and ivory, eventually taken to Constantinople, where it was destroyed in a fire in AD462.

2 The Temple of Artemis at Ephesus – a marble temple, which was left to decay, due to the rise of Christianity. It was pulled down in AD401.

3 The Mausoleum at Halicarnassus – a grandiose tomb built by King Mausolus of Caria. It survived until 1522, when the stones were used for a Crusader castle.

2 Ephesus
3 Halicarnassus
1 Olympia
7 Rhodes
5 Babylon
4 Alexandria
6 Giza

4 The Pharos of Alexandria – the famous lighthouse which acted as a beacon for ships sailing into the busy trading port.

7 The Colossus of Rhodes – a huge statue, of legendary dimensions, that straddled the entrance to the port. It was damaged in an earthquake in 226BC and then sold to a Syrian trader.

6 The Great Pyramid at Giza (see pages 104-105). Built as a tomb for Egyptian Pharaoh Khufu, this is the only one of the Seven Wonders that is still standing.

5 The Hanging Gardens of Babylon (see pages 38-39) – beautiful terraced gardens that adorned the city of Babylon in the 6th century BC.

INQUIRING MINDS

The ancient Greeks were responsible for many of the ideas about art, literature, philosophy, science, politics and history that laid the foundations of European civilization. From about the 6th century BC, scholars began to ask questions and make observations about the world around them. The people who did this are known as philosophers, from the Greek word *philosophos*, meaning 'lover of wisdom'.

This is a carved head of Plato, one of the most famous Athenian philosophers.

PHILOSOPHY

For the ancient Greeks, philosophy wasn't just the study of ideas about the meaning of life. It covered almost everything - from every branch of science to moral questions, such as how people should behave and what an ideal political system would be.

EVOLUTION

One scholar, Anaximander, concluded that much of the Earth had once been covered in water, and that people had developed from other animals - possibly fish. Another scholar, Xenophanes, discovered that fossils were the remains of plants and animals preserved in rock.

This drawing shows a model of an early steam machine, designed by Hero, a Greek from Alexandria. Fire boiled the water inside a metal ball. Steam escaped, which made the ball rotate.

This medieval manuscript is supposed to show Aristotle, one of the great Athenian philosophers, teaching Alexander the Great.

HISTORY

When the Greeks were involved in the Persian Wars, they realized the importance of knowing more about their enemies. They began to keep records of their history, and that of other peoples.

The first real historian was probably Herodotus, often described as the 'father of history'. Herodotus wrote an account of the Persian Wars after interviewing survivors to find out what had actually happened. Most earlier histories were far less accurate.

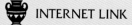

🏺 INTERNET LINK

For links to websites where you can find out about ancient Greek thinkers, inventors and achievements, go to www.usborne-quicklinks.com

MATHEMATICS AND PHYSICS

Many basic mathematical rules were first thought out by Greek scholars, such as Euclid, Pythagoras and Archimedes. Pythagoras devised a theorem for calculating the size of the angles in triangles and introduced the symbol p for determining the area and the circumference of a circle.

MEDICINE

The first "doctors" were priests of Asclepius, the god of healing. Sick people visited one of his temples, where priests tried to cure them with prayers. The first man to adopt a more practical, scientific approach was Hippocrates of Kos. He tried to search for the causes of illnesses and to find out how the body worked. His followers opened schools where his ideas were taught. They prescribed herbal medicines, a special diet, rest or exercise. They performed operations too - but without painkillers, so this was both dangerous and painful.

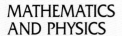

These pages are from Elements, a famous book by Euclid. Part of the book sums up the work of the mathematicians before him.

ASTRONOMY

An astronomer named Aristarchus reckoned that the Earth revolved on its axis and that it moved around the Sun. At this time, most people believed that the Sun moved around the Earth, and so his ideas were rejected as he had no evidence to prove them.

Archimedes discovered an important law of physics when he noticed that the water in his bath tub overflowed. From this, he deduced that an object displaces its own volume of water.

This is a demonstration of one of Archimedes' inventions: a large screw which acts as a water pump, raising water from one level to another.

Another astronomer, named Anaxagoras, realized that the Moon did not produce its own light, but reflected the light of the Sun. He also calculated that eclipses were caused by the Moon blocking the light as it passed between the Sun and the Earth.

THE ROMAN CONQUEST

While Alexander's inheritance was in political disarray, there was a formidable new power rising in the west: Rome. By 200BC, the Romans dominated much of Italy and were pushing their frontiers in all directions. It was just a matter of time before they would threaten the stability of the fragile Hellenistic kingdoms.

Although this portrait of Cleopatra VII was carved in Egyptian style, the Ptolemies kept their Greek culture. Cleopatra was the only ruler who learned the Egyptian language.

THE CONQUEST OF GREECE

At the end of a long series of wars against the Romans, the Antigonid rulers were defeated and removed from power in 168BC. Greece was split into Roman provinces in 147-146BC.

THE END OF THE SELEUCIDS

Meanwhile, the Seleucids were finding it impossible to control the vast, rambling territory they had inherited, and their empire was gradually falling apart. The final blow came in 64BC. After two years of successful campaigning, the Roman general Pompey conquered the remaining Seleucid territory and added it to the ever-expanding Roman empire.

ANTONY AND CLEOPATRA

Ptolemaic Egypt was caught up in a power struggle between two Roman leaders: Octavian and Mark Antony, who was having an affair with the Queen of Egypt, Cleopatra VII. Octavian defeated them at Actium in 31BC and landed in Alexandria the following year. Antony and Cleopatra comitted suicide and the last of Alexander's kingdoms fell into Roman hands (see pages 282-283).

The face on this coin is Mark Antony.

THE GRAECO -ROMAN WORLD

Although the Romans were the conquerors, they were influenced by the Greeks' ideas and culture. So many aspects of Greek art, architecture, religion and customs survived, even after the Hellenistic Age (see page 340). Greek remained a major language, and cities like Athens became financial and administrative bases within the Roman empire.

These are Roman legionaries, the well-trained soldiers who conquered a huge empire.

 INTERNET LINK

For links to websites where you can explore an online exhibit about Cleopatra and read how the Greeks influenced Roman culture, go to www.usborne-quicklinks.com

ANCIENT GREECE
FACTFINDER

Statue of a young woman holding a tray with sacrificial objects, probably Greek, 2nd century BC.

GODS AND GODDESSES

The ancient Greeks believed in many different gods and goddesses, sometimes described as Immortals, each one concerned with particular aspects of life or death. People thought of them as being very like humans, with feelings such as love, hate, or anger. Here are the most important ones. In brackets, you can see how to pronounce their names.

AEOLUS (ee-oh-luss)
Aeolus was the keeper of the winds. He was usually helpful, but was sometimes unable to keep the winds under control.

APHRODITE (aff-ro-die-tee)
Aphrodite, the daughter of Uranus and wife of Hephaestos, was the goddess of love and beauty. She was born in the sea and rode to shore on a shell. Charming but vain, she had many admirers because of her great beauty.
One of them was Ares, which made Hera very jealous. Aphrodite was thought to have provoked the Trojan War, by promising Helen, the wife of Menelaus, to Paris, if he judged her the most beautiful goddess. Her symbols were roses, doves, sparrows, dolphins and rams.

APOLLO (a-poll-o)
Apollo was the god of the Sun, light and truth, and controlled the Sun's movement across the sky. Apollo was also patron of the Arts and was a skilled musician. He was the twin brother of Artemis, and very protective of his mother and sister. He killed his mother's enemy, the serpent Python, when it was sheltering in the shrine at Delphi, and made Delphi his Oracle. His symbol was a laurel tree.

ARES (air-eez)
Ares was the god of war. He had a violent temper and was always picking fights. He was young, strong and handsome, and an expert but jealous lover. He once had to stand trial for murder in Athens, on the hill of the Areopagus, which was named after him. His symbols were a burning torch, a spear, dogs and vultures.

ARTEMIS (are-tem-iss)
Artemis was the moon goddess and huntress. She never married, was fiercely independent and could be merciless in her vengeance. Her silver arrows brought plague and death, but she also had healing powers. She protected young girls and pregnant women and was the mistress of wild animals. Her symbols were cypress trees, deers and dogs.

ASCLEPIUS (ass-klep-ee-us)
Asclepius, the god of medicine, was the son of Apollo and Coronis. He had been a mortal and a very successful doctor. But he went too far by bringing the dead back to life. He was killed by Zeus and then revived to become a god himself.

ATHENE (a-thee-nee)
Athene was born from the head of Zeus after he swallowed the Titaness Metis in the form of a fly. Athene was the goddess of wisdom and war and the patron goddess of Athens. She rarely lost her temper, but if angered she could be deadly. Her symbols, also used by the city of Athens, were the owl and the olive tree.

DEMETER (de-meet-a)
Demeter was the goddess of the earth, plants and harvests. She was helped by her daughter, Persephone, but when Persephone was kidnapped by Pluto to be his wife, Demeter abandoned her duties to go in search of her. Her symbol was a sheaf of wheat or barley.

DIONYSUS (die-on-eye-sus)
Dionysus was born from the thigh of Zeus. He was the god of wine and plays. He journeyed around the world, teaching people how to make wine from grapes. He led a wild, pleasure-filled life, attended by fanatical followers, especially female creatures called Maenads. He became cup-bearer to the gods.

EOS (ee-oss)
Eos was goddess of the dawn, and made the Sun rise every morning when she drove her chariot across the skies. She had been cursed by Aphrodite to fall in love with many different men, after she had an affair with Aphrodite's lover, Ares.

ERIS (air-iss)

Eris was the daughter of Zeus and Hera, and goddess of spite. She was troublesome and vengeful and helped to cause all sorts of conflicts, including the Trojan War.

EROS (ear-oss)

Eros made couples fall in love, even if they were unsuited to each other. He could be mischievous, but got into trouble himself by falling in love with the mortal (human) Psyche, when he was accidentally grazed with his own arrow. The problem was solved when Zeus made Psyche immortal.

HEBE (hee-bee)

Hebe was the daughter of Zeus and Hera, and cup-bearer to the gods. She was thought to have married the Greek hero Heracles after he was made a god.

HEPHAESTOS (heff-eye-stoss)

Hephaestos, the patron of craftsmen, was hard-working, skilled at making things and kind, but life was unkind to him. As a child he was crippled after being thrown from Olympus by his bad-tempered mother, Hera. Aphrodite was forced to marry him against her will and he suffered ever after from her constant infidelities.

HERA (hear-a)

Hera was the daughter of Cronos and Rhea, and the sister and wife of Zeus. As the protector of women and marriage, she was proud and jealous, and spent much of her time chasing her husband's many lovers and punishing them in ingenious and cruel ways. Hera's symbols were the pomegranate and peacock.

HERMES (her-meez)

Hermes was energetic and mischievous as a child and stole cattle from Apollo. But he won Apollo's forgiveness by inventing the lyre and giving it to him. To keep him out of trouble, Zeus made him messenger to the gods, and patron of voyagers and thieves. He wore a winged hat and carried a staff with entwined snakes.

HESTIA (hess-tee-a)

Hestia, goddess of the hearth, was very popular, as she protected people's homes. Every family had a shrine dedicated to her. Hestia was quiet and gentle and did not get involved in the jealous quarrels that blew up all the time on Mount Olympus. She eventually gave up her place on Olympus to Dionysus.

PAN (pan)

Pan, son of Hermes, was god of nature, shepherds and sheep. He fell in love with a nymph (a type of lesser goddess) called Syrinx, but she escaped him by turning into a bed of reeds. Pan used them to make musical pipes to play on.

PERSEPHONE (per-seff-on-nee)

Persephone was the daughter of Zeus and Demeter, and helped her mother with growing things and harvests. She was kidnapped by Pluto to be Queen of the Underworld, but she was very unhappy. So a bargain was struck: she spent half the year with her mother (spring and summer), and half with Pluto (autumn and winter). According to the Greeks, this was the origin of the seasons.

PLUTO (plue-toe)

Pluto was the brother of Zeus and Hera, and King of the Underworld (beneath the Earth). He drove a gold chariot with black horses and guarded the dead jealously. Pluto was extremely rich, as he owned all the precious stones and metals inside the Earth. Persephone was his queen.

POSEIDON (poss-eye-don)

Poseidon was the brother of Zeus and Hera, and King of the Oceans. He lived in an underwater palace, rode a gold chariot with white horses, and controlled storms, sea monsters and earthquakes. His symbols were a trident, dolphins and horses.

URANUS (you-rain-us)

Uranus was the sky. He and Mother Earth created all living things, including some monstrous children. Heartless and cruel, he imprisoned some of his children and Mother Earth turned against him.

ZEUS (zyooss)

Zeus, the ruler of the gods, was married to his sister, Hera. He had one son and two daughters by her: Ares, Eris and Hebe. But his relationship with Hera was very explosive. This was because he had many love affairs with mortal (human) women, appearing to them in many different disguises - as a bull, a swan, or a shower of gold. His symbols were the thunderbolt, the eagle and the oak tree.

GREEK MYTHS

Myths are old, traditional stories which often try to explain the things that happen in the natural world. They usually involve the adventures of gods, goddesses and heroes. Ancient Greek myths are among the most famous in the world. As well as gods and heroes, they are full of monsters, magic and amazing feats. Many Greek plays (see pages 258-259) retold the traditional Greek myths, and to this day people still write plays, poems and even TV series based on the stories.

PROMETHEUS

Prometheus upset Zeus, the king of the gods, by teaching the gods' secrets to humans. He showed them how to grow crops, tame horses and use plants as medicines. When he gave humans the secret of fire, Zeus was furious and devised a terrible punishment. Prometheus was chained to a rock on Mount Caucasus, and every day a vulture came and tore out his liver. Every night, it grew back. After many years of this torture, Prometheus was finally rescued by Heracles (see opposite).

PANDORA'S BOX

Zeus created Pandora, the first woman, as a wife for Prometheus (see above). He asked Hephaestos, the blacksmith of the gods, to shape her out of clay, and then breathed life into her. He gave her a beautiful box, which he forbade her to open. But one day her curiosity overcame her, and she opened the lid. With a terrible rushing sound, out of the box flew all the evils of the world - sin, sickness, age and death. Finally, one last thing flew out. It was Hope, and it meant that despite these horrors, people should not despair.

PERSEPHONE

Demeter, the goddess of crops and harvests, had a beautiful daughter, Persephone. When Pluto, god of the Underworld, saw Persephone he fell in love with her and wanted to marry her. But nobody ever wanted to live in the Underworld, so he kidnapped Persephone.

Demeter was so upset that she neglected her duties and no crops grew. She begged Zeus to help her get Persephone back, but Zeus could only persuade Pluto to return her for half of each year. For the six months Persephone spent with her mother, Demeter was happy, and the sun shone and the crops grew. This became spring and summer. But when Persephone was in the Underworld, it became winter.

APOLLO AND DAPHNE

Apollo fell in love with a beautiful nymph (a kind of half-goddess) named Daphne. But she didn't want his attention, and she ran away, praying to Mother Earth to save her. Just as Apollo was about to catch her, her prayers were answered and she was turned into a laurel tree. From then on, Apollo wore a wreath of laurel leaves in her memory.

THE WEAVING CONTEST

Athene was the goddess of wisdom and war, and also of handicrafts. When a princess called Arachne boasted that she was an even better weaver than the goddess, Athene was so annoyed that she challenged Arachne to a contest. But her irritation turned to fury when she discovered that Arachne really could weave as beautifully as she could. Athene tore up Arachne's weaving, and Arachne was so frightened that she tried to hang herself. Ashamed of what she had done, Athene saved Arachne from death by turning her into a spider. Ever since, spiders have woven beautiful webs.

DAEDALUS AND ICARUS

Daedalus, a great Athenian inventor, was so jealous of his clever nephew Talos that he killed him. Then he fled with his son Icarus to Crete, to work for King Minos. He built the Labyrinth, a maze for a monster named the Minotaur to live in. But Minos turned against Daedalus, so he had to escape. He built wings out of feathers and wax for himself and Icarus and they flew away. But Icarus flew too near the Sun. The wax melted, his wings fell apart, and he fell into the sea and died. Daedalus landed at Cumae and built a temple.

THESEUS AND THE MINOTAUR

Theseus was the son of King Aegeus of Athens. Once a year the Athenians were forced to send fourteen young men and women to Crete as food for the Minotaur, a monster which lived in a maze called the Labyrinth, built by Daedalus (see above).

Theseus decided to sail to Crete with the victims to kill the Minotaur. He told his father that when he came home he would put white sails on his ship if he had been successful. If the ship had its usual black sails, Aegeus would know Theseus was dead.

In Crete, King Minos's daughter Ariadne fell in love with Theseus. She gave him a sword to kill the Minotaur and a ball of thread, which Theseus tied to the entrance of the Labyrinth to help him find his way out. He found the Minotaur, killed it and escaped. Then he, Ariadne and the other Athenians fled from Crete.

On the way back to Athens, they stopped at the island of Naxos. By now Theseus was bored of Ariadne and one night, when she was asleep, he set sail without her. The gods punished him for his cowardice by making him forget to hoist his white sails. Aegeus saw the black sails and, believing his son was dead, threw himself off a cliff. The sea where he died is now called the Aegean Sea.

PARIS AND THE TROJAN WAR

When the sea goddess Thetis married a human, Peleus, they did not invite Eris, the goddess of spite and discord. Furious, she turned up anyway with a golden apple. Written on it were the words "for the fairest". The goddesses Hera, Athene and Aphrodite started arguing about who should own it, so Zeus sent them to ask a Trojan shepherd boy, Paris, to judge which of them was the most beautiful. He chose Aphrodite. As a reward she told him that he would have the most beautiful woman in the world as his wife.

Years later, Paris went to compete in the games in Troy. He did so well that the king and queen asked to see him. They realized that he was their own son. A prophecy had said that he would cause the downfall of Troy, so they had sent him away. But they were so glad to see him that they welcomed him back.

Paris was sent on a mission to visit Menelaus, King of Sparta in Greece. He fell in love with Menelaus's wife Helen, the most beautiful woman in the world. While Menelaus was away, Paris and Helen escaped to Troy.

This led to the Trojan War (see page 164). All Greece's armies sailed to Troy to get Helen back. After ten years of fighting, the Greeks won. Troy was destroyed, and many people were killed, including Paris and Achilles, the son of Thetis and Peleus. Helen was reunited with Menelaus and taken back to Sparta.

THE ODYSSEY

After the Trojan War, King Odysseus of Ithaca, one of the Greek leaders, set off for home. But his ships were blown off course and he wandered the seas for ten years. He met many monsters on his journey, or 'odyssey'. His men were killed, and he arrived home alone, to find his palace full of princes trying to force his wife Penelope to marry them. Odysseus killed the princes in a huge battle and reclaimed his kingdom.

AGAMEMNON

Agamemnon, King of Mycenae, led the Greek armies in the Trojan War. While Agamemnon was at Troy, his wife Clytemnestra, who hated her husband for sacrificing their daughter Iphigenia to help the Greeks win the war, fell in love with Aegisthus, Agamemnon's cousin and enemy. When Agamemnon came home, the couple pretended to welcome him as a hero but then murdered him.

Agamemnon's son Orestes, supported by his sister Electra, took revenge on the murderers by killing them both. But by killing his mother, Orestes had committed a terrible crime, and he went insane. At last, as he had suffered enough, the gods forgave him and he became the King of Mycenae.

HERACLES

Heracles, known as Hercules by the Romans, was the Greeks' most popular hero. He was the son of Zeus and a human named Alcmene. Zeus' wife Hera was jealous of Alcmene and so she tried to kill Heracles. When he was still a baby, she sent two deadly serpents to bite him in his cradle. But he amazed everyone by strangling the serpents with his bare hands.

Heracles married Megara, and became famous for his great strength and courage. But Hera was jealous of his happiness and drove him insane, so that he killed his wife and children. When he saw what he had done, he was horrified and asked the Oracle at Delphi how he could make amends. He was told to offer himself as a slave to King Eurystheus, who gave Heracles twelve "impossible" tasks (known as the Twelve Labours of Heracles) involving killing monsters and finding rare objects. If he was able do them all he would be cleansed of his guilt. With the help of the gods, Heracles succeeded and became immortal.

One of Heracles' tasks was to fight the Nemean Lion. He strangled the beast and wore its skin as a cloak.

OEDIPUS

Oedipus was the son of King Laius and Queen Jocasta of Thebes. An oracle predicted that Oedipus would kill his father and marry his mother, so he was left on a mountain to die. A shepherd found him and took him to Corinth where the king and queen adopted him. Years later, Oedipus heard the oracle's prophecy and ran away from Corinth, believing the king and queen were his real parents.

On the way to Thebes, he killed a stranger in a fight, not realizing that it was his real father Laius. Then, after solving a riddle and defeating a monster called the sphinx, he became King of Thebes and married the queen, Jocasta - his real mother. When the truth came out, Jocasta hanged herself in shame and Oedipus blinded himself. He fled from Thebes and died at Colonus.

PERSEUS AND THE GORGON

Perseus was the son of Zeus and a woman named Danae. Polydectes, King of Seriphos, sent him to kill Medusa, a gorgon. She had snakes for hair and her eyes could turn people to stone. But the gods helped Perseus, and Athene gave him a mirror so he wouldn't have to look directly at the gorgon. Perseus killed Medusa, cut off her head and gave it to Athene to stick in the middle of her shield.

ANDROMEDA

Andromeda was a beautiful princess, the daughter of King Cepheus of Ethiopia and his wife Cassiopeia. Cassiopeia boasted that Andromeda was more beautiful than the Nereids (sea nymphs, or half-goddesses), and they complained to the sea god Poseidon. He sent a sea-monster to ravage Cepheus's lands. An oracle told Cepheus to sacrifice Andromeda to the monster to stop the attacks, so she was tied to a rock by the seashore. The hero Perseus rescued her by turning the monster to stone, using the gorgon's head (see left). Then he married her.

JASON AND THE ARGONAUTS

Jason was the son of Aeson, the rightful King of Iolkos. When he grew up, Jason went to claim the throne of Iolkos from Aeson's brother Pelias, who had seized it. Pelias said Jason must first fetch the golden fleece, a magic ram's fleece which hung in the grove of Ares, guarded by a dragon. Jason took a ship, the *Argo*, and a band of heroes, the Argonauts, and set off to get the fleece. He married Medea, an enchantress, and she helped him win the fleece. But she then killed Pelias, and she and Jason had to leave Iolkos to escape Pelias's angry brother Acastus.

BELLEROPHON

Bellerophon was the son of King Glaucus of Corinth, and served at the court of another king, King Proteus of Argos. But unfortunately Proteus's wife, Anteia, fell in love with Bellerophon. When he rejected her, she was furious and told Proteus that Bellerophon was in love with her and wouldn't leave her alone. Proteus was angry and wanted to kill Bellerophon, but he didn't dare. Instead he sent Bellerophon to visit Iobates, the King of Lycia, with a sealed letter. The letter asked Iobates to kill Bellerophon.

However, when Iobates read the letter, he didn't want to commit murder either. Instead he sent Bellerophon to kill the Chimaera - a fierce, fire-breathing monster with a lion's head, a goat for a body, and a snake for a tail - knowing he would probably die. But the gods helped Bellerophon by lending him the magical winged horse, Pegasus. Riding on its back, Bellerophon managed to kill the Chimaera.

Then Proteus sent Bellerophon to fight the Solymi, a tribe of mighty warriors, and the Amazons, a tribe of fierce women, but he conquered them both. At last Bellerophon made friends with Iobates and married his daughter Philonoe.

Later, Bellerophon tried to fly to Mount Olympus, the home of the gods, on the back of Pegasus. Zeus, furious at his impudence, made Pegasus throw him off. Bellerophon became an outcast and died alone.

Bellerophon fighting the Chimaera on the back of his winged horse, Pegasus

GREEK PHILOSOPHY

Ancient Greek philosophers like Plato and Socrates are very famous. But what exactly was Greek philosophy? In fact, philosophy (which is Greek for 'love of knowledge') is not as complicated as it sounds. In ancient Greece, it simply meant trying to explain how the world worked, and trying to decide how people should behave and how society should be run. Of course, different philosophers had different ideas. As time went on, different systems or 'schools' of philosophy developed. The most important ideas and schools are explained here.

THE EARLY THINKERS
Greek philosophy probably started in around 600BC in Ionia (the area of ancient Greece which is now part of Turkey), when **Thales of Miletus** developed a theory that the whole universe was made of water. It could appear in the form of objects, plants, animals and people, but these were all really just different types of water.

After Thales, **Anaximander** (c.610-545BC) also argued that everything was made of one substance - not water, but an everlasting force called the *apeiron*. Anaximander had some other ideas too - he said the Earth was drum-shaped, and that life had begun when mud was warmed by the Sun (which is not so far from what some scientists believe today). Another philosopher, **Anaximenes** (c.546BC), suggested the substance everything was made of was air.

However, all these early thinkers had one thing in common - they were trying to work out how the universe was constructed and what made it tick.

THE CULT OF PYTHAGORAS
Pythagoras (c.580-c.500BC) was a philosopher and religious leader. He thought that when people died, they were reincarnated (born again) as other people or animals. But he also had scientific ideas: he said that the Earth was a sphere, and that the way the universe worked was based on mathematics and the relationships between numbers. He had a large cult (group of followers) who passed on his ideas after he died. Many of Pythagoras's theories influenced other Greek philosophers and are also still important to our understanding of science today.

THE ELEATIC SCHOOL
Following on from **Anaximander**, several philosophers had new ideas about the force that made up the universe. **Xenophanes** (c.570BC-c.475BC) saw it as a great godlike being. **Parmenides** (c.515BC-c.445BC) argued that the changing, varied everyday world was just an illusion and that in fact the universe was constant and unchanging. His follower **Zeno** (c.490BC-c.440BC) claimed it was impossible for many different things to exist. 'Things' were just different aspects of one universe. This approach was called the **Eleatic School**, because Zeno and Parmenides lived in Elea in Italy.

ELEMENTS, SEEDS AND ATOMS
Some philosophers strongly disagreed with the Eleatic School. **Empedocles** (c.495BC-c.435BC) said that far from being one single thing, the universe was made up of four elements - air, earth, fire and water. **Anaxagoras** (c.500BC-c.428BC) had another view: he thought the universe was made up of tiny 'seeds' of different substances, while **Leucippus** (5th century BC) and **Democritus** (c.460BC-357BC) thought it was made up of invisible atoms. These philosophers are sometimes called the **atomists** or **pluralists**.

SOCRATES
In Athens in the 5th century BC, **Socrates** (469BC-399BC) invented a new philosophy. He was concerned with *arete*, which means 'goodness'. He held sessions in which he questioned other

A medieval illustration of a book by Aristotle

people's ideas of what goodness really was. He also believed that being good made people happy. But Socrates upset politicians with all his questions, and was executed. After his death, his pupils wrote down his ideas and passed them on. The debate over what is good and what is bad became known as **ethics**.

PLATO
Plato (c.429-347BC) was a pupil of Socrates, but slowly developed his own ideas. Like Socrates, he was interested in the nature of goodness. He said that states should be run by 'philosopher-kings' who knew better than most people what goodness was. He is also famous for his theory of **ideals**. He said that an ideal version of each thing existed in a 'World of Ideas'. A real thing, such as a chair, a dog or a human, could never be as good as the ideal version, but humans could try to get nearer to ideals through philosophy. Plato's ideas spread across the world and are still important today.

ARISTOTLE
Aristotle (384BC-322BC) was Plato's pupil, but disagreed with him about ideals, which he did not believe in. However, he too thought that people could reach towards goodness by using the power of their minds, or *nous*, for thinking philosophical thoughts. Aristotle also wrote about many other subjects.

GREEK PLAYS

Greek plays were mainly divided into tragedies, comedies and satyrs. Tragedies were meant to show people how or how not to behave. They often retold traditional stories about heroes and gods. Comedies were mostly funny and dealt with politics or the battle between men and women. Satyrs were rude, biting comedies, which mocked serious themes. However, tragedies could be funny too, and some even had happy endings.

Although hundreds of plays were written, only a few, including those by Aeschylus, Sophocles, Euripides and Aristophanes, survive. The plots of some of the most famous ones are summarized here.

ALCESTIS

This play by Euripides is a tragedy with a happy ending. Admetus has been granted a long life by the gods, as long as he can persuade someone else to die for him. His parents refuse, so his dutiful wife Alcestis dies for him instead. Admetus is very upset and regrets her death. When his friend, the hero Heracles, finds out what has happened, he goes to rescue Alcestis from the Underworld, and brings her back to life.

ANTIGONE

A tragedy by Sophocles. Antigone buries her brother Polyneices, who has died in a fight to win control of Thebes. King Creon, who has ordered that the body should not be buried, has Antigone left to die in a cave as punishment. Her fiancé, Creon's son Haemon, is outraged and leaves to go to her. Creon also goes to the cave, where he finds that Antigone has hanged herself. Haemon stabs himself to death. When Creon goes home, his wife Eurydice has also killed herself.

THE BIRDS

A comedy by Aristophanes. Two Athenians, Peisetairos and Euelpides, are looking for a better place to live. They persuade the birds to build a kingdom in the air, called Cloud-cuckooland. For food, they plan to steal sacrifices intended for the gods. All goes well until the goddess Iris comes to complain. Peisetairos demands Zeus's daughter Basilaeia as his wife in return for an agreement. At last the birds and the gods make peace, and Peisetairos replaces Zeus as king of the gods.

THE CYCLOPS

This play by Euripides tells the story of Odysseus and the Cyclops, a one-eyed giant. Arriving at the Cyclops's island, Odysseus and his crew bargain with the giant's captive Silenus. The Cyclops returns and locks them in his cave. Odysseus and his men blind him by driving a stake into his eye, and escape from the cave by hiding under his sheep.

DYSCOLUS

In this comedy by Menander, a rich young man named Sostratus falls in love with a country girl, but fails to impress her grumpy old father Cnemon (the *dyscolus*, or 'bad-tempered man', of the title). The girl's brother Gorgias helps Sostratus, but to no avail. However, after falling down a well, Cnemon has a personality change and hands over control of his affairs to Gorgias, who allows Sostratus to marry his sister. Sostratus's own sister marries Gorgias, and the play ends with a party.

ECCLESIAZUSAE

A political comedy by Aristophanes. By disguising themselves as men, the women, led by Praxagora, take over their city and rule that everyone should have a fair share of love and marriage, including old and ugly people. Praxogara explains this to her husband, who is stuck at home because she has stolen his clothes. Back at the assembly, a young man arrives to find his girlfriend; but he is seized by three old women who fight over him. One wins and carries him away. The play ends with a feast.

ELECTRA

Sophocles and Euripides both wrote tragedies about Electra, daughter of Agamemnon, the king killed by his wife Clytemnestra and her lover Aegisthus (see page 255). In Sophocles' version, Orestes, Agamemnon's son, arrives to avenge the murder. To trick his mother, he sends news that he is dead. Meanwhile, Clytemnestra sends her daughter Chrysothemis to tend Agamemnon's grave. Electra, her other daughter, is furious. They are all arguing at the tomb when they receive the news of Orestes's death. Clytemnestra is delighted, but Electra is devastated and resolves to kill her mother herself. Then Orestes and a friend arrive and kill Clytemnestra and Aegisthus.

Euripides' version is similar, but Electra is married to a farmer. She also helps Orestes to kill their mother.

THE FROGS

This comedy by Aristophanes is one of his most famous. When the play begins, the three great tragic poets, Aeschylus, Sophocles and Euripides, are all dead and the war-weary city of Athens needs good advisers. So the god Dionysus disguises himself as the hero Heracles, and sets off for Hades to fetch Euripides, accompanied by a chorus of frogs.

After many adventures, he is asked to judge a dispute between Aeschylus and Euripides over who is the best poet. Each of them speaks a line of poetry into a pair of scales. Aeschylus wins, as his poetry is the weightiest. However, neither poet has much good advice for Athens.

HIPPOLYTUS

A tragedy by Euripides. When Theseus marries his second wife, Phaedra, she falls in love with his son Hipploytus instead. But the noble Hippolytus refuses to see her, so she hangs herself, leaving a note for Theseus accusing Hippolytus of seducing her. Theseus is furious and banishes his son, calling on the sea god Poseidon to curse him. A monster rises out of the sea and frightens Hippolytus's horses, and he is thrown from his chariot and killed. Theseus finds out too late that Hippolytus was innocent.

MEDEA

One of Euripides's most famous tragedies. The enchantress Medea, wife of the adventurer Jason, has murdered Pelias, one of Jason's enemies. The pair flee to Corinth to escape Pelias's vengeful son. There, Jason decides to leave Medea and marry the daughter of Creon, the King of Corinth. Medea is furious at his ingratitude. King Creon, afraid of her magic, tries to banish her, but she stays long enough to murder Creon and his daughter. Then, to hurt Jason, she kills their own two children, and escapes to Athens.

OEDIPUS TYRANNUS

A tragedy by Sophocles, also called *Oedipus Rex*. Terrified by a prophecy that he will kill his father and marry his mother, Oedipus (or 'swollen-foot', named for his damaged feet) has left his parents, the King and Queen of Corinth. On the road to Thebes he kills a man in a fight, but then wins the hand of the Queen of Thebes, Jocasta, by answering a riddle, so becoming King of Thebes.

But Thebes is troubled by plagues, and an oracle reveals that the killer of Laius, Jocasta's first husband, is in the city. A servant from Corinth arrives to call Oedipus home, as his father has died. Oedipus is afraid of the prophecy, but the servant says Oedipus was not his parent's real son ~ he had been found as a baby. A shepherd reveals that Laius and Jocasta had had a son, but after a prophecy that the son would kill his father, the shepherd had been sent to leave the baby out to die, its feet disabled with a spike. In pity, he had given the baby to a Corinthian instead. Oedipus realizes he was this child. The man he killed was Laius, his father, and his wife is his mother. He goes to find Jocasta, but she has hanged herself. Oedipus blinds himself. Her brother Creon is left to manage the kingdom.

THE ORESTEIA TRILOGY

Many Greek plays were written in groups of four (tetralogies) or three (trilogies). This trilogy of tragedies is by Aeschylus.

Agamemnon Agamemnon returns from the Trojan War with Cassandra, who can see into the future. But his wife Clytemnestra has a new lover, Aegisthus. She also hates Agamemnon for sacrificing their daughter to the gods before the war. She pretends to welcome her husband but then murders him and Cassandra.

Choephoroe Agamemnon's son Orestes, comes with a friend, Pylades, to avenge his father. His sister Electra finds out he has arrived and together they plot against the murderers. Orestes kills first Aegisthus, then Clytemnestra. He sees the Furies, or Eumenides, the spirits of vengeance, coming for him, and runs away.

Eumenides Clytemnestra's ghost urges the Furies to avenge her. Orestes asks the goddess Athene to judge between them, and Athene asks the citizens of Athens to vote on the issue. They are equally divided, and Athene rules that Orestes should be acquitted.

PEACE

A comedy by Aristophanes, set during the war between Athens and Sparta. Trygaios, a vine-grower who is sick of food shortages, rides to heaven on a giant dung-beetle to visit the gods. Hermes explains that most of the gods have gone away to avoid the fighting. War is in charge, and has thrown Peace into a cave. Trygaios and his friends help Peace out of the cave and take her back to Greece. The war ends, and everyone is happy except the weapon-makers.

THE SEVEN AGAINST THEBES

A tragedy by Aeschylus. Oedipus's sons Polyneices and Eteocles are fighting over Thebes. Eteocles holds the city, and Polyneices has a plan for seven champions to lead seven attacks on the city's seven gates. Eteocles picks seven men to defend the gates: he himself will fight his own brother. Both of them die in the battle. It is decreed that Polyneices should not be buried because he attacked his own city. His sister Antigone vows to bury him herself.

THE WASPS

A comedy by Aristophanes. An old man, Philocleon, loves to serve on juries. His son Bdelycleon tries to stop him by keeping him at home, but his friends (dressed as wasps, to show their love of punishing people) try to help him escape. Eventually Bdelycleon lets his father put the family dog on trial for stealing some cheese. After this, the old man changes his ways and goes to a wild party.

BATTLES AND BATTLE FORMATIONS

The Greeks were well-known throughout the ancient world for their superior military skills. Training, discipline and the careful use of battle formations often enabled them to win victories even when they were outnumbered. Here is a list of sites of the most important battles fought by the ancient Greeks, with maps showing what happened at some of the most famous ones.

AEGINA An island between Athens and southern Greece, the site of a naval war between Aegina and Athens in the early 5th century BC.

AEGOSPOTAMI A town near the Hellespont in Turkey. In 405BC, the Athenian navy was virtually wiped out here by the Spartans. It was the last great battle of the Peloponnesian Wars.

CHAERONEA A town in central Greece, the site of Philip II of Macedon's decisive victory over the Greek cities in 338BC.

GAUGAMELA A town on the east side of the Euphrates river, now in Iraq. Here, in 331BC, Alexander the Great won his third victory over King Darius III of Persia.

GRANICUS RIVER A river in northwest Turkey, the scene of Alexander's first victory over the Persians in 334BC.

HYDASPES A river in northwest India and the scene of Alexander's battle against the Indians in 326BC.

ISSUS A river near the borders of present-day Syria and Turkey. It was the site of Alexander's second victory over the Persians in 333BC.

LEUCTRA A town in central Greece, where the Thebans won a victory against the Spartans in 371BC.

MANTINEA A town in southern Greece, where the Thebans won a victory over the Spartans, in 362BC, although they lost the war.

MARATHON

A plain in Attica, northeast of Athens. In 490BC, the combined armies of the Athenians and their allies, the Plataeans, won a great victory against the Persians.

This diagram shows the positions of the two armies at the Battle of Marathon.

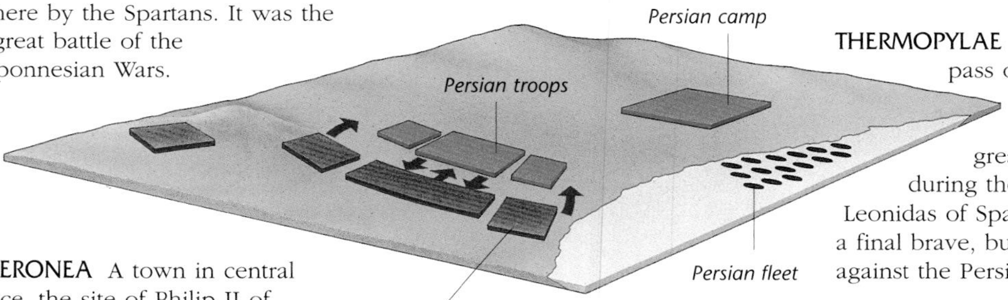

Persian camp

Persian troops

Persian fleet

Greek forces begin to encircle the Persians.

PLATAEA A town in central Greece, the site of a Spartan victory over the Persians in 479BC.

PYDNA The site of the battle in 168BC in which the Romans defeated the Macedonians and took over control of Greece.

RAPHIA A town in Palestine, the scene of a battle in 217BC between the Seleucids and the Ptolemies.

SALAMIS An island just off the coast of Greece, near Athens. In 480BC, the Greeks won a great naval victory here against the Persians during the long-running Persian Wars.

This diagram of the Battle of Salamis shows the positions of the Greek and Persian fleets before the battle began.

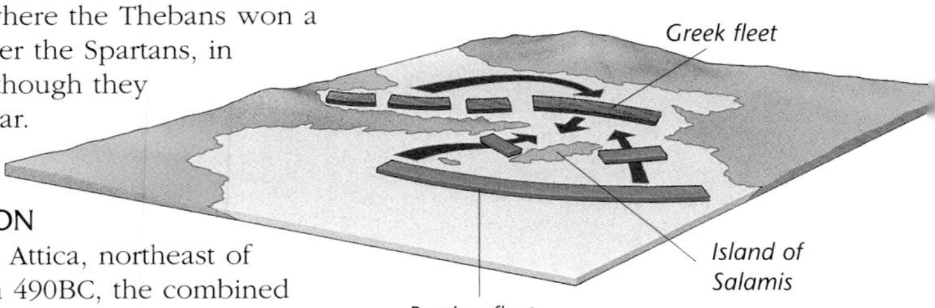

Greek fleet

Island of Salamis

Persian fleet

The Greeks are hiding in the bay behind the island, waiting for the Persian fleet to sail up the narrow stretch of water before they attack.

THERMOPYLAE A narrow mountain pass on the east coast of Greece, where the Persians won a great victory in 480BC, during the Persian Wars. King Leonidas of Sparta led his troops in a final brave, but hopeless, battle against the Persians.

This diagram shows the positions of the Spartans and the Persians at the Battle of Thermopylae.

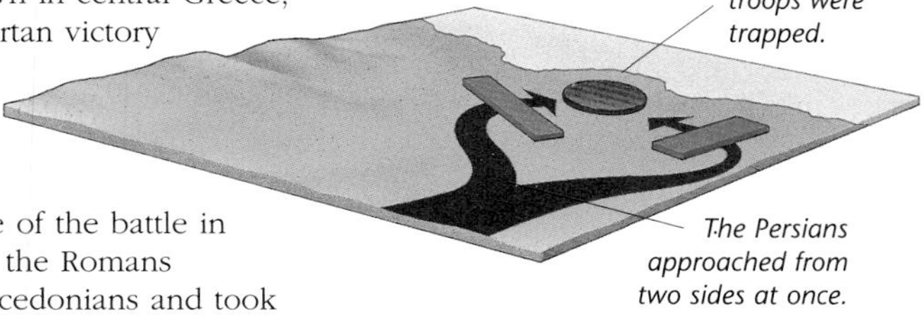

The Spartan troops were trapped.

The Persians approached from two sides at once.

TROY The site of nine cities in Asia Minor, each built on the ruins of its predecessor. The seventh was besieged by the Greeks in about 1250BC, during the Trojan War.

BATTLE FORMATIONS

Greek hoplite soldiers fought in a formation called a phalanx, which consisted of a long block of soldiers (see page 179). For a phalanx to be effective, it was important for the men to stay in line and move as a unit. Flute music was sometimes used to keep them in step with each other and keep the phalanx in line.

A phalanx was usually 8 rows deep, but it could be more or less than that.

Each hoplite was partly protected by his own shield and partly by the shield of the man to his right. This left the man at the right-hand end of the line partly exposed. In a battle, a general would often try to attack the enemy's right wing, as this was the most vulnerable to attack.

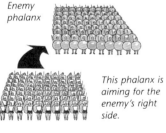

Enemy phalanx

This phalanx is aiming for the enemy's right side.

ALEXANDER'S PHALANX

Alexander the Great often used the phalanx in a oblique formation, shown below, as a way of attacking his enemy's weaker right side, while keeping the right side of his own phalanx protected.

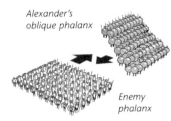

Alexander's oblique phalanx

Enemy phalanx

THE MACEDONIAN PHALANX

The phalanx worked very well, but it was vulnerable if heavy pressure was put on a single point. The Macedonians strengthened the design of the phalanx by using a very long pike, called a sarissa, and a two-handed spear. When the phalanx was charging, the pikes of the first four or five rows of men extended beyond the front line. The rest of the phalanx held their pikes in the air to break the impact of enemy missiles.

The Macedonian syntagma (shown below) had 16 rows, with 16 men in each row.

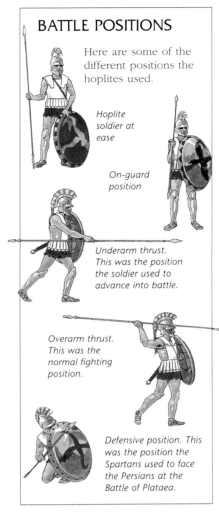

BATTLE POSITIONS

Here are some of the different positions the hoplites used.

Hoplite soldier at ease

On-guard position

Underarm thrust. This was the position the soldier used to advance into battle.

Overarm thrust. This was the normal fighting position.

Defensive position. This was the position the Spartans used to face the Persians at the Battle of Plataea.

This is a syntagma, made up of 256 men, the smallest unit of a Macedonian phalanx.

Soldiers at the back held their pikes upright.

A fresco of a garden with fruit trees, from the Villa of Livia, near Rome

ROMAN WORLD

THE TOWN OF POMPEII

O ne of the best places to learn about the Romans is the town of Pompeii in southern Italy. In AD79, Pompeii was buried under layers of ash from a violent volcanic eruption, but the ash that destroyed the town also preserved it for archaeologists. Buildings, furniture, tools and possessions survived almost intact, clearly showing what life was like on the day disaster struck.

Many lively mosaics and paintings have been uncovered at Pompeii. This sign warned people to beware of the fierce dog.

A LIVELY TOWN

Pompeii was a thriving town close to the Bay of Naples. Its wealth came mainly from exporting wine, olive oil and wool, and several of its more important citizens were rich enough to own luxurious villas. The town's bustling streets were lined with busy workshops, inns and shops, and the townspeople liked to relax by visiting the public baths, watching plays at the theatre, or cheering on the gladiators in the town's arena.

ERUPTION!

One clear summer's morning in AD79, a massive explosion rocked the streets of Pompeii, as the nearby volcano Mount Vesuvius erupted into life. Soon, the town was engulfed in dust, lumps of burning rock fell from the sky, buildings shook, and the streets were filled with terrified people running in all directions.

The destruction continued throughout the night and into the next day. The writer Pliny recorded that the sky grew blacker than the darkest night. Many people were suffocated by hot, dusty winds, and Pompeii was gradually buried under a blanket of ash.

Here you can see how Pompeii would have looked at the time that Mount Vesuvius erupted.

REMARKABLE REMAINS

The ash gradually became rock-hard and the town remained buried until the 18th century, when archaeologists began to uncover its buildings. They were amazed at what they found. Statues, furniture and lamps had survived, as well as smaller objects such as dishes and rings. People who had died suddenly from suffocation had left a perfect imprint in the hardened ash - caught forever in the act of escaping, or huddled close together for comfort.

This plaster cast of a man was made by filling the hollow shape left by his body.

INTERNET LINK

For links to websites where you can browse an exhibit on Pompeii and see photo galleries of everyday life, go to www.usborne-quicklinks.com

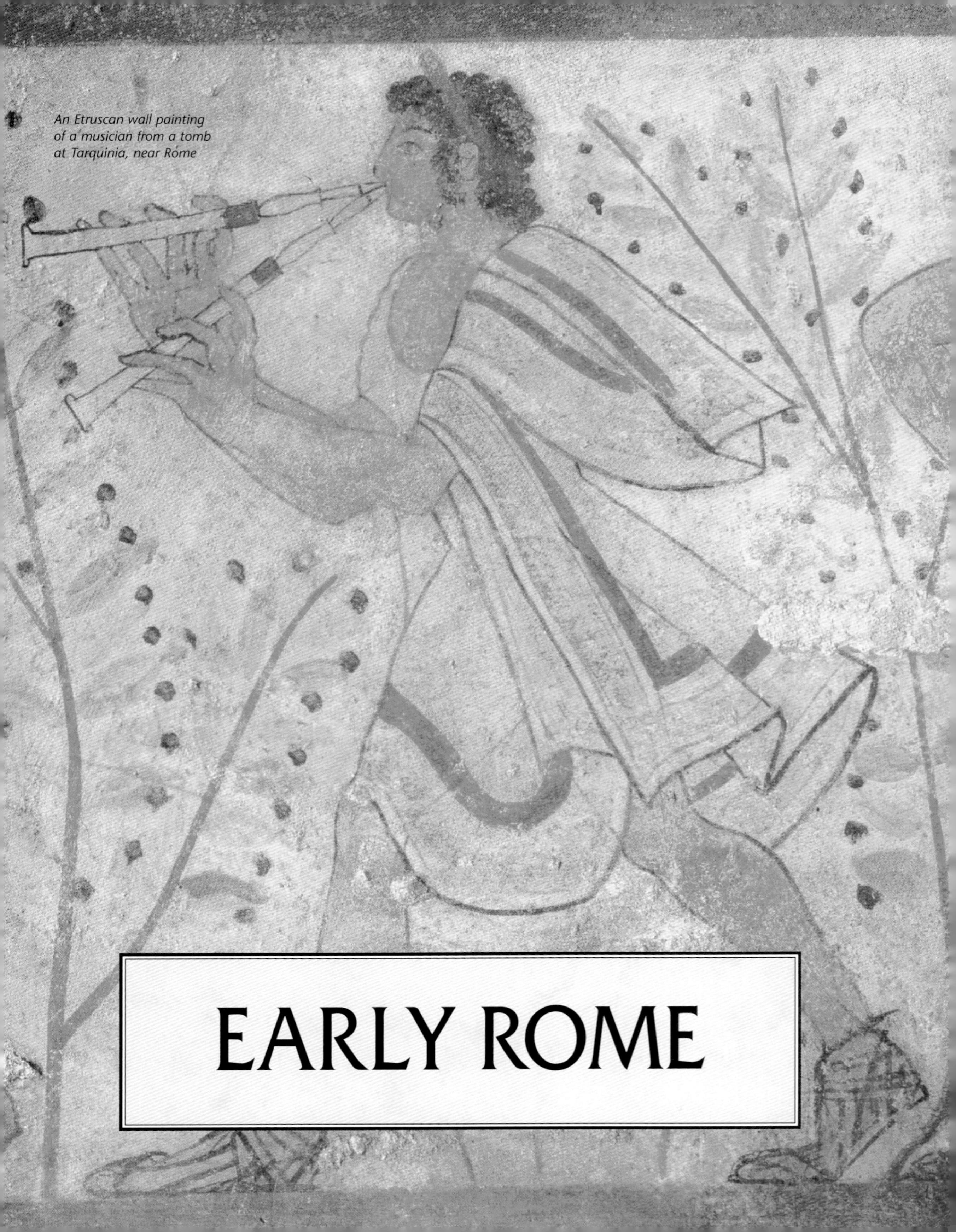

An Etruscan wall painting
of a musician from a tomb
at Tarquinia, near Rome

EARLY ROME

THE FOUNDING OF ROME

Around 3,000 years ago, a tribe of people known as the Latins settled on the hilltops above the banks of the Tiber, in the land that is now Italy. This cluster of small villages eventually grew to become the city of Rome - one of the most splendid cities in the ancient world and the capital of the mighty Roman empire.

Urns like this, in the shape of a house, were used by the Latins for burying the ashes of their dead.

LAND OF THE LATINS

The Latins lived on a fertile plain on the west coast of Italy. They spoke an earlier form of the language which is now known as Latin, and the area of Italy where they lived became known as Latium. The Latins grew crops and kept animals, and around 1,000BC they began building the first small hilltop villages on the future site of the great city of Rome.

The site had lots of natural advantages. At just that spot the Tiber narrowed, and there was an island in the middle, making it possible for people to cross the river. The coast was 25km (about 15 miles) away - close enough to reach the sea by boat, but far enough away to be safe from the pirates who roamed the Mediterranean. And from the hills above the river, it was easy to spot enemies coming and fight them off.

Here, you can see an early Latin settlement on the Palatine Hill, one of the seven hills which later became the site of Rome.

The Latins lived in simple, wooden huts with thatched roofs. They built their homes on the hilltops above the Tiber and used the marshy valleys below as cemeteries for burying their dead. Gradually, these small villages spread down the hillsides and, some time during the 8th century BC, they merged to form a single town - Rome.

INTERNET LINK

For links to websites where you can read more about the founding of Rome and the legend of Romulus and Remus, go to **www.usborne-quicklinks.com**

A wooden fence helped to protect the village from enemies.

The marshy valley below the Palatine Hill became a meeting place for people from the surrounding villages.

MYTHS AND LEGENDS

Much later, Roman historians, such as Livy, combined a Greek myth and a Roman folktale to provide a far grander and more interesting account of how their great city was founded.

The story began with Aeneas - a mythical hero from Greek legend who had escaped from the conquered city of Troy. After many adventures, Aeneas finally arrived in Italy, where he married a Latin princess and started a new line of kings.

According to Roman tradition, two of Aeneas's descendants were twin boys named Romulus and Remus. The boys' great-uncle, Amulius, wanted them out of the way and ordered them to be drowned in the Tiber. But Amulius's men took pity on the babies and set them afloat in a cradle. They drifted ashore where they were found by a she-wolf, who fed them with her milk until they were rescued by a kindly shepherd.

A later Roman coin showing a portrait of Romulus

When the boys grew up, they killed their wicked great-uncle and decided to build a new city on the banks of the Tiber. But as the city walls were being built, Remus mocked his brother, and they had a violent argument. Romulus killed Remus and became king of the new city, which was named 'Rome' after him. According to tradition, this happened in 753BC.

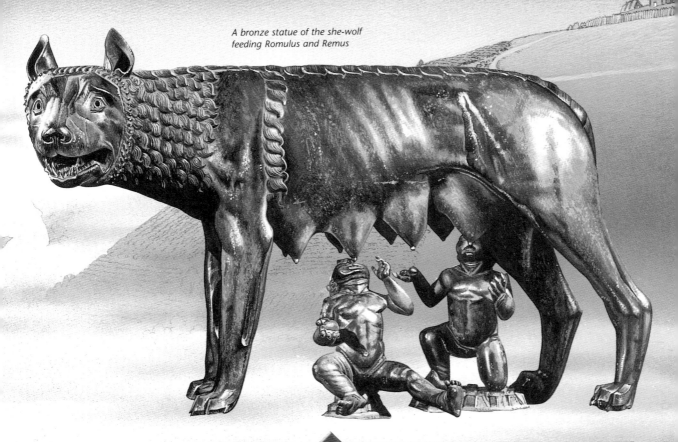

A bronze statue of the she-wolf feeding Romulus and Remus

THE GROWTH OF ROME

In the 8th century BC, while Rome was growing into a city, the Latins were just one of many groups of people who lived on the Italian peninsula. To the north of the Latins lay the great Etruscan civilization, while the south was dominated by the Greeks who had set up colonies there. In between were numerous tribes of hill-farmers, such as the Sabines. All these people had a part to play in the history of Rome in its early years.

THE SABINE WOMEN

According to the Roman historian Livy, who lived much later, the newly founded city of Rome suffered from a shortage of women. So the Latins invited the nearby Sabines to take part in a festival of games, and then kidnapped all their daughters. Although the story is unlikely to be true, some of the early inhabitants of Rome were Sabines. Perhaps the legend may have grown up later on to explain how they came to be there.

Map showing some of the different groups of people who lived in Italy

GREAT GREECE

As early as 750BC, Greek colonists began setting up cities in southern Italy and on the coast of Sicily. The Greeks had such a strong influence in this area that the Romans later called it *Magna Graecia* - or 'Great Greece'.

As well as bringing goods to trade - such as fine pottery, metalwork and wine - the Greeks also brought with them their science, literature, drama, art and architecture. All of these had a huge effect on Roman culture.

The ruins of a typical Greek temple, built by Greek colonists at Segesta, on the island of Sicily

THE ETRUSCANS

The people who had the greatest influence on early Rome were the Etruscans, who controlled the area of the Italian peninsula north of the Tiber. No one is quite sure where the Etruscans came from. Some experts think they were native to Italy, while others think they came from the eastern Mediterranean. Their civilization, based on a group of large, well-planned cities, was at its peak between 800BC and 400BC.

A gold perfume bottle, found in the tomb of an Etruscan nobleman

The Etruscans traded with the Greeks in southern Italy, and adopted the Greek alphabet, which they passed on to the Romans. They were also highly skilled artists, who created elaborate sculptures in bronze and terracotta, and decorated the walls of their tombs with brightly painted frescoes.

Many of the things we think of as typically Roman were actually inherited from the Etruscans. They enjoyed chariot races and gladiator fights, built arches, aqueducts and sewers, and invented the toga. They also played a part in shaping the early government of Rome.

THE KINGS OF ROME

Early Rome was ruled by a king, who was chosen and advised by a council of elders - or *senes*. According to Roman tradition, there was a series of seven kings, but there are no written records from the time to back this up. The last three kings were said to be Etruscans.

Rome was situated on a route used by Etruscan traders to cross the Tiber, and experts believe that around 600BC the Etruscans took control of the city. Under the Etruscans, Rome grew into an impressive city with a public square surrounded by temples, a proper drainage system and huge defensive walls to protect it.

INTERNET LINK

For links to websites where you can watch short movies about the Etruscans and the growth of Rome, go to **www.usborne-quicklinks.com**

The Etruscans often decorated the lids of their coffins with terracotta sculptures, such as this one of a man and his wife.

ROMAN WORLD

Internet link for a link to a website where you can see a timeline of ancient Rome, go to www.usborne-quicklinks.com

THE LAST KING OF ROME

The Romans resented the Etruscan kings who ruled over them, and the last king - Tarquinius Superbus, or 'Tarquin the Proud' - was particularly unpopular. His story is told by the Roman historian Livy, who was writing 500 years later, and it is probably based on folktales handed down by generations of Romans.

A REIGN OF TERROR

Tarquin became the ruler of Rome after murdering the previous king by throwing him down the steps of the Senate House. He was a ruthless tyrant, who ruled without consulting the council of elders and who put to death anyone he pleased.

Late one night, Tarquin's son brutally attacked a Roman noblewoman named Lucretia, while her husband was away. This was the final straw for the Romans. Outraged by this cowardly act against a woman, they drove Tarquin and his family out of the city.

HORATIO THE HERO

Tarquin appealed to the Etruscans for help, and finally persuaded the king of Clusium (an Etruscan city farther north) to attack Rome. But to reach the city, the Etruscan army first had to cross a wooden bridge over the Tiber.

A fearless Roman soldier named Horatio held the Etruscans back, while the Romans destroyed the bridge behind him. Horatio then jumped into the river and swam back to his friends - Rome was saved.

Here you can see Horatio defending the bridge against the Etruscan army.

THE BIRTH OF THE REPUBLIC

Although all these stories are legend, rather than fact, the Romans did eventually drive out their Etruscan rulers. The reign of the last king ended in 510BC or 509BC, and Rome became an independent republic.

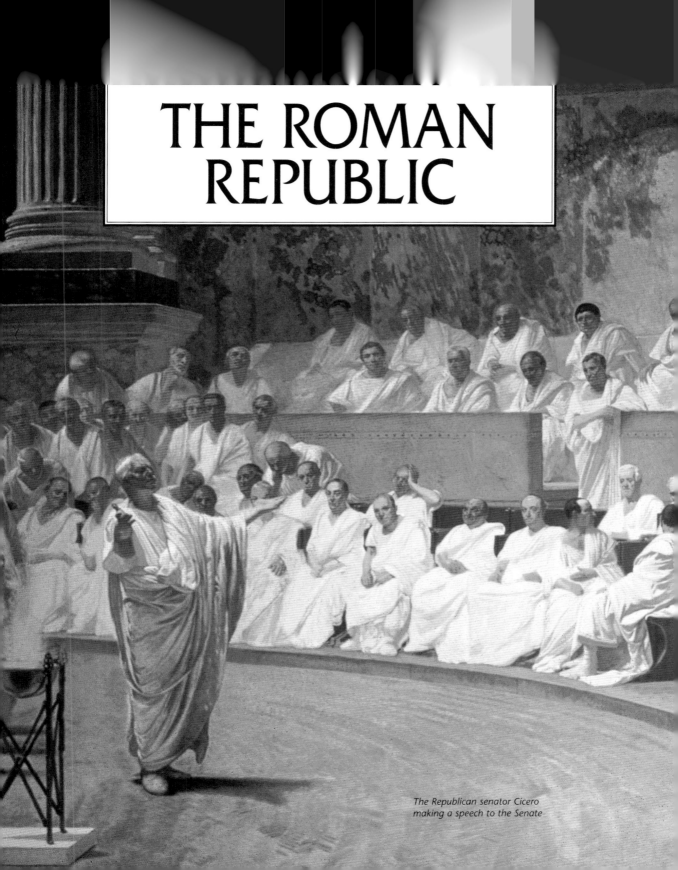

THE ROMAN REPUBLIC

The Republican senator Cicero making a speech to the Senate

Internet link *for a link to a website where you can find a clear account of the early history of Rome, go to* **www.usborne-quicklinks.com**

THE CONQUEST OF ITALY

The Roman Republic was surrounded on all sides by enemies in its early years. To the north were the powerful Etruscans, while central Italy was swarming with fierce mountain tribes, such as the Volsci, the Aequi and the Samnites. At times, Rome was also at war with rival Latin cities nearby. By using a mixture of military power and clever politics, the Romans gradually mananged to fight off their enemies and take control over their land.

Roman lands
Roman allies

Veii
Rome
LATIUM

ITALY

Tarentum

Thurii

Map of Roman lands in 264BC

Here you can see an army of Gauls climbing the Capitol Hill to attack Rome at night.

Roman soldiers, woken by the cackling of geese, rushed to defend the Capitol.

GETTING STARTED

At first, the Republic wasn't strong enough to defeat the mountain tribes by itself and was forced to accept the help of a group of Latin cities, known as the Latin League. By 400BC, Rome was the leading city in the League, and the Republic had doubled in size. Soon, the Romans began expanding to the north as well, defeating the nearby Etruscan city of Veii in 396BC.

ROME UNDER ATTACK

Then, disaster struck. An army of Gauls - a Celtic tribe from central Europe - swept south through Italy and defeated the Romans in a fierce battle at the Allia river. In 390BC, the Gauls attacked Rome, burned most of its buildings to the ground, and besieged the Capitol Hill - the religious heart of the city.

According to legend, the Gauls tried to creep up on the Capitol late one night, but they disturbed some geese that were kept at one of the temples. The cackling geese woke the Romans just in time. The Capitol was besieged for seven months, and when the Gauls eventually moved away, they left the city in ruins.

BACK ON TRACK

Gradually, the Romans rebuilt their city and began to win back the land they had lost. The other cities in the Latin League resented Rome's increasing power, and war broke out. In 338BC, Rome defeated the League and took control of Latium.

At the same time, Rome was involved in three wars against a nearby hill tribe called the Samnites. The Samnites won several spectacular victories against Rome, but they were eventually defeated - along with their allies the Gauls and the Etruscans. By 290BC, Rome controlled most of central and northern Italy.

The Gauls were fierce warriors, who fought with swords and spears.

This fresco shows two Samnite warriors wearing helmets decorated with feathers.

KEEPING CONTROL

The Romans could be very generous to people they conquered. Any city that surrendered quickly was offered an alliance, and its people were given some of the privileges of Roman citizens. But those who resisted were brutally killed or sold as slaves. These tactics helped the Romans keep their growing lands under control.

THE PYRRHIC WARS

In 282BC, Rome was drawn into a dispute between rival Greek cities in the south, and agreed to help defend the city of Thurii. But Tarentum - another Greek city nearby - was suspicious of Rome's motives, and appealed to a Greek king named Pyrrhus for help. In the war that followed, Pyrrhus defeated the Romans twice, but lost vast numbers of his own soldiers. He is supposed to have remarked grimly: "Another victory like that, and I'll be ruined."

Pyrrhus was eventually defeated in 275BC, and by 264BC the Romans dominated all of Italy. Rome was now one of the most powerful states in the Mediterranean.

This is a statue of King Pyrrhus. The phrase 'a Pyrrhic victory' is still used today when the cost of winning is too high.

MASTERS OF THE MEDITERRANEAN

While Rome was gaining control of Italy, the western Mediterranean was dominated by the great trading empire of Carthage, on the coast of North Africa. As long as they weren't competing for trade, the Romans and the Carthaginians left each other in peace. But in 264BC, a series of bitter wars broke out between them. These wars - called the Punic Wars - would eventually decide who ruled the Mediterranean.

Coin showing Hamilcar Barca, who led the Carthaginian army during the First Punic War

ALL AT SEA

The First Punic War began when both Rome and Carthage stepped in to sort out a dispute on the island of Sicily, off the coast of Italy.

To win the war, Rome would have to defeat the powerful Carthaginian navy, but the Romans had very few ships and no experience of fighting at sea.

Luckily, they found a stranded Carthaginian warship and used it as a model to build a fleet of their own. The Romans won two early sea battles - but twice lost all their ships in violent storms.

Having rebuilt their fleet, the Romans finally defeated the Carthaginians in 241BC. Carthage was forced to pay a huge fine and also agreed to let Rome have control of Sicily - its first overseas territory. The Romans later seized Sardinia and Corsica as well.

HANDLING HANNIBAL

In search of a new empire, the Carthaginians invaded Spain. In 219BC, they attacked the Spanish city of Saguntum - an ally of Rome - provoking the Second Punic War. The next year, the Carthaginian general, Hannibal, set off with 35,000 men and 37 elephants to invade Italy.

INTERNET LINK

For links to websites with information on Hannibal and an animated map of the Second Punic War, go to www.usborne-quicklinks.com

The Romans added a spiked drawbridge - called a corvus - to their ships. Here, you can see it being used to board a Carthaginian ship.

When the corvus was dropped onto the enemy's ship, Roman soldiers could charge across.

Hannibal led his troops across two huge mountain ranges - the Pyrenees and the Alps - losing 10,000 men and all but one of the elephants on the way. But Hannibal was an outstanding general, and his men won battle after battle. At the famous Battle of Cannae in 216BC they wiped out an entire Roman army.

Hannibal leading his army over the Alps

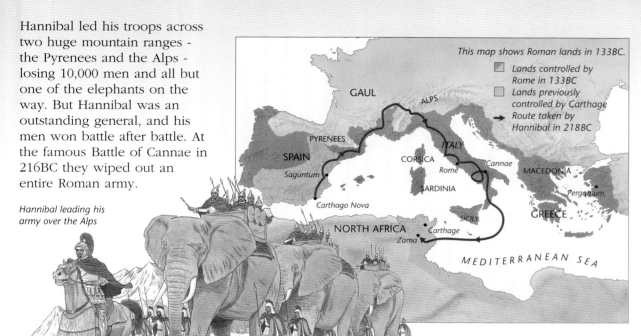

This map shows Roman lands in 133BC.
- Lands controlled by Rome in 133BC
- Lands previously controlled by Carthage
→ Route taken by Hannibal in 218BC

GAUL
ALPS
PYRENEES
SPAIN
Saguntum
Carthago Nova
ITALY
CORSICA
Rome
SARDINIA
Cannae
MACEDONIA
Pergamum
SICILY
NORTH AFRICA
Carthage
Zama
GREECE
MEDITERRANEAN SEA

Unable to defeat Hannibal in Italy, the Romans invaded Spain and then attacked Carthage itself. Hannibal had to return home, and in 202BC he was finally defeated at Zama by the Roman general Scipio. Carthage was forced to pay another massive fine and had to give its Spanish lands to Rome.

CARTHAGE DESTROYED

Although the Carthaginians were no longer a threat, some Romans were suspicious of what they might do in the future. For four years, a senator named Cato ended every speech he made with the words: "Carthage must be destroyed." In 149BC, war broke out again, and three years later Carthage was defeated and burned to the ground. Its people were sold as slaves, and the soil was sown with salt so that nothing could ever grow there again.

ROME RULES

Winning the Punic Wars gave the Romans large areas of land in Spain and North Africa. But during this period, they also conquered parts of southern Gaul (present-day France) and were drawn into wars in the eastern Mediterranean.

In 168BC, the Romans took over the Greek state of Macedonia, and by 146BC they controlled all of Greece. In 133BC, the King of Pergamum (in present-day Turkey) died, leaving his kingdom to Rome. With lands stretching from Spain to Asia, the Romans were indeed masters of the Mediterranean.

Internet link for links to websites where you can find out more about the people and the city of Rome, go to **www.usborne-quicklinks.com**

CITIZENS AND SENATORS

As far as the Romans were concerned, there were two kinds of people - citizens and non-citizens. Citizens had special rights and privileges, and were given extra protection under the law, so citizenship was highly prized. But in return, all citizens were expected to serve Rome by voting in elections, fighting in the army, and perhaps working for the government.

CITIZENS AND NON-CITIZENS

Originally, in order to qualify as a citizen, you had to have been born in the city of Rome and have parents who were Roman citizens. Non-citizens included people known as provincials - who lived outside Rome itself but within Roman territory - and slaves. Provincials couldn't vote in elections and, unlike citizens, they had to pay taxes. Slaves were owned by other people and had no rights at all of their own.

Roman women, like the one shown here with her slave, weren't classed as full citizens and weren't allowed to vote.

PATRICIANS AND PLEBEIANS

Roman citizens were divided into two groups - the patricians and the plebeians. In early Rome, the heads of the richest and most powerful families were known as *patres* - or 'fathers'. The patricians were descended from these men and they were the leading citizens in the city of Rome.

A statue of a patrician holding busts of two of his ancestors

Everyone who wasn't a patrician was classed as a plebeian. Many plebeians had no land or skills and were extremely poor. Others made their living as shopkeepers or craftworkers, while one group - known as *equites* - were bankers or merchants. These wealthy men were descended from the first Roman cavalry officers.

RICH RULERS

During the Republic, Rome was ruled by the Senate - a group of 300 men drawn from important patrician families. To qualify for the Senate, a man had to own a vast amount of land, but once appointed he held the job for life. It was considered a great honour to be chosen. Senators were expected to spend lots of money on entertaining, providing for their supporters and paying for public buildings, and some senators ended up bankrupt.

A coin showing the Senate House in Rome

TOP JOBS

After being consul, it was possible a man could become a proconsul and govern one of the Roman provinces abroad. Some were considered more important and pleasant to govern than others. Another important job was done by the two censors, who made sure there were enough senators and checked that anyone claiming to be a Roman citizen genuinely was one. In dire emergencies, the Senate sometimes appointed one man to be dictator for a time. He had absolute authority over everyone else.

The fasces - an axe tied to a bundle of rods - was the symbol of a consul's power.

POWER TO THE PLEBS

Very early in Rome's history, the plebeians - especially the wealthy ones - began to resent the patricians' power and wanted a share in governing the city.

In 494BC, the plebeians actually threatened to leave Rome and start a city of their own. So the Senate agreed that the plebeians could set up their own council, and elect officials - called tribunes - to protect their interests.

In 450BC, after riots by the plebeians, a list of laws known as the Twelve Tables was drawn up and displayed in the Forum. This meant that everyone knew what the laws were and could check if the judges were following them.

Over the years, plebeians won the right to become senators and stand for government positions themselves. The first plebeian consul was elected in 366BC, and after 287BC all decisions of the Plebeian Council had to become law - even if the Senate didn't agree with them.

THE CAREER LADDER

For a young Roman who wanted a career in politics, the road to the top was long, difficult and very expensive. After spending a few years in the army, the budding politician had to get himself elected to a series of government positions. The most senior position was that of consul. The pictures on the right show the usual career path for an ambitious Roman.

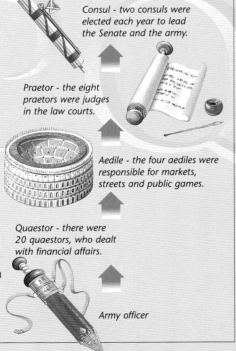

Consul - two consuls were elected each year to lead the Senate and the army.

Praetor - the eight praetors were judges in the law courts.

Aedile - the four aediles were responsible for markets, streets and public games.

Quaestor - there were 20 quaestors, who dealt with financial affairs.

Army officer

SPQR

These letters stand for Senatus Populusque Romanus (the Senate and people of Rome). They are often found on Roman carvings.

THE REPUBLIC IN CRISIS

By the 3rd century BC, the plebeians were playing a much bigger part in the government of Rome. Some patrician senators began to feel threatened, and tensions grew between the people and the patricians. From the 2nd century BC, one crisis followed another, plunging the Republic into a period of turmoil and bloodshed.

Great Roman generals were given a parade - or triumph - to celebrate their victories. This scene shows a typical triumph.

LAND MATTERS

As Rome began building up an empire, men had to spend long periods of time overseas fighting in the army, and they weren't able to farm their land. The farms fell into disrepair, and many of them were bought up by rich landowners, who used slaves to do all the work.

Without land or jobs, lots of country people drifted into Rome, where they remained out of work and desperately poor. Since only landowners were allowed to fight in the army, there was soon a shortage of soldiers too.

Soldiers wearing laurel wreaths shouted, "Io triomphe!" (behold the triumph).

In 133BC, a tribune named Tiberius Gracchus suggested that any land that had been illegally seized by the rich should be given to poor city dwellers. But many senators were violently opposed to this, because a lot of the land belonged to them. Riots broke out, and Tiberius was clubbed to death. In 123BC, Tiberius's brother Gaius was elected tribune. He also planned to help the poor, but - like his brother - he was murdered.

A slave held a laurel wreath over the general's head. It was his job to repeat in the general's ear, "Remember, you are just a man."

The general rode in a golden chariot. His face was painted red and he carried an olive branch.

MARIUS AND THE ARMY

In 107BC, one of Rome's greatest generals - Gaius Marius - took charge of a war that was raging in North Africa at the time. Marius won the war and became a national hero when he also defeated some tribes from Gaul who were threatening Rome. But he wasn't as skilled at politics as he was at fighting, and he angered many senators by supporting reform.

Marius is famous for reorganizing the army, allowing all citizens to enlist - not just those who owned land. These new soldiers were very poor and they relied on their generals to provide for them when they retired. This accidentally brought about a dramatic change in Roman politics, as some generals began using their own loyal armies to win power for themselves.

MURDER AND MAYHEM

In 88BC, Cornelius Sulla became consul and was asked to lead an army against the King of Pontus (now part of Turkey). Marius thought he should have been chosen instead and he challenged Sulla. Sulla promptly marched his army to Rome, took control of the city and drove Marius out.

Sulla then set off for Pontus. As soon as he had gone, Marius reappeared with an army of his own, took over the city and put Sulla's supporters to death. Marius died in 86BC, but when Sulla returned to Rome he found Marius's men still in charge. He had all of them killed and ruled Rome as a dictator from 82BC to 80BC.

POMPEY THE GREAT

One of the generals who had served under Sulla's command was Gnaeus Pompeius, known as Pompey the Great. Pompey won victories in Spain in 72BC and helped the senator Crassus to crush a slave rebellion led by a gladiator named Spartacus. In 70BC, he and Crassus became consuls.

A sculpture of Pompey the Great

Soon, Pompey was a hero. In just three months, he managed to clear the seas of the fearsome pirates who had been plaguing the Italian coast. He then reorganized Rome's lands in the Middle East and conquered several large areas of new territory. But when he returned to Rome, the Senate refused to support what he had done. Frustrated, Pompey looked around for new allies - one of these was a talented politician named Gaius Julius Caesar.

Prisoners of war were displayed on a platform, along with their weapons.

White oxen were sacrificed when the procession reached the temple of Jupiter, on the Capitol Hill.

Treasures captured in battle

The procession was led by senators.

Internet link for a link to a website where you can find out more about Julius Caesar, go to www.usborne-quicklinks.com

THE LIFE OF CAESAR

Gaius Julius Caesar came from an old patrician family which claimed to be descended from the goddess Venus and the legendary hero Aeneas. He was a skilled politician, a talented public speaker and an outstanding general. Today, he is regarded as one of the most remarkable figures in Roman history.

A coin showing Julius Caesar

A RISING STAR

In 60BC, Caesar formed an alliance with Pompey and Crassus, and with their support he became consul the following year. After his year in office, he persuaded the Senate to give him command of Rome's lands in southern Gaul. This gave him a chance to prove himself, and soon he conquered the rest of Gaul, extending Roman territory as far as the English Channel. His popularity in Rome soared.

TROUBLE AHEAD

After the death of Caesar's daughter Julia, who was married to Pompey, the bond between the two men began to weaken. Afraid of Caesar's growing power, the Senate decided to support Pompey and turn the two men against each other. Caesar was ordered to give up his command in Gaul and return home without his army. If he refused, it would mean war.

TRIUMPH AND DISASTER

In January 49BC, Caesar defied the Senate and led his army across the Rubicon river into Italy. Pompey retreated to Greece, and Caesar took control of Rome. He defeated Pompey in 48BC and then crushed rebellions in North Africa and Spain. By 45BC, Caesar was the most powerful leader Rome had ever known.

Once in power, Caesar passed new laws to help the poor and improve the way Rome's lands were run. But he took decisions without consulting the Senate, and in 44BC he became dictator for life. Some politicians were worried that he had grown too powerful, and on March 15, 44BC, a group of senators stabbed him to death. Soon after, a civil war broke out which would finally bring the Republic to an end.

A scene showing the murder of Caesar, from a modern production of Shakespeare's play Julius Caesar

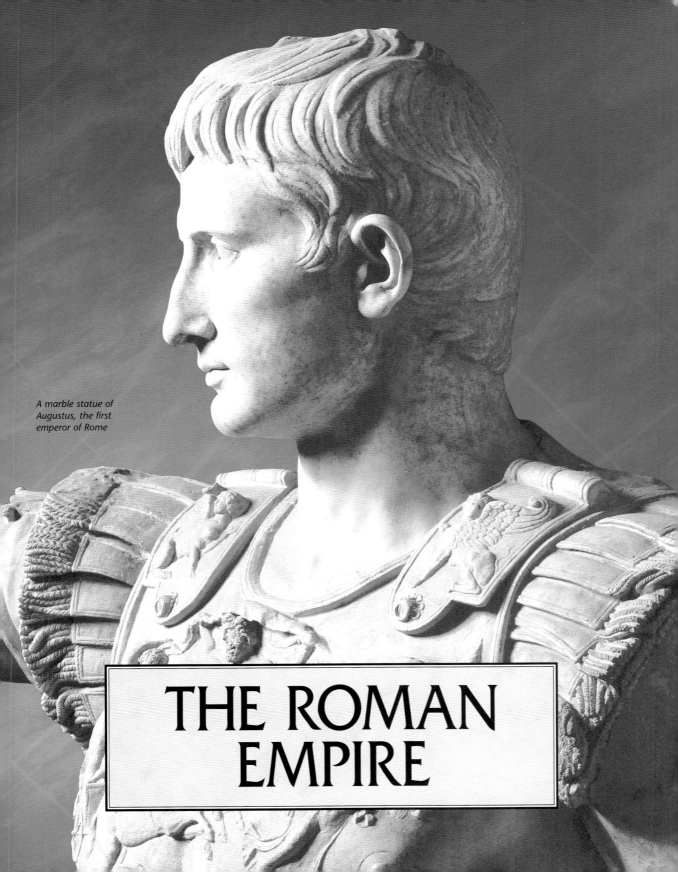

A marble statue of
Augustus, the first
emperor of Rome

THE ROMAN EMPIRE

Internet link for a link to a website where you can find out about the life of *Augustus and the growing Roman Empire, go to* **www.usborne-quicklinks.com**

THE BIRTH OF THE EMPIRE

After Julius Caesar's murder in 44BC, his friend Mark Antony seemed poised to become the next Roman ruler. Caesar's adopted son and heir, Octavian, was only 18, and most people assumed that he was still much too young to take power. But when Octavian heard of Caesar's death, he rushed to Rome, where he was welcomed by many people who had supported Caesar. Soon, a chaotic struggle for power began between the two groups.

A Roman coin showing a portrait of Antony

EARLY BATTLES

Mark Antony, by contrast, had many enemies in the Senate, and they managed to persuade the other senators to declare him an outlaw in order to stop him from gaining power in Rome. With the Senate's support, Octavian led an army against Mark Antony and defeated him at Mutina, in northern Italy.

Octavian then demanded to be made a consul, but the Senate refused, so he changed his plans. He joined forces with Antony and Lepidus - Antony's ally - and the three men stormed into Rome with a huge army. They forced the Senate to accept them as rulers, and executed thousands of their opponents. Lepidus soon retired, leaving Octavian and Antony in charge of Rome and its territories.

THE TWO RULERS

By 42BC, Antony and Octavian had crushed all their enemies and were free to rule. But they disliked each other so much that they couldn't work together, so they decided to divide up Rome's territory between them. Octavian ruled the western part, while Antony took the east.

This map shows how Antony and Octavian divided up Rome's lands.

Octavian's territory
Antony's territory

Many of Antony's ships were sunk.

The two sides tried to destroy each other's boats with metal rams.

This carving shows the Egyptian queen Cleopatra wearing a royal headdress.

For ten years, Antony lived in Egypt with Cleopatra, the Egyptian queen. Meanwhile, Octavian stayed in Rome, and made himself popular with the Senate and the people. The two rulers became more and more suspicious of each other, and the situation became very tense.

In 31BC, war finally broke out. Octavian defeated Antony and Cleopatra in the sea battle of Actium, off the western coast of Greece, and the despairing lovers fled back to Egypt. When Octavian pursued them there, they both committed suicide.

This scene shows part of the Battle of Actium.

Octavian had more ships than Antony, and used them to surround his opponent's fleet.

HAIL AUGUSTUS!

Octavian seized control of Egypt and became sole ruler of all the Roman lands. In 27BC, he offered to let the Senate take over, but this was just for show. Octavian was supported by the army, and everyone knew that only he could unite the Roman people. The Senate gave Octavian the new name Augustus, which means 'deeply respected one', and he gradually gained total control over the Roman world.

The Romans called Augustus by the military title *imperator*, from which we get the word 'emperor'. He is usually regarded as the first emperor of Rome, and the period of Roman history that began with his rule is known as the Empire.

Augustus ruled wisely and efficiently, bringing peace after decades of civil war. By the time he died in AD14, most people had accepted the idea of being governed by a single powerful ruler. The Republic was over forever.

A statue of Augustus wearing the uniform of a Roman general

Catapult

EMPERORS OF ROME

Augustus was the first in a long series of emperors who ruled the Roman world for over 400 years. Most emperors made a show of consulting the Senate, but in fact they had the power to rule exactly as they pleased. Even though the emperor controlled a huge empire, his life could be in danger if he became unpopular. Jealous rivals and assassins were never very far away.

BRUTAL BODYGUARDS

The emperor had his own special group of soldiers called the Praetorian Guard, whose job was to protect him and his family. However, these supposedly loyal bodyguards sometimes had their own ideas about who should rule Rome, and several emperors were actually murdered by their own protectors.

MAD, BAD AND DANGEROUS TO KNOW

After Augustus's death in AD14, the imperial family was plunged into a turbulent time of scheming and betrayal, and some of the emperors from this period behaved with extreme cruelty.

Augustus's stepson, the Emperor Tiberius (AD14-37), was a ruthless and corrupt man, and having power as the emperor made him worse. Worried that people were plotting to assassinate him, he executed dozens of important Romans and then fled to the island of Capri. He stayed there for the last 11 years of his rule, and any visitor he didn't like was thrown over the cliffs to his death.

This coin shows the Emperor Tiberius wearing a laurel crown - a symbol of military victory often worn by Roman emperors.

The next emperor, Caligula (AD37-41), may have been insane. He believed he was a god, and it was said that he tried to have his horse elected consul. He once made his soldiers attack the sea, because he was angry with the sea god Neptune.

Here you can see the actor John Hurt as the Emperor Caligula in the television production I, Claudius

The Emperor Nero, who was thought by many to have started the Great Fire of Rome

The Emperor Nero (AD54-68) was viciously cruel, and had his wife and mother murdered, as well as anyone who dared to oppose him. He also loved art, music and poetry, and shocked his people by playing the lyre and singing in public. (Musicians weren't considered respectable.) Nero's performances could be very long, and the audience was forbidden to leave before the end. Sometimes, people pretended to be dead so that they could be carried out.

THE YEAR OF THE FOUR EMPERORS

After Nero's death came a period of incredible turmoil. In AD69, Rome was ruled by no fewer than four emperors within a single year. The last of these emperors, Vespasian, was a general in the Roman army. With the support of his soldiers, he finally brought stability back to the Empire.

REASONABLE RULERS

Many emperors were sensible, fair rulers who did their best to keep an enormous empire running smoothly.

Tiberius's nephew, the Emperor Claudius (AD41-54), had been left crippled by a childhood disease, and most people thought he wasn't capable of ruling Rome. In fact, he turned out to be an excellent emperor, although he was eventually murdered. Some historians think his wife gave him poisoned mushrooms to eat.

The Emperor Claudius was a shy and nervous man, but an efficient ruler. He conquered Britain in AD43.

In AD96, Nerva became emperor, and ruled Rome and the empire wisely and fairly. After him came four capable emperors, and together these rulers are known as the five good emperors. They expanded the Empire, improved its organization, and won the support of senators by treating the Senate with respect.

PASSING ON POWER

At first, a man could only become emperor if he was related to the last ruler. But Nerva started a new tradition, when he chose and adopted the man he thought would be most suitable to rule after him. (See page 355 for a full list of Roman emperors.)

THE CITY OF ROME

Ancient Rome - the capital of the Empire and home of the Roman emperors - was a city of huge contrasts. As well as many huge, splendid public buildings, there were plenty of rickety, overcrowded apartment blocks, and while wealthy citizens enjoyed a life of incredible luxury, many ordinary Romans were desperately poor.

INTERNET LINK

For links to websites where you can explore an interactive map of the Roman Forum, and find out more about the great fire, go to www.usborne-quicklinks.com

CITY OF MARBLE

Rome was constantly changing, as each emperor tried to leave his mark on the city by putting up impressive new buildings and monuments. The Emperor Augustus spent huge amounts of money on transforming Rome completely, boasting proudly that he had found it a city of bricks and left it a city of marble.

At the heart of the city was the Roman Forum - a large, open space used as a market square and meeting place. Around the Forum, there were basilicas - large buildings used as law courts - and grand temples. Near one end was the *Curia* - or Senate House. As Rome grew, the Roman Forum was no longer big enough for everyone to meet, so some emperors built their own larger *fora* nearby.

Here, you can see a reconstruction of the Roman Forum at the height of the Empire.

WALKING THE STREETS

Most streets in Rome were extremely narrow, unbearably crowded and incredibly noisy. Carts were banned from the city during daylight hours to try and make more room, and shopkeepers displayed their goods in the streets. The main streets were swept clean, but the smaller alleys could be ankle-deep in waste. People often threw their refuse out of the window - an added hazard for anyone passing by.

NIGHT LIFE

As soon as dusk fell, an endless stream of delivery carts began rumbling through the city. Rome had no streetlights, so at night the city was plunged into darkness. Thieves and murderers lurked on street corners, and wealthy citizens wouldn't leave home without a group of slaves to guard them. The poet Juvenal joked that it would be foolish to go out after dark without first making a will.

The buildings were faced with thin slices of gleaming white marble.

The temple of Castor and Pollux was dedicated to the twin sons of the god Jupiter.

The temple of the goddess Vesta, where the Vestal Virgins kept a sacred fire burning

ON THE DOLE

By the first century AD, there were over a million people living in Rome, and many of them were too poor to survive without special help from the government. Rations of free grain - known as the corn dole - were handed out to the poorest 200,000 citizens and their families, so they could eat. Most of the grain came from Egypt, and if the grain ships were late arriving, violent riots could break out.

FIRE! FIRE!

Most Romans lived in flimsy apartment blocks heated by metal braziers filled with burning wood. Fire was a constant danger, so Augustus organized groups of firefighters - called *vigiles* - to tackle blazes in the city. But, equipped only with buckets of water and basic hand pumps, the *vigiles* couldn't cope with the largest fires.

In AD64, Rome was devastated by the worst fire in its history. Only four of the city's fourteen districts were left undamaged, and three were completely burned to the ground. At the time, many Romans blamed the Emperor Nero for starting the fire so that he could build himself a vast palace in the ruins of the city. Nero was said to have sung and played his lyre as he watched Rome burn, but in fact he may have tried to help put out the fires.

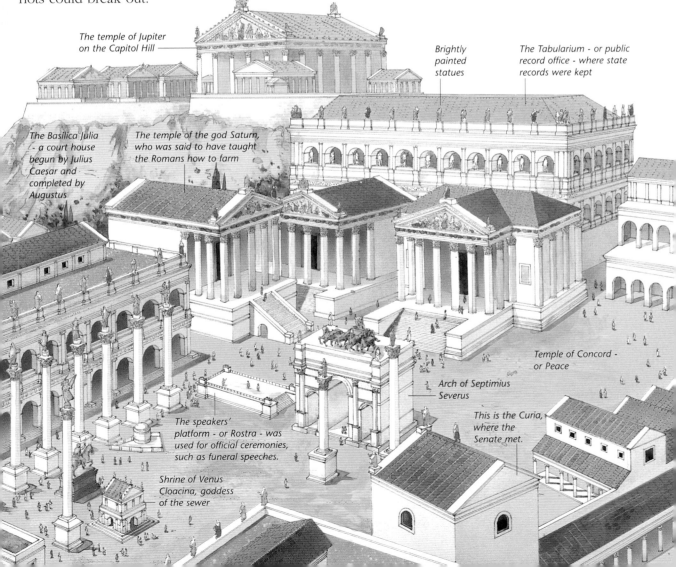

The temple of Jupiter on the Capitol Hill

Brightly painted statues

The Tabularium - or public record office - where state records were kept

The Basilica Julia - a court house begun by Julius Caesar and completed by Augustus

The temple of the god Saturn, who was said to have taught the Romans how to farm

Temple of Concord - or Peace

Arch of Septimius Severus

The speakers' platform - or Rostra - was used for official ceremonies, such as funeral speeches.

This is the Curia, where the Senate met.

Shrine of Venus Cloacina, goddess of the sewer

THE ROMAN ARMY

Without the mighty Roman army, the empire could never have been created at all. Well-trained and highly disciplined, this formidable fighting force was one of the most feared and successful armies in history. For hundreds of years, it seemed unbeatable.

Here you can see men dressed as Roman soldiers. The man in the plumed helmet is a centurion - an officer who led a century (a group of 80 men).

THE EARLY ARMY

In the early Republic, Rome didn't have a professional army. Only Roman citizens who owned land were allowed to fight for Rome, and very few of these were full-time soldiers. When a war started, thousands of men were called up, but they had to provide their own weapons and equipment, and they mostly returned home as soon as the fighting was over, to get on with their lives back in Rome.

Each century had a decorated staff, called a standard.

TURNING PROFESSIONAL

As the Romans began to fight wars overseas and expand their territory, they needed a bigger and better army to conquer faraway lands and control distant provinces. In the 2nd century BC, the army was completely transformed by a commander named Gaius Marius, who turned it into a full-time, professional fighting force.

INTERNET LINK

For links to websites where you can watch videos of soldiers training for battle and command a Roman legion of your own, go to **www.usborne-quicklinks.com**

MARIUS'S MULES

Marius allowed all Roman citizens to enlist, whether they owned land or not, and each man was given the same weapons and training. Soldiers also began to receive wages for the first time, so lots of poor men joined the army to earn a living. Marius made Roman soldiers carry so much heavy equipment that they became known as 'Marius's mules'.

ORGANIZING THE ARMY

The Roman army was divided into groups of 6,000 men, called legions. The soldiers, known as legionaries, were very well trained and highly organized.

A combat helmet made of bronze and iron worn by a Roman cavalry soldier

Every legion had a gold or silver eagle that was carried by a soldier called an aquilifer, shown in this bronze statue.

Most soldiers fought and travelled around on foot, but the army also had a cavalry - mounted soldiers who rode alongside the legions and could move ahead to surround enemies. (For more about the army's organization, see pages 356 and 357.)

WEAPONS OF WAR

The Romans fought most of their battles on open ground, attacking their enemies with javelins and swords. But the Roman army was also highly skilled at besieging and capturing cities. First, the soldiers surrounded the city so that no one could escape and no food or equipment could be brought in. Then, they used catapults to launch rocks at the defenders, and tried to demolish the walls with battering rams and siege engines.

FOREIGN FIGHTERS

The Romans recruited soldiers from all the areas they conquered, so the army had an almost endless supply of men. These foreign warriors, known as auxiliaries, often had special skills which made them useful. For example, warriors from the Middle East were skilled archers, and many other auxiliaries fought in the cavalry. By the 2nd century AD, there were more auxiliaries in the army than legionaries. When they retired, auxiliaries were given Roman citizenship as a reward for their loyalty and bravery in fighting for Rome.

This stone carving shows archers from the Middle East serving as auxiliaries in the Roman army.

A SOLDIER'S LIFE

Although the Roman Army is famous for its triumphs on the battlefield, there was much more to a soldier's life than just fighting. Many legionaries spent a lot of their time in camps and forts guarding the frontiers of the empire, or building roads and bridges to help the army move around quickly.

ON THE MOVE

In times of war, legions often had to march for many days to reach a battlefield. The soldiers marched at the same pace for hours, and covered up to 30km (18 miles) a day. When the ground was too boggy or hilly to use carts, they had to carry all their equipment on their backs. If there was no way across a river, they built their own bridge from tree trunks.

Marching soldiers were weighed down with weapons, food, cooking pots and tools for digging.

SETTING UP CAMP

When a legion was on the move, the soldiers stopped each night and built a camp. They dug a deep rectangular ditch with rounded corners, and used the soil from the ditch to make a rampart - or wall - all around the camp. They strengthened the rampart with sharpened wooden stakes, and then put up tents in neat rows. The next morning, the soldiers took everything apart and carried it away with them.

LIVING IN A FORT

In the 2nd century AD, the Romans realized they had conquered as much land as they could rule, so most legions were based at permanent frontier forts to protect the borders of the empire. Life in a Roman fort was strictly organized. Loud trumpet blasts rang around the fort to wake the men in the morning and to announce meal times. Each day, the legionaries were all given a new password, to prevent enemy spies from sneaking into the fort.

INTERNET LINK

For links to websites where you can tour a Roman fort and find online activities about a soldier's daily life, clothing and weapons, go to www.usborne-quicklinks.com

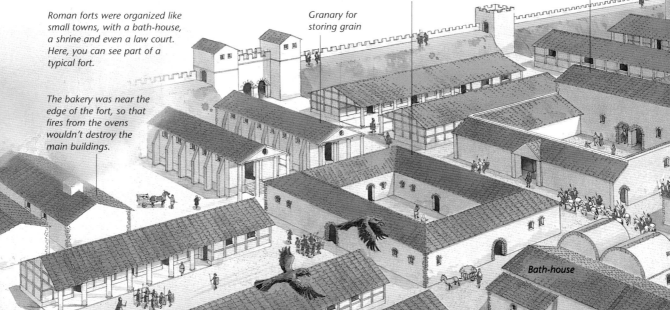

In the middle of the fort was the principia, or headquarters building.

There was always a large hospital, since it was vital to keep the soldiers healthy.

Granary for storing grain

Roman forts were organized like small towns, with a bath-house, a shrine and even a law court. Here, you can see part of a typical fort.

The bakery was near the edge of the fort, so that fires from the ovens wouldn't destroy the main buildings.

Bath-house

Soldiers fighting mock battles on horseback wore a metal mask and helmet like this.

GOOD AND BAD

Life held many advantages for a Roman soldier - good pay, the chance to keep captured treasure, and better medical treatment than most people received. Retired soldiers were given a large sum of money or a piece of land, and soldiers could also belong to a funeral club, which guaranteed them a proper burial for a small fee.

But there were disadvantages too. During a war, the men lived under the constant threat of injury or death, and in the long stretches of peace, life could become boring, especially since many soldiers served as long as 25 years.

The entire legion had to train every day - an exhausting routine of running, swimming, javelin-throwing and fencing. Soldiers also had to fight mock battles to prepare them for war. Discipline was very strict - if a soldier disobeyed his orders he was beaten, and if a whole legion tried to rebel, one in every ten men was killed.

MASTER BUILDERS

Many soldiers were not only skilled fighters, but also trained builders. In peacetime, they helped to construct canals, bridges and buildings in local towns, and they also built roads throughout the empire.

How a Roman road was made

Stone slabs formed the road surface.

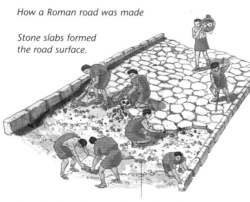

Beneath the surface were layers of sand, gravel and stones packed into a trench.

Roman roads were always as straight as possible, so that a legion could take the most direct route to a troubled area. Even today, many roads in Europe still follow the routes laid down by the Romans.

A high stone rampart surrounded the fort.

The commanding officer lived in a large house.

Each side of the fort had a heavily guarded gateway.

Most soldiers lived in small rooms in a barracks. Eight men had to share each bedroom.

Workshops where weapons were made

Ditches were dug around the rampart to make it harder to attack the fort.

EXPANDING THE EMPIRE

By the end of the Republic in 27BC, the Romans already controlled large areas of Europe, as well as parts of Africa and Asia. Conquering new lands brought Rome wealth and slaves, and emperors were always eager to win glorious victories. Over the next 150 years, Roman territory grew even more, until Rome ruled one of the biggest empires the world has ever seen.

INTO BRITAIN

Britain was first invaded in 55BC by Julius Caesar and his troops, but the native tribes refused to accept Roman rule, and Caesar eventually had to withdraw. In AD43, the Emperor Claudius finally succeeded in conquering the Britons. To celebrate this achievement, Claudius held a grand victory parade in Rome and named his son 'Britannicus'.

TRAJAN'S TRIUMPHS

The empire reached its greatest extent under the Emperor Trajan, who came to power in AD98. One of the most talented commanders in Roman history, Trajan led his legions on daring campaigns in regions far from the centre of the Roman empire and won huge new areas of land. First, he conquered the mountainous land of Dacia (present-day Romania). Then, he led a dangerous mission to the east, creating three new Roman provinces - Armenia, Assyria and Mesopotamia - in just four years.

By AD117, the empire was at its height. It stretched 4,000km (2,500 miles) from west to east, and was home to more than 50 million people. In Trajan's time, it was possible to travel all the way from the windswept moors of northern Britain to the sunbaked deserts of the Middle East without ever leaving Roman territory.

A statue of the Emperor Trajan

Map of the Roman Empire in AD117, showing all the provinces

BRITANNIA
GERMANIA INFERIOR
GERMANIA SUPERIOR
BELGICA
GALLIA LUGDUNENSIS
RAETIA
AQUITANIA
NORICUM
MOESIA INFERIOR
PANNONIA
DACIA
NARBONENSIS
DALMATIA
MOESIA SUPERIOR
BITHYNIA AND PONTUS
CAPPADOCIA
LUSITANIA
TARRACONENSIS
ALPES COTTIAE
ITALIA
ALPES MARITIMAE
THRACIA
ARMENIA
BAETICA
CORSICA
MACEDONIA
GALATIA
SARDINIA
EPIRUS
ASIA
MESOPOTAMIA
MAURETANIA CAESARIENSIS
SICILIA
ACHAEA
CILICIA
ASSYRIA
CRETA
Cyprus
SYRIA
MAURETANIA TINGITANA
LYCIA AND PAMPHYLIA
JUDEA
AFRICA
ARABIA
CYRENAICA
AEGYPTUS

Roman Empire at its largest

REBELLIOUS REGIONS

As the empire grew larger, it became harder to control, even with the mighty Roman army patrolling its frontiers. As early as AD9, Rome suffered a terrible shock when three whole legions were massacred by tribes deep in the forests of Germany. In AD60, the province of Britain was suddenly plunged into chaos when Boudicca, queen of the native Iceni tribe, led a daring and violent rebellion against the Romans occupying Britain. It took a year to crush the revolt.

A much later artist's view of Queen Boudicca, who poisoned herself after being defeated by the Romans

Another serious revolt broke out in AD66, in the Middle Eastern province of Judea. Thousands of Jews rebelled, so the Romans destroyed the Jewish capital city, Jerusalem.

Then, in AD73, the legions surrounded the remote mountain-top fortress of Masada, the last stronghold of Jewish resistance. After a siege that lasted an entire year, the Romans stormed the fortress, but found that most of the rebels inside had committed suicide rather than surrender.

HADRIAN'S WALL

In AD117, Hadrian became emperor, and immediately decided that the empire had grown too vast to control. So he gave up some of the land that Trajan had conquered, and built large permanent fortresses along the new frontiers. To defend Roman Britain against tribes invading from the north, Hadrian built a great wall stretching 130km (80 miles) across the province. Some sections of Hadrian's Wall are still standing today.

INTERNET LINK

For links to websites where you watch a short movie about Trajan, take a virtual tour of a fort on Hadrian's wall, and find out more about Boudicca, go to www.usborne-quicklinks.com

Here you can see part of Hadrian's Wall, in northern England.

RUNNING THE EMPIRE

The Roman empire was so vast, and was home to so many different peoples, that holding it all together from the centre was an enormous task. To make this easier, the Romans organized their territory into lots of different provinces, built a network of roads to link the provinces together, and based lots of soldiers near the empire's borders to keep out invaders.

KEEPING THE PEACE

The rule of the Emperor Augustus was the beginning of a 200-year period without any major wars inside the empire. The Romans kept this peace, known as the *Pax Romana*, with the help of their formidable army. Rebellions were crushed mercilessly and swiftly to serve as an example to others who might be thinking of rebelling. If barbarian tribes began gathering together armies outside the empire, the legions quickly launched an attack to break up the tribes and stop them from uniting against the Romans.

SHOWING RESPECT

Brute force alone wasn't always enough to control such a huge area of land, and the Romans also tried to keep the people they governed happy by treating them with respect. People in different areas were often allowed to continue following their own local customs and worshipping their own gods.

This stone carving shows a sun god from a temple in England. It combines elements of British and Roman gods.

INTERNET LINK

For links to websites where you can find an animated map of the expansion of the Roman Empire and learn about Roman roads, go to **www.usborne-quicklinks.com**

RUNNING THE PROVINCES

Each province was ruled by a governor, who usually came from Rome. Some governors and regions were more important than others. A few vital provinces were ruled by legates, chosen by the emperor himself, while other significant provinces were run by special governor appointed by the Senate.

Less important provinces were run by procurators, who were usually wealthy bankers or merchants. There were also many civil servants sent from Rome, who worked alongside the governor and helped him with running the provinces.

Early governors weren't paid, and some of them tried to use their important position to get rich by stealing precious works of art and taking bribes. To stop this from happening, the Emperor Augustus brought in a new system - from then on the governors were paid a salary, and officials were regularly sent out from Rome to check up on them.

KEEPING IN TOUCH

Roman roads were used by the army and by traders, but also by imperial messengers, who carried government information on horseback from one part of the empire to another. All the main roads had post-houses where messengers could stop when their horses were tired to to get fresh ones. In an emergency, news could travel as far as 240km (150 miles) within a single day.

A stone carving showing a Roman tax collector at work

Imperial messengers were sometimes attacked by rebels from native tribes. Here, you can see a messenger being ambushed by warriors.

COLLECTING TAXES

The Romans collected taxes from all over the empire, but people in the provinces had to pay much more than those who lived in Italy. At first, the money was collected by tax collectors, but many of these men were corrupt and kept lots of money for themselves. So the Emperor Augustus put the local governors in charge of tax collection.

The taxes helped to pay for the army and for public buildings, such as bath-houses and aqueducts. All this was very expensive and, despite the taxes, the State sometimes ran short of money. The Emperor Marcus Aurelius once had to sell some of his own furniture to raise funds.

CITIZENS OF THE EMPIRE

In 89BC, the Romans allowed anyone living in Italy to become a Roman citizen. Some provincial leaders were also given this privilege, but most people in the provinces were still classed as non-citizens.

The Emperor Caracalla

Then, in AD212, the Emperor Caracalla granted citizenship to every free man living within Roman territory. This gave people a sense of belonging, and helped to unite the different parts of the empire.

Internet link for links to websites with activities and information about Roman trade, go to www.usborne-quicklinks.com

TRAVEL AND TRADE

Travel was vital for the smooth running of the empire, and every corner of the Roman world was linked to the city of Rome by road, river or sea. Officials came to Rome with reports from distant provinces, important legal cases were brought to the city's courts, and trade goods of every description poured in from all over the empire and beyond.

Amber for precious objects, like this ring, came from the Baltic coast.

ON THE ROAD

The main purpose of Roman roads was for official business, such as moving troops and supplies around the empire or carrying messages to and from the emperor and his officials in distant places. But the roads were also used by ordinary citizens. Local traders took goods from town to town, while wealthy Romans made frequent trips to the country or the seaside.

Vehicles ranged from light, two-wheeled carriages to heavy, four-wheeled coaches big enough to carry a whole family. If the nearest town was too far away to reach in one day, people could spend the night at a state-run inn. But the rich often preferred to stay with friends, while some Romans took a tent with them or just slept in their carriage. They could also travel by horse or on foot.

IRELAND

BRITAIN

BALTIC SEA

GERMANIA

ATLANTIC OCEAN

GAUL

SPAIN

SARDINIA

Rome
Ostia

ITALY

SICILY

AFRICA

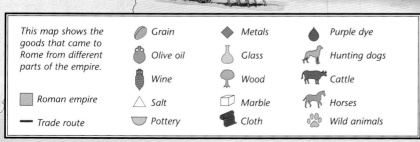

This map shows the goods that came to Rome from different parts of the empire.	Grain	Metals	Purple dye
	Olive oil	Glass	Hunting dogs
	Wine	Wood	Cattle
Roman empire	Salt	Marble	Horses
— Trade route	Pottery	Cloth	Wild animals

UNDER SAIL

Despite the excellent roads, it was often easier and cheaper to transport goods by boat. Where possible, the Romans sailed along rivers, but they also had a huge fleet of sea-going merchant ships, which carried goods all over the Mediterranean and as far away as India.

The Mediterranean could be very dangerous to cross, especially in winter. Ships frequently ran into terrible storms, and shipwrecks were common. Roman ships were strong, but they were clumsy and rather slow. With a top speed of only 7km (4 miles) an hour, a ship could take as long as three weeks to sail from Egypt to Italy.

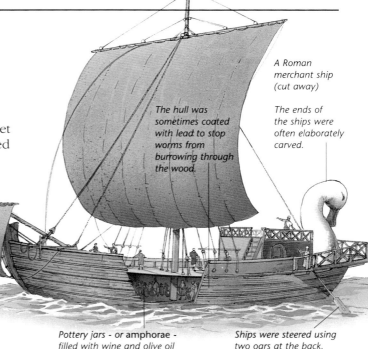

A Roman merchant ship (cut away)

The ends of the ships were often elaborately carved.

The hull was sometimes coated with lead to stop worms from burrowing through the wood.

Pottery jars - or amphorae - filled with wine and olive oil

Ships were steered using two oars at the back.

THE PORT OF OSTIA

Most merchant ships were too big to sail up the Tiber to Rome. Instead, they docked at the port of Ostia, at the mouth of the river. There, the cargo was unloaded onto barges and taken the final 25km (15 miles) upriver to Rome. As Rome's main seaport, Ostia was vital to the city's economy and was a busy place packed with merchants, shipbuilders and officials.

WAREHOUSE OF THE WORLD

By the time of the Empire, Rome was at the heart of a vast trading network. Such huge quantities of goods reached the city that one writer described Rome as the 'warehouse of the world'. While grain, olive oil and wine were the most important items, wealthy Romans could buy an array of luxury goods, such as ivory from East Africa, spices and gems from India and silks from China.

Pepper - the dried fruit of the pepper plant - was a very popular spice.

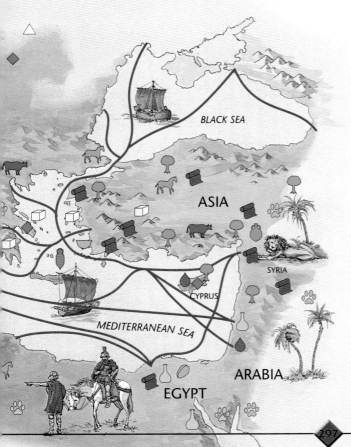

BLACK SEA

ASIA

SYRIA

CYPRUS

MEDITERRANEAN SEA

ARABIA

EGYPT

CRIME AND PUNISHMENT

Everyone in the empire had to obey the Roman laws, and these were usually very strict. People who committed crimes were punished severely, to try to discourage other people from breaking the law. The poor received particularly brutal punishments, which were often carried out in public, but rich and important citizens were normally treated less harshly.

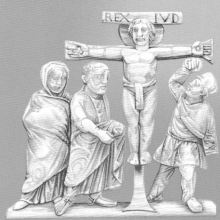

This ivory carving shows Jesus Christ being crucified. The Romans executed many people in this agonizing way.

ON TRIAL

Anyone accused of committing a crime was put on trial in the town law court, known as the basilica. There was a judge in charge of each trial, and a group of citizens - known as the jury - decided whether the accused person was innocent or guilty. At important trials, as many as 75 citizens could be asked to serve on the jury at the same time.

If the accused could afford it, he paid a lawyer to speak for him. Lawyers often made dramatic and emotional speeches on behalf of their clients, to win over the jury. Sometimes, people who were on trial smeared their hair with ashes and wore ragged clothes to make the jury feel sorry for them.

This is a sculpture of Cicero, the most famous of all Roman lawyers. His style of speaking and writing was imitated for centuries after his death.

PAINFUL PUNISHMENTS

When someone was found guilty of a crime, the judge decided what the punishment should be. Wealthy Romans who hadn't paid debts or taxes were often given huge fines. If they couldn't pay up, they lost their property and their citizenship. Other wealthy criminals were exiled to distant parts of the empire and forbidden to come home.

Many poor people were sold as slaves, forced to work in mines deep underground, or sent out into the arena to fight as gladiators. Some punishments were even worse, and lots of criminals were beheaded, torn apart by wild beasts, or put to death on a cross. (See page 365 for more about the legal system.)

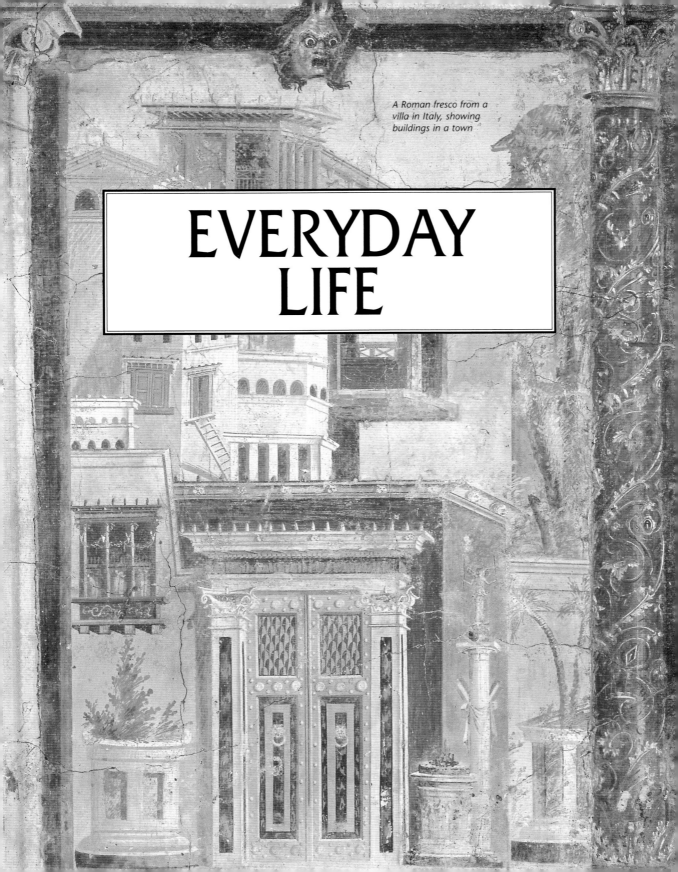

A Roman fresco from a
villa in Italy, showing
buildings in a town

EVERYDAY
LIFE

FAMILY LIFE

The family was an important part of Roman life, and most Romans took their duty to their families very seriously. Families were larger than we are used to today, and normally included the head of the family - known as the *paterfamilias* - his wife and children, his sons' wives and children, and all their slaves.

A FATHER'S POWER

It was a father's duty to look after his family and lead their worship of the household gods (see page 329). During the Republic, the *paterfamilias* was a very powerful figure. He had the right to whip or imprison his children, and could even put them to death or sell them as slaves. But most fathers were affectionate parents, and during the Empire it became a crime for a father to sell or execute his children.

CLIENTS AND PATRONS

As well as the family members who lived with him, a wealthy Roman would also have lots of supporters - or clients - who relied on his help. He was known as their patron. Clients were expected to visit their patron every morning, accompany him whenever he went out, and vote for him if he decided to enter politics. In return, he would sometimes lend his clients money, help them with their careers and occasionally ask them to dinner.

An engagement ring engraved with two clasped hands

WEDDINGS...

Young Romans didn't have very much choice about who they got married to. Their parents usually chose husbands or wives for them - often in order to make an alliance with another powerful or wealthy family. Girls could get married at the age of 12, but their husbands were often much older than this. When a couple became engaged, a family party was held, and the girl was given a ring for the third finger of her left hand.

A 19th century artist's impression of a couple making offerings on their wedding day

Garlands of myrtle were traditional at Roman weddings.

The night before her wedding, the bride offered her childhood toys to the gods at the household shrine. The next morning, she was dressed in a white tunic, a saffron-yellow cloak and shoes, and a flame-red veil. On her head, she wore a garland of flowers. When the bridegroom and guests arrived, an animal was sacrificed and a priest examined its insides to find out if the gods approved of the marriage.

Then, the marriage contract was read and signed - this gave details of the dowry to be paid by the bride's father to the groom. The bride and groom joined hands and made their vows. After a party at the house of the bride's family, the bride and groom led a procession of flute-players and torch-bearers to the groom's house. The groom carried his bride over the threshold, and the couple began their life together.

...AND FUNERALS

Death was commonplace in Roman families. Many women died in childbirth, and lots of diseases that are curable today were fatal in Roman times. When an important Roman died, the body was washed and covered in oil. If the person was a senator, he was dressed in his official robes. Then, the body lay on display for several days, so visitors could pay their last respects.

On the day of the funeral, the body was carried in a procession to the forum, where a speech was made in praise of the dead person. The body was then either buried or cremated. It was against the law to bury a person's body or ashes inside the city, so Roman tombs were always built outside the city walls.

When a body was cremated, the ashes were placed in an urn like this before being taken to the family tomb.

GROWING UP

Children from all but the poorest homes were brought up to serve the State and help to improve their family's position in society. Boys were trained for service in the army or the government, while girls were expected to marry well and produce children who would become loyal Roman citizens in their turn.

Marbles were made from glass or pottery.

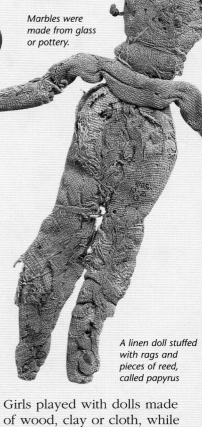

A linen doll stuffed with rags and pieces of reed, called papyrus

STARTING LIFE

When a child was born, its father would lift it in his arms to show that he accepted it into the family. Every Roman parent wanted a healthy baby boy - baby girls and sickly boys were sometimes left outside to die. Babies were named at eight or nine days old and were given a lucky charm - called a *bulla* - to ward off evil spirits. But many children died in the first few years of life - a woman might have as many as six or seven babies and still end up childless.

A gold bulla like this would have belonged to a child from a very wealthy family.

FUN AND GAMES

Roman children played a wide variety of games, Including hide-and-seek, leapfrog and hopscotch. A baby's first toy was usually a pottery rattle, often shaped like a bird, with small pebbles inside. Older children had toy animals to play with, as well as seesaws, swings, hobbyhorses, marbles and hoops for rolling along the ground.

Girls played with dolls made of wood, clay or cloth, while boys had wooden swords. Some lucky children even had miniature chariots pulled by goats or geese.

This carving shows a boy riding in a tiny chariot pulled by a goat.

INTERNET LINK

For links to websites where you can find out about different Roman ball games, and discover what life was like for Roman children, go to **www.usborne-quicklinks.com**

SCHOOL DAYS

Children from poor families had to go out to work at an early age, but families who could afford it sent their children to school when they were seven. Girls and boys were taught together at a school called a *ludus*, where they learned reading, writing and arithmetic. Younger pupils had to recite the alphabet and copy out simple proverbs, while older children read the works of Greek or Roman authors.

Many teachers and tutors were Greeks.

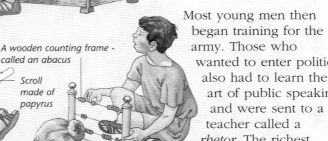

A wooden counting frame - called an abacus

Scroll made of papyrus

Small children scratched writing on pieces of broken pottery.

A scene in a typical Roman ludus

Most pupils wrote on a wax tablet using a pointed metal pen - called a stylus.

Pupils left the *ludus* at the age of 11. Boys could continue their education at a secondary school - or *grammaticus* - where they studied Greek and Roman literature, history, geography, astronomy, music, mathematics and athletics. Girls stayed at home and began preparing for marriage. Most Roman men didn't like their women to be too well educated - the poet Juvenal declared: "I hate a woman who reads."

A slave called a *paedagogus* took the children to school and kept an eye on them in class. Most schools only had about 12 pupils, and the school day lasted from dawn until noon without a break. Discipline was very strict, and beatings were common.

A portrait of a young girl holding a wax tablet and a stylus

BOYS TO MEN

When a boy was about 14, he officially became an adult at a special ceremony held in the forum. He put aside the clothes and *bulla* he had worn as a child and was given an adult's toga. He also had his first shave and was registered as a Roman citizen.

Most young men then began training for the army. Those who wanted to enter politics also had to learn the art of public speaking and were sent to a teacher called a *rhetor*. The richest families sent their sons away to Athens or Rhodes to study with the best Greek teachers who lived there. This training could continue throughout life - even an experienced politician would take time off work if a good teacher was in town.

ROMAN WOMEN

The ideal Roman woman was a good housekeeper, a caring mother and an obedient wife. She ran the home, took care of her children's early education, and supported her husband in his career. In theory, Roman women had very few rights, but most of them had lots of power behind the scenes.

These mosaic pictures show two Roman women exercising.

WOMEN'S RIGHTS

A Roman husband had the right to divorce his wife if she could not have children, if she became ugly or if she argued with him too much. He could even sentence her to death if she was unfaithful. A wife, on the other hand, could only divorce her husband if he deserted her, joined the army or became a prisoner of war. But although the law was very unfair, Roman history is full of examples of respectful and devoted husbands who got on well with their wives.

WORKING WOMEN

Not all Roman women could afford to stay at home and look after the family. Some had jobs as midwives or hairdressers, while many helped out in the family shop or farm. A few women worked as acrobats or dancers, but these jobs weren't considered respectable.

CHANGING TIMES

During Republican times, most women had large families and stayed at home, spinning and weaving cloth. But by the time of the Empire, some wealthy wives had different ideas about how they wanted to spend their time. Several Roman writers complained about idle women who neglected their duty to have children, and spent their time pampering themselves and attending dinner parties.

POWERFUL WOMEN

Rich women supervised large households with lots of slaves, and a wife often ran her husband's business while he was away. Many politicians' wives took an active interest in their husbands' careers. By crafty plotting and scheming, they made sure that their husbands succeeded in public life, and that their enemies were dealt with mercilessly.

A statue of Livia - wife of Augustus - who was famous for her ruthless scheming. She ended up being declared a goddess.

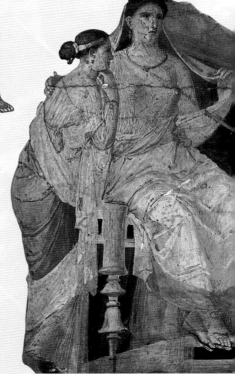

SLAVES AND FREEDMEN

Most Roman families relied on slaves to help them run their homes, keep their businesses going and farm their land. Slaves were usually bought from dealers or were born into a slave family - they had no rights and belonged entirely to their master or mistress.

HOUSEHOLD SLAVES

Many slaves worked in private homes, doing the household shopping, cooking and cleaning. They also served at meals and helped their mistress with her hair, her clothes and her makeup.

In this painting, you can see a slave arranging a girl's hair.

In many Roman homes, slaves were treated kindly, and sometimes the children of a trusted slave were brought up as companions for their master's children. In the country, slaves worked as labourers on farms, and in towns they helped in shops and workshops.

Slaves wore an identity tag inscribed with the name and address of their master.

EDUCATED SLAVES

Many slaves from Greece had a good education and were expensive to buy. They worked in wealthy Roman homes as private tutors, doctors and librarians, or were employed by the government. Well-educated government slaves helped run the empire, and they often rose to important positions.

A HARD LIFE

For many slaves, life was very hard. Some were made to work in appalling conditions in the mines, while others had to stoke the burning-hot furnaces in the public baths. Many worked on building sites, where they were given all the most dangerous jobs, and some trained as gladiators and had to fight to the death in the arena against wild animals or other gladiators.

A statuette of a slave cleaning a boot

BECOMING FREE

Slavery wasn't always for life, and some slaves were granted freedom as a reward for loyal service. Other slaves managed to save small amounts of money and buy their own freedom. Very occasionally, a gladiator was freed because he had fought bravely and survived many fights.

Freed slaves were given the status of 'freedmen' and could buy property and keep their own slaves. Under some emperors, freedmen could even become Roman citizens. Some of the emperor's freed slaves worked as his personal secretaries and gained great power in the Empire.

LIVING IN A TOWN

The Romans spread their way of life to all the areas they conquered, and built towns all over the empire. These towns had grand temples, bath-houses and arenas, as well as lots of shops and restaurants. The wealthiest Roman families owned elegant town houses, but most people lived in apartment blocks, which were called *insulae*.

HOME COMFORTS?

Apartment blocks could be up to seven floors high, and in poor areas of town they were often dark, crowded and dirty. Some of these buildings were so badly built that they collapsed without any warning, killing many of the people inside.

Most apartments had no running water or toilets, so many people used public lavatories. These were very sociable places where people sat side by side and chatted, but you had to pay to use them - poorer people simply used a bucket at home.

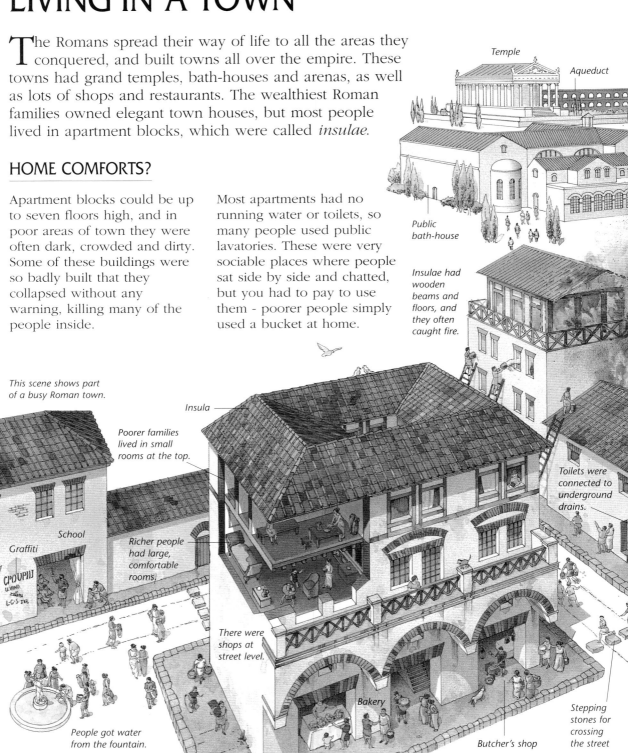

Temple

Aqueduct

Public bath-house

Insulae had wooden beams and floors, and they often caught fire.

Toilets were connected to underground drains.

This scene shows part of a busy Roman town.

Insula

Poorer families lived in small rooms at the top.

School

Graffiti

Richer people had large, comfortable rooms.

There were shops at street level.

People got water from the fountain.

Bakery

Butcher's shop

Stepping stones for crossing the street

RUNNING WATER

Each town needed lots of fresh water to supply its bathhouses, toilets and drinking fountains. This water was carried to the towns through a system of pipes and channels, called aqueducts.

STREET LIFE

Most towns had straight, paved streets laid out in a neat grid pattern. The main streets were broad, but there were many narrow alleys too. Often, the streets were full of waste, which people had thrown out of windows, so stepping stones were built to let people cross without getting filthy.

The streets of a town were lined with dozens of different shops, from butchers and fruit sellers to carpenters and sandal makers. There were also taverns and restaurants, as well as markets where people could buy anything from vegetables to slaves.

This photograph shows part of the ruined Roman town of Pompeii.

MEETING AND GREETING

In the middle of town was a large market square, or forum, where everyone could mingle. There, merchants bought and sold goods, taxes were collected, and people played games. The forum also had a raised platform where town officials stood to make speeches to the crowds.

Around the forum were statues, monuments and temples, and along one side was a huge building called a basilica. The basilica was used as a law court, a town hall and a public meeting place.

There were no drains upstairs, so some people threw their dirty water out of the window, though this was against the law.

Slaves for sale

Pharmacist's shop

Apartments had no stoves for cooking, so people bought hot food from snack bars.

Slaves did most of the shopping.

Sandals for sale

Rich people were carried around in litters.

INTERNET LINK

For links to websites where you can take a virtual tour of Pompeii, and see inside a merchant's home, go to **www.usborne-quicklinks.com**

307

A HOUSE IN TOWN

Most wealthy Roman families had a comfortable house in town. Although these houses varied in size, each house - or *domus* - followed the same basic design, and was sturdily built from stone, cement and wood. Houses were peaceful, private places, designed to keep cool in the hot Roman summers, but they were also designed to welcome visitors. Important people spent lots of money and made their homes look very grand to impress their guests.

INVITING INTERIORS

Although town houses looked quite plain from the outside, they could be lavishly decorated inside. The walls were smoothly finished with plaster and were often adorned with beautiful paintings known as frescoes. The floors were laid with stunning mosaics made from baked clay, glass or stone tiles. Lifesize statues in marble or bronze helped make the rooms look even more dramatic.

FURNITURE

Grand houses were extravagantly furnished with intricately carved marble tables, couches decorated with ivory and gold, and gleaming bronze lamp stands. Sometimes, the floors were covered with leopard skins or fine Egyptian rugs. However, most Roman houses had just a few simple pieces of wooden furniture.

"DO COME IN..."

A 19th century painting showing a Roman family welcoming guests in their atrium

A typical *domus* was arranged around a hall - called the *atrium* - where guests were received. The central part of the ceiling was open to the sky, and beneath the opening was an ornamental pool, known as the *impluvium*. The *atrium* usually had a shrine to the household gods as well.

Around the *atrium* were the dining room, kitchen and study, and the wealthiest homes also had a bathroom. (People who had no bathroom at home used the public bath-house.) The rooms next to the street were often rented out as shops.

Part of this Roman house has been cut away, so you can see inside.

The rooms at the front were rented by shopkeepers.

KEEPING WARM

Wealthy Romans had toilets and running water in their homes, as well as a central heating system, called a hypocaust. This ingenious Roman inventi on was powered by a furnace in the basement, and once the house heated up, it stayed warm for a long time.

IN THE GARDEN

At the back of the house was a peaceful walled garden called a peristyle. The peristyle was often planted with neat hedges, bay trees and rose bushes, and might be decorated with elegant statues, a fountain, or a fish pond. Romans loved to relax and chat in these tranquil, shady places, away from the hustle and bustle of city life.

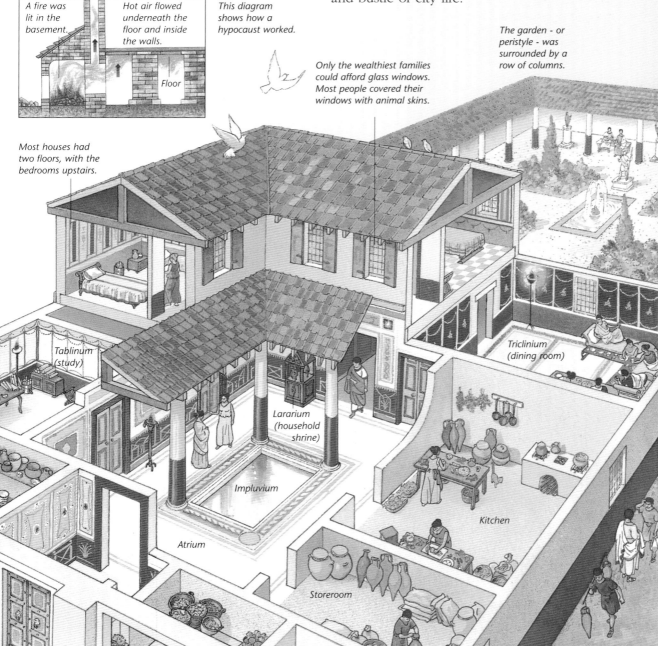

A fire was lit in the basement.

Hot air flowed underneath the floor and inside the walls.

Floor

This diagram shows how a hypocaust worked.

Only the wealthiest families could afford glass windows. Most people covered their windows with animal skins.

The garden - or peristyle - was surrounded by a row of columns.

Most houses had two floors, with the bedrooms upstairs.

Tablinum (study)

Triclinium (dining room)

Lararium (household shrine)

Impluvium

Atrium

Kitchen

Storeroom

LIVING IN THE COUNTRY

Although the Roman empire is famous for its towns, most people actually lived in the country. Many townspeople saw life in the countryside as a peaceful alternative to living in a crowded city. But the reality was anything but relaxing for most country people, and the slaves who worked on farms had to endure hours of backbreaking toil in the fields.

EARLY FARMS

In the early days of the Republic, most farms were small and family-owned. Farmers grew grain, grapes and olives, and kept a few sheep, goats, pigs and cattle. Most farmers produced just enough to feed their families, and any leftover crops were sold in local markets.

This statue shows a Roman farmer using oxen to prepare the land for sowing.

THE RISE OF THE LANDOWNERS

In the 3rd century BC, lots of farmers had to leave Italy to go and fight wars overseas. Many of these men never returned, and their farms fell into ruin. Other farms were devastated by wars in Italy itself.

Rich landowners bought up lots of these ruined farms, combined them to make large estates, and used slaves to work on the estates. Farming became very profitable, and the landowners were some of the wealthiest men in the Roman world.

SLAVES IN THE COUNTRYSIDE

By the time of the Empire, almost all farmworkers were slaves, and they did a variety of exhausting jobs. They had to plant and harvest crops with just a few simple tools, chop down trees to clear new fields, and look after animals.

One of the hardest jobs was being a shepherd. Sheep were often kept in remote highland areas, and the shepherd had to cope with loneliness, bad weather and thieves trying to steal his animals.

A reconstruction of a Roman estate

Fish was a very popular food, and many farms had a pond.

Shepherds often led lonely, isolated lives.

Sheep were kept for their wool and milk.

SUPPLYING THE CITIES

Roman cities depended on the countryside for food, building materials, and wood to burn. During the Empire, the most important farm products were grapes and olives - used to make wine and olive oil - and cereals, such as wheat, oats and barley. Farm animals provided townspeople with meat, milk, cheese and wool.

Wine was made by trampling grapes to squeeze out the juice, as shown in this stone carving.

Grapes were a very popular fruit, and were also used to make wine.

Crops such as fruit and vegetables were usually sold to local towns, but olive oil, wine and grain were exported in huge quantities to cities all over the empire. As Rome grew, farms in Italy could no longer provide enough grain to feed everyone. At the height of the Empire, two-thirds of Rome's grain was imported from Egypt.

Slaves cleared woodland to make new fields.

Farmers grew many different vegetables, such as lettuce, radishes, carrots and beans.

Pigeons were kept to use as food during the winter.

Olive oil was made by crushing olives in a machine like this.

Farmers kept flocks of chickens, ducks and geese for their eggs and meat.

Since the Romans had no sugar, food was sweetened with honey made by bees.

Oxen were used to push threshing machines that harvested wheat.

Pork was a popular meat, so farmers kept large herds of pigs.

A COUNTRY VILLA

Many wealthy Roman families had a large house - or villa - in the countryside, where they went to escape from the stress of city life and the hot summers in town. The family usually owned all the farmland around their villa, and made lots of money by selling produce from their farm.

EARLY VILLAS

The first villas, built during the Republic, were simple farmhouses surrounded by orchards, vineyards and fields for growing crops and keeping animals. Most of these farms were run by a manager, as the owner usually lived in town.

MAGNIFICENT MANSIONS

As Rome became more prosperous, and more people became wealthy, grand country villas were built all over the empire. The rooms of these villas were often decorated with beautiful mosaics and wall paintings, some of which survive to this day. Some rooms showed scenes of everyday life, while others depicted events from Greek or Roman mythology. The most luxurious houses also had underfloor heating, a bakery, a bath-house and even a swimming pool. The villas near Rome, owned by the most wealthy citizens, were particularly impressive.

This fresco from the villa of the Empress Livia shows a large Roman villa and part of its garden.

The villas of the wealthy were lit by intricately carved oil lamps like this.

Oil and a wick were placed in here.

Most villas were still part of a farm - or estate - but many were situated well away from the fields. A few of the largest villas had no connection with farming, and were built simply as lavish country homes. The nearby fields only grew food for the owner and his family.

The grandest villas had spacious gardens full of statues and ornamental pools. People relaxed in courtyards surrounded by elegant columns, and the silence was broken only by birdsong and the rippling water of fountains.

INTERNET LINK

For a link to a website where you can take a photo tour of a Roman villa in Germany and find out how the remains of the villa were discovered, go to **www.usborne-quicklinks.com**

This is an ornamental pool in the gardens of the Emperor Hadrian's villa, near Rome. Known as the Canopus, this part of the villa was inspired by a city in Egypt.

PEACE AND QUIET

Although the Romans were very sociable, they also valued the privacy of their country homes. The Roman writer Pliny remarked that he enjoyed not having to wear a formal toga at his villa. He also appreciated having no one living nearby: "There's peace and quiet all around, which is just as good for your health as the clear sky and pure air."

HADRIAN'S VILLA

One of the most amazing villas was built by the Emperor Hadrian at Tivoli, near Rome. Hadrian designed a group of impressive buildings including a stadium, a library and two bath-houses - all surrounded by splendid gardens. He based some of the buildings on sights he had seen during his travels to Egypt, Greece and other parts of the empire.

BESIDE THE SEASIDE

Some of the most attractive villas were situated on beautiful stretches of coastline, where their owners could spend summer days bathing in the sea. Fashionable Romans flocked to resorts such as Baiae, on the Bay of Naples, where several emperors built lavish villas. The Emperor Tiberius had no fewer than 12 villas on the island of Capri, just off the Italian coast.

FOOD AND COOKING

Some foods which we take for granted today, such as potatoes, tomatoes and chocolate, were unknown to the Romans. Likewise, many Roman dishes are unheard of now. The menu at a lavish banquet could include sows' udders, stuffed dormice and larks' tongues, though most people never ate such extravagant meals. A lot of the recipes which survive use simple meats and vegetables.

Glass bottles like these were used to store oils and sauces.

THREE MEALS A DAY?

Poorer Romans and slaves had to live on basic food, such as bread, porridge and stew, but wealthier people had a more varied diet. For breakfast, they ate a snack of bread or wheat biscuits with honey, and lunch was a simple meal of eggs, cheese, cold meat and fruit.

Many people hardly ate at all during the day, waiting instead for the evening meal. For average Romans, this was roast poultry or fish, but the wealthy often enjoyed lavish dinner parties.

INTERNET LINK

For a link to a website where you'll find a selection of tasty Roman recipes, go to **www.usborne-quicklinks.com**

WINE AND WATER

The Romans drank lots of wine, and people in Rome could choose from around 200 types which were made all over the empire. Wine was often spiced, or sweetened with honey, and was usually diluted with water - drinking it undiluted wasn't considered respectable.

In the early days of the Republic, women were forbidden to drink wine, but during the Empire this rule was dropped. Other popular drinks included grape juice and goat's milk, and people could also drink water from public fountains.

IN THE KITCHEN

A Roman kitchen was equipped with many of the same utensils that we use today - saucepans, cheese graters, and strainers to drain water away. These items were usually made of bronze, which can make food taste strange, so some expensive pans were coated with silver.

Food was boiled, fried, grilled, stewed, or roasted on a spit. With no freezers or cans to keep food fresh, it had to be smoked, pickled or salted to preserve it.

This scene shows slaves preparing a meal in a Roman kitchen.

Wine and oil were stored in tall earthenware pots called amphorae.

SPICES AND SAUCES

Rich Romans loved spicy food, and most of their meals were highly seasoned or eaten with a strong sauce. One of the most popular sauces was a thick, salty concoction called *liquamen*, made from pickled fish.

Because there was no chimney, smoke often billowed around the kitchen.

Most dishes were seasoned with herbs.

Meat was roasted on a spit.

Food was cooked in earthenware or bronze pots.

Charcoal was burned in the stove.

Slaves often spent all day preparing the evening meal.

Ingredients for sauces were ground up with a pestle and mortar.

EATING OUT

In towns, very few people did their own cooking. Most people lived in apartment blocks with wooden beams and floors, and it was forbidden to light cooking fires inside, in case the building burned down. Instead of cooking at home, people usually bought hot food, such as pies, sausages and stews, from snack bars in the street.

AT A DINNER PARTY

Wealthy Romans loved to eat fancy food and they often threw lavish dinner parties. Hosting a party was a great way for people to show off their wealth and power, and important Romans tried to outdo each other by making their banquets more and more extravagant.

THE PARTY BEGINS

A dinner party usually began in the early evening. The guests would remove their sandals at the door and have their feet washed by a slave, before being announced by an usher. They would then be shown to their places and have their hands washed with perfumed water. Having clean hands was important since people usually ate with their fingers.

Wealthy Romans reclined on cushioned couches while they ate - only slaves and children sat on chairs to eat. Men and women ate together, with up to nine people around the table, on couches arranged to form three sides of a square.

The host of the party sat here.

Romans didn't have forks, but they sometimes used knives and spoons.

People ate straight from a serving dish, rather than using plates.

Between courses, slaves washed the guests' hands with perfumed water.

This scene shows wealthy Romans at a dinner party.

The guests reclined on three couches.

Musicians entertained the guests.

FUN AND GAMES

Between courses, the guests were entertained by poets, musicians, conjurors or clowns, and after dinner there would often be games. For example, the host would pick a number, and everyone would have to swallow that number of drinks.

TABLE MANNERS

To show that they had enjoyed a meal, guests would belch loudly, and if they were too full to finish their food, they could wrap the leftovers in a napkin to take home. Really greedy guests would simply tickle their throats with a feather until they were sick, and then start eating all over again. The writer Seneca was disgusted by guests who indulged in this habit, and wrote scornfully: 'They vomit to eat, and eat to vomit.'

Beautifully decorated drinking cups like this were used at grand parties.

FRIGHTENING FEASTS

Guests had to be careful what they talked about at parties, as the emperor's spies were everywhere. If people were overheard criticizing the emperor, they might suddenly be tied up in chains and dragged away. Some parties were even more dangerous - the crazy emperor Elagabalus once smothered his guests to death with thousands of rose petals falling from the ceiling.

A 19th-century painting of Elagabalus's guests being smothered in petals. The petals were released from a net above the table.

MARATHON MEALS

A full Roman banquet was made up of seven courses, and could last as long as ten hours. It started with a few cold courses, such as eggs, sardines and mushrooms, before moving on to more exciting dishes, like dormice in honey, flamingoes' tongues or even elephants' trunks.

The way the food looked was just as important as how it tasted, and chefs particularly enjoyed disguising one type of food as another. The writer Petronius boasted that his chef could make a pig's belly look just like a fish.

Internet link for links to websites where you can print out and shade in pictures of Roman clothing and find out more about Roman fashion, go to www.usborne-quicklinks.com

FASHION AND BEAUTY

Looking good was very important to the Romans, and wealthy men and women spent a lot of time on their appearance. Fashions were often influenced by what the emperor and his wife wore, and people tried hard to keep up with the latest trends.

TUNICS AND TOGAS

The main garment for men was a tunic, made out of two rectangles of wool stitched together and tied with a belt. Underneath, men wore a loincloth - an ancient version of underpants made from a strip of wool or linen.

Most men wore short, undyed tunics like this.

Men often wore a cloak over their tunic.

Men and women wore open sandals made of leather.

Over their tunic, Roman citizens sometimes wore a toga - a large piece of woollen cloth wrapped carefully around the body. But the toga was so uncomfortable that it was usually only worn on important public occasions.

A statue of the Emperor Augustus wearing a toga

STOLAS AND PALLAS

Underwear for women consisted of a loincloth and sometimes a simple leather bra. On top of these went a long robe called a stola and a large rectangular shawl, known as a palla.

A woman in a bright silk stola

Women often wore their palla draped around their shoulders.

The palla could also be looped over the head like a hood.

During the Empire, fashionable Roman ladies began to wear brightly dyed stolas and pallas, made from Indian cotton or Chinese silk. These materials were incredibly expensive, and silk was literally worth its weight in gold.

STATUS SYMBOLS

Clothes were an important way of showing a person's status, and there were strict rules about what different people were allowed to wear.

Only Roman citizens could dress in a toga - foreigners and slaves were forbidden to wear one. Purple was the most expensive dye, and only the wealthiest people could afford it. Senators wore a toga with a broad purple stripe, but it was a crime for anyone except the emperor to dress entirely in purple.

HAIR CARE

For most of the Roman era, men were clean-shaven and had simple, short haircuts - although the Emperor Hadrian later started a fashion for beards. Most men went to the barber every morning for a shave. This was a good opportunity to hear the latest gossip, but it was also very painful because barbers didn't use any soap or oil to protect the skin. Some men removed the hair from their arms and legs too.

During the Republic, women usually tied their hair in a simple bun, but in later times many had extremely elaborate hairstyles. Their hair would be curled with heated tongs, then arranged in an intricate pile on top of the head, held firmly in place by dozens of hairpins. Some women cut off a slave's hair and had it made into a wig.

This statue shows a popular women's hairstyle from the 2nd century AD. The poet Juvenal mocked hairstyles like this, saying they made women look much taller from the front than the back.

RINGS ON THEIR FINGERS

Rich Roman men and women wore lots of expensive rings, sometimes several on each finger. Wealthy women also wore a glittering variety of gold and silver brooches, bracelets, necklaces and earrings, studded with precious stones and jewels.

A gold ring set with a carved gemstone

A necklace set with emeralds and mother-of-pearl

A pair of intricately carved earrings, shaped like dolphins

A bracelet shaped like a snake

AMAZING MAKEUP

A wealthy Roman woman would spend hours every morning being made up by her slaves. It was fashionable to look pale, so women whitened their faces and arms with powdered chalk. They used ash to darken their eyebrows, and painted their lips red with plant dye. Some even used a face cream made from crushed snails.

Wealthy women wore perfume, which they kept in beautiful bottles like this.

Internet link for links to websites where you can spend a day at the Roman baths and find out more about them with online activities, go to www.usborne-quicklinks.com

AT THE BATHS

Very few Roman houses had a bathroom, so most people made a daily trip to the public bath-house. But a visit to the baths involved much more than just a good wash. The largest bath-houses were vast leisure complexes where people could exercise, meet friends, discuss business and politics, or simply relax.

POOLS OR PALACES?

By AD300, the city of Rome had 11 public baths - or *thermae* - and about 1,000 privately owned bath-houses where people could bathe in greater privacy. Some emperors built spectacular public baths, gleaming with gold and marble, to show off their wealth and power. The most impressive baths were those built by the Emperor Caracalla, which could hold up to 1,600 people at a time.

PAYING YOUR WAY

Entrance to the baths was extremely cheap, especially for men, who were only charged a *quadrans* - the smallest Roman coin. Women had to pay four times that amount for entry, but children got in free. Wealthy politicians sometimes tried to bcome popular and win votes by paying everyone's bath fees for a day.

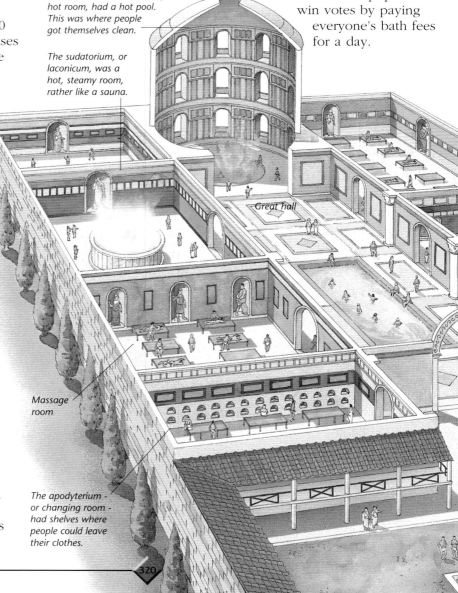

The caldarium, another very hot room, had a hot pool. This was where people got themselves clean.

The sudatorium, or laconicum, was a hot, steamy room, rather like a sauna.

Great hall

This reconstruction shows the different rooms in a Roman bath-house.

Massage room

The apodyterium - or changing room - had shelves where people could leave their clothes.

BATH TIME

The baths were usually open from mid-morning until sunset, and most Romans went every day - women in the morning and men in the afternoon. For most of the Roman period, mixed bathing was considered scandalous.

WORKING OUT

Many Romans began their visit to the baths by working up a sweat in the exercise yard - or *palaestra*. Men enjoyed weight-lifting, wrestling, fencing and ball games, while women played a game called *trochus*, which involved rolling a metal hoop with a hooked stick.

GETTING CLEAN

The Romans didn't have soap, so instead they smeared their bodies with perfumed oil. The oil was then scraped off, along with the dirt, using a curved stick called a *strigil*. Scraping yourself wasn't easy, so wealthy Romans usually brought a slave to do the scraping for them.

This is a metal strigil - the long, curved end was scraped over the skin.

THE HOTTEST SPOT IN TOWN

The baths were heated by a central heating system, or *hypocaust*. Hot air, warmed by a furnace in the basement, ran under the floors and inside the walls. Some of the floors were so hot that people had to wear wooden-soled sandals to stop their feet from getting burned, while the slaves who stoked the furnaces often fainted from the heat.

Bath-houses often had a public toilet, like this, where people sat together and chatted.

"...AND RELAX!"

Roman men often stayed at the baths until closing time. After their bath, they could buy a snack at one of the food stalls, then stroll in the gardens, read quietly in the library, or listen to a concert or poetry recital. Some sat in the shade playing board games, such as chess or backgammon, or gambling with dice.

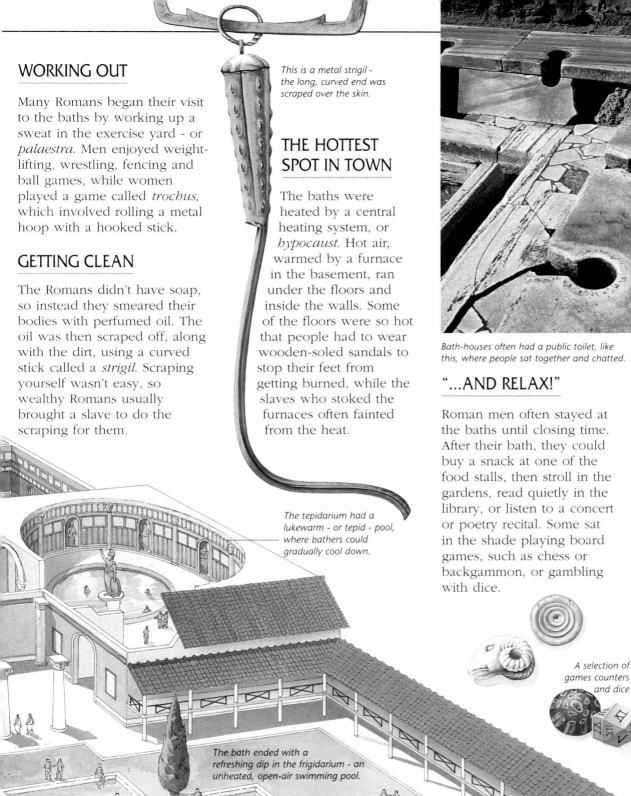

The tepidarium had a lukewarm - or tepid - pool, where bathers could gradually cool down.

The bath ended with a refreshing dip in the frigidarium - an unheated, open-air swimming pool.

A selection of games counters and dice

AT THE GAMES

Most Roman citizens had a lot more free time than people do today, because most of the heavy work was done by slaves. In fact, there were so many slaves working in Rome that many poorer Romans couldn't find jobs at all. To keep people entertained - and leave them less time for stirring up trouble - the emperor put on bloodthirsty shows known as 'the Games', where people could watch fights between armed gladiators and wild-beast hunts.

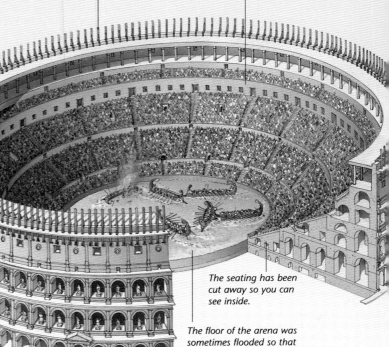

On sunny days, a huge awning was hung from poles around the top of the Colosseum.

Women weren't allowed to sit with men. They had to watch from behind this wall.

The seating has been cut away so you can see inside.

The floor of the arena was sometimes flooded so that gladiators could take part in mock sea battles.

THE GROWTH OF THE GAMES

Gladiator fights were originally held as part of ancient funeral ceremonies. But during the Republic, politicians realized they could win votes by putting on lavish shows, and the number of days given over to games grew. By imperial times, there were 93 days of games in the year, and more were added by emperors eager to make themselves popular.

The Games took place in a huge stone stadium with an oval arena in the middle. The largest stadium in the empire was the Flavian Amphitheatre in Rome - now known as the Colosseum - which could hold up to 50,000 people at a time. It had a maze of tunnels underneath the floor, where wild animals were kept before a show.

A BEASTLY PASTIME

A day at the arena began with a grand parade of gladiators, musicians, dancers, jugglers and priests. Then, the wild beasts were brought out. Rare animals were put on display or were made to perform circus tricks. According to the Roman historian Suetonius, one emperor introduced the amazing spectacle of tightrope-walking elephants.

Most animals were forced to fight each other or were hunted down with spears, daggers, bows and arrows. Sometimes, unarmed criminals were dragged into the arena to be torn to pieces by lions, tigers or bears.

In beast hunts, like the one shown here, as many as 5,000 animals might die in a single day.

GLADIATORS

Gladiator fights took place in the afternoon. Most gladiators were slaves, criminals or prisoners of war who were forced to fight each other, but some were paid volunteers. A very small number of gladiators were women. There were many types of gladiators, each with different weapons and costumes, and different types were usually pitted against each other.

Gladiators often fought to the death, although anyone who was badly wounded could appeal to the emperor for mercy. After consulting the crowd, the emperor gave a signal with his thumb. Experts think the 'thumbs up' sign meant that the gladiator should be allowed to live.

Victorious gladiators received money and a crown, and those who survived long enough could become rich and famous - a little like today's rock stars. After many victories, a gladiator might be given a wooden sword, which meant that he was a free man. Many freed fighters became trainers at special gladiator schools.

The retiarius fought with a net and trident.

The murmillo was a heavily armed gladiator who wore a helmet crowned with a fish.

The Samnite carried a sword and shield, and wore a helmet with a visor.

The Thracian had a curved dagger and a small, round shield.

INTERNET LINK

For links to websites where you can prepare a gladiators for battle, see their weapons and tour the Colosseum, go to www.usborne-quicklinks.com

AT THE RACES

Chariot races were originally part of religious festivals, but soon became incredibly popular as entertainment. Races were held at specially designed racetracks, called circuses, and regularly attracted huge crowds. The largest racetrack was the Circus Maximus in Rome, which could seat 250,000 people - more than any sports stadium in the world today.

THE DAY BEGINS

Only Roman citizens and their families could go to the races, and people started arriving at dawn to get a good seat. Unlike at the Games, men and women were allowed to sit together. The poet Ovid wrote that the circus was a good place to find a girlfriend or boyfriend!

The spectacle began with a parade, as musicians led in the official who was to start the races. This might be an important senator, or even the emperor himself on special occasions. He and his attendants were followed by singers, and priests carrying images of the gods.

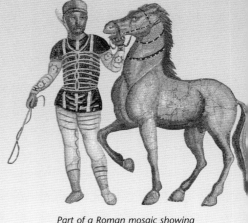

Part of a Roman mosaic showing a champion driver and his horse

Chariots raced around the central barrier - or spina - which had three pillars at each end.

The poorest citizens stood at the back.

Marble seats for senators

Imperial box

"...AND THEY'RE OFF!"

At the blast of a trumpet, the official in charge raised a white cloth and let it fall to the ground. The starting gates at one end of the track flew open, and the drivers charged out on their lightweight chariots, racing counter-clockwise around the track.

The chariots were normally pulled by two or four horses, but for added excitement six or eight horses might be used. The more horses there were, the harder the chariot was to control. To stop themselves from falling off, drivers wound the reins around their bodies. Each driver wore a light helmet and carried a dagger, so he could cut himself free from the wreckage if his chariot overturned.

TAKING THE CORNER

The most hair-raising part of the race came as the drivers turned the tight corner at each end of the track. Jostling for position, they tried to stay as close as possible to the central barrier - or *spina*. Chariots often collided, resulting in spectacular crashes, and it was quite common for drivers to be badly injured or even killed.

FAME AND FORTUNE

Most drivers were slaves, but some were professionals who were paid large amounts of money to compete. Race winners were rewarded with more money, a palm leaf of victory and, of course, instant fame. The life of a chariot-driver was glamorous, but could be short - many drivers died in their early 20s.

TEAM SPIRIT

Most chariot-drivers belonged to one of four teams - red, blue, white or green - and the best drivers were idolized by their team's supporters. Fans placed bets on their favourite team before a race, and cheered their drivers on noisily. Passions ran so high that serious riots sometimes broke out between rival groups of supporters.

The palm leaf was the Roman symbol of victory.

Here you can see chariots rounding the corner in a race at the Circus Maximus.

At the end of each of the seven laps, a marker in the shape of an egg or a dolphin was turned over.

Up to 12 chariots competed in each race, with as many as 24 races in a day.

This Egyptian monument, called an obelisk, was brought to Rome by the Emperor Augustus.

The track measured 550m x 180m (1,800ft x 600ft).

PLAYS AND PANTOMIMES

The idea of drama came from Ancient Greece, and plays based on Greek tragedies and comedies became popular in Rome during the 3rd century BC. But the Romans gradually developed their own style of drama - one that could compete with the thrills and spills of chariot races and gladiator shows.

TRAGEDY AND COMEDY

The first plays seen in Rome were translations of Classical Greek plays - both tragedies and comedies. Tragedies were about Greek gods and heroes, while comedies dealt with ordinary people. Roman writers soon began adapting these plays to make them more interesting for a Roman audience. The most famous playwrights are Plautus and Terence, whose comedies were popular during the 2nd century BC.

DRAMATIC CHANGES

At first, plays were staged in temporary wooden buildings, as part of a festival for a god or goddess, and the whole building was taken down as soon as the festival was over. The first permanent auditorium in Rome - the Theatrum Pompeii - was built in 55BC, and similar buildings were soon put up in towns all over the empire.

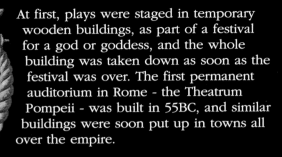

Plays were accompanied by music performed on instruments such as the lyre.

Classical plays, with their complicated plots and dialogue, remained popular among some educated Romans, but most people wanted something much less demanding. So speeches were cut and plays were reduced to a series of songs sung by a chorus, with actors miming the action. This type of drama was called pantomime.

MASKS AND COSTUMES

Each play featured the same kind of characters, such as the 'wise old man' or the 'smiling fool', and the actors wore striking masks to show which character they were playing. Female characters wore pale masks, but behind the masks all the actors were men.

Different characters could also be identified by the actors' robes - red for a poor person, purple for a rich citizen and white for an elderly character.

In this mosaic, a group of actors is getting ready to perform a play. The man on the left is being helped into his costume.

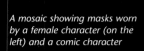

A mosaic showing masks worn by a female character (on the left) and a comic character

MIME OR MURDER?

During the Empire, a style of drama known as mime became very popular. Mime actors wore normal clothes, without masks, and women were allowed to take part. Plays were either very rude or very violent, and the action was as realistic as possible.

At the end of one particular play, a criminal took the place of an actor and was actually tortured to death on stage.

STARS OF THE SHOW

The Romans didn't think acting was a respectable profession, so actors were usually slaves or freedmen.

But famous actors were treated like heroes, and some became so popular that they were mobbed by their fans. Women weren't allowed to sit near the stage, in case they were tempted to run off with one of the performers.

INTERNET LINK

For a link to a website with a reconstruction of a Roman auditorium and more information about Roman plays, go to **www.usborne-quicklinks.com**

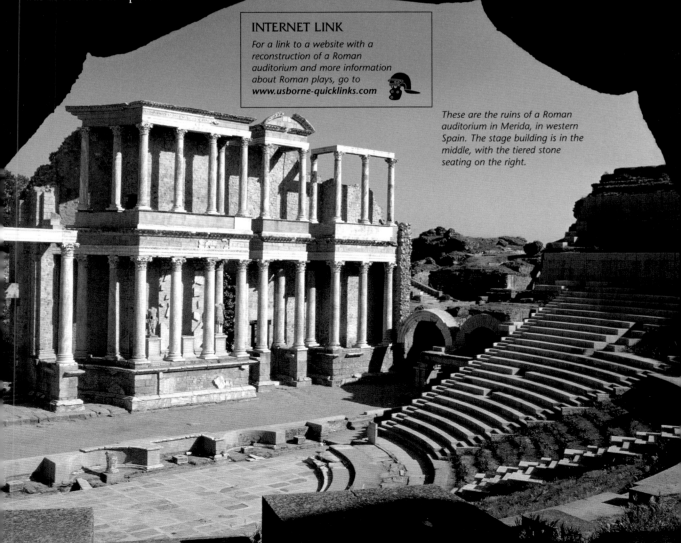

These are the ruins of a Roman auditorium in Merida, in western Spain. The stage building is in the middle, with the tiered stone seating on the right.

GODS AND GODDESSES

The Romans had two kinds of gods - the powerful gods and goddesses of the state religion and the friendly household spirits who protected their homes. Temples were built for important state gods, and people were expected to attend public sacrifices. At home, the Romans prayed to their own household spirits and offered them simple gifts.

MANY GODS

There were dozens of Roman gods and goddesses, but the three most important ones were Jupiter, Juno and Minerva. Most Roman gods were borrowed from the Greeks - Jupiter was originally the Greek god Zeus, Juno was Hera and Minerva was Athene.

Each god controlled a different aspect of life or nature. Jupiter ruled the sky, Juno was the goddess of women, and Minerva looked after soldiers and school children. There were even household spirits responsible for things as small as mildew. You can see a list of Roman gods on page 358.

The Romans believed that thunderstorms were caused by their chief god, Jupiter, hurling thunderbolts from the sky.

MAKING SACRIFICES

Offerings to the gods ranged from simple cakes and flowers to elaborate statues, but the most popular gifts were animals. Sacrificing a valuable animal was meant to show the gods how much people cared about them. Priests sacrificed oxen, sheep, pigs and doves on open-air altars in front of temples.

Once the creature had been killed, its internal organs were taken out and examined. The Romans believed that this would help them find out the will of the gods. Then, the organs were burned on the altar, and the rest of the meat was served up as a feast for the god's followers.

Bacchus was the god of wine. This statue shows him with bunches of grapes entwined in his hair.

PRIESTS AND PRIESTESSES

Most Roman priests had other jobs too, and by the time of the Empire, the chief priest - or *Pontifex Maximus* - was the emperor himself. But one group of priestesses - the Vestal Virgins - devoted most of their lives to their goddess. Vesta was goddess of the hearth, and the Vestal Virgins kept a constant fire burning in her temple in Rome.

A priest leading a bull to be sacrificed outside a temple

One of the leading Roman priests was the *Flamen Dialis*, or Priest of Jupiter. His life was made very complicated by a huge number of rules. For example, he couldn't touch or even talk about goats, ivy or beans.

INTERNET LINK

For links to websites where you can find out about lots of Roman gods and goddesses, and test your knowledge with online quizzes, go to www.usborne-quicklinks.com

FESTIVALS

Religious festivals took place throughout the year, but especially at sowing and harvest times. Some festivals were very solemn occasions, but others were great fun. During the mid-winter feast of Saturnalia, masters waited on their slaves, people exchanged gifts, and a mock-king ruled over the merrymakers.

EMPEROR GODS

Very soon after the Emperor Augustus died, he was declared a god by the next emperor, Tiberius. After this, many emperors became gods when they died, and statues were put up all over the empire so people could worship their past rulers.

Praying to dead emperors was really just a way of showing respect for Rome, but the Emperor Caligula actually believed he was a god. According to the Roman historian Suetonius, Caligula often dressed up as Jupiter and even carried a metal thunderbolt to make himself seem more frightening.

GODS AT HOME

In their own homes, the Romans prayed to two main groups of gods. The *lares* were spirits who protected the home, while the *penates* looked after the larder and the food cupboards.

A statuette of a lar, guardian of the home

Each house had a shrine - called the *lararium* - where the family held daily prayers and offered food and wine to their gods. On special occasions, such as birthdays and weddings, the spirits were given extra gifts.

The lararium shown here was found in a house at Pompeii. The family would have placed their gifts in front of the statuettes.

BELIEFS AND SUPERSTITIONS

By the time of the Empire, most Romans felt that the worship of the state gods had become formal and empty, but this didn't mean that religion was dead. People still believed that gods and spirits could affect their lives, and the Romans saw signs - or omens - everywhere.

A bronze sculpture of a hand covered with symbols to ward off evil spirits

SIGNS AND SUPERSTITIONS

The Romans were incredibly superstitious. They believed that some days were unlucky, and that owls, snakes and black cats were messengers of disaster. Even educated Romans were terrified of ghosts. People wore lucky charms to ward off evil spirits, and performed complex rituals to bring themselves good fortune.

TELLING THE FUTURE

People tried many ways of looking into the future. Priests named augurs interpreted the patterns made by birds, clouds and stars. Soothsayers carefully inspected the entrails of sacrificed animals for signs of disease which might spell bad fortune. Army generals tried to predict success in battle by watching the way sacred chickens ate their food, and anxious emperors questioned astrologers to learn if they would be assassinated.

At times of national crisis, the Romans consulted the writings of the Sibyl of Cumae. She was a wise woman who lived in a cave at the time of the Roman kings and claimed to be able to see into the future.

FOREIGN FAITHS

By the 1st century AD, many people were looking for a faith that would give their lives more meaning, and thousands of Romans turned towards the religions of the Middle East.

Unlike the Roman state religion, these foreign faiths had strict rules on how their followers should try to live. They also offered believers the promise of life after death, which the Roman religions did not.

MOTHER GODDESSES

Romans throughout the Empire became passionate followers of Isis, from Egypt, and Cybele, from Turkey. These powerful mother goddesses attracted mainly female followers, and their priests held elaborate rituals on the themes of death and rebirth. Worship of Isis became especially popular after the Egyptian queen Cleopatra spent a year in Rome in 45BC.

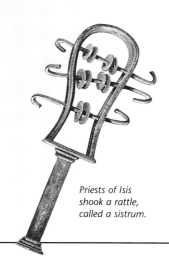

Priests of Isis shook a rattle, called a sistrum.

This picture shows a ceremony outside a temple of the Egyptian goddess Isis.

Temples were decorated with Egyptian-style statues.

The chief priest chanted prayers to Isis.

Sacred birds called ibises were kept at the temple.

Priests played musical instruments and sang songs.

MIGHTY MITHRAS

Followers of the Persian god Mithras met in underground temples and suffered terrifying ordeals, such as being locked in a coffin for several hours. Only men could worship Mithras, and his religion was especially popular with the Roman army.

Here, Mithras is shown slaying a sacred bull, whose blood was believed to have given birth to the Earth.

JEWS AND CHRISTIANS

The Middle Eastern religions of Judaism and Christianity each had a single god, which meant that their followers couldn't worship the Roman gods as well. This led to fierce campaigns against Christians and Jews in the empire. Thousands of Christians were persecuted and put to death, and the Emperor Hadrian tried to get rid of Judaism completely.

CELTIC GODS

In the Celtic countries of Britain and Gaul (present-day France), the Romans prayed to many native gods, and sometimes combined these gods with their own Roman deities. But the Romans loathed the Celtic priests - called druids - because they performed human sacrifices, and also because they encouraged the Celts to resist Roman rule.

INTERNET LINK

For links to websites where you can take a virtual tour of a temple of Mithras and watch a slide show about Roman religious beliefs, go to www.usborne-quicklinks.com

HEALING THE SICK

In Roman times, no one knew exactly what caused diseases, so if people became sick they often blamed evil spirits, or thought that the gods were punishing them. The Romans tried many ways to cure themselves from their illnesses, including asking their gods for help.

SPELLS AND PRAYERS

Many Romans tried to drive away diseases by chanting magic spells, or by praying to Aesculapius, the god of healing.

Offerings like this model leg and eye have been found in temples of Aesculapius. They were either thanks for a cure or reminders of a request for healing.

Some people were so desperate for a cure that they spent all night in the temple of Aesculapius in Rome. They hoped that the god would visit them in a dream, and show them how to make themselves well.

HERBAL MEDICINES

This carving shows a pharmacist's shop. Unusually for Roman times, the pharmacist is a woman.

Most Roman medicines were made from herbs and plants. In the early days of the Republic, people brewed their own medicines, using traditional recipes, but by the time of the Empire pharmacists had set up shops selling ready-made herbal remedies.

Pharmacists ground up plants and minerals with a pestle and mortar and made them into pills or sticks of ointment to sell to people. They also made a kind of alcoholic cough mixture by combining wine and herbs.

Rosemary was used in remedies for bad eyesight.

INTERNET LINK

For links to websites where you can read about Roman doctors, medicine and remedies, and try to solve a mysterious death, go to **www.usborne-quicklinks.com**

VISITING THE DOCTOR

Wealthy Romans paid for a doctor to come to see them in their house, but most people had to visit the doctor themselves. Medical treatment wasn't free, but in AD100 a state health service was set up, so the poor could see a doctor free of charge.

Surgeries were held in shops or private rooms, and patients lay on a couch while a doctor examined them. Doctors prescribed herbal medicines, advised on a healthy diet, and recommended exercise and visits to the baths. However, they also believed in the helpful effects of blood-letting, and drained away cupfuls of their patients' blood.

Sage was an important ingredient in cough mixture.

EYES AND TEETH

Some doctors specialized in treating eyes. They made sticks of eye ointment from lead, zinc or iron and even performed operations to remove cataracts. Dentists extracted rotten teeth, and supplied false ones to fill in the gaps.

False teeth made from ivory or bone were attached to a gold band which wouldn't rust.

SCARY SURGERY

Surgeons who had trained in the army performed basic operations in state hospitals. These doctors were expert at sawing off limbs and setting bones, but they were less successful at what we would see as simple operations, such as removing an appendix.

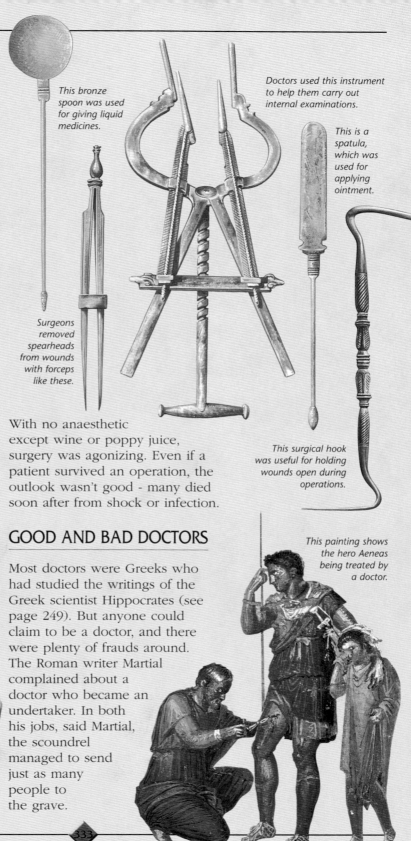

This bronze spoon was used for giving liquid medicines.

Surgeons removed spearheads from wounds with forceps like these.

Doctors used this instrument to help them carry out internal examinations.

This is a spatula, which was used for applying ointment.

This surgical hook was useful for holding wounds open during operations.

With no anaesthetic except wine or poppy juice, surgery was agonizing. Even if a patient survived an operation, the outlook wasn't good - many died soon after from shock or infection.

GOOD AND BAD DOCTORS

Most doctors were Greeks who had studied the writings of the Greek scientist Hippocrates (see page 249). But anyone could claim to be a doctor, and there were plenty of frauds around. The Roman writer Martial complained about a doctor who became an undertaker. In both his jobs, said Martial, the scoundrel managed to send just as many people to the grave.

This painting shows the hero Aeneas being treated by a doctor.

Mustard seeds were used to treat snakebites.

Fennel was supposed to calm the nerves.

Lemon balm was believed to cure headaches.

Garlic was given to soldiers to keep them healthy.

CRAFTS AND TRADES

All the heavy work in a Roman town was done by slaves, so ordinary citizens had to earn their living in other ways. Most townspeople worked as shopkeepers or craftworkers, and Roman towns and cities were filled with bustling shops and workshops.

SHOPKEEPERS

Each town had several bakers, butchers, fishmongers, olive oil sellers and wine merchants, who supplied people's daily needs. The baker was especially important because everyone needed fresh bread each day.

In this picture of a busy baker's shop, the roof has been cut away so you can see inside.

CRAFTWORKERS

Roman craftworkers produced a huge variety of goods, ranging from basic clothes and tools to fancy goblets and statues. Usually, the craftworkers were men, but Roman wives and daughters also helped in the family workshop. Sons learned their trade by working with their fathers, but slaves were kept to do the nastiest jobs.

A carving of a knife-maker and his wife at the counter of their workshop

The same essential craftworkers were found in every town. Carpenters made beds, tables and storage chests, potters produced a range of basic pots and dishes, while smiths shaped tools, pans and weapons from iron, copper and bronze.

The baker served his bread from a counter at the front of the shop.

Wheat was ground into flour in a mill.

The flour was mixed with yeast and water to make dough.

The bread was baked on shelves above a roaring fire.

CLEANING CLOTH

Most Romans took their woollen cloth to the fuller's workshop, where it was cleaned and treated before being made into clothes. First, the cloth was stiffened by soaking it in urine, and then it was cleaned by rubbing it with a kind of clay, known as fuller's earth. After this, the cloth was beaten, stretched and bleached to make it soft and white. Fullers also cleaned and mended clothes for the richer townspeople.

Here you can see a fuller soaking cloth in urine.

GREAT GLASS

By the 1st century AD, the Romans had learned how to blow glass. Some glaziers made simple glass jars and sheets of glass for windows, while others produced exquisite goblets and dishes from delicate patterned glass. Precious glass objects were used at grand dinner parties, or were placed in graves as funeral offerings.

Glass bowl and flask from the 1st century AD

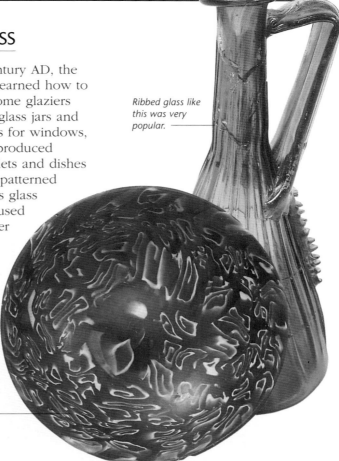

Ribbed glass like this was very popular.

Swirls of white glass

LUXURY CRAFTS

As well as the everyday craftworkers, there were also many fine artists who specialized in luxury goods. Goldsmiths and silversmiths produced elaborate necklaces, flasks and ornaments, ivory carvers made intricate covers for writing tablets, and engravers carved delicate cameos for brooches and rings.

This cameo was carved from a gemstone called sardonyx. It shows the Emperor Tiberius.

CRAFT CLUBS

Each Roman trade and craft had its own *collegium* - a kind of social club which held regular meetings and occasional banquets. Belonging to a *collegium* was a great source of pride, and members who contributed to their club's burial fund were given a dignified funeral and an impressive tombstone.

AFTERNOONS OFF

Although the Romans worked hard at their trades and crafts, they also made sure that they enjoyed themselves. By the end of the 1st century AD, most city shops and workshops closed in the afternoon, leaving their owners free to enjoy themselves at the baths, the games or the races.

INTERNET LINK

For links to websites where you can take an interactive journey to Londinium and find out more about Roman trade, go to www.usborne-quicklinks.com

BUILDERS AND ENGINEERS

All over the empire, Roman builders and engineers constructed vast public buildings, bridges and water systems. These magnificent structures were certainly built to last - many Roman buildings are still standing today.

INCREDIBLE CONCRETE

In the 2nd century BC, the Romans invented concrete - an amazing new building material that was strong, light and easy to use. It was made by mixing volcanic ash with water, and then adding stones to give it extra strength.

Cutaway picture of a Roman wall filled with concrete

At the top, the concrete was mixed with small, light stones.

Hollow wall built from bricks

At the base, the stones in the concrete were larger and heavier.

By filling the walls of their buildings with concrete, the Romans could build tall, strong structures that were light enough not to collapse under their own weight. These buildings were often faced with stone or marble to make them look beautiful.

ROUNDED ARCHES

Roman buildings are famous for their rounded arches - a feature that was copied from the Etruscans. These arches are surprisingly strong because each stone in an archway pushes hard against the stones next to it, which helps to hold the arch together.

Here you can see how a Roman arch was built around a wooden frame.

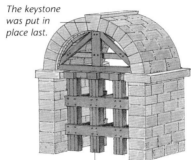

The keystone was put in place last.

The frame was removed once the arch was completed.

BUILDING BRIDGES

The Romans used arches to build huge public buildings and to construct bridges that spanned wide valleys. Building a bridge was an engineering challenge that required very careful planning.

This picture shows a simple Roman bridge being built.

VIADUCTS AND AQUEDUCTS

Some of the most stunning achievements of the Roman engineers were their multi-layered bridges, known as viaducts and aqueducts. Viaducts carried roads high above the ground, while aqueducts carried water in raised stone channels. Amazingly, some of these structures are still being used today.

Roman aqueducts formed part of a complex system of pipes and channels that delivered water from mountain springs direct to the towns and cities. Some of the Roman water systems were over 40km (25 miles) long. Because they relied entirely on gravity, the water in them had to flow downhill all the way. This is why aqueducts were needed, to keep the water high up so that it could get over hills.

1 First, the builders laid a temporary bridge across a row of boats.

2 Next, they drove a ring of wooden stakes into the river bed.

The Pont du Gard aqueduct in southern France was part of a system that carried mountain water to the city of Nîmes.

WATER FOR ALL

Once the water reached a city, it was collected in huge tanks and fed through a network of lead pipes into the public fountains, toilets and baths. Only wealthy people could afford to have water piped to their homes, but some resourceful Romans attached their own illegal pipes to the public water system.

STUPENDOUS SEWERS

Roman engineers designed elaborate networks of underground drains to take away sewage and waste from their cities. The most famous Roman sewer was the *Cloaca Maxima* in Rome. It was so enormous that one city engineer made his tour of inspection by sailing a boat through it.

INTERNET LINK

For links to websites where you can design your own aqueduct and find out more about Roman tools and building skills, go to **www.usborne-quicklinks.com**

A wooden crane was used for lifting and lowering building materials.

4 When the columns were tall enough to support the bridge, wooden frames were nailed between them.

3 Water was pumped out of the ring of stakes, and blocks of stone were placed inside, forming a set of solid columns.

5 Once the frames were complete, wooden planks were laid over them, and the bridge was ready to use.

AMAZING ARCHITECTURE

The elegant temples of the Greeks were an inspiration to Roman architects, and the builders of the Republican period copied the Greek style closely (see pages 212-213). But by imperial times, the Romans had developed their own style of architecture, along with new building techniques. Throughout the Roman world, grand public buildings were erected to celebrate the glory of Rome.

COPYING THE GREEKS

Greek temples were rectangular in shape with an outer row of columns supporting the roof, and most early Roman temples followed this plan. But the Romans tried to make their temples grander than the Greeks', by raising them up on a platform and increasing the size of the inner room - or *cella*.

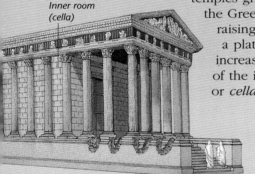

Inner room (cella)

In most Roman temples the outer columns, known as the peristyle, were attached to the cella.

(see pages 212-213)

USING ARCHES

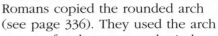

Arch *Vault*

From the Etruscans, the Romans copied the rounded arch (see page 336). They used the arch for doorways and windows, and for high, curved roofs, called vaults. They also used arches as a frame to build the first circular domes.

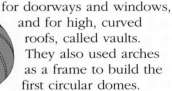

Dome

By the 2nd century AD, the Romans had learned how to build a roof from a series of crossed vaults supported by columns. This meant that they could create huge rooms inside their basilicas and bath-houses.

Crossed vaults

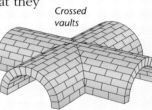

(see page 336)

The Romans copied the three types of columns used by the Greeks, but made them chunkier and more richly decorated. They also created two styles of their own - Tuscan and Composite.

Types of columns used by the Romans

Ionic (Greek)

Tuscan (Roman)

Corinthian (Greek)

Doric (Greek)

Composite (a Roman combination of Corinthian and Ionic)

The Greek Corinthian style of column, shown here, was the most popular.

BIG BUILDINGS

By using arches, domes and vaults combined with lightweight concrete (see page 336), the Romans could build huge structures that were both light and strong. Every Roman city had a set of public buildings - temples, bath-houses, basilicas and arenas - all built on a grand scale with massive walls and pillars, rounded arches and roofs, and large, airy rooms where many people could gather together.

This is the Pantheon in Rome, an enormous temple devoted to all the gods. Its vast dome, measuring 43m (140ft) across, was the largest in the ancient world.

TRIUMPHAL ARCHES

All over the empire, the Romans built grand triumphal arches and set up victory columns topped by statues. These impressive monuments were intended to celebrate great Roman victories, and their marble sides were covered with carvings showing battles, heroes and scenes from the glorious history of Rome and its empire.

INTERNET LINK

For links to websites where you can see amazing reconstructions of Rome's ancient buildings and take a photographic walking tour of Rome's ruins today, go to **www.usborne-quicklinks.com**

PAINTING AND SCULPTURE

The Romans loved to decorate their buildings with dramatic paintings and sculpture. Even quite humble homes had striking wall paintings, and Roman towns and cities were filled with larger-than-life statues of emperors, generals and gods.

A bronze sculpture of a middle-aged Roman, showing him as he really looked

ART EDUCATION

The Romans learned their love of art from the Greeks (see page 216-217). When they started to conquer Greece, they were amazed by the treasures they found, and seized thousands of Greek carvings and statues to send back to Rome. Soon, it was fashionable to collect Greek art, and many Greek sculptors set up studios in Rome, to copy earlier masterpieces and produce new works for Roman tastes.

CHANGING FACES

By the time of the late Republic, sculptors had started to create realistic portraits in bronze, stone or marble. These statues were partly based on the death-masks of the Etruscans - likenesses made by taking a cast from the face of a dead person. They showed people as they really were - double chins, wrinkles, warts and all.

Around the beginning of the 1st century AD, the Emperor Augustus introduced a new, idealized style for portraits of leaders, and for the next 300 years emperors and generals were shown as handsome, calm and commanding. However, ordinary people continued to be portrayed in a realistic way.

In this marble statue, the Emperor Marcus Aurelius appears noble and dignified.

INTERNET LINK

For links to websites where you can watch movies and see examples of Roman sculpture and art, go to **www.usborne-quicklinks.com**

SCENES IN STONE

Like the Greeks before them, the Romans carved dramatic scenes in stone and marble, but Roman sculptors concentrated on events from the glorious history of Rome. Roman carvings usually look crowded and action-packed, with lively figures set against dark, dramatic shadows.

A carved scene from Trajan's Column showing Roman soldiers in battle

By the time of the Emperor Constantine, Roman sculptors had lost much of their earlier inspiration. Although some fine work was still produced, many later Roman carvings show flattened, stumpy figures arranged in rigid ranks.

Fruit from a fresco in a Roman town house

PAINTED WALLS

Roman temples, palaces and villas were all decorated with frescoes - a kind of mural that is painted directly onto the wall while the plaster is still wet. Frescoes are very long-lasting and many Roman paintings have stayed remarkably bright and clear.

The subjects of Roman frescoes ranged from imposing arches and columns to exotic landscapes, gardens and country scenes. In temples and grand houses, artists showed gods and goddesses, while the walls of middle-class homes were often painted with scenes from daily life.

PAINTED PORTRAITS

Many Romans paid for their portraits to be painted on wooden panels or on the walls of their houses, and some Roman homes had whole galleries of ancestors. Portraits were believed to contain the spirit of the person they portrayed, and if someone was disgraced, their face would be scratched out.

This Roman portrait was found attached to a coffin in Egypt.

MAGNIFICENT MOSAICS

Roman mosaics were made from thousands of cubes of stone, marble, pottery or glass. These tiny cubes, or *tesserae*, were pressed into wet cement to make a flat, patterned surface which was very hardwearing. Many Roman mosaics still look magnificent today.

PATTERNS AND SCENES

Mosaic floors were laid in temples, palaces and villas, and their subjects ranged from simple, geometric patterns to elaborate scenes. Many mosaics depicted myths and legends, but scenes from daily life were also a popular subject. Sometimes, a mosaic was designed to suit the particular room it was in - some Roman dining rooms had a floor that looked just like a pond of tasty fish.

A mosaic of a musician beating a tambourine

SPECIAL EFFECTS

Creating a picture from thousands of tiny cubes is a difficult and awkward job, but Roman mosaics were often very realistic. By using a range of subtle shades, with highlights and shadows to create a feeling of shape, the craftsmen really made their subjects come to life.

By the 4th century AD, Christian artists were using mosaics to decorate their churches. Some of these churches look very dramatic, with glittering figures of saints and angels covering their ceilings and walls.

This stunning mosaic ceiling was created for a church in Ravenna, Italy.

MAKING MOSAICS

This picture shows a mosaic border being laid.

The master craftsman drew up a plan for his assistants to follow.

Simple mosaics were laid on site, but the more elaborate pictures were assembled in a workshop inside a wooden frame. When a picture was completed, the frame was taken to the site and set in position. Then a decorative border was laid around it.

INTERNET LINK

For links to websites where you can take a fly-through of a Roman villa and see close-ups of Roman mosaics, go to www.usborne-quicklinks.com

342

THE END OF THE EMPIRE

A 6th-century mosaic from Ravenna in Italy, showing
Theodora, the wife of the Byzantine Emperor Justinian

THE EMPIRE WEAKENS

For 150 years, the mighty Roman Empire seemed unbeatable, but by the mid-2nd century AD, it was showing signs of strain. The Emperor Marcus Aurelius spent most of his reign fighting off invaders, and caused widespread resentment by raising taxes to pay for the army. To make matters worse, in AD166 a terrible plague spread from the east, plunging the empire into chaos. For the first time, people began to doubt the power of Rome.

Here, Septimius Severus is shown with his family. One of his sons, Caracalla, murdered the other, then ordered that his brother's image be removed from all pictures. You can see the smudge where his face used to be.

TROUBLED TIMES

After Marcus Aurelius died in AD180, things became much worse. His son Commodus ignored the attacks on the empire's borders and squandered huge sums of money arranging public games and races. Commodus was assassinated and his successor lasted only three months before he was murdered too.

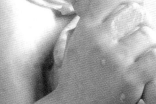

The Emperor Commodus loved to fight in the arena. He is shown here dressed as the mythical warrior Hercules.

In AD192, the Praetorian Guard sold the job of emperor to the highest bidder, but the winner was soon replaced by Septimius Severus, an army commander. Severus was an efficient emperor who defended the empire's borders for 14 years. He was followed by three more members of his family, but each of them was assassinated, and civil war broke out in AD235.

THE ANARCHY

In the 50 years between AD235 and AD284 there was a series of over 20 emperors, most of whom were murdered. During this turbulent period - known as the Anarchy - the Empire was also struck by plague and famine. Taxes and prices rose, life got much harder for farmers and traders, and many people became outlaws to escape taxation.

Some Roman governors took advantage of the chaos to seize power for themselves. For eight years, Postumus, the governor of Lower Germany, controlled his own empire in western Europe, and set up an independent Senate in the German city of Trier.

ATTACKS ON THE EMPIRE

During the Anarchy, the Roman empire was often under attack from Germanic tribes in the north and Sassanian Persians in the east. The lowest point came in AD260, when the Emperor Valerian was captured by the Sassanians, who later stuffed his body with straw and displayed it in one of their temples.

Sassanian warriors fought with long, heavy spears.

This scene shows Roman troops defending the empire against Sassanian invaders.

The Roman soldiers and horses were less well protected than their opponents.

THE EMPIRE DIVIDES

In AD284, a general named Diocletian was proclaimed emperor by his troops. Realizing that the empire was too large for him to control, he split it in two, and ruled the eastern half himself, while another general, Maximian, became emperor in the west. Each emperor chose a deputy to help him rule - the emperors took the title of 'Augustus' while their deputies were known as 'Caesar'.

Map of the Roman empire at the time of Diocletian

Diocletian increased the size of the army by a third, and built up a mobile fighting force which could move swiftly to crush rebellions. He divided the empire into smaller provinces and made sure that they were run efficiently. Diocletian worked hard at restoring the status of the emperor, declaring himself a god and always taking care to appear remote and godlike. He wore a pearl crown, and made visitors kneel and kiss his robe.

A NEW CAPITAL

In AD305, Diocletian and Maximian retired, and their two deputies became the new emperors. But this arrangement didn't last long, and eventually Constantine fought his way to power. Constantine reunited both halves of the empire, but concentrated on the east. He moved the empire's capital to Byzantium, at the entrance to the Black Sea, and renamed the city Constantinople.

THE RISE OF CHRISTIANITY

The Christian religion began when a Jew named Jesus started preaching in Judea, a small Roman province in the Middle East. After Jesus died, around AD30, his followers continued to spread his teachings, and by the end of the 1st century AD Christianity had reached as far as Rome itself.

SPREADING THE WORD

Jesus taught that people should give up their old, sinful ways, and devote their lives to God and to helping other people. The followers of Jesus believed that he had risen from the dead and hoped they would have eternal life too. These beliefs attracted many Romans, and Christianity became especially popular with poor people and slaves.

KEEPING SECRETS

Many powerful Romans were suspicious of the new religion, so most early Christians kept their faith a secret. They met in private houses, and used secret signs to show other Christians that they shared the same faith.

In this portrait of an early Christian family, there is a Christian symbol above the child's head.

In Rome, groups of Christians gathered in the catacombs - a series of tunnels under the city that were used as burial vaults. But all this secrecy only encouraged wild stories about the mysterious Christians and their strange ceremonies.

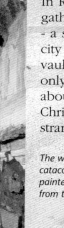

The walls of the catacombs were painted with scenes from the Bible.

PUNISHMENT AND PERSECUTION

Because the Christians believed there was only one god, they refused to worship the emperor or the state gods. This made some emperors see them as rebels against Rome and the empire.

The Emperor Nero blamed his Christian subjects for the Great Fire of Rome, claiming that they had made the gods angry, and he sent hundreds of Christians into the arena to be torn apart by wild animals.

Other emperors also had Christians arrested, tortured and killed, but the Emperor Diocletian carried out the most savage persecution. In AD303, he began executing thousands of Christians for refusing to give up their faith.

This scene shows a group of Christians being attacked by wild animals in the arena.

CONSTANTINE AND THE CHRISTIANS

In AD312, Constantine became sole ruler of the Western Roman empire after defeating his rival for the throne at the Battle of the Milvian Bridge. Before the battle, Constantine saw a cross of light in the sky, which he believed was a sign from Christ.

Constantine was the first Roman emperor to allow Christians to worship openly. He gave Christians important jobs, paid for their churches, and made sure that his new capital at Constantinople was a Christian city. Finally, on his deathbed, Constantine was baptized as a Christian.

Part of a colossal statue of the Emperor Constantine which originally measured over 15m (50ft) high

CHRISTIANITY GROWS

About 25 years after Constantine's death, the Emperor Julian tried to bring back the state gods, but it was too late to stop the spread of Christianity. All the emperors after Julian supported the Christians, and in AD391 the Emperor Theodosius declared that Christianity was the empire's official religion.

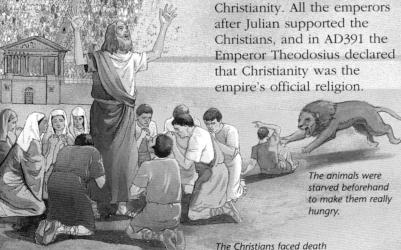

The animals were starved beforehand to make them really hungry.

The Christians faced death bravely, singing hymns and praying together.

BISHOPS AND POPES

By the end of the 4th century AD, the leaders of the Christian Church - known as bishops - had become very powerful. They built beautiful churches and cathedrals, and sent out missionaries to teach people about Christianity. One of the most important leaders was the Bishop of Rome, who came to be known as the Pope. As the emperors grew weaker, the popes became steadily stronger.

This golden cross was a gift from a Roman emperor to an early pope.

HERMITS AND MONKS

Some of the early Christians escaped from persecution into the desert where they lived alone as hermits, devoting their lives to God. Later, these holy men gathered together to form the first monasteries. Many of these monasteries became places of learning, where monks kept the traditions of writing alive while the Roman empire crumbled around them.

INTERNET LINK

For links to websites where you can find out about early Christians and see the catacombs where Christians hid, go to www.usborne-quicklinks.com

BARBARIANS AND BYZANTINES

Ever since the second century AD, the empire had been threatened by a group of tribes from the northeast, known as the Germani. The Romans called all these Germanic people 'barbarians' and fought fiercely to keep them out of their lands. But the struggle grew much harder in AD370, when a warlike tribe called the Huns swept west from Central Asia into Europe, pushing the Germani inside the bounds of the empire itself.

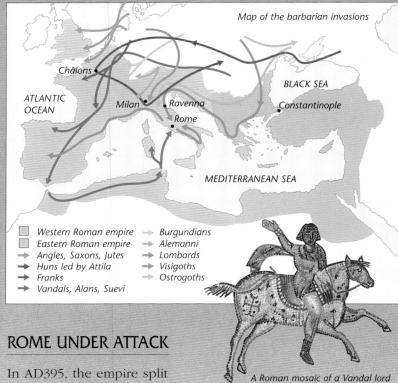

Map of the barbarian invasions

ATLANTIC OCEAN

Châlons

Milan · Ravenna
Rome

BLACK SEA

Constantinople

MEDITERRANEAN SEA

▢ Western Roman empire	→ Burgundians
▢ Eastern Roman empire	→ Alemanni
→ Angles, Saxons, Jutes	→ Lombards
→ Huns led by Attila	→ Visigoths
→ Franks	→ Ostrogoths
→ Vandals, Alans, Suevi	

A Roman mosaic of a Vandal lord

THE BARBARIANS MOVE IN

The Romans allowed some barbarians, such as the Visigoths, to settle inside the empire, but in return these settlers had to help fight off other tribes. Many Germanic warriors fought in the Roman army, but they kept their own commanders, and sometimes groups of barbarians rebelled against the Romans.

This eagle brooch was made by Visigoth goldsmiths, and probably dates from the 4th century AD.

ROME UNDER ATTACK

In AD395, the empire split permanently into east and west (see map). The empire in the east remained secure, but the western empire was soon overrun by barbarians. In AD401, an army of Visigoths, led by Alaric, attacked the city of Milan, where the Emperor Honorius had his palace. Honorius fled to Ravenna and set up a new capital city there.

Alaric and his warriors invaded Italy again in AD410 and attacked the city of Rome, rampaging through the streets for three days. This was a crushing blow for the Romans.

ADVANCING TRIBES

While Alaric was invading Italy, hordes of Vandals, Suevi, Alans and Burgundians were streaming into Germany and Gaul (present-day France). In AD409, the Vandals invaded Spain, and 20 years later they crossed into North Africa, one of the richest areas in the empire. There, they set up a Vandal kingdom ruled by their leader, Gaiseric.

ATTILA THE HUN

One of the fiercest enemies of the empire was Attila, leader of the Huns. Attila stormed through Gaul, killing thousands of people, but in AD451 he was defeated by a combined force of Romans and barbarians at the Battle of Châlons. This was the last great victory for the Romans.

Hun archers, like the one shown here, could strike down their opponents from a distance of 100m (330ft).

INTERNET LINK

For links to websites where you can see examples of Byzantine art, and read an eyewitness account of Attila the Hun, go to www.usborne-quicklinks.com

THE FALL OF THE WESTERN EMPIRE

In AD455, Gaiseric and his Vandals invaded Italy and spent 12 days looting Rome. After this, the western empire was plunged into chaos. Powerful barbarian generals took control of the army, while the emperors in Ravenna became increasingly helpless.

The end finally came in AD476, when a Germanic general named Odoacer sent the last emperor, Romulus Augustulus, into exile. Odoacer declared himself King of Italy, and the western empire collapsed.

AFTER THE FALL

After the fall of Italy, the western empire split into lots of small barbarian kingdoms. In most of these kingdoms, people still tried to keep on living like the Romans, but the once grand public buildings soon fell into ruins, and the Roman way of life gradually died out.

THE EMPIRE IN THE EAST

While the western empire was in ruins, the eastern empire continued for another thousand years, preserving many Roman traditions in its army, laws and government. The empire in the east was known as the Byzantine empire because its capital city, Constantinople, was originally called Byzantium.

A coin showing the Emperor Justinian

The high point of the Byzantine empire came in the 6th century AD, when Emperor Justinian won back many lands that had once been part of the western empire. Justinian encouraged trade and learning, and filled the city of Constantinople with spectacular churches.

This picture shows part of the city of Constantinople as it would have looked in Justinian's time.

THE LEGACY OF ROME

Although the western empire collapsed in AD476, the customs, ideas and inventions of the Romans continued to influence people's lives. The Catholic Church kept many Roman traditions alive, countries all over the world based their governments and laws on ancient Roman models, and Roman buildings were copied everywhere.

ROMAN CATHOLICS

After the fall of Rome, the Catholic Church in the west continued to be controlled from Rome by the Bishop of Rome, later known as the Pope. Church services were held in Latin, and Roman learning was preserved by Christian monks who studied ancient Latin texts and copied them out for others to read.

Monks copied Latin texts and illustrated them with pictures like this.

ANCIENT FEASTS

Many Christian customs have their origins in the feasts and festivals of ancient Rome. For example, the Christian celebration of Christmas includes some elements of the midwinter feast of *Saturnalia*, when the Romans cooked huge meals, played lively games and exchanged gifts.

EMPIRES AND REPUBLICS

Rulers throughout history have tried to recreate the glory of the Roman Empire. In AD800, Charlemagne, King of the Franks, was crowned Emperor of the Romans, and in 955 King Otto of Germany declared himself Holy Roman Emperor. The Holy Roman Empire lasted until the 1800s and had as its symbol the Roman imperial eagle.

Coat of arms of the Holy Roman Emperor

In this portrait, the French emperor Napoleon wears a golden crown based on the Roman crown of victory, made from laurel leaves.

The titles 'Kaiser' and 'Czar' - used by the emperors of Germany and Russia - both came from the Roman 'Caesar'. Napoleon Bonaparte tried to rule 19th-century France like a Roman emperor, and during the 1930s the Italian leader Mussolini attempted to create a new Roman empire.

Some people have been inspired by the Roman Republic, rather than the Empire. In the 18th century, Republicans in France and America saw the Roman Republic as a shining example of a state without a monarch, and America today still has a Senate and senators - based on the Roman Senate at the time of the Republic.

LAW AND ORDER

The Roman system of justice is often seen as particularly good and fair. In most Roman law courts, cases were tried by a judge and a jury - a type of trial that has been copied all over the world. Roman lawyers also built up a vast set of laws, and these have provided a model for the laws of many modern countries.

LIVING LIKE ROMANS

After the Empire collapsed, many buildings, roads and water systems survived, showing how the Romans once lived. For several hundred years, these structures were allowed to fall into ruin, but they helped people rediscover ancient ways of building, and in the 15th century people began to copy Roman styles as well.

Today, cities and towns all over the world have grand public buildings in the Roman style of architecture, while their water and sewage systems are similar to those built by ancient Roman engineers. People live in houses with central heating, eat fast food at snack bars, and visit public swimming pools - just as the Romans did 2,000 years ago.

The Arc de Triomphe in Paris - a 19th-century copy of a Roman triumphal arch

LASTING LATIN

The Romans had an enormous impact on the language we use today. Italian, French, Spanish, Portuguese and Romanian all come from Latin, and even the English language, which isn't so closely related to Latin, includes thousands of words that are based on Latin.

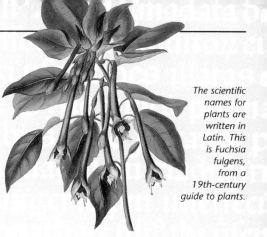

The scientific names for plants are written in Latin. This is Fuchsia fulgens, from a 19th-century guide to plants.

LETTERS AND NUMBERS

Of the 26 letters in our alphabet, 22 come from the Roman alphabet. The Romans had no W or Y, the letters I and J were both written as I, while U and V were written as V. Roman letters and numbers were mainly made from straight lines so that they were easy to carve in stone.

Latin inscriptions can be found on Roman buildings, monuments and tombs. On this gravestone for 'Rinnio Novicio, mule driver', the carver wasn't able to fit the man's name onto one line.

The numbers that we use today are based on Arabic numerals which are much easier to use than Roman ones. But Roman numerals are often used on the faces of clocks and watches. (See page 363 for a guide to Roman numerals.)

A 24-hour stone clock with carved Roman numerals

WORDS AND PHRASES

Although no one speaks Latin as a first language anymore, it hasn't been forgotten. All over the world, scientists identify plants and animals by their Latin names, and some children still study Latin at school.

The English language contains several Latin phrases, such as *ad infinitum* ('to infinity') and *et cetera* ('and the rest'). It also includes many words that are based on Latin. For example, the word 'urban' comes from the Latin *urbs*, meaning 'city'.

REMEMBERING THE GODS

Our calendar is based on the Roman system (see page 362). Some of our months take their names from Roman gods, such as Mars (March) and Juno (June), while July and August are named after Julius Caesar and the Emperor Augustus. The Romans also gave the names of their gods to the planets Jupiter, Venus, Mars, Mercury and Saturn.

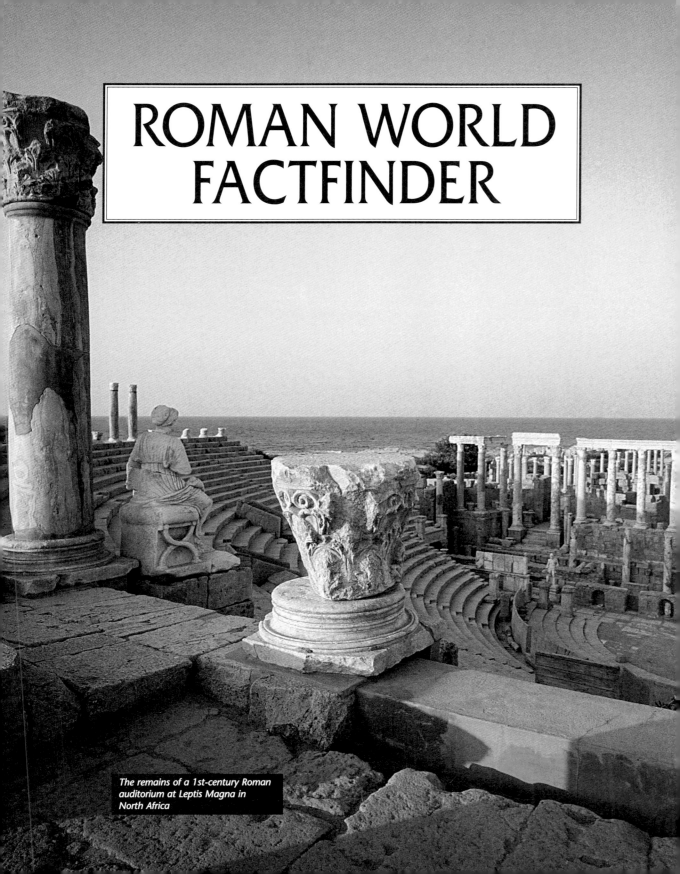

ROMAN WORLD
FACTFINDER

The remains of a 1st-century Roman auditorium at Leptis Magna in North Africa

MORE ABOUT THE EMPIRE

Here you can discover which modern countries once belonged to the Roman empire, and where you can go to visit Roman ruins today. You can also see a list of Roman emperors.

THE ROMAN EMPIRE TODAY

At its height, the Roman empire covered most of Europe, and extended into Africa and Asia. Today, this area is divided into 40 different countries, from Portugal in the west to Iran in the east, and from northern Britain to southern Egypt.

ROMAN SITES

These are just a few of the places with interesting Roman remains that can still be seen today:

ITALY
Herculaneum
Ostia
Piazza Armerina
Pompeii
Ravenna
Rome
Tivoli
Verona

FRANCE
Arles
Glanum
Nîmes
Orange
Vienne

GERMANY
Saalburg
Trier

SPAIN
Alcantara
Italica
Merida
Segovia

UNITED KINGDOM
Bath
Caerleon
Chedworth Villa
Fishbourne Palace
Hadrian's Wall
Housesteads Fort
St Albans
York

TUNISIA
Dougga
El-Djem

CROATIA
Split

TURKEY
Aphrodisias
Ephesus
Side

SYRIA
Palmyra

JORDAN
Jerash

ALGERIA
Djemila
Timgad

LIBYA
Leptis Magna

This map shows which countries were once part of the Roman empire.

☐ Roman empire at its largest

These Roman baths at Leptis Magna, on the coast of Libya, survived virtually intact beneath the sand dunes.

EMPERORS OF ROME

This list shows most of the emperors of Rome. A few emperors who seized power for themselves, and who ruled for only a very short time, have not been included. Some emperors appointed a co-ruler; those who ruled jointly for a time are marked with an asterisk (*).

27BC-AD14	Augustus
AD14-37	Tiberius
37-41	Gaius (Caligula)
41-54	Claudius
54-68	Nero
68-69	Galba
69	Otho
69	Vitellius
69-79	Vespasian
79-81	Titus
81-96	Domitian
96-98	Nerva
98-117	Trajan
117-138	Hadrian
138-161	Antoninus Pius
161-180	*Marcus Aurelius
161-169	*Lucius Verus
180-192	Commodus
193	Pertinax
193	*Didius Julianus
193-194	*Pescennius Niger
193-211	*Septimius Severus
195-197	*Clodius Albinus
209-212	*Geta
211-217	*Caracalla
217-218	*Macrinus
218-222	*Elagabalus
222-235	Severus Alexander
235-238	Maximinus I
238	*Gordian I
238	*Gordian II
238	*Balbinus
238	*Pupienus
238-244	Gordian III
244-249	Philip the Arab
249-251	Trajan Decius
251-253	*Trebonianus Gallus
251-253	*Volusian
253-260	*Valerian
253-268	*Gallienus
268-270	Claudius II
270-275	Aurelian
275-276	Tacitus
276	*Florian
276-282	*Probus
282-283	Carus
283-284	*Carinus
283-284	*Numerian
284-286	Diocletian

WESTERN EMPIRE		EASTERN EMPIRE	
286-305	Maximian	286-305	Diocletian
305-306	Constantius I	305-311	*Galerius
306-307	*Severus II		
306-312	*Maxentius	309-313	*Maximinus II
307-324	*Constantine I	308-324	*Licinius
324-337	Constantine I *ruled both East and West*		
337-340	*Constantine II		
337-350	*Constans		
350-353	Magnentius	337-353	Constantius II
353-361	*Constantius II *ruled both East and West*		
360-363	*Julian the Apostate *ruled both East and West*		
363-364	Jovian *ruled both East and West*		
364	Valentinian I *ruled both East and West*		
364-375	*Valentinian I	364-378	Valens
367-383	*Gratian		
375-392	*Valentinian II		
392-394	Eugenius	379-394	Theodosius I
394-395	Theodosius I *ruled both East and West*		
395-423	Honorius	395-408	*Arcadius
423-425	Johannes	402-450	*Theodosius II
425-455	Valentinian III	450-457	Marcian
455-456	Avitus		
457-461	Majorian	457-474	*Leo I
461-465	Severus III		
465-467	*No emperor*		
467-472	*Anthemius	473-474	*Leo II
472	*Olybrius	474-475	Zeno
473-474	Glycerius	475-476	Basiliscus
474-475	Julius Nepos	476-491	Zeno
475-476	Romulus Augustulus	491-518	Anastasius
		518-527	Justin
		527-565	Justinian

THE ORGANIZATION OF THE ARMY

The structure of the Roman army changed a lot over the centuries. These two pages explain how the army was organized in the early days of the Republic, and later under the Empire. You can also find out about different types of soldiers and battle formations.

THE REPUBLICAN ARMY

At the start of the Republic, the army was organized very simply, and soldiers were divided into groups called centuries, each containing 100 men. Later, as the army grew, soldiers were grouped into much larger units, called legions, of about 4,200 men. Each legion was divided into groups known as maniples, containing 120 men.

THE IMPERIAL ARMY

During the Empire, the army reached the peak of its organization. It was successful because each legion was divided into lots of small, highly disciplined groups.

This diagram shows the structure of a legion in the imperial army.

CONTUBERNIUM (8 MEN)

A group of eight soldiers was known as a *contubernium*. The members of each *contubernium* shared a tent together when the army was on the move, and shared a pair of rooms in the army fort.

CENTURY (80 MEN)

Ten *contubernia* (80 men) made up a century, which was smaller than in Republican times when it had got its name from having 100 men. This new, smaller century was easier to control and more effective in battle. Each century was commanded by a centurion.

COHORT (480 MEN)

A cohort was usually made up of six centuries (480 men), but the first cohort in every legion had ten centuries (800 men). Some of these extra men were cooks and clerks, who didn't usually fight.

LEGION (6,000 MEN)

A legion was made up of ten cohorts, nine of the usual size and one of 800 men, making over 5,000 soldiers in all. Each legion also included more than a hundred horseback messengers, as well as builders, engineers, doctors and a catapult maker. The Roman army had a total of 25 to 35 legions - the exact number varied over time.

TYPES OF SOLDIERS

By the time of the Empire, there were many different types of soldiers in the army. Here are some of the most common ones:

Legate - An experienced officer who commanded a legion.

Tribune - An officer who helped the legatus to run the legion. Each legion had six tribunes.

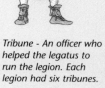

Praefectus Castrorum - A senior officer in charge of the training and organization of a legion.

Primus Pilus - The senior centurion in a legion.

Centurion - The leader of a century.

Nine ordinary cohorts
(480 men in each)

First cohort
(800 men)

Contubernium
(8 men)

Century (80 men)

Legionary - A foot soldier. Only Roman citizens could be legionaries.

Auxiliary - A non-citizen who fought in the army. Each legion had its own groups of auxiliaries.

Aquilifer - The standard-bearer who carried the legion's precious golden eagle during battle.

Cavalry soldier - A soldier who fought on horseback.

Cornicene - A horn-blower who sent signals during battles.

Signifer - A standard-bearer who carried the emblem of a century.

THE UNSTOPPABLE TORTOISE

During the Empire, groups of soldiers advanced in a cunning formation called the *testudo*, or tortoise. The soldiers locked their shields together to form a solid barrier over their heads and around the edges of the group. This protected them from spears and arrows, and allowed the soldiers to get close to the enemy while remaining safe.

Men dressed as Roman soldiers, in the testudo formation

GODS, GODDESSES AND FESTIVALS

The Romans prayed to dozens of different gods and goddesses and celebrated more than 100 festivals a year. Here is a list of gods and goddesses and a brief description of the main Roman festivals.

GODS AND GODDESSES

Most of the Roman gods were borrowed from the Greeks. In this list of major Roman gods and goddesses, their Greek names are given in brackets.

Apollo *(Apollo)* - god of the Sun, music, healing and prophecy

Bacchus *(Dionysus)* - god of wine

Ceres *(Demeter)* - goddess of crops and harvests

Cupid *(Eros)* - god of love

Diana *(Artemis)* - goddess of the Moon and hunting

Dis *(Pluto)* - god of the Underworld

Flora - Roman goddess of Spring and flowers

Fortuna *(Tyche)* - goddess of good luck

Janus - Roman god of doorways and bridges

Juno *(Hera)* - queen of the gods, goddess of women and childbirth

Jupiter or **Jove** *(Zeus)* - king of the gods, god of the sky, thunder and lightning

Mars *(Ares)* - god of war

Mercury *(Hermes)* - Jupiter's messenger, god of trade and thieves

Minerva *(Athena)* - goddess of science and wisdom, crafts and war

Neptune *(Poseidon)* - god of the sea

Roma - goddess of Rome

Saturn *(Chronos)* - god of farming

Venus *(Aphrodite)* - goddess of love and beauty

Vesta *(Hestia)* - goddess of the hearth

Vulcan *(Hephaestus)* - god of blacksmiths and craftworkers

A Roman fresco showing the goddess Flora picking flowers

FESTIVALS AND FEASTS

These are some of the main festivals of the Roman year. Their names and dates are given where they are known.

January 1
After 153BC, this day marked the start of the Roman New Year. Bulls were sacrificed to Jupiter to give thanks for the god's protection in the past year, and two new consuls took up their positions as leaders of the Senate.

Early January - *Compitalia*
In the country, farmers sacrificed an animal to purify their farms for the coming year. In towns, people made sacrifices at crossroads, and then enjoyed three days of celebrations.

February 13-21 - *Parentalia*
Romans placed flowers, milk and wine on the graves of their dead parents. This was to stop the dead from feeling hungry and returning to haunt the living.

February 15 - *Lupercalia*
Two teams of young men raced around the Palatine Hill in Rome, dressed in the skins of sacrificed goats. As they ran, they whipped the spectators with strips of goatskin. It was believed that any woman touched by them would soon have a baby.

February 22 - *Caristia*
Families gathered for a meal to mark the end of *Parentalia*.

March 1
Originally the start of the Roman year, on this day the fire in the temple of Vesta in Rome was relit by the Vestal Virgins. This was also the first day of the dances of the priests. Twelve young priests danced around Rome holding sacred shields. The dancing lasted for 19 days and the dancers feasted at a different house each night.

March 15 - *Anna Perenna*
People ate picnics on the banks of the Tiber to celebrate the feast of Anna Perenna, goddess of the year. Some Romans believed that they would live for as many years as they could drink cups of wine.

March 23 - *Tubilustrium*
The sacred trumpets of war were purified in a ceremony dedicated to Mars, god of war. This was meant to bring success in battle.

April 4-10 - *Ludi Megalenses*
Games were held in praise of Cybele, the Great Mother Goddess from Turkey.

April 12-19 - *Ludi Ceriales*
Games were held for Ceres, goddess of crops and harvests.

April 21 - *Parilia*
Parilia began as a country festival when all the sheep were washed, but later it was celebrated in Rome as the city's birthday. People in Rome threw offerings onto bonfires and then danced around the flames. The celebrations ended with a large outdoor feast.

April 28-May 3 - *Floralia*
This celebration in praise of Flora, goddess of Spring, was also known as *Ludi Florales*. Tables were piled high with flowers, and people wore garlands and performed dances.

June 9 - *Vestalia*
On this day, married women visited the temple of Vesta in Rome, bringing gifts of food for the goddess. *Vestalia* was a holiday for bakers, because the Vestal Virgins baked a special bread made from salted flour.

June 24 - *Fors Fortuna*
This was a great public holiday in Rome. In the morning, people rowed down the Tiber to watch sacrifices to the goddess Fortuna,

which were held just outside Rome. The rest of the day was spent picnicking and drinking.

July 6-13 - *Ludi Apollinares*
During the Republic, this festival was connected with ceremonies to the god Apollo. But by imperial times, it was just an excuse for theatrical shows, games and races.

August 13
This was the feast day of Diana, goddess of hunting. Slaves had a holiday and it was traditional for women to wash their hair.

September 5-19 - *Ludi Romani*
This 15-day festival of games, races and plays was held in praise of Jupiter. On September 13, a cow was sacrificed at Jupiter's temple and a grand banquet was held there. Statues of Jupiter, Juno and Minerva were dressed up and placed on couches so that they could share in the feast.

November 4-17 - *Ludi Plebeii*
During this 13-day celebration in praise of Jupiter, people watched plays, games and races. On November 13, there was a banquet for senators and magistrates.

Early December - *Rites of the Bona Dea*
This was a women-only festival in praise of Bona Dea, the 'Good Goddess' and protector of women. Men were forbidden to attend these secret ceremonies, which may have involved dancing, drinking and the worship of sacred objects.

December 17 - *Saturnalia*
At first, *Saturnalia* lasted only one day, but later it was extended to about a week. The festival began with a sacrifice at the temple of Saturn, god of farming. People played games and gave each other gifts, and masters changed places with their slaves for a day.

LEGENDS OF ROME

Today, historians concentrate on facts, but Roman historians, such as Livy, also included many legends in their writings. These helped to shape the way the Romans saw themselves. Roman poets, such as Virgil, were also inspired by these ancient stories and wrote poems about them. On these two pages, you can read some of the myths that grew up around the early history of Rome.

TARPEIA THE TRAITRESS

While Romulus was King of Rome, the Romans kidnapped some Sabine women who lived nearby (see page 268). The Sabines were determined to seek revenge, but this was no easy task, as Rome was very well defended. The strongest place of all was the fortress on top of the steep, rocky Capitol Hill.

It so happened that the commander of the fortress had a daughter named Tarpeia, who was in love with a young Sabine man. Tarpeia agreed to open the gate of the fortress and let the Sabines in. But the Sabines were so disgusted by her betrayal of Rome - even though she had helped them - that as they entered the fortress, they crushed her to death beneath their shields. Ever after, the Romans punished traitors by hurling them off the high rock on top of the Capitol Hill. This rock was named the Tarpeian Rock, after Tarpeia the traitress.

NUMA AND THE NYMPH

Numa - the second king of Rome - was famous for his wisdom. But in fact, he was getting some help from the gods. The king had fallen in love with Egeria - one of the nymphs who served the goddess Diana. The two lovers would meet on the wooded slopes of Mount Albanus, near Rome, and when Numa had a problem, he would consult Egeria to find out the will of the gods. When Numa died, Egeria was heartbroken. As a nymph, she was immortal and could never join him in death. She wept so much that she turned into a stream that cascaded down Mount Albanus and into the Alban Lake.

THE SIBYLLINE BOOKS

In ancient times, there were several priestesses in Italy known as Sibyls. It was believed that the gods spoke through the Sibyls, solving people's problems and making prophecies. The most famous of these priestesses was the Sibyl of Cumae.

According to legend, Tarquin the Proud - the last king of Rome - was approached by the Sibyl of Cumae, who offered to sell him 12 books of prophecies about the future of Rome. Tarquin thought her price was too high, so he refused. Then, before his very eyes, she burned three of the books and offered him the remaining nine - at the same price. This happened twice more.

Finally, Tarquin was so intrigued that he bought the three surviving books - at the original price. These were the famous Sibylline Books, which were consulted by future generations whenever Rome was faced with a crisis.

MUCIUS THE LEFT-HANDED

After Tarquin the Proud was driven out of Rome, Porsena - king of the Etruscan city of Clusium - agreed to help put him back on the throne. The Etruscans advanced on Rome, but were held back by the Roman hero Horatio (see page 270). Unable to attack the city, the Etruscans besieged it instead.

A young Roman noble, named Caius Mucius, was determined to save Rome. He swam the Tiber and entered the Etruscan camp, intending to kill King Porsena. But, by mistake, he killed a secretary who was sitting next to the king. Seized by the king's bodyguards, Mucius had to think quickly. He hinted that he wasn't alone and that the king had reason to be afraid.

Porsena was furious and threatened to burn Mucius alive if he didn't explain what he meant. To prove he wasn't afraid, Mucius thrust his right hand into the fire. Porsena was so impressed by Mucius's courage that he spared his life and made peace with Rome. From then on, Mucius was known as Mucius Scaevola - or 'Mucius the Left-handed'.

THE STORY OF CORIOLANUS

During the early days of the Republic, Rome was at war with an Italian hill tribe called the Volsci. On one occasion, the Roman army attacked the Volscian town of Corioli and surrounded it.

While the Romans were busy besieging Corioli, they were suddenly attacked from behind by another Volscian army. At the same moment, the gates of Corioli opened and a band of Volscian soldiers rushed at the Romans head on. The situation looked grim.

A young Roman soldier named Gnaeus Marcius was on guard at the time. Marcius fought his way through the open gates of Corioli and set fire to the town. Seeing the flames, the Volscians thought the town had already been captured, and their attack faltered. The Romans won the battle and took control of Corioli. Gnaeus Marcius became a hero and was known from then on as 'Coriolanus'.

VIRGIL'S AENEID

The Aeneid - a long poem written by the poet Virgil - is one of the most famous works in Roman literature. It tells the story of the legendary Trojan hero Aeneas, his escape from the burning city of Troy, and his journey to find a new homeland. There, he was destined to start a new race of people - the Romans - who would rule the world in peace and prosperity. On the rest of this page, you can read a brief outline of the *Aeneid*.

DIDO AND AENEAS

After Aeneas and his fellow Trojans escaped from Troy, they were shipwrecked off the coast of North Africa, near the city of Carthage. There, they were welcomed by Dido, the Carthaginian queen. As Aeneas told her about the fall of Troy and his search for a new home, she fell hopelessly in love with him. The two of them spent several happy months together, until the god Jupiter commanded Aeneas to continue his voyage.

Dido was heartbroken. Once Aeneas had gone, she called for the sword he had given her, and stabbed herself. She died cursing Aeneas and prophesying eternal hatred between his descendants and Carthage. From his ship, Aeneas could see the flames of her funeral pyre.

AENEAS IN THE UNDERWORLD

Aeneas finally reached the shores of Italy and went to see the Sibyl of Cumae. He asked her how to get to the Underworld, so he could consult his dead father about the future. She told him he had to find a golden branch to take as a gift to Proserpine, queen of the Underworld. Helped by his mother - the goddess Venus - Aeneas found the branch and hurried back with it to the Sibyl.

Then, the Sibyl led Aeneas down into the Underworld. There, they met Charon the ferryman, whose job was to take the souls of the dead across the River Styx. When he saw the golden branch, Charon agreed to ferry Aeneas and the Sibyl across the river. On the other side, they encountered the three-headed dog Cerberus, which had snakes bristling around its three necks. The Sibyl threw the dog a piece of drugged cake, which it ate greedily. Cerberus fell fast asleep, and the Sibyl and Aeneas continued their journey.

Eventually, they came to the Elysian Fields - a blissful place where the souls of the good would live forever. There, Aeneas met his dead father, who revealed the future to him, including the great leaders who would make Roman history. Inspired by what he had seen, Aeneas followed the Sybil back to the world of the living.

AENEAS IN ITALY

Aeneas rejoined his friends and they sailed up the coast of Italy. When they landed at the mouth of the Tiber, Aeneas recognized this as their new homeland.

At first, the Trojans were welcomed by the local people - the Latins - but soon a long and bitter war broke out. Aeneas eventually killed the leader of the Latin army in a duel, bringing the war to an end.

The Trojans and the Latins became one people, and Aeneas married the daughter of the Latin king. It was one of their descendants - Romulus - who later founded the city of Rome (see page 267).

This mosaic shows Virgil writing The Aeneid. On either side of him are two of the muses (goddesses of learning) who inspired him.

DATES, TIME AND NUMBERS

The calendar we use today is based on the Roman calendar. On these two pages, you can find out about Roman months and weeks, and discover how the Romans calculated their dates. There is also information on how the Romans measured time and a quick guide to Roman numerals.

ROMAN DATES

Within each month, dates were counted from special days, known as *Kalends*, *Ides* and *Nones*. These special days were as follows:

Kalends - the 1st day of each month
Ides - the 15th day of March, May, July and October, and the 13th day of all the other months
Nones - the 7th day of March, May, July and October, and the 5th day of all the other months

Dates were counted back from the *Kalends*, *Ides* or *Nones*:

ROMAN DATE		MODERN DATE
V *Kalends Maius* =	5 days before the 1st day of May	= April 25
II *Nones October* =	2 days before the 7th day of October	= October 5

Julius Caesar, shown here, was assassinated on March 15 - the Ides of March.

THE ROMAN CALENDAR

According to Roman legend, Romulus - the founder and first king of Rome - divided the Roman year into ten months. Here is a list of Roman months with an explanation of their names:

Martius	the month of the god Mars
Aprilis	origin uncertain
Maius	the month of Maia, mother of Mercury
Junius	the month of the goddess Juno
Quintilis	the fifth month
Sextilis	the sixth month
September	the seventh month
October	the eighth month
November	the ninth month
December	the tenth month

With this system, each year only had 304 days, so King Numa later added two new months: *Januarius* (the month of the god Janus) and *Februarius* (the month of purification). In 153BC, the start of the New Year was moved from March to January 1. But even with the two new months, each year still had only 355 days, so the Romans had to keep adding in extra days to make the calendar work.

THE JULIAN CALENDAR

During 46BC and 45BC, Julius Caesar reformed the calendar, ordering that each year should have 365 days, with an extra day every four years. This idea still survives today in our leap year. Julius Caesar's simplified system of calculating the days of the year has become known as the Julian calendar.

Finally, during the reign of the Emperor Augustus, the months of *Quintilis* and *Sextilis* were renamed *Julius* and *Augustus* after Julius Caesar and Augustus himself.

DAYS OF THE WEEK

For most of their history, the Romans didn't have a week as we understand it, though they did have a market day every eight days. Then, in AD321, the Emperor Constantine introduced a new seven-day week, with Sunday as the first day.

The Romans believed that the Sun and the Moon were planets and thought that there were seven planets altogether. The planets had been named after Roman gods and goddesses, and the days of the week were named after the seven planets:

Sunday	*dies Solis* (Sun day)
Monday	*dies Lunae* (Moon day)
Tuesday	*dies Martis* (day of Mars)
Wednesday	*dies Mercurii* (day of Mercury)
Thursday	*dies Jovis* (day of Jove or Jupiter)
Friday	*dies Veneris* (day of Venus)
Saturday	*dies Saturni* (day of Saturn)

TELLING THE TIME

The early Romans had no way of telling the exact time of day so they had to rely on the Sun's position in the sky. Only three points in the day could be accurately known - sunrise, midday and sunset. The Romans divided the day into two parts on either side of midday, or *meridies*. The time before midday was called *ante meridiem* (a.m.), and the time after midday was *post meridiem* (p.m.) - terms that we still use today to describe the times before and after noon.

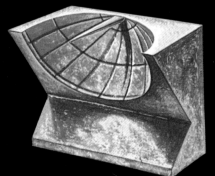

Sundials were set up in public squares so that people could check the time.

By the mid-3rd century BC, the Romans were using sundials to tell the time. Each day lasted as long as the daylight and was divided into 12 hours, with midday at the end of the sixth hour. The Romans didn't use minutes, and because the hours of daylight varied over the year, an hour was much longer in the summer than in the winter. The night was also divided into 12 hours, and summer nights were much shorter than winter nights.

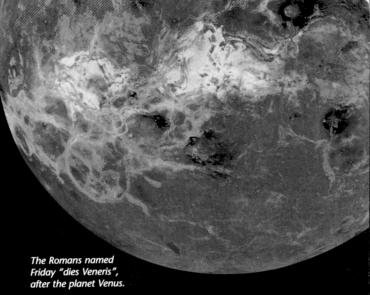

The Romans named Friday "dies Veneris", after the planet Venus.

ROMAN NUMERALS

Roman numerals are made up of a combination of the letters I, V, X, L, C, D and M. They follow a logical pattern, based on addition and subtraction. For example, 4 is written IV, meaning 1 less than 5 (V); 7 is VII, meaning 5 (V) plus 2 (II). However, this way of writing numerals meant that many numbers became extremely long. For example, the Romans needed 7 letters to write the number 78:

50 + 20 + 5 + 3 = 78

GUIDE TO ROMAN NUMERALS

1	I	11	XI	25	XXV
2	II	12	XII	50	L
3	III	13	XIII	75	LXXV
4	IV	14	XIV	100	C
5	V	15	XV	200	CC
6	VI	16	XVI	500	D
7	VII	17	XVII	700	DCC
8	VIII	18	XVIII	1000	M
9	IX	19	XIX	1500	MD
10	X	20	XX	2000	MM

MONEY AND BANKING

Here, you can find out about Roman money and banking, and also learn about some of the different weights and measures which were used by the Romans.

COINS OF THE REPUBLIC

In the early Republic, people didn't use money, but simply swapped - or bartered - one thing for another. As the Romans became richer and began to trade more, they needed a more precise way to pay. First, small bronze blocks were used as a kind of money, then the idea of using coins was copied from the Greeks (see page 211). The first Roman coin-making factory - or mint - opened around 290BC. Soon, there were several mints in different parts of Italy.

COINS OF THE EMPIRE

When Augustus became emperor in 27BC, he declared that gold and silver coins could only be made in Rome, although the less valuable bronze and copper coins could still be made in the provinces. Eventually, the same money was used all over the empire.

BANKERS AND MONEY-LENDERS

By the time of the Empire, the Romans controlled a huge trading network. Merchants or traders who needed money to set up businesses could borrow what they needed from money-lenders and bankers. Some money-lenders worked for the government, while others were independent and became extremely rich. Some people borrowed so much money that they couldn't pay back the loan. This meant they had to give up their homes, or even be sold as slaves.

Here are the most common Roman coins:

aureus: gold - the most valuable Roman coin

denarius: silver - 25 denarii in an aureus

sestertius: bronze - 4 sestertii in a denarius

dupondius: bronze - 2 dupondii in a sestertius

as: copper - 2 as in a dupondius

semi: bronze - 2 semis in an as

quadrans: copper - 4 quadrans in an as

LOSING VALUE

During the Empire, prices kept rising, so coins gradually became less and less valuable. New ones of higher value were made, but since precious metals were expensive, many new coins were made of copper and just coated with gold or silver. There were also many forged coins, and all this gradually made people suspicious of government money. Near the end of the Empire, some Romans abandoned coins altogether and went back to bartering.

MESSAGES ON MONEY

Stamping pictures on coins was one of the best ways to communicate with people all over the empire. In imperial times, every coin showed the emperor's face on one side, and special batches of coins were made to publicize victories. When an unpopular emperor was killed, coins bearing his image were covered with scratches or taken out of use.

WEIGHTS AND MEASURES

Here are some of the most common Roman weights and measures:

The *libra* was the basis of all Roman weights, and was equivalent to about 335g (12oz).

The *pes* was used to measure length, and was equivalent to about 30cm (12in). *Pes* is Latin for 'foot'.

A larger unit of length was the *passus*, equivalent to about 1.5m (5ft).

The *jugerum* was a measure of area, and was equivalent to about 2,530m2 (27,230ft2). It was based on the area of land that two oxen could prepare for sowing in one day.

The *modius* was the main measure of volume, used to measure goods such as salt and wheat, and was equivalent to about 9l (2gal).

ROMAN LAW

Roman law changed a lot during Rome's history. On this page, you can find out how the legal system worked under the Republic and during the time of the Empire.

THE TWELVE TABLES

In 450BC, a long list of Roman laws - called the Twelve Tables - was published. It listed laws about inheriting money, owning property, and many other aspects of daily life. Although the laws kept changing throughout the Roman period, they were always based on the Twelve Tables. One law in the Twelve Tables prevented patricians from marrying plebeians, and another gave fathers the power of life and death over their children.

REPUBLICAN LAW

During the Republic, laws were made by the Senate and the Plebeian Council (see page 277). These laws were often quite vague, so local judges had to decide how to apply them in court. When a man became a judge, he wrote a document called an edict which explained his interpretation of each law. This was usually based on the edict of the judge before him. Judges took local customs into account when writing their edict, so the laws were slightly different in each province.

If someone accused another person of committing a crime, the accuser had to summon the accused to court. If the accused refused to come, the accuser could use force to make him attend, and this often led to fights before trials.

A jury of Roman citizens listened to the charges, and both the

Professional lawyers were talented speakers, or orators. This statue shows a Roman orator.

accuser and the accused had the chance to present their side of the argument. Wealthy people employed a lawyer - called an *advocatus* - to speak for them. Anyone found guilty of lying in court was executed. At the end of the trial, the jury decided whether the accused was innocent or guilty. When someone was found guilty, the judge decided what the punishment should be.

IMPERIAL LAW

At the start of the Empire, the Emperor Augustus wanted to give firmer guidelines on how to interpret laws, so he asked some leading lawyers for their opinions. Although different provinces still had different laws, all judges now had to follow the official interpretation, instead of making their own decisions. Most new laws were made by the emperor. The Senate still suggested laws, but the emperor decided whether they should be passed or not.

During the imperial period, changes were also made in the courtroom. At the start of each trial, the judge placed the accused in one of two categories: *honestiores* or *humiliores*. The *humiliores* were usually poorer, and were punished more severely if found guilty.

LAWS FOR ALL

In the 2nd century AD, the Emperor Hadrian collected all the regional edicts and made them into a single set of laws that governed all Roman citizens. If citizens living in the provinces thought they had been wrongly judged by a local court, they had the right to appeal to the legal authorities in Rome.

WHAT'S NEW?

New information on Roman life is being uncovered all the time. On these two pages, you can learn about a few recent discoveries made by archaeologists, and find out about exciting new ways of looking at the ancient world.

TREASURES OF ZEUGMA

In Spring 2000, a team of archaeologists raced against time to uncover as much as possible of a buried Roman city, before it was drowned in floodwater from a newly constructed dam.

The city of Zeugma, in present-day Turkey, was one of the richest cities in the eastern Roman empire. But it was destroyed by Persians in the 3rd century AD, and gradually became buried under layers of soil.

Using magnetic detecting equipment, a group of experts traced the outlines of Zeugma's city walls, while another team explored the network of sewage tunnels underneath its streets. The most exciting discovery was a lavish 14-room villa, decorated with beautiful wall paintings and spectacular mosaic floors.

Before they left the site, the archaeologists managed to rescue the mosaics, removing them gently section by section. These mosaics will be carefully reconstructed, although most of the city of Zeugma is now underwater.

FINDS AT HERCULANEUM

The port of Herculaneum in southern Italy was destroyed at the same time as Pompeii, when Mount Vesuvius erupted in AD79 (see page 264). Until recently, archaeologists have concentrated mainly on Pompeii, but exciting new finds have now been made at Herculaneum.

The remains of 48 victims of the eruption have been found on the beach at Herculaneum. These remains show that people weren't choked by ash, as experts used to believe, but instead died suddenly from a blast of suffocating heat.

SECRETS OF THE SCROLLS

During the 1750s, hundreds of burned and blackened scrolls were discovered inside a villa at Herculaneum. These scrolls contained important works of philosophy, but most of them were impossible to read.

Now, however, camera techniques originally developed by the NASA space team have made it possible to distinguish between the black of the charred scrolls and the black of the ink. These techniques will help experts in the future to read other scrolls and uncover more secrets.

READING THE BONES

By studying Roman skeletons, experts known as palaeopathologists can discover a great deal about disease in Roman times. For example, they now know that at the time that the barbarians were attacking Rome, malaria was raging through northern Italy.

Studies of Roman skeletons in Britain have revealed that some Romans living in Britain suffered from gout - a painful disease that attacks the joints. Palaeopathologists have also suggested that Roman soldiers carried leprosy from the east and introduced the disease into western Europe.

INTERNET LINKS

For links to websites where you can find out more about the latest discoveries of Roman life, go to www.usborne-quicklinks.com

Find out more about the discoveries at Zeugma, see photos of the amazing mosaics, and learn how archaeologists explored the site.

Learn more about the eruption of Vesuvius and the bodies found at Herculaneum.

Find out more about the specialized techniques scientists are using to read the damaged scrolls discovered at Herculaneum.

Discover how archaeologists managed to reconstruct a Roman bath-house in Turkey, and look at photos of each stage of the building.

Take a virtual tour of the Forum of Trajan in ancient Rome and see incredible 3-D architectural reconstructions and short movies about Roman life.

Find out how Roman remains in London are excavated and processed.

Read about the latest archaeological discoveries.

INVESTIGATING SHIPWRECKS

The exploration of the ocean bed has led to the discovery of many lost Roman ships. Marine archaeologists dive deep underwater to investigate wrecks, climbing inside ancient vessels to take photographs and rescue treasures.

Over the past 50 years, marine archaeologists have explored Roman warships, merchant ships and barges, discovering coins, weapons, furniture and many tall terracotta jars - known as *amphorae* - that were once used to hold olive oil and wine. A few of these Roman shipwrecks held incredibly precious cargoes - statues and pillars looted from Greece by a victorious Roman army.

ROMAN RECONSTRUCTIONS

Some archaeologists try to learn more about Roman machines and buildings by reconstructing them with the same materials the Romans used. For example, experts have built full-size copies of wooden catapults, and experimented with them to see how far they can fire metal bolts.

Archaeologists have also reconstructed reaping machines and other farming equipment, and one group of experts recently recreated a Roman bath-house. These projects help us to understand how ancient technology worked, and reveal the problems Roman engineers had to overcome.

COMPUTER TECHNOLOGY

In recent years, powerful computers and the growth of the World Wide Web have brought many important changes to the way archaeologists work. Now, experts all over the world can share their ideas, findings and photographs through the Internet, combining their different discoveries to form a more complete picture of the Roman world.

Using computer graphics, archaeologists can also create amazing three-dimensional images of Roman buildings and towns. Many of these can be viewed on the Internet, giving us a far more vivid understanding of how these places once looked.

This photograph shows a diver holding a Roman amphora found at a shipwreck in the Mediterranean Sea.

18th dynasty wall painting from a tomb near Thebes, showing the nobleman Nebamun hunting birds; a popular aristocratic pastime

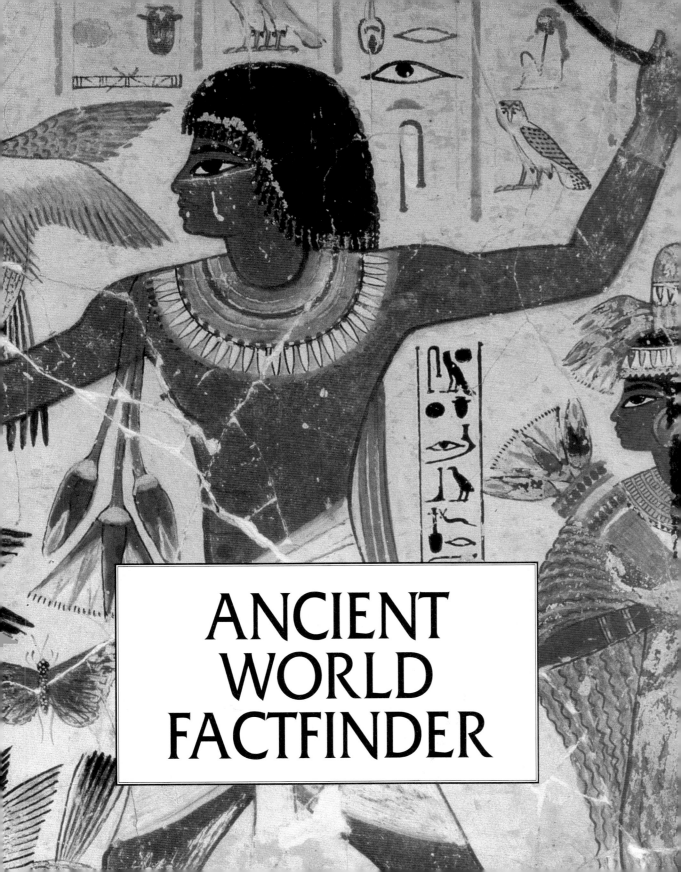

ANCIENT
WORLD
FACTFINDER

WHO'S WHO IN THE ANCIENT WORLD

The next six pages give you a quick guide to some of the most famous and important people in the ancient world. Names that appear in bold type also have their own entries. The dates given are for life spans except for the Egyptian and Persian kings where the dates are their reigns.

AESCHYLUS (C.525BC-456BC)
Greek playwright, known as the founder of Greek tragedy. He wrote over 80 tragedies, only seven of which have survived. His most famous work is the *Oresteia*, a group of three plays about Agamemnon (see page 255). According to legend, he died when an eagle dropped a tortoise on his head.

AGRIPPINA (AD15-59)
Mother of Roman emperor **Nero**. Intelligent and ambitious, she had a great influence on her son, and may even have poisoned her husband, Emperor **Claudius**, so that Nero could take over. Nero later had her stabbed to death.

AHMOSE (C.1552-1527BC)
King of Egypt. First king of Dynasty XVIII and the New Kingdom. Son of Tao II and Ahhotep I, he came to the throne as a child, with his mother as regent. He liberated Egypt from the Hyksos and began the reconquest of Nubia.

AKHENATEN/AMENHOTEP IV (C.1364-1347BC)
King of Egypt (Dynasty XVIII). One of the most controversial figures in ancient history. He abandoned the traditional gods and introduced the worship of one god, the disc of the sun, known as Aten. He changed his name to Akhenaten and built a new capital, Akhetaten. After his death, all Akhenaten's monuments were destroyed and he was branded a heretic.

ALARIC (C.AD370-410)
King of the Visigoths, a warlike tribe from northeast Europe. He served in the Roman army under Theodosius but later invaded Italy, attacking Rome in AD410.

ALCIBIADES (C.450BC-404BC)
Athenian politician and *strategos* (military commander). Brought up by **Pericles** and a pupil of **Socrates**. He persuaded the Athenians to attack Sicily, but before the attack he was recalled to face charges against him by personal enemies. So he betrayed Athens by fleeing to Sparta. Despite this, the Athenians re-elected him as *strategos* in 407BC, but he was held responsible for their defeat at the Battle of Notium. He was assassinated in Persia.

ALEXANDER THE GREAT (356BC-323BC)
King of Macedonia and brilliant military commander. A pupil of **Aristotle**, he learned military tactics in the army of his father, **Philip II**. He became king in 336BC, at the age of 20. After taking control of Greece and the areas to the north, he invaded Asia and built up the largest empire in the ancient world. He died in Babylon at the age of 32 - possibly poisoned. His heirs were murdered and his empire divided between his generals: **Ptolemy**, **Antigonas** and Seleucus.

AMENHOTEP III (C.1402-1364BC)
King of Egypt (Dynasty XVIII). Son of Tuthmosis IV and father of **Akhenaten**. Some of the religious ideas and artistic styles of Akhenaten's reign may have begun to develop in his father's reign.

ANAXAGORAS (C.500BC-C.428BC)
Early Athenian philosopher and friend of **Pericles**. His book, *On Nature*, tried to explain how the universe worked. His theories influenced later philosophers: he calculated that the Sun was a mass of flaming material and that the Moon reflected its light, and he was the first person to explain a solar eclipse.

ANTIGONAS I (C.382BC-301BC)
Macedonian king who fought for control of the empire of **Alexander the Great**. He was killed at the Battle of Ipsus in 301BC, but his descendants founded the Antigonid dynasty, ruling most of Greece until its conquest by Romans in 146BC.

ANTONY, MARK (82-30BC)
Roman soldier and politician. After **Julius Caesar's** death in 44BC, he led the alliance that defeated Caesar's murderers. Struggled for power with **Octavian**, until the two men agreed to divide the empire between them. For ten years, he ruled the eastern empire and lived with **Cleopatra**, the Egyptian queen. He was defeated by Octavian at the Battle of Actium in 31BC, and he and Cleopatra committed suicide.

APOPHIS (C.1585-1542BC)
One of the greatest Hyksos kings of Egypt (Dynasty XV). After war broke out with Tao II, King of Thebes, the Hyksos, including their king, were expelled and the New Kingdom began.

ARCHIMEDES (C.287-212BC)
Greek mathematician, astronomer and inventor, who studied at the Museum in Alexandria. He invented a type of pulley for lifting objects, and the Archimedes screw, a device for pumping water. Famous for shouting "Eureka!" ("I have found it!") when he discovered a major law of physics while taking a bath.

ARISTEIDES (C.520BC-C.467BC)
Athenian politician and general, known as 'the Just'. A prominent leader during the Persian Wars and a commander at the Battle of Marathon, he also helped to set up the Delian League, an alliance of Greek states against the Persians.

ARISTOPHANES (C.445BC-C.385BC)
Athenian playwright, writer of about 40 comedies, of which eleven survive. Most make fun of the political events, and some mock other, more serious playwrights such as **Euripides**. His most famous plays are *The Wasps*, *The Birds* and *The Frogs*.

ARISTOTLE (384BC-322BC)
Best-known Greek philosopher. Aristotle was the son of a doctor to the King of Macedonia. He studied for 20 years at the Academy, the school run by **Plato**, researched the lives of animals in the eastern Mediterranean, and spent three years in Macedonia as the tutor of **Alexander the Great**. In 335BC, he set up a school in Athens, the Lyceum, for the study of science and literature. His writings cover many areas: he divided up knowledge into different subjects, such as biology, psychology and meteorology, and his ideas about drama and rhetoric (the power of persuasive speech) are still influential. Some of Aristotle's most famous works are *Poetics*, *Politica* and *Metaphysica*. He died in exile in Euboea.

ATTILA (C.AD406-453)
King of the Huns, a warlike tribe from Central Asia. Famous for his cruelty, Attila invaded Gaul in AD451, but was defeated by a combined army of Romans and barbarians at the Battle of Châlons.

AUGUSTUS (63BC-AD14)
First Roman emperor 27BC-AD14. He was the great-nephew and adopted son of **Julius Caesar**. After Caesar's death, Augustus and **Mark Antony** struggled for power before agreeing to divide the empire between them. In 31BC, Augustus defeated Antony and **Cleopatra** at the Battle of Actium, and gradually became supreme ruler of the Roman world. Originally named Octavian, he was given the military title 'Augustus' as a mark of respect. A wise and fair ruler, he worked closely with the Senate and brought peace after years of civil war. He passed laws to help the poor, and built splendid new buildings in Rome. After his death, he was declared a god by **Tiberius**.

BRUTUS (84-42BC)
Roman soldier and politician. A strong believer in the traditions of the Roman Republic, he led the plot to murder **Caesar** in 44BC, because he thought Caesar was going to make himself king. Brutus committed suicide after losing a battle against **Mark Antony**.

CAESAR, JULIUS (C.100-44BC)
Roman politician, general and writer. From 58BC to 49BC, he led troops in Gaul and Illyricum, extending Roman territory as far as the English Channel. He wrote about these campaigns in seven books, called *De Bello Gallico* (The Gallic Wars). In 49BC, following disputes with **Pompey** and the Senate, Caesar returned to Italy with his army. After defeating his enemies, he was declared dictator for life. Some politicians feared he had grown too powerful, and in 44BC he was murdered by a group of senators, led by **Brutus**.

CALIGULA (AD12-41)
Roman emperor AD37-41. Famous for his wild and cruel acts, he may have become insane following a serious illness. He grew up in the army, and was nicknamed Caligula ('little boots') because of the miniature soldier's uniform he wore as a child. His real name was Gaius.

CAMBYSES (C.525-521BC)
King of Persia. Son of **Cyrus II**. He conquered Egypt in 525BC. Some claim

he was both cruel and insane. He was said to have offended the Egyptians by breaking into a pharaoh's tomb and burning the corpse, and desecrating temples and wounding the Apis bull.

CARACALLA (AD188-217)
Roman emperor AD211-217. He bribed barbarian tribes to stay away from the empire's borders and he extended Roman citizenship to all free men living in the empire. Cruel and extravagant, he was assassinated by his personal bodyguard.

CATO (234-149BC)
Roman politician and writer. His book *De Agri Cultura* is the oldest existing work in Latin and describes the traditional Roman values of dignity and simplicity. He also wrote *Origines* - a history of the Roman people.

CATULLUS (C.84-54BC)
Roman poet. He wrote love poems and vivid descriptions of Roman life, and was one of the first to adopt the forms and style of Greek poetry. His most famous poems were written to his beloved Lesbia.

CICERO (106-43BC)
Roman politician, lawyer and writer. The greatest public speaker of his day, he became a famous lawyer and consul. He accused the senator Catiline of plotting against the Republic, and had several of the conspirators executed. Cicero made enemies by speaking out against important men, and was murdered by the troops of **Mark Antony**. His style of writing and speaking was imitated by scholars for centuries after his death.

CIMON (C.510BC-450BC)
Athenian soldier and statesman, renowned for his amazing height and shaggy hair. The son of **Miltiades**, a sworn enemy of the Persians, he led successful campaigns to free the Greek islands from Persian rule. In 462BC, he persuaded Athens to support Sparta, but when the Spartans refused Athenian help, Cimon's prestige suffered and he was ostracized. (He was later called back to Athens to negotiate peace.) He died during an expedition to recapture Cyprus from the Persians.

CLAUDIUS (10BC-AD54)
Roman emperor AD41-54. After his nephew **Caligula's** murder, Claudius was found hiding in the imperial palace and was declared emperor by the Praetorian

Guards. He limped and stuttered and many people thought he wasn't very intelligent, but he turned out to be a capable ruler. Claudius conquered Britain in AD43 and wrote books about Roman and Etruscan history. He may have been poisoned by his wife, **Agrippina**.

CLEISTHENES (DIED C.500BC)
Athenian politician and aristocrat. He took power in Athens after the overthrow of the tyrant Hippias in 510BC, introducing reforms that led to the political system known as democracy (see page 192-193). He also introduced ostracism (the practice of banishing unwanted politicians).

CLEOPATRA VII (51-30BC)
Queen of Egypt (Ptolemaic Period). Sister-wife of both Ptolemy XIII and Ptolemy XIV and lover of **Julius Caesar**, she later married his friend **Mark Antony**. They were defeated at Actium in 31BC by Caesar's heir **Octavian**. In 30BC Cleopatra committed suicide along with Mark Antony and Egypt was absorbed into the Roman empire.

COMMODUS (AD161-192)
Roman emperor AD180-192. The son of **Marcus Aurelius**, he made peace with the barbarian tribes and spent most of his reign in Rome, living a life of luxury. He loved to fight as a gladiator in the arena and was killed in a wrestling match.

CONSTANTINE (C.AD274-337)
First Christian Roman emperor AD307-337. Became sole ruler of the western empire after defeating his rival, Maxentius, at the battle of Milvian Bridge. He reunited the empire and moved the capital to Byzantium, which he renamed Constantinople. In AD313, he issued the Edict of Milan, allowing Christians to worship freely.

CRASSUS (C.112-53BC)
Roman soldier and politician. He defeated a rebellion led by the slave Spartacus in 71BC. In 60BC, he made an alliance with **Pompey** and **Caesar**, and used his wealth to support Caesar's ambitions. He was killed in battle.

CYRUS II (559-529BC)
King of Persia and founder of the Achaemenid dynasty. In 550BC, he defeated his grandfather Astyages of Media and united the kingdoms of Persia and Media under his rule. He conquered the kingdoms of Lydia and Babylon.

DARIUS I 'THE GREAT' (C.521-485BC)
King of Persia. Under him the Persian empire reached its greatest extent. He established a fair and efficient law code and divided the empire into provinces, each run by a satrap (or governor).

DIOCLETIAN (AD245-313)
Roman emperor AD284-305. He made radical changes to coinage, taxation, the civil service and the army. After splitting the Empire in two, he ruled the eastern empire while Maximian ruled the west.

DJOSER (C.2630-2611BC)
King of Egypt (Dynasty III). The first pyramid, the step pyramid at Saqqara, was designed for him as a tomb by his architect **Imhotep**.

DOMITIAN (AD51-96)
Roman emperor AD81-96. Strengthened the frontiers of the empire against barbarians, and restored many of Rome's buildings. Efficient but tyrannical and unpopular, he despised the Senate and persecuted many Christians and Jews. His wife Domitia had him stabbed to death.

DRACO (7TH CENTURY BC)
Athenian politician and legal reformer. He made existing laws much more severe, introducing the death penalty for minor crimes - including laziness. He promoted public trials so people could see that justice had been done. The word 'Draconian', meaning 'very severe', comes from him. But the Athenians soon became unhappy with his laws, and most of Draco's system was abolished by **Solon**.

ESARHADDON (680-667BC)
King of Assyria. He rebuilt the city of Babylon, which had been destroyed by his father **Sennacherib**. In 671BC he invaded the Nile Delta and installed Assyrian governors in Egypt. But his empire was huge and the Assyrians were cruel and unpopular with their subjects.

EUCLID (LIVED C.300BC)
Greek mathematician, working in Alexandria in Egypt. In his greatest work, *Elements*, he explained many aspects of geometry and mathematics, and summed up the teachings of earlier mathematicians. Several of his theories and discoveries are still in use today.

EURIPIDES (C.485BC-406BC)
Athenian playwright, and (along with **Aeschylus** and **Sophocles**) one of the three great writers of Greek tragedies. He wrote over 90 plays, of which 19 have survived, including *Medea*, *Bacchae* and *Electra*. He was famous for his natural style and for depicting his characters' inner thoughts and feelings.

GRACCHUS, GAIUS (C.160-121BC)
Roman soldier and politician, and brother of **Tiberius Gracchus**. Known for introducing the corn dole, where cheap grain was given to the poor and unemployed. He was murdered in 121BC.

GRACCHUS, TIBERIUS (C.169-133BC)
Roman soldier and politician, and brother of **Gaius Gracchus**. In 133BC, he forced through a new law, giving land to the poor that had been illegally seized by the rich. Many senators were opposed to his ideas, and a group of them started a riot in which he was murdered.

HADRIAN (AD76-138)
Roman emperor AD117-138. Believing the empire had become too big to control, he gave up some of Rome's lands, and built fortresses and walls to protect the borders, the most famous of which is Hadrian's Wall, in northern England. A cultured man, Hadrian spent time visiting the provinces.

HANNIBAL (247-182BC)
Carthaginian general, who commanded the army against Rome in the Second Punic War. In 218BC, he invaded Italy and defeated the Romans at Lake Trasimene and Cannae. He was finally defeated by **Scipio** at Zama, in North Africa, in 202BC, and later committed suicide to avoid being captured by the Romans.

HATSHEPSUT (1490-1468BC)
Queen of Egypt (Dynasty XVIII). Daughter of Tuthmosis I and Queen Ahmose and sister-wife of Tuthmosis II. Appointed regent for her son **Tuthmosis III**, she seized power and reigned as 'king' for over 20 years. Evidence of her reign is scarce, as her official inscriptions were destroyed after her death.

HERODOTUS (C.490BC-425BC)
Greek historian, writer of a history of the Persian Wars, he known as 'the father of history' because he was the first to establish historical facts and write about them as a sequence of linked events. Born in Ionia, he settled in Athens, and later in Thurii in southern Italy.

HESIOD (C.700BC)
One of the earliest Greek poets. He claimed that the Muses (nine goddesses of the arts) visited him as he was tending sheep on Mount Helicon, and gave him the gift of poetry. His most famous book, *Works and Days*, includes practical details of farming, a calendar of lucky and unlucky days and an explanation of religious ceremonies.

HIPPOCRATES (C.460BC-C.370BC)
Greek doctor. His teachings formed the basis of medical practice throughout the ancient world. (Doctors still take the Hippocratic Oath, in which they promise to treat patients well.) Unlike earlier doctors, he based his work on close observation, rather than religious rituals. His writings (collected long after he died, so may not all be by him) discuss such things as the effect of environment on illness. He founded an important medical school on the island of Kos.

HOMER (C.8TH CENTURY BC)
The most famous Greek poet. Little is known about his life. He was a bard - an entertainer who recited poems - and his work was passed on by word of mouth. Eventually fragments were written down (and probably added to), centuries after his death. He may have come from the island of Chios, and was blind. His poems *The Iliad* and *The Odyssey* describe events during and after the Trojan War.

HORACE (65-8BC)
Roman poet and government clerk before he began writing poetry. His most famous works are the *Odes* - short poems on the joys of food, wine and the countryside.

IMHOTEP
Egyptian official (Dynasty III). Doctor, High Priest and architect of the step pyramid of Saqqara, he may also have introduced the calendar. Later revered as a god, the Greeks identified him with their god of medicine, Asclepius.

JOSEPHUS (C.AD37-100)
Jewish historian and general, who led a revolt against Roman rule in Judea in AD66. When the rebellion was crushed he joined the Romans, and wrote a famous account, *History of the Jewish War*.

JULIAN (AD332-363)
Roman emperor AD360-363. Known as 'the Apostate', he tried to restore the old Roman gods 50 years after Christianity had been accepted. He improved the civil service, but was unpopular because of his old-fashioned religious views.

JUVENAL (C.AD60-C.AD130)
Roman poet, author of the Satires, biting attacks on corruption in Roman society. These may have caused him to be banished from Rome for a time.

KAMOSE (C.1555-1552BC)
King of Egypt (Dynasty XVII: the Theban kings). Son of Tao II and Ahhotep I. He fought the Hyksos and extended his frontier as far as the Faiyum.

KHAFRE OR KHEPHREN (C.2520-2494BC)
King of Egypt (Dynasty IV). Son of **Khufu**, he succeeded his brother Ra'djedef. His pyramid is the second one of the three at Giza.

KHUFU OR CHEOPS (C.2551-2528BC)
King of Egypt (Dynasty IV). Son of **Seneferu** and Hetepheres I. His pyramid, the Great Pyramid at Giza, is the largest ever built and was the oldest of the Seven Wonders of the Ancient World.

LIVIA (58BC-AD29)
Wife of Roman emperor **Augustus**. A wealthy and intelligent aristocrat, she had a great influence on Augustus's rule. After her husband's death, Livia made sure that **Tiberius** - her son by an earlier marriage - became the next emperor.

LIVY (59BC-AD17)
Roman historian and author of *Ab Urbe Condita* - a vast history of the city and its people, originally consisting of 142 books, only 35 of which have survived.

MARCUS AURELIUS (AD121-180)
Roman emperor AD161-180. Most of his reign was spent fighting off barbarian invaders. He was an outstanding general, peace-loving philosopher, and author of journals called *Meditations*.

MARIUS (157-86BC)
Roman general and politician. He won wars in Spain, Africa and Gaul and was consul seven times. He is best known for reorganizing the Roman army. A power struggle between him and **Sulla** in 88BC was one of the causes of the civil war that led to the collapse of the Republic.

MARTIAL (C.AD40-104)
Roman poet. Born in Spain, but lived in Rome for many years. His short poems - the *Epigrams* - describe daily life and some of Rome's livelier characters. Much of his poetry was bitterly satirical, but he also wrote affectionate poems to friends.

MENES or NARMER (C.3100BC)
Early king of Upper Egypt, conqueror of Lower Egypt and probably first king of a united Egypt under Dynasty I. Menes and Narmer may have been one and the same, or two separate kings.

MENKAURE or MYCERINUS (C.2490-2472BC)
King of Egypt (Dynasty IV). Son of **Khafre**. His pyramid is the smallest of the three pyramids at Giza.

MENTUHOTEP II (C.2040-2010BC)
King of Thebes in Upper Egypt (Dynasty XI). He defeated the King of Lower Egypt (Dynasty X) and reunited Egypt under his rule. This began the Middle Kingdom.

MERENPTAH (C.1224-1204BC)
King of Egypt (Dynasty XIX). He was in his fifties when he succeeded his father **Ramesses II**, who had outlived his first 13 sons. A great military commander, he fought the Sea Peoples and the Libyans.

MILTIADES (C.550BC-489BC)
Athenian soldier and politician, and father of **Cimon**. Supported the Ionian revolt against Persian rule in 499BC and led the Athenians at the Battle of Marathon.

NECHO I (C.672-664BC)
Prince of Sais (Lower Egypt). His family had never accepted the Nubian Dynasty XXV, and he sided with the Assyrians when they invaded Egypt in 664BC. He was captured and executed, but his son Psamtek restored Egypt's independence, founding Dynasty XXVI. The Egyptians called him Necho I, because they counted him as the first king of the dynasty.

NECTANEBO I (C.379-361BC)
King of Egypt (First of Dynasty XXX).

NEFERTARI
Chief queen of Egyptian pharaoh, **Ramesses II** (Dynasty XIX). One of the temples at Abu Simbel was built for her.

NEFERTITI
Egyptian Queen (Dynasty XVIII). Wife of **Akhenaten** and mother of Akhesenamun.

NERO (AD37-68)
Roman emperor AD54-68. He ruled well at first, but later became tyrannical, and had his own wife and mother murdered, as well as anyone who dared oppose him. He enjoyed playing the lyre and singing, and taking part in chariot races. Nero built an extravagant palace in Rome, known as the Golden House. He may have started the Great Fire of Rome in AD64 to make room for this new palace.

NERVA (C.AD30-98)
Roman emperor AD96-98. A fair and peaceful ruler, he brought stability after **Domitian's** turbulent reign. He started a new tradition by adopting as a son the man he wanted to rule after him: **Trajan**.

OCTAVIAN see Augustus

ODOACER (C.AD434-493)
Ruler of Italy AD476-493. A barbarian general who sent the last Roman emperor, Romulus Augustulus, into exile in AD476, and declared himself king.

OVID (43BC-AD18)
Roman poet, who originally studied law. His work became very popular in Rome, but in AD8, **Augustus** banished him to the Black Sea and he never returned. His most famous work is *Metamorphoses* - 15 books of poems on myths and legends.

PEISISTRATUS (C.600BC-527BC)
Athenian politician. In 546BC, he declared himself tyrant (unelected ruler). The city prospered under him: trade improved and he reorganized public finances, spent money on roads, a water supply, and rebuilding. Succeeded by his son Hippias.

PEPI II (C.2246-2252BC)
King of Egypt (Dynasty VI). He reigned for 94 years; the longest recorded reign in history. After his death, Egypt collapsed into civil conflict and confusion and the Old Kingdom came to an end.

PERICLES (C.495BC-429BC)
Athenian statesman and great public speaker. He became the most powerful politician of his day, and was elected *strategos* (war commander) every year from 443BC to 429BC. He improved the democratic system, and built the Parthenon; but in 430BC he was charged with stealing public money to fund his building projects. He died after becoming ill with a plague.

PHEIDIAS (C.490BC-432BC)

Athenian painter and sculptor, employed by **Pericles** to provide new sculptures for the city, including a bronze statue of Athene which stood on the Acropolis, an ivory and gold statue of Athene inside the Parthenon, and his masterpiece, Zeus at Olympia. In 432BC, he was accused of stealing gold intended for work on the Parthenon. He proved his innocence, but was sent to prison, where he died.

PHILIP II OF MACEDONIA (C.382BC-336BC)

Macedonian king, who reorganized the army and showed great skill as a military commander and diplomat. He united the country, extended the frontiers, and made Macedonia into the greatest military power of its day. He was murdered, and succeeded by his son **Alexander**.

PINDAR (C.518BC-438BC)

Greek poet, born in Boeotia, he was famous for verses celebrating sporting heroes, and great leaders.

PLATO (427BC-347BC)

Athenian philosopher, aristocrat and pupil of Socrates, he wrote *The Apology*, in answer to Socrates' enemies. He set out his ideas for an ideal state in *The Republic* and *The Laws*, and founded a school near Athens, called the Academy. The school, whose pupils included **Aristotle**, was famous throughout the ancient world, but was closed in AD529 by the Roman emperor Justinian, who thought it politically dangerous. Plato's ideas have remained influential to the present day.

PLAUTUS (C.254-184BC)

Roman playwright. He is said to have written over 130 plays, but only 21 have survived. These are all based on Greek comedies, though they include aspects of Roman life. His works inspired many later playwrights, including Shakespeare.

PLINY (C.AD61-113)

Roman writer, lawyer, and consul under **Trajan**. Published nine volumes of letters, including an eyewitness account of the eruption of Vesuvius in AD79.

PLUTARCH (AD46-126)

Roman writer, who wrote on many different subjects, including science, literature and philosophy. His best-known work is *Plutarch's Lives* - pairs of biographies comparing Greek and Roman soldiers and statesmen.

POMPEY (106-48BC)

Roman general and politician. He helped **Crassus** to put down the slave revolt led by Spartacus, cleared the Mediterranean of pirates and won great victories in the Middle East. In 60BC, he joined an alliance with Crassus and **Caesar**, but this broke down and he was eventually defeated and murdered in Egypt.

PRAXITELES (BORN C.390BC)

Athenian sculptor, who developed a new, delicate style of sculpture, in contrast to the grand, formal style of earlier artists.

PTOLEMY I (305-284BC)

King of Egypt. A general in the army of **Alexander the Great**, he was appointed governor of Egypt after Alexander's death, ruling on behalf of Alexander's son and mentally handicapped brother. When they were both murdered, Ptolemy became king and founder of the Ptolemaic dynasty.

PYTHAGORAS (C.580BC-500BC)

Greek philosopher, mathematician and mystic. He believed in reincarnation and taught his followers that they must not eat meat or beans (no one knows why). He studied mathematics, astronomy and music, and is best-known for his discoveries about right-angled triangles.

RAMESSES/RAMSES II (c.1289-1224BC)

King of Egypt (Dynasty XIX). He built a large number of fortresses, temples and monuments, including two temples cut into the rock at Abu Simbel. During the early part of his reign he was engaged in a struggle with the Hittites, but fear of the Assyrians brought an end to the conflict.

RAMESSES/RAMSES III (c.1184-1153BC)

King of Egypt (Dynasty XX). Last great king of the New Kingdom. He fought the Libyans, overcame an attack by the Sea Peoples, and built a huge mortuary complex at Medinat Habu.

SAPPHO (C.610BC-650BC)

Greek poet. Born and lived on the island of Lesbos. Famous for her lyrical, emotional style, she wrote nine books of poetry, mostly about love or family and friends, but only fragments survive.

SCIPIO (237-183BC)

Roman general. Led the Roman invasion of Carthage during the Second Punic War, and defeated **Hannibal** at Zama, in North Africa. After this victory, he was given the name Scipio Africanus.

SENECA (C.5BC-AD65)

Roman writer, philosopher and lawyer. He was born in Spain, but spent most of his life in Rome. He became **Nero's** tutor and had a great influence on the early part of Nero's reign, but in AD65 he was accused of plotting against the emperor and was forced to commit suicide. His *Moral Letters* set out his ideas and beliefs.

SENEFERU (C.2575-2551BC)

King of Egypt (Dynasty IV). He built two pyramids: the 'Bent' Pyramid and the Red Pyramid (the first straight-sided pyramid).

SENNACHERIB (C.704-681BC)

King of Assyria. Son of Sargon II. He sacked Babylon in 689BC, put down revolts in other provinces, and invaded Egypt, but had to withdraw after an outbreak of plague. Murdered by his son who crushed him with a statue of a god.

SENUSRET III (C.1878-1841BC)

King of Egypt (Dynasty XII). He led campaigns against the Kushites who were threatening the frontiers of Nubia, began a huge rebuilding operation, to strengthen the fortresses there, and claimed to have established his frontier further south than any previous king.

SHUPPILULIUMA (C.1380-1340BC)

The greatest Hittite king: a wily and able ruler and diplomat and a successful soldier. Under him the Hittite empire reached its greatest extent. He conquered the Mitanni empire and encouraged discontented Egyptian vassals to rebel.

SOCRATES (469BC-399BC)

Athenian philosopher. He didn't write any books, but taught by word of mouth, discussing philosophy and questioning weaknesses in the government and in people's beliefs. Famous for having an ugly face but a magnetic personality, his teachings made him unpopular with politicians. He was charged with impiety (refusing to believe in the gods) and corrupting the young, and sentenced to death by poison. His ideas were passed on by his pupils, who included **Plato**.

SOLON (C.640BC-558BC)

Athenian politician. Came to power in about 594BC, and overturned many of the harsh laws created by his predecessor **Draco**. He set up a court of appeal, and reformed the way the government took decisions. Solon encouraged craftsmen to come and live in Athens, and aided the development of trade and industry.

SOPHOCLES (C.496BC-405BC)
One the great Greek tragic playwrights, he wrote 123 plays. Only seven survive: the most famous are *Electra*, *Antigone* and *Oedipus Tyrannus*. He was the first to use more than two actors in his plays, was one of the first to use scenery, and was admired for his realistic characters.

SUETONIUS (C.AD69-140)
Roman historian, lawyer and official. He wrote *Lives of the Twelve Caesars* - a lively account of Roman rulers from **Caesar** to **Domitian**, which included details about their looks, personalities and habits.

SULLA (138-78BC)
Roman general and politician. Lieutenant to **Marius**, who later became his fiercest rival. From 88BC to 86BC, the two men were involved in a bitter power struggle. When Marius died, Sulla seized control and made himself dictator, using his position to increase the Senate's power.

TACITUS (C.AD55-116)
Roman historian, army officer and official. His most famous works are the *Annals* and the *Histories* - which cover the period from **Tiberius** to **Domitian**.

TERENCE (C.195-159BC)
Roman playwright. Originally a slave, he was freed by his master, he wrote six plays, all adapted from Greek comedies. Roman audiences often found Terence's plays dull, but his work was still performed in imperial times.

TETI (C.2323-2291BC)
King of Egypt. Founder of Dynasty VI, he established a claim to the throne through his wife, Queen Ipwet, daughter of King Unas, the last king of Dynasty V. He built a pyramid at Saqqara and was murdered by his guards, in mysterious circumstances.

TETI-SHERI
Queen of Thebes (Dynasty XVII). Wife of Tao I. A woman of great influence, she may have encouraged the men of her family to rebel against the Hyksos. They were driven out by her grandson **Ahmose**, who provided her with a burial at Thebes and a monument at Abydos.

THEMISTOCLES (C.524BC-459BC)
Athenian statesman and war commander. He persuaded the Athenians to build up their navy, and led the Greeks at the Battle of Salamis in 480BC, helping them

to win. But public opinion turned against him and in c.471BC he was banished and fled to Argos. He was then accused of treason and fled to Asia Minor.

THEODOSIUS (C.AD346-395)
Roman emperor AD379-395. He allowed some barbarian tribes to settle in the empire as long as they helped to fight off other tribes. For a time, he ruled both the east and the west, but after his death the empire split permanently in two. Under Theodosius, Christianity became the official religion of the empire.

THUCYDIDES (C.460BC-399BC)
Athenian politician and historian. Elected strategos in 424BC, but he was blamed for a military defeat and fled into exile for over 20 years. While he was away, he wrote an account of the Peloponnesian Wars which is considered to be one of the first history books. As well as describing battles and political events, it reveals a lot about everyday life in ancient Greece.

TIBERIUS (42BC-AD37)
Roman emperor AD14-37. He had already retired from a life in the army when he was called to Rome to become emperor. An unpopular ruler, who was frightened that people were plotting to assassinate him. He executed many important Romans and fled to the island of Capri, for the last 11 years of his rule.

TITUS (AD39-81)
Roman emperor AD79-81. A generous emperor, he gave money to the people of Pompeii and Herculaneum when their towns were destroyed by a volcanic eruption. He was also an outstanding military commander, capturing Jerusalem in AD70. The Arch of Titus in Rome was later built to commemorate this victory.

TRAJAN (C.AD53-117)
Roman emperor AD98-117. One of Rome's finest military leaders, Trajan won huge areas of new land in Dacia and the Middle East, enlarging the empire to its greatest ever extent. He built many new roads, bridges, canals and towns, and an enormous forum in Rome, surrounded by markets, libraries and baths. Trajan's Column - a monument carved with scenes from the emperor's Dacian campaigns - still stands in Trajan's Forum.

TUTANKHAMUN (C.1347-1337BC)
King of Egypt (Dynasty XVIII). Son of **Akhenaten**. He came to the throne aged

only about nine and married his half-sister Ankhesenamun. A general named Horemheb and a courtier named Ay became regents. Although Tutankhamun died young, he is famous for the treasures found in his tomb in the Valley of the Kings by egyptologist Howard Carter in the 1920s. Many of the tombs of the Dynasty XVIII kings had been robbed over the centuries, but Tutankhamun's tomb had escaped attention.

TUTHMOSIS III (C.1490-1436BC)
King of Egypt (Dynasty XVIII). Son of Tuthmosis II and nephew of **Hatshepsut**, who was regent and kept him from power for the first twenty years of his reign. Probably the greatest of the New Kingdom warrior pharaohs, he enlarged the Egyptian empire to its widest limits.

VESPASIAN (AD9-79)
Roman emperor AD69-79. He brought peace and stability after the death of **Nero**. Strict but fair, he strengthened the empire's borders and granted citizenship to many people in the provinces. He began many ambitious building projects, including the Colosseum in Rome.

VIRGIL (70-19BC)
Roman poet. His work includes a long poem, the *Georgics*, a celebration of country life, and the *Aeneid*, which tells of the history of Rome in 12 books. Virgil was considered one of Rome's greatest poets, and by imperial times his works were being taught in schools.

VITRUVIUS (C.70BC-EARLY 1ST CENTURY AD)
Roman architect and engineer. He wrote *De Architectura* - 10 books on building styles and construction, which contain examples drawn from Greek architecture.

XENOPHON (C.428BC-354BC)
Athenian writer, and a pupil of **Socrates**. He fought for the Persians and Spartans against Athens, and was banished to Sparta. There he wrote many books, including *The Anabasis*, about his time with the Persians, and *The Hellenica*, a history of the events of his day.

ZENOBIA (3RD CENTURY AD)
Queen of Palmyra (part of the Roman province of Syria). She led a rebellion against Roman rule. After several victories, she was defeated and captured in AD272. Brought to Rome as a prisoner, she lived on for many years in comfort and style.

TIME CHART

This time chart outlines the dates of important periods and events in the history of the ancient world.

c.10000-2000BC Farming develops in the Middle East, then spreads to western and northern Europe.

c.5500BC People start to settle on the banks of the river Nile in Egypt.

c.5000BC Farming begins in China and central America.

c.4000BC Uruk culture develops in Sumer in Mesopotamia.

c.4000BC Farming communities settle in the Indus Valley, India.

From 4000BC The first people settle in Greece, hunting and gathering food.

c.3500BC Sumerians develop writing, invent the wheel and learn how to make bronze.

c.3500-3100BC Farming and irrigation begin in Egypt. Two separate kingdoms emerge: Upper Egypt in the south and Lower Egypt in the north. Hieroglyphic (picture) writing develops; Upper and Lower Egypt are united by King Menes around 3100BC.

c.3000-2000BC Independent city-states flourish in Sumer, Akkad and Canaan.

c.3000BC Pottery is in use in Ecuador, South America.

c.2900-1000BC Population of Greece increases; towns develop; metal is widely used.

c.2900-2400BC Early dynasties develop in Sumer.

c.2590BC The Great Pyramid of Giza is built in Egypt.

c.2500BC Longshan culture in China.

c.2500BC Troy is founded.

c.2500BC-1800BC Indus Valley civilization in India. People build cities and develop writing.

c.2000BC Building of Stonehenge is begun in England.

c.2000-1000BC Hurrians form an aristocratic caste in Canaan ruling the Amorites and Canaanites.

c.2000-1000BC Beginning of Mayan culture in central America.

c.2000BC Evidence of farming, metal-working and pottery in Peru.

c.2000BC Horses and wheeled vehicles are used in eastern Europe.

c.1900BC The rise of the Minoan civilization on Crete.

c.1813-1781BC Reign of Shamshi-Adad of Assyria. He builds up an empire from Mari to Babylon.

c.1792-1750BC Reign of Hammurabi, founder of the Babylonian empire.

c.1766-1027BC Shang dynasty rules China: a feudal state with walled cities, ruled by priest-kings.

c.1700BC Cretan palaces destroyed by earthquakes and rebuilt.

Young Minoan man from a wall-painting in the palace of Knossos in Crete

Bust of Nefertiti, chief queen of the pharaoh Akhenaten

c.1674BC Nile Delta is overrun by Hyksos: people from the Middle East.

c.1640-1552BC Egypt rules Kush (modern Sudan).

c.1600BC Towns and cities begin to develop in China.

c.1595BC The Hittites, a people from Anatolia, plunder Babylon and destroy the Amorite kingdom.

c.1552-1069BC Royal tombs built in the Valley of the Kings, Egypt.

c.1550BC Indo-Europeans known as Aryans settle in northern India.

c.1500BC Writing is in use in China. The earliest examples are found on bones used as oracles, thought to reveal the future.

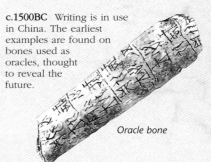

Oracle bone

BC, AD AND c.

Many of the dates in this book have the letters **BC**, **AD** or **c.** next to them.
- **BC** stands for 'Before Christ'. BC dates are counted backwards from the birth of Christ ~ so 300BC means 300 years before the birth of Christ.
- **AD** is used with dates after the birth of Christ, such as 50AD. It stands for *Anno Domini*, which in Latin means 'in the Year of the Lord'. It is often used for dates from Greek and Roman times.
- Some dates have a **c.** in front of them. It stands for *circa* ~ the Latin word for 'about'. It means that the date is not exact, but only a rough guess. It is used when experts are not sure exactly when something happened.

c.1500BC Mitanni people unite and rule the Hurrian kingdoms.

c.1500BC Aryans settle in Persia, now called Iran.

c.1500BC Farming reaches the southeast of North America.

c.1500BC Decline of the Indus Valley civilization in India.

c.1500-600BC Vedic Period in India: the Hindu religion is gradually established.

Statue of Shiva, one of the many Hindu gods

c.1500BC-AD200 Rise of the Olmec culture in Mexico: they use picture writing and calendars, and build huge temples and stone heads.

c.1490-1468BC Reign of Queen Hatshepsut, woman pharaoh of Egypt.

c.1450BC Volcanic eruption on Thera. Crete is taken over by Mycenaeans.

c.1450-1390BC The Mitanni conquer Assyria and build an empire. They make a peace treaty with Egypt in 1440BC.

1380BC Accession of Shuppiluliuma, one of the greatest Hittite kings. He overthrows the Mitanni and captures Syria, part of the Egyptian empire.

c.1300BC Bronze Age culture in Europe known as Urnfield.

c.1250BC Main fortifications are built at Mycenae and other sites.

c.1200BC Mycenaean power declines. Migration of the Sea Peoples, raiders and settlers from Greece and the Mediterranean islands.

Reconstruction of the city of Troy in Mycenaean times

c.1200BC The Olmecs build a great city at San Lorenzo in Mexico.

c.1200BC Hebrews arrive in Canaan (Palestine) led by Moses and Joshua.

c.1200-300BC Chavín people create the first civilization in South America, building temples and working in gold.

1196-1195BC The Sea Peoples destroy the Hittite empire. Some Hittites establish small neo-Hittite states.

1184-1153BC Reign of Ramesses III in Egypt: the last great warrior pharaoh.

c.1158BC Kassite rulers are thrown out of Babylon. Babylonian rule is restored.

c.1150BC Peleset, or Philistines, a group of Sea Peoples, settle in Canaan, later known after them as Palestine.

c.1100BC Phoenicians are established in Canaan. They found colonies with cities at Byblos, Sidon, Beirut and Tyre.

By 1100BC The Mycenaean way of life has collapsed.

c.1100BC Phoenicians spread throughout the Mediterranean and develop a form of alphabetic writing.

c.1085BC Nubia and Kush regain independence from Egypt.

1027-221BC Zhou dynasty overthrows the Shang in China. A period of trade and growth, but also of instability and wars.

c.1020-1010BC Reign of Saul, first King of the Israelites.

c.1010-926BC Kingdom of Israel.

c.1000-900BC Etruscans are established in northern Italy. They are skilled at working in metal.

c.1000BC The Latin people first settle on the Palatine Hill in Rome.

c.1000-300BC Adena people build earth mounds in North America.

Portrait of one of the Sea Peoples from an Egyptian temple

c.966-926BC Reign of King Solomon of the Israelites. Israelite power reaches its greatest height.

c.900BC The *Rig Veda* (Hindu religious text) is composed in India.

c.850-750BC Greek poet Homer probably lived at this time.

c.814BC Phoenicians found the city of Carthage in north Africa.

c.800BC The Hindu religion spreads south in India.

c.800BC Celtic way of life spreads in western Europe.

c.800-400BC Etruscans flourish in central and northern Italy.

c.800BC Greeks resume trading contacts with other peoples. They adapt Phoenician writing.

776BC Traditional date of the first Olympic Games in Greece.

c.750-650BC People start to emigrate from Greece, founding colonies in the Mediterranean.

c.726-722BC Reign of Shalmaneser V of Assyria who conquers Israel.

c.722-481BC Spring and Autumn Period in China; small states fight for supremacy.

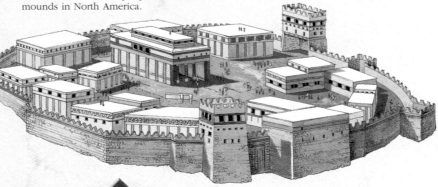

c.700BC Scythians move into eastern Europe from Asia.

c.670BC Kingdom of Media is set up near Persia.

664-525BC Saite dynasty rules Egypt: Egyptian independence is restored.

668-627BC Reign of Ashurbanipal II of Assyria; he sacks Thebes (in Egypt), Babylon and Susa (Persia).

c.650BC The first coins are introduced in Lydia.

621BC Draco introduces very strict laws in Athens.

612BC The Assyrian cities of Ashur and Nineveh fall to an alliance of the Medes and Babylonians.

605-562BC Nebuchadnezzar II rules the Babylonian empire, and rebuilds the city of Babylon.

c.600-500BC The Nubians abandon their capital at Napata and move south to set up a capital at Meroë.

c.600BC Introduction of Taoism in China by Lao-zi, the Chinese philosopher.

597-568BC Nebuchadnezzar II of Babylon occupies Jerusalem and carries off its leading citizens to Babylon. After a further revolt in 587-568BC, he sacks Jerusalem and deports many more people to Babylon.

c.594BC Solon is made archon of Athens and reforms the political system.

c.563-483BC The life of Gautama Siddhartha, known as the Buddha.

Carving of the Buddha's head

551-479BC The life of Kong Zi (also known as Confucius), the Chinese philosopher and prophet.

c.550BC Media and Persia are united by Cyrus II of Persia. He conquers Lydia and takes over the Babylonian empire.

c.546BC The Persians conquer Greek colonies in Ionia (Turkey).

525BC Egypt is conquered by Cambyses II of Persia.

By 521BC Darius I has expanded Persian empire as far as the Nile and the Indus rivers.

A Persian elite warrior from the palace at Susa

c.510BC Rome becomes a republic.

508BC Cleisthenes seizes power in Athens and introduces reforms which lead to democracy.

500-494BC Greek colonies in Ionia revolt against Persian rule.

496BC The Romans are defeated by an alliance of Latin cities at Lake Regillus.

494BC Roman plebeians go on strike and threaten to set up their own city.

490BC The Greeks defeat the Persians at the Battle of Marathon.

c.481-221BC Warring States Period in China: seven major states destroy each other in struggles for power.

480BC The Persians defeat the Greeks at Thermopylae. The Greeks defeat the Persians at the Battle of Salamis.

479BC The Persians are defeated at Plataea and expelled from Greece.

478BC Athens and other Greek states form the Delian League to fight against the Persians.

c.465BC Persia declines.

461-429BC Pericles plays a leading role in Athenian politics: he is elected *strategos* every year from 443BC until his death in 429BC.

460-457BC The Long Walls are built around Athens and Piraeus. The Acropolis is rebuilt.

c.450BC Start of the Celtic culture known as La Tène.

447-438BC The Parthenon temple is built in Athens.

431-404BC The Peloponnesian Wars between the Athenians and the Spartans.

421BC 50 Years' Peace negotiated between Sparta and Athens.

413BC War breaks out again between Athens and Sparta.

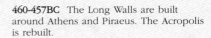

Bronze Celtic shield found in the Thames at London

407BC The Athenian fleet is defeated at the Battle of Notium by the Spartans.

405BC Athens is defeated by Sparta at the Battle of Aegospotami.

404BC Final Spartan victory over Athens.

404-343BC The Egyptians throw the Persians out of Egypt.

403BC Democracy is restored in Athens.

By 400BC Rome is the leading city in the Latin League.

c.400BC The Olmec culture comes to an end in central America.

399BC The Greek philosopher Socrates is condemned to death.

395-387BC Corinthian War in Greece: Corinth, Athens, Argos and Thebes fight against Sparta.

394BC Persians defeat the Spartans at the Battle of Cnidus.

394-391BC The Long Walls are rebuilt around Athens.

Statue of a Spartan soldier

390BC The city of Rome is attacked by an army of Gauls and most of its buildings are destroyed.

387BC The Corinthian War ends, negotiated by the Persians; Greek colonies in Ionia pass to the Persians.

371BC Thebans defeat the Spartans at the Battle of Leuctra.

366BC The first plebeian consul is elected in Rome.

362BC The Spartans and Athenians defeat the Thebans at Mantinea.

359BC Philip II is King of Macedonia.

Head of Philip of Macedonia

347BC Rome begins making coins.

343-331BC The Persians retake Egypt.

340BC Greek states form a Hellenic League against Philip of Macedonia.

338BC Rome defeats the Latin League and takes control of Latium.

338BC Philip II defeats the Hellenic League at Chaeronea and becomes ruler of Greece. This marks the end of the independent Greek city-states.

337BC Greek states join the Corinthian League, led by Philip II of Macedonia, which declares war on Persia.

336BC Philip II dies, and is succeeded by his son, Alexander the Great.

333BC Alexander defeats the Persians at the Battle of Issus.

332BC Alexander conquers Egypt, Phoenicia, Samaria, Judea and Gaza.

331BC Alexander destroys the Persian army at the Gaugamela and advances into India.

323BC Alexandria becomes the new capital of Egypt. Alexander dies. His general Ptolemy becomes ruler of Egypt.

323-322BC Lamian Wars: Greek city-states fight for independence from Alexander's empire, but are defeated.

323-281BC Wars of the Diadochi (between Alexander's 'successors').

321BC Mauryan Empire is founded in northern India by Chandragupta Maurya.

312BC First Roman road: the Appian Way, leading south from Rome.

301BC Battle of Ipsus: four rival Diadochi kingdoms are established.

c.300BC Mayan people begin building stone cities in central America.

c.300BC The Chavín civilization in South America comes to an end.

c.300-200BC Alphabetic script develops in Meroë, in Sudan.

281BC Alexander's empire is divided into three kingdoms: Macedonia (ruled by Antigonas); Asia Minor (ruled by Seleucus); and Egypt (ruled by Ptolemy).

c.272-231BC Emperor Asoka of the Maurya dynasty unites most of India under his rule.

264BC Rome now dominates Italy.

247BC The Kingdom of Parthia is set up in Persia.

241BC Sicily becomes Rome's first overseas territory.

221BC Unification of China under the first Qin (or Ch'in emperor) Shi Huangdi. The Great Wall of China is begun.

216BC The Romans are defeated by the Carthaginians at the Battle of Cannae.

Greek soldiers shown on a vase painting

215BC Philip V of Macedonia allies with Hannibal of Carthage to fight against the Romans.

206BC-AD222 The Han dynasty is in power in China.

202BC The Roman general Scipio defeats Hannibal at Zama.

202-197BC Philip V of Macedonia is defeated by the Romans and surrenders Greece to them.

c.200BC Nazca people make giant drawings in the deserts of Peru.

171-168BC Romans defeat the last Macedonian king, Perseus, at Pydna and set up four Roman republics.

149-146BC The Third Punic War ends with the destruction of Carthage by the Romans.

147-146BC The Romans destroy Corinth after a Macedonian revolt, and impose direct Roman rule on Greece.

133-31BC The Romans expand throughout the Mediterranean.

123BC Gaius Gracchus becomes Roman tribune and introduces the corn dole to feed the poor in Rome.

Reconstruction of the Pharos or lighthouse at Alexandria

c.112BC The opening of the Silk Road trade route, linking China with the West.

107BC Marius becomes Roman consul and begins reorganizing the Roman army.

102-101BC Marius manages to defeat tribes of Gauls invading Roman lands.

c.100BC The pyramid city of Teotihuacán is begun in central America

c.100BC Paper is invented in China.

82-80BC Sulla becomes dictator in Rome.

73-71BC The gladiator Spartacus leads a revolt of 90,000 slaves against the leaders of Rome.

63BC The Roman general Pompey conquers four provinces in the Middle East, including Syria and Judea.

Carved stone bust of Julius Caesar

58-51BC Julius Caesar, a Roman general, conquers Gaul (France). He invades but withdraws from Britain in 55-54BC.

49BC Caesar returns to Rome and seizes power. Civil war breaks out between him and Pompey. By 45BC he is the leader of the Roman world.

44BC Caesar is murdered by Roman senators, led by Brutus and Cassius.

42BC Brutus and Cassius are defeated at Philippi. Mark Antony and Octavian divide up the Roman empire: Antony rules the east, Octavian the west.

c.33BC Civil war between Octavian and Mark Antony.

31BC Octavian defeats Antony and Queen Cleopatra of Egypt at Actium.

30BC Egypt becomes a province of the Roman empire.

27BC Octavian becomes the first Roman emperor and takes the name Augustus.

c.5BC Jesus of Nazareth is born in Bethlehem, in Judea.

c.AD1 Moche culture begins in Peru.

c.AD1-100 Buddhism spreads from India throughout Asia.

AD9 Three Roman legions are massacred by Germanic tribes.

c.AD30 Jesus of Nazareth is crucified in Jerusalem, in Judea.

AD43 The Roman emperor Claudius conquers Britain.

AD58-60 The Christian missionary Paul of Tarsus travels to Rome.

AD60 Boudicca, Queen of the Iceni, rebels against the Romans in Britain.

Wall-painting of a couple, found in the ruins of Pompeii, Italy

AD64 Great Fire of Rome. Nero blames the Christians for the fire and starts persecuting them.

AD66-73 The Jewish people of Judea rebel against Roman rule.

AD68-69 Year of the Four Emperors in Rome. Galba, Otho and Vitellius are briefly in charge, until Vespasian seizes power for himself.

AD70 The Roman commander Titus captures the city of Jerusalem, in Judea. Christianity reaches Alexandria, in Egypt.

AD73 Roman army defeats the Jewish rebellion by capturing the last stronghold of Jewish resistance at Masada.

AD79 The Colosseum is opened in Rome. Mount Vesuvius erupts, destroying Pompeii and Herculaneum.

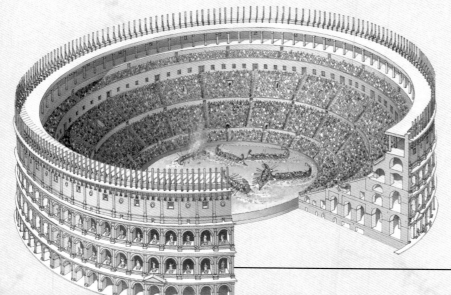

Reconstruction of a mock sea-battle at the Colosseum in Rome

AD100-700 The Champa kingdom is set up in Southeast Asia.

AD100-700 The kingdom of Axum, in present-day Ethiopia, flourishes.

AD117 The Roman empire reaches its largest extent, after Trajan's conquests of Dacia and Parthia.

AD122-127 Hadrian's Wall is built by the Romans in northern England.

AD132-135 The Romans put down a revolt in Judea. The Jewish nation comes to an end, and Jews spread out around Europe and the Middle East.

c.AD200 Germanic tribes attack the borders of the Roman empire.

c.AD200-600 A civilization grows around the city of Tiahuanaco, in Bolivia.

AD235-284 The Anarchy in Rome - short reigns of many emperors. Barbarians attack from the north and east. Plagues sweep Europe.

AD238 Revolt against Roman rule in North Africa.

c.AD250-750 The Zapotec civilization flourishes in Mexico, Central America.

c.AD250-900 Mayan civilization in Central America is at its peak.

AD260 Romans are defeated by the Persians, and the Emperor Valerian is taken prisoner.

AD268-272 Queen Zenobia of Palmyra captures Syria and parts of Egypt.

A Yamato warrior

AD271 The Aurelian Wall is built around Rome to protect the city.

AD284 Roman emperor Diocletian splits the empire into east and west.

c.AD285 The first Christian monasteries are set up in Egypt.

c.AD300 Leaders of the Yamato tribe become the first emperors of Japan.

AD303 Diocletian begins his campaign to persecute Christians.

AD304 Huns break through the Great Wall of China.

AD312 Constantine defeats Maxentius at the Battle of the Milvian Bridge, and becomes the sole ruler of the western Roman empire.

AD313 Constantine allows Christians to worship freely.

AD320 Gupta empire founded in India.

AD324-337 Constantine reunites the Roman empire. In AD330 he moves the capital to Byzantium, which is renamed Constantinople.

AD325 First Council of the Christian Church meets in Nicaea.

c.AD330 King Ezana of Axum (Ethiopia) becomes the first Christian king in Africa.

AD337-361 Emperor Julian ('the Apostate') tries to restore the old Roman gods.

AD367 Barbarian tribes set up kingdoms inside the Roman empire.

c.AD370 The Huns invade Europe from Central Asia.

AD378 The Roman emperor Valens is killed by Goths at Adrianople.

AD383-410 The Roman legions withdraw from Britain and Gaul.

AD394-395 Emperor Theodosius reunites the Roman empire.

AD394 Christianity becomes the Roman empire's official religion.

AD395 The Roman empire splits permanently into east and west.

c.AD400 First towns built south of the Sahara Desert.

c.AD400 Settlers from southeast Asia reach Easter Island in the Pacific Ocean.

AD402 Goths invade Italy. The Roman emperor Honorius moves his court to the city of Ravenna.

AD404 First Latin version of the Bible - known as the Vulgate - is completed.

AD409 Vandals invade Spain.

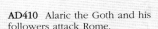

A Hun archer on horseback

AD410 Alaric the Goth and his followers attack Rome.

AD429 Vandals set up a kingdom in North Africa.

AD430-470 Huns invade the Gupta empire, in India.

AD449 Vortigern, King of the Britons, invites the Saxons into Britain to help him fight the Picts and the Scots. Angles and Jutes, from northern Europe, follow.

By c.AD450 Franks settle in Gaul.

AD451 The Romans and Franks defeat the Huns at the Battle of Châlons.

AD455 Vandals invade Italy from Africa, and destroy Rome.

AD475 Visigoths declare an independent kingdom in Spain.

AD476 Romulus Augustulus, last emperor of the western Roman empire, is defeated by Odoacer, a barbarian general who declares himself King of Italy. The empire in the west ends. The empire in the east continues, and is known as the Byzantine empire.

Mosaic showing Constantine holding a model of his capital city, Constantinople

GLOSSARY

This glossary explains some of the specialized words used in this book. If a word used has its own separate entry, it is shown in *italic type*.

acropolis Fortified city located on high ground.

aedile Roman government official.

agora Central, open marketplace in a Greek city.

akh One of the three aspects of an Egyptian person's spirit.

alabaster A translucent, white stone used for vases and lamps.

Amphidromia A Greek ceremony held after the birth of a baby.

amphora (plural: amphorae) Greek two-handled jar for wine or olive oil.

amulet A good luck charm in the form of a god, or sacred object.

andron Dining room in a Greek private house, used only by men.

ankh An Egyptian *amulet* shaped a little like a cross; the symbol of life.

Anthesteria A Greek spring festival.

apis bull A sacred bull associated with the Egyptian god Ptah.

aqueduct (1) A Roman pipe for carrying water. (2) A large bridge with a water channel along the top.

Arabs A *Semitic* people living in Arabia and surrounding territory.

archon An Athenian official.

arena Middle of a Roman stadium, where *gladiator* fights took place.

aristocrat A member of a powerful, land-owning family.

Aryan The language or people of the Iranian and Indian branches of the *Indo-European* group.

Asia Minor The historical name for Anatolia, the Asian part of Turkey.

Asphodel Fields In Greek mythology, a drab, misty place where most people went after they died.

atef crown A tall crown worn by the pharaoh for religious ceremonies.

atrium Main hall of a Roman *domus*, open to the sky.

ba An Egyptian word for a person's life force; part of their spirit.

barbarian The Greek and Roman name for any foreigner who spoke a different language or who lived outside the *empire*.

basilica Large rectangular building with two rows of columns, used as law courts and offices by Romans.

bedouin *Nomads* inhabiting the deserts of North Africa and Arabia.

black-figure ware A style of Greek pottery with black figures painted on a red background.

bulla A charm worn by Roman children to protect against evil spirits.

Byzantines People who lived in the Byzantine or eastern Roman empire.

cameo A miniature Roman carving on a semi-precious stone.

capital The top part of a column.

Carthaginians People from the city of Carthage, in North Africa.

caryatid A statue of a woman used in place of a Greek column.

catacombs Tunnels under the city of Rome, used as burial vaults.

cella The main room of a Greek temple, holding the god's *cult* statue.

centurion A Roman army officer, who commanded a group of soldiers, known as a **century**.

Chaos In Greek mythology, the state of nothingness before the world began.

chiton A Greek woman's dress.

chorus A group of men, speaking, singing and dancing in Greek plays.

circus A large racetrack where Roman chariot races were held.

citizen A free man who could participate in the government of the *city-state* in which he was born.

city-state A self-governing city and its surrounding territory, forming the basis of an independent state.

concubine A woman who lived with a man without being married to him.

consul The most senior Roman government official.

Corinthian column A style of column with an ornate, leafy-patterned *capital*.

corn dole Free grain handed to the poorest *citizens* in Rome.

cornice The ledge on a Greek temple above the *pediment*.

corvée The work tax imposed by the pharaohs on Egyptian men.

cuirass A breastplate and backplate used by Greek *hoplite* soldiers.

cult The worship of a particular god or goddess, or the following of a particular system of religious rites.

cuneiform Writing system developed in Mesopotamia, using signs made with a wedge-shaped tool to represent objects, ideas or sounds.

Curia The Senate House, where the Roman *Senate* met.

Delian League An alliance formed by Athens and its allies, in 478-477BC, to fight the Persians.

democracy A political system, introduced by the Greeks, in which all *citizens* had a say in running their state.

demotic Shorthand Egyptian script that evolved during the Late Period.

Diadochi The generals who took over different parts of Alexander the Great's empire after his death.

Dionysia A dramatic festival, held by the Athenians, from which the idea of plays probably developed.

domus Roman private house, usually for one family and its slaves.

Dorians A people who dominated southern Greece in c.1100BC.

Doric column A Greek column with a plain *capital*; the distinguishing feature of a style of architecture called the **Doric order**.

dowry Money or property brought by a woman to her husband at marriage.

dynasty A succession of rulers from the same family.

electrum A natural mixture of gold and silver, used for the first coins.

Elysian Fields The equivalent of Heaven in Greek mythology.

emperor The supreme ruler of all Roman lands. Augustus became the first emperor in 27BC.

empire All the different lands controlled by the Romans.

Empire The period 27BC to AD476 when Rome was ruled by *emperors*.

ephor A Spartan official.

equites Roman *citizens* descended from Rome's first cavalry officers.

Etruscans People whose civilization flourished in northwest and central Italy from c.800-400BC.

exile Enforced absence from a home or country.

faience Glazed earthenware, made by heating powdered quartz.

Fertile Crescent An arc of rich and well-watered land around *Mesopotamia*, where farming first began.

forum (plural: fora) Central open space in a Roman town, used for law courts, markets and political meetings.

fresco A wall painting made by applying paint to wet plaster.

frieze Band below the pediment on a Greek temple, often decorated with painted sculpture.

fuller A Roman craftsman who cleaned and prepared woollen cloth, and cleaned and mended clothes.

Gauls The people of a Celtic tribe from central Europe.

gerousia A Spartan council, consisting of two kings and 28 council members, elected for life.

gladiator A Roman slave or prisoner who fought to entertain people.

gorgon In Greek mythology, one of three monstrous, winged sisters whose looks turned people to stone.

governor An official who ran a Roman *province*.

grammaticus (1) A Roman school where boys from rich families continued their education after the age of 11. (2) A teacher who taught in a *grammaticus*.

grammatistes A Greek teacher of reading, writing and arithmetic.

greave A bronze leg covering used by Greek *hoplite* soldiers.

gymnasium (plural: gymnasia) In Greece, a sports hall for athletic training; later, often a place of intellectual activity equipped with a lecture hall and a library.

gynaeceum The women's rooms in a Greek private house.

Heb Sed An Egyptian festival.

Hebrew An ancient *Semitic* language and people, the people also known as Israelites and Jews.

Hellene A member of the Greek race.

helot A Spartan slave, descended from the indigenous people of Sparta, who had resisted Spartan rule.

hetaira (plural: hetairai) A woman educated to entertain men at a Greek dinner party.

hieratic An Egyptian shorthand script, used mainly by priests.

hieroglyphics The Egyptian system of writing using pictures or signs, known as **hieroglyphs,** to represent objects, ideas or sounds.

himation A cloak or shawl, worn by both Greek men and women.

Hittites An *Indo-European* speaking people from Anatolia (in Turkey), who built up a great empire in *Asia Minor*.

hoplite A heavily armed foot soldier, in the armies of the Greek *city-states*.

Hyksos A group of *Semitic* peoples, probably mostly *nomads*, who invaded and conquered Egypt.

hypocaust A Roman central heating system, where hot air flowed through gaps between walls and under floors.

hypostyle hall The central hall in an Egyptian temple.

Immortal Another word for a Greek god or goddess.

Indo-European A group of languages including Iranian, Armenian and Sanskrit, as well as most modern European languages.

insula A Roman apartment building.

inundation The annual flooding of the Nile river in Egypt.

Ionic column A Greek column, with a *capital* with a curling decoration; the main feature of the **Ionic order** of Greek architecture.

Israelites The *Hebrew* inhabitants of the Kingdom of Israel.

Jews Another name for the *Semitic* people also known as *Israelites* and *Hebrews*; followers of Judaism.

ka One of the three aspects of an Egyptian person's spirit.

khephresh A bright blue crown worn by the Egyptian pharaoh, symbolizing his role as a warrior.

kitharistes A Greek teacher of music and poetry.

kore A Greek sculpture depicting a young woman.

kouros A Greek sculpture depicting a young man.

krater A large Greek vase in which wine was mixed with water.

Kush A kingdom in southern *Nubia*.

labrys A double-headed weapon used in the *Minoan* religion.

labyrinth A mythical underground maze at Knossos on Crete, home of the *Minotaur*, a bull-headed monster.

lararium A *shrine* in a Roman house, with statues of the household gods.

legate (1) A senior Roman in charge of an important *province*. (2) A Roman officer commanding a *legion*.

legionary A Roman *citizen* in the army. About 5,000 legionaries made up a **legion**.

libation An offering of wine, milk or blood, poured onto an altar or the earth during a religious ceremony.

Libyans A people from a land to the west of Egypt.

Linear A Early *Minoan* writing.

Linear B Writing used by the *Mycenaeans*, adapted from *Linear A*.

Long Walls The walls which were built to enclose Athens and its port at Piraeus from 460-404BC.

ludus (1) A Roman game. (2) A school for boys and girls aged 7-11.

lyre A stringed musical instrument.

mastaba A brick building containing tombs, used for Egyptian royal burials before the introduction of pyramids.

Medjay A *Nubian* tribe.

megaron A large hall in a *Mycenaean* palace.

Mesopotamia The area in the present-day Middle East, between the Tigris and the Euphrates. From the Greek, meaning 'between the rivers'.

metic A free man living in Athens, but born outside the city.

millennium One thousand years. The first millennium BC refers to the thousand year period before Christ.

mime A type of Roman drama acted by men and women without masks.

Minoan The name given by archaeologist Arthur Evans to the civilization he discovered on Crete.

Minotaur The legendary bull-headed monster who lived in the *labyrinth* at Knossos on Crete.

mortuary A building where dead bodies are placed before burial.

mosaic A design or picture made up of small pieces of glass or stone.

mummy An embalmed body.

museum The Latin name for a temple to the Muses, goddesses of the arts and creativity.

Mycenaean A civilization on mainland Greece, dating back to around 1900BC, named after the city of Mycenae.

mystery cult A religious *cult*, with secret rituals and ceremonies.

naos The inner sanctuary at the back of an Egyptian temple, where the statue of the god was kept.

necropolis A cemetery.

Next World Another name for the afterlife; where people thought they went after death.

nomads People who travel from place to place.

nome The Greek name for an Egyptian administrative district, governed by a **nomarch**.

Nubians People from the land south of Egypt (now Sudan).

obelisk A tall stone pillar, erected in Egypt to the sun god.

oligarchy A political system involving rule by a small number of people.

omen A sign from the gods which warned of good or evil to come.

oracle (1) A message given by a god or goddess. (2) The priest or priestess who spoke for the god or goddess. (3) The place where this happened.

orientalizing style A Greek pottery style in use from c.720-550BC, with motifs popular in Middle Eastern art.

ostraca (singular: ostracon) Pieces of broken pottery or stone, used for drawing or writing on.

ostracism A vote held in the Athenian Assembly to banish unpopular politicians; from *ostraca*, on which their names were written.

paedagogus A Roman private tutor.

paidagogos A slave in Greece or Rome used to escort children to school and to supervise them.

paidotribes A Greek teacher of dancing and athletics.

palla A large, rectangular shawl worn by Roman women.

pankration A dangerous sport, combining wrestling and boxing.

pantomime Roman drama, in which men in masks mimed the action, accompanied by music and singing.

papyrus A reed used to make a form of writing paper (also called papyrus) used by the Egyptians.

paterfamilias The head of a Roman family group.

patrician A Roman *citizen* descended from one of the oldest noble families.

patron A wealthy person who helped others by providing money or a job.

patron deity A god or goddess who protects a place, person or group.

pectoral A decorated ornament, worn on the chest on a chain.

pediment The triangular part on a Greek temple above the *frieze* and below the *cornice*.

peltast A lightly armed foot soldier, used in the Greek armies.

pentathlon An event in the Olympic Games: running, jumping, wrestling and discus and javelin throwing.

periokoi Descendants of the people who had surrendered to Spartan rule.

peristyle (1) Row of columns round a courtyard or building. (2) A garden or courtyard within the columns.

phalanx A battle formation used by Greek *hoplite* soldiers.

philosopher From the Greek for 'lover of knowledge', scholars who studied all aspects of the world.

Phoenicians A people from the coast of what is now Lebanon.

Phrygians *Indo-European* speaking people from Phrygia, in *Asia Minor*.

pictograph A picture of an object or idea, used in some writing systems.

pithos (plural: pithoi) A large pottery storage jar used in Crete.

plebeian Ordinary Roman *citizen*.

polis An independent Greek state, consisting of a city and the countryside surrounding it.

praetor A Roman official, who served as a judge in the law courts.

Praetorian Guard A group of soldiers whose job was to protect the Roman *emperor* and his family.

proconsul A former Roman *consul*, sent as a *governor* to one of the *provinces* of the *empire*.

procurator A Roman official who helped to run the *empire*.

province A region of the Roman *empire* outside Italy, controlled and governed by a Roman *governor*.

provincial Any free person in Roman territory who was not a Roman *citizen*.

psiloi Auxiliary Greek soldiers, armed with clubs and stones.

pylon The main gateway leading into an Egyptian temple.

Pythia The priestess who spoke on behalf of the god Apollo at the *oracle* of Delphi in Greece.

quaestor A Roman government official in charge of financial affairs.

red-figure ware A style of Greek pottery, with red figures painted on a black background.

regent Someone who rules on behalf of a ruler who is either absent, incapable or too young to rule.

relief A sculpture with the carving raised up from a flat background.

republic A country without a king or queen, whose rulers are elected by the people, often for a fixed period.

rhapsode A Greek man who made his living by reciting poetry at religious festivals or private parties.

rhetor A Roman teacher who taught the art of public speaking. The study and art of public speaking is still known as **rhetoric**.

rhyton A Greek pot in the shape of a horn or an animal's head. It was used to pour out *libations* at religious ceremonies.

Romans A people from the city of Rome in central Italy, founded in the 8th century BC, which became the heart of a great civilization.

Rostra The speaker's platform in the Roman *forum*.

sacrifice A gift or offering made to a deity; this often consisted of fruit, vegetables or flowers, but could involve the killing of animals or humans.

sarcophagus A stone coffin or tomb, often with inscriptions or carvings.

scribe A person employed to write and copy texts and keep records.

Sea Peoples The name of various groups of peoples who, in about 1190BC, settled around the eastern Mediterranean.

Seleucid A dynasty and kingdom in Mesopotamia founded by Seleucus Nicator, a Macedonian general serving under Alexander the Great.

Semites Groups of people who occupied an area which stretched from northern Mesopotamia to the eastern borders of Egypt from c.2500BC. They spoke related dialects which form part of the **Semitic** language group. Early Semites include the Akkadians and the Babylonians. *Arabs* and *Jews* are modern Semites.

Senate The group of men who governed Rome during the *Republic*.

senator A member of the *Senate*.

shaft grave An early form of *Mycenaean* tomb.

shrine A place where people worship a god or goddess, or the container where the figure of the god is kept.

slave A person owned by someone else. Used for work, slaves had no rights and could be bought and sold.

soothsayer Someone who was thought to be able to predict the future from dreams, signs and events.

sophist A Greek teacher of public speaking and debating skills.

sphinx An Egyptian statue, with the body of an animal and the head of a lion, ram or pharaoh.

SPQR (Senatus Populusque Romanus) Meaning 'the *Senate* and people of Rome', found on many Roman coins and sculptures.

stela (plural: stelae) An upright stone with inscriptions.

stoa (plural: stoae) A long, roofed passageway, usually built around a Greek *agora*.

stola A long robe worn by Roman women, tied at the waist.

strategos (plural: strategoi) An army commander and political leader in ancient Athens.

strigil A Roman curved stick for scraping oil and dirt from the skin.

Styx In Greek mythology, the river a dead person had to be ferried across in order to reach the afterlife.

symposium A Greek dinner party for men, which included drinking, intellectual conversation and music.

Tartarus The equivalent of Hell in Greek mythology.

terracotta Baked red clay, used to make tiles and small statues. The statues are also known as terracottas.

Thirty Tyrants The group of pro-Spartan *aristocrats* who ruled Athens after the Peloponnesian Wars.

tholos A type of *Mycenaean* grave. It was built of stone in a beehive shape.

Titan One of a family of giants, children of the first gods and goddesses in Greek mythology: Gaea, mother Earth, and Uranus, the sky.

toga A long piece of cloth draped around the body, worn by Roman *citizens* on official occasions.

tribune (1) An official elected by the *plebeians* to speak for them in the *Senate* and to protect their interests. (2) A senior officer in the Roman army.

trireme A powerful Ancient Greek warship with three rows of oarsmen.

triumph A victory parade through the streets of Rome.

tyrant From the Greek word for 'ruler', someone who governed with absolute power. Later, a tyrant meant any cruel, oppressive ruler.

udjat-eye The eye of Horus, an *amulet* used for healing in Egypt.

Underworld Another name for the *Next World*, thought to be in the far west or deep underground. Known as Hades in Greek mythology.

Vestal Virgins Six priestesses who kept a fire burning in the temple of the goddess Vesta in Rome.

viaduct A Roman bridge to carry a road across a river or a valley.

villa A large Roman country house.

vizier Chief advisor to the pharaoh.

wepet renpet The Egyptian New Year, the time the Nile began to rise.

ziggurat A Mesopotamian stepped temple, built in 'steps', or layers, with smaller layers on top of larger ones.

INDEX

ACKNOWLEDGEMENTS

(t=top, b=bottom, l=left, r=right, c=central, m=middle, wp=whole page):

Cover *(l)* ©AKG London/Erich Lessing/Regio Clabria, Muzeo Nazionale, ©Larry Lee/CORBIS;

pp2-3 *(wp)* ©Araldo de Luca/CORBIS; **pp6-7** *(bl)* ©Mimmo Jodice/CORBIS, *(background)* ©Digital Vision; **p8** *(t)* ©Archivio Iconigrafico/CORBIS; **p9** *(l)* ©Jonathan Blair/CORBIS; **pp10-11** ©Vanni Archive/CORBIS; **pp12-13** ©Nik Wheeler/CORBIS; **p15** ©David Lees/CORBIS; **p17** *(t)* ©Copyright The British Museum, *(r)* ©Copyright The British Museum; **pp16-17** ©V. Theakston/Robert Harding; **p18** *(b)* ©Roger Wood/CORBIS; **p22** *(br)* ©Copyright The British Museum, *(bl)* ©Bettman/CORBIS; **p23** *(l)* ©Copyright The British Museum, *(r)* Heritage Image Partnership/British Museum; **p24** *(l)* ©Gianni Dagli Orti/CORBIS, *(c)* ©Gianni Dagli Orti/CORBIS; **p26** *(l)* Head of a king, possibly Hammurabi, King of Babylon, Mesopotamian, found at Susa, Iran, c.1750BC (diorite) Louvre, Paris, France/Bridgeman Art Library; **p27** *(br)* ©Gianni Dagli Orti/CORBIS; **p29** *(b)* ©O. Alamany and E. Vicens/CORBIS; **p30** *(tc)* ©Gianni Dagli Orti/CORBIS, *(bl)* ©Gianni Dagli Orti/CORBIS; **p31** *(tr)* ©Archivio Iconigrafico/CORBIS; **p33** *(r)* ©Wolfgang Kaehler/CORBIS; **p34** *(l)* ©Copyright The British Museum, *(bc)* Timelife/Rex; **p36** *(cl)* ©Gianni Dagli Orti/CORBIS, *(c)* ©Copyright The British Museum; **p37** *(c)* ©Archivio Iconigrafico/CORBIS; **pp36-37** *(t)* Timelife/Rex; **p37** *(c)* ©Archivio Iconigrafico/CORBIS; **p39** *(tl)* ©Francoise de Mulder/CORBIS; **p40** *(bl)* ©Paul Almasy/CORBIS; **p41** *(b)* ©CORBIS; **pp42-43** *(wp)* Art Directors and TRIP/Helen Rogers; **p44** *(b)* ©Copyright The British Museum, *(tr)* ©Jim Zuckerman/CORBIS; **p45** *(bl, mt)* Photo Peter Clayton, *(br)* The Petrie Museum of Egyptian Archaeology, University College London; **p46** *(l)* Photo Scala, Florence, *(tr)* ©Werner Forman Archive: Egyptian Museum, Cairo, *(b)* Griffith Institute, Ashmolean Museum, Oxford; **p47** ©Gianni Dagli Orti/CORBIS; **pp46-47** ©Robert Holmes/CORBIS; **p48** *(tl, tr)* ©Dave Bartruff/CORBIS, *(l)* Photo Peter Clayton, *(b)* Photo Scala, Florence; **p49** *(bl)* ©Ludovic Maisant/CORBIS, *(r)* ©Otto Lang/CORBIS; **pp48-49** ©Historical Picture Archive/CORBIS; **p50** Popperfoto/Reuters; **p51** Popperfoto/Reuters; **p53** ©Archivo Iconografico, S. A./CORBIS; **p54** Brooklyn Museum of Art, Museum Collection Fund 07.447.505; **p55** *(bl)* ©Werner Forman Archive: Egyptian Museum, Cairo, *(b)* Digital image ©1996 CORBIS: Original image courtesy of NASA/CORBIS; **p56** *(tl)* ©Charles and Josette Lenars/CORBIS, *(t)* ©Copyright The British Museum, *(b)* ©Michael Nicholson/CORBIS; **p57** *(tl)* Photo Scala, Florence, *(m)* ©Roger Wood/CORBIS, *(r)* ©Charles and Josette Lenars/CORBIS; **p58** ©Gianni Dagli Orti/CORBIS; **p61** ©Archivo Iconografico, S.A./CORBIS; **pp60-61** *(b)* ©Michael Nicholson/CORBIS; **p62** Photo Scala, Florence; **p63** *(t)* ©Carmen Redondo/CORBIS, *(m)* ©O. Alamany & E. Vicens/CORBIS; **p64** *(tl)* ©Gianni Dagli Orti/CORBIS, *(l)* ©Richard T. Norwitz/CORBIS; **p65** ©Gianni Dagli Orti/CORBIS; **p66** *(bl)* ©Archivo Iconografico, S. A./CORBIS, *(m)* ©Roger Wood/CORBIS; **p67** *(t)* Ashmolean Museum, University of Oxford, *(b)* ©Archivo Iconografico, S. A./CORBIS, *(mr)* ©Gianni Dagli Orti/CORBIS; **p68** ©Gianni Dagli Orti/CORBIS; **p69** ©Gianni Dagli Orti/CORBIS; **pp68-69** ©Charles and Josette Lenars/CORBIS; **p71** Photo Peter Clayton; **p72** *(tl, mr)* ©Roger Wood/CORBIS, *(bl)* Robert Partridge: The Ancient Egypt Picture Library; **p74** *(tl, bl)* ©Copyright The British Museum, *(ml)* ©North Carolina Museum of Art/CORBIS; **p75** *(t)* ©Araldo de Luca/CORBIS, *(b)* ©Adam Woolfitt /CORBIS, *(wp)* Digital Vision; **p76** *(b)* ©North Carolina Museum of Art/CORBIS, *(br)* ©Bettman/CORBIS; **p77** Photo Scala, Florence; **p78** ©Gianni Dagli Orti/CORBIS; **p80** *(tl, l)* ©Roger Wood/CORBIS, *(b)* ©Copyright The British Museum; **p82** Photo Scala, Florence; **p83** *(tr)* ©Dr E. Strouhal, *(bl)* The Ancient Egypt Picture Library; **p84** The Art Archive/Egyptian Museum Cairo/Dagli Orti (A); **p85** ©Copyright The British Museum; **p86** Photo Scala, Florence; **p87** ©Copyright The British Museum; **p90** ©Gianni Dagli Orti/CORBIS; **p92** ©Christine Osborne/CORBIS; **p94** ©Yann Arthus-Bertrand/CORBIS; **p96** ©Copyright the British Museum; **p97** ©Copyright The British Museum; **p98** *(tl, b)* Vanni Archive/CORBIS, *(l)* Photo Scala, Florence, *(tr)* ©Copyright the British Museum; **p99** ©Copyright The British Museum; **p100** ©Bettman/CORBIS; **p101** *(l)* Ancient Art and Architecture, *(r)* ALEXANDER TSIARAS/SCIENCE PHOTO LIBRARY, *(br)* ©THE TRUSTEES OF THE NATIONAL MUSEUMS OF SCOTLAND; **p102** ©Gianni Dagli Orti/CORBIS; **p103** *(tl)* ©Burnstein Collection/CORBIS, *(m)* ©Copyright The British Museum, *(br)* ©Charles and Josette Lenars/CORBIS; **p104** ©Yann Arthus-Bertrand/CORBIS; **p106** ©Roger Wood/CORBIS; **p107** *(tl)* ©Werner Forman Archive/CORBIS, *(bl)* ©Gianni Dagli Orti/CORBIS, *(br)* ©Roger Wood/CORBIS; **pp106-107** Powerstock Zefa; **p108** *(tl)* ©Roger Wood/CORBIS, *(m)* ©Eye Ubiquitous /CORBIS; **p109** *(tl)* ©Vanni Archive/CORBIS, *(br)* ©Roger Wood/CORBIS; **p110** *(t)* ©Robert Partridge: The Ancient Egypt Picture Library *(m)* ©Nik Wheeler/CORBIS, *(b)* ©Carmen Redondo/CORBIS; **p111** ©Gianni Dagli Orti/CORBIS; **p113** *(ml, b)* ©Copyright The British Museum, *(tr)* ©Gianni Dagli Orti/CORBIS; **p114** *(tl)* ©Burstein Collection/CORBIS, *(l)* ©Gianni Dagli Orti/CORBIS; **p115** *(br)* ©Gianni Dagli Orti/CORBIS, *(br)* Burstein Collection/CORBIS; **p116** ©Gianni Dagli Orti/CORBIS; *(tr)* ©Robert Partridge: The Ancient Egypt Picture Library; **p117** *(t)* The Art Archive /Egyptian Museum Cairo/Dagli Orti, *(ml)* ©Gianni Dagli Orti/CORBIS; **pp116-117** Art Directors & TRIP/Bob Turner; **p118** *(tl, br)* ©Gianni Dagli Orti/CORBIS, *(ml)* Reproduction by permission of the Syndics of The Fitzwilliam Museum, Cambridge; **pp118-119** ©Copyright The British Museum; **p119** The Art Archive/Egyptian Museum Cairo/Dagli Orti; **p120** *(tl)* ©Michael T.